Bransk, Book of Memories

(Brańsk, Poland)

Translation of

Bransk, sefer hazikaron

Editors: Alter Trus and Julius Cohen

Brainsker Relief Committee of New York,

Originally published in New York

1948 (Yiddish 440 pages)

Published by JewishGen Press

JewishGen Inc.
An Affiliate of the Museum of Jewish Heritage - A Living Memorial to the Holocaust
New York

Cover Credits

Cover photo and creative filters by Rachel Kolokoff Hopper

Poem on the back cover by Yosef Khaim Heftman (page 140)

Photos on the back cover as follows:
Woman in the top left: Khaye Esther the Gabai'ete (page 100)
Man in top middle: Yosef Khaim Heftman (page 139)
Man in top right: Rabbi Shmaryahu Margolis (page 29)
Man in bottom left: Khone Kashtan (page 227)
Woman in bottom right: Khone Kashtan's wife (page 227)
Man in bottom middle: Ruven Katsev, age 95 (page 17)

Bransk, Book of Memories   -   (Brańsk, Poland)
Translation of Bransk, *sefer hazikaron*

Copyright © 2017 by JewishGen, Inc.
All rights reserved.
First Printing: August 2017, Av 5777
Second Printing: August 2019, Av 5779

Translation Project Coordinator: Rubin Roy Cobb
Layout: Joel Alpert and Lynn Mercer
Cover Design: Rachel Hopper
Indexing: Randall Tenor

Published by JewishGen, Inc.
An Affiliate of the Museum of Jewish Heritage
A Living Memorial to the Holocaust
36 Battery Place, New York, NY 10280

"JewishGen, Inc. is not responsible for inaccuracies or omissions in the original work and makes no representations regarding the accuracy of this translation. Digital images of the original book's contents can be seen online at the New York Public Library Web site."

The mission of the JewishGen organization is to produce a translation of the original work and we cannot verify the accuracy of statements or alter facts cited.

Printed in the United States of America by Lightning Source, Inc.

Library of Congress Control Number (LCCN): 2016944514
ISBN: 978-1-939561-53-4 (hard cover: 492 pages, alk. paper)

JewishGen and the Yizkor-Books-in-Print Project

This book has been published by the **Yizkor-Books-in-Print Project,** as part of the **Yizkor Book Project** of **JewishGen, Inc.**

JewishGen, Inc. is a non-profit organization founded in 1987 as a resource for Jewish genealogy. Its website [www.jewishgen.org] serves as an international clearinghouse and resource center to assist individuals who are researching the history of their Jewish families and the places where they lived. JewishGen provides databases, facilitates discussion groups, and coordinates projects relating to Jewish genealogy and the history of the Jewish people. In 2003, JewishGen became an affiliate of the **Museum of Jewish Heritage - A Living Memorial to the Holocaust** in New York.

The **JewishGen Yizkor Book Project** was organized to make more widely known the existence of Yizkor (Memorial) Books written by survivors and former residents of various Jewish communities throughout the world. Later, volunteers connected to the different destroyed communities began cooperating to have these books translated from the original language—usually Hebrew or Yiddish—into English, thus enabling a wider audience to have access to the valuable information contained within them. As each chapter of these books was translated, it was posted on the JewishGen website and made available to the general public.

The **Yizkor-Books-in-Print Project** began in 2011 as an initiative to print and publish Yizkor Books that had been fully translated, so that hard copies would be available for purchase by the descendants of these communities and also by scholars, universities, synagogues, libraries, and museums.

These Yizkor books have been produced almost entirely through the volunteer effort of researchers from around the world, assisted by donations from private individuals. The books are printed and sold at near cost, so as to make them as affordable as possible. Our goal is to make this important genre of Jewish literature and history available in English in book form, so that people can have the personal histories of their ancestral towns on their bookshelves for themselves and for their children and grandchildren.

A list of all published translated Yizkor Books in the project with prices and ordering information can be found at:
http://www.jewishgen.org/Yizkor/ybip.html

Lance Ackerfeld, Yizkor Book Project Manager

Joel Alpert, Yizkor-Book-in-Print Project Coordinator

JewishGen
Yizkor Book Project

This book is presented by the
Yizkor Books in Print Project
Project Coordinator: Joel Alpert

Part of the
Yizkor Books Project of JewishGen, Inc.
Project Manager: Lance Ackerfeld

These books have been produced solely through volunteer effort
of individuals from around the world. The books are printed and
sold at near cost, so as to make them as affordable as possible.

Our goal is to make this history and important genre of Jewish
literature available in English in book form so that people can have
the near-personal histories of their ancestral towns on their bookshelves for themselves and for their children and grandchildren.

Any donations to the Yizkor Books Project are appreciated.

Please send donations to:
Yizkor Book Project
JewishGen
36 Battery Place
New York, NY 10280

JewishGen, Inc. is an affiliate of the
Museum of Jewish Heritage
A Living Memorial to the Holocaust

BRANSK YIZKOR BOOK
BRANSK SEFER HAZIKARON

A written description of her home, people, heroes, leaders of the religious, social, political and economic institutions. How Bransk lived under the various occupations of both World Wars, her eventual horrific demise as a Jewish community.

Translation Project Coordinator, Editor and Compiler

Rubin Roy Cobb

Based on the Preliminary and Unfinished Translations from the Yiddish by Mindle Crystal Gross and Polish by Ania Zilberkant.

Thanks to Michael L. Redd, Lance Ackerfeld and especially Joel Alpert and their respective teams of volunteers without whose assistance it would not have been possible to publish this Bransk Yizkor Book.

Including

1 Extensive corrections and missing pages, paragraphs and words added in the preliminary Yiddish translation and confirming the Polish translation.
2 Maps - details and anecdotes indicated thereon, drawn up from information given by a survivor, Jack (Yankel) Rubin z"l (passed away on 2/13/2011), a cousin of Rubin Roy Cobb (RRC), on flight from New York to Warsaw to film the documentary "Shtetl" for PBS on 10/11/1991 to RRC; thereafter edited by walk through Bransk a few days later with VHS video by Jack Rubin to RRC and further editing with Jack Rubin on 2/15/1992; and editing audio tapes recorded by RRC on 4/15/1996.
3 Map of Bransk immediately before the liquidation of the ghetto on November 2, 1942 sketched by Zbigniew Romaniuk, a Polish historian/teacher living in Bransk, as well as sketches of ca 1905 and 1932 obtained by him from the Grodno, Belarus archives after the fall of the Soviet Union in 1991.
4 Comprehensive notes and anecdotes throughout.
5 References from personal recollections of RRC, Wikipedia, Johannesburg Bransker Society.

PREFACE TO THE TRANSLATION

I remember when the photo of the Bransker Organization in Johannesburg was taken at our home in 1947 (see page 417) when I was eleven years old. The following year the Bransk Yizkor Book, in Yiddish, was published, and my father pointed out to me that he had first cousins living in Atlanta (see pp. 412-413). This took less than a minute, but for a reason that I cannot explain, I recalled it only 28 years later when my wife and I were searching for a place to settle in the United States in the aftermath of the Soweto, Johannesburg uprising. The uprising took place when some 20,000 black school children protested in response to the introduction of Afrikaans (the language of the Apartheid government) as the medium of instruction in local schools and were met by fierce police brutality. The number of protesters killed by the (mainly) white police was approximately 700. The Apartheid government openly supported the Nazis during World War II and almost 100% of South African Jewry was against this Apartheid government. We felt that 'the writing was on the wall'. As my parents taught me when they emigrated to South Africa in 1929, better ten years too early than ten minute too late!

The first time that I visited Bransk was in 1974. As an attorney, I had to settle a deceased estate in in Poland, and it took me three attempts to obtain a visa. There was no love lost between the governments of Apartheid South Africa and Communist Poland, but one thing that they did share was hatred for the Jews. I was granted a five day visa and managed to engage an English-speaking car owner to take me out to Bransk from Warsaw. There we met an elderly Polish couple who pointed out where most of the Jews lived, location of the mikva (ritual bath), the five synagogues and the home of the Skorniks (my mother's family), just a few yards away from them.

On October 11, 1991, I again visited Bransk, this time with a surviving cousin of mine from Baltimore, Yankel Rubin. He was 26 when the war broke out in 1939 and had a remarkable memory of where almost every Jewish family lived on the day they were transported to the gas chambers of Treblinka on November 2, 1942. I took a video camera and tape recorder with me as we walked through the shtetl and later edited them with him on February 15, 1992 and again on April 15, 1996.

I was also fortunate to meet Zbigniew Romaniuk, a gentile historian and high school teacher, and now a professor of History at the University of Bialystok, who took a great interest in the Jewish community in Bransk before the liquidation after he came across a medieval seal with Hebrew letters. This prompted him to study the Hebrew alphabet; he spent five months in Israel for that purpose, also meeting with survivors who informed him on the life, customs, liquidation and survivorship hardships of Bransk's Jewish community. Prior to the discovery of this seal, he didn't even know that Jews existed! I met with him in Israel, Bransk and Atlanta; his knowledge and research were invaluable. In Bransk, he helped to clean up the two Jewish cemeteries and to replace some 80 tombstones that were used as paving and grinding stones

In 2013 a number of Bransk descendants in Atlanta got together and decided to have the Bransk Yizkor Book translated. But as in most Jewish organizations, one committee meeting after another took place and nothing was done. I thereupon decided to do so on my own and sent the same page out to various translators for comparison. Of course, none agreed with each other and I decided to choose Mindle Crystal Gross who did a splendid job. Unfortunately she also made many errors, left out paragraphs, had no knowledge of Hebrew words or abbreviations, never fully checked out the translations resulting in an irreconcilable muddling of words, etc.

It took me about two and a half years to complete in early 2017 the correcting and editing of the translation.

I dedicate this translated book to the memory of my parents, Jospa Skornik Cobb (Kobylanski) and Henry (Lapidot Khlawne) Cobb (Kobylanski) and to their parents, siblings, nephews and nieces who were murdered by the Nazis and their collaborators during the Shoah:

Treblinka November 7, 1942:

Akiva Ha'koheyn Skornik   Henye Rivka (Anni) Piekuck

Bella Ziesel Skornik Wasser   Yitzkhak Wasser

Khone Wasser   Ruven Wasser

Shoshana Wasser   Shulamit Wasser

Chaya Rivka Kobylanski Klamentinowski

Zvi Herschel lamentinowski

Yokheved Klamentinowski

Faigel Klamentinowski
Shaynste (Yaffa) Kobylanski Zagel   Dov (Berel) (Segal) Zagel
Yossele Zagel

Auschwitz January/February 1943

Shimeon Kobylanski   Tzvia Shtern Kobylanski

I also dedicate this translated book to Renee Davidoff Cobb, my beloved wife of 56 years; our children Jody Frankel (David), Sheli Feldman (Sam) and Gavin Cobb (Melinda); our grandchildren Adam Frankel (Miriam-Leah), Talia Feldman, Shana Frankel, David Feldman, Ariel Frankel, Justin Cobb, Micah Frankel and Nicole Cobb; our great-grandchildren Nechama Zisl Frankel, Avraham Ephraim Frankel and Sarah Vichna Frankel; and to all the future generations.

WE SHALL NOT FORGET

מיר טאָן ניט פֿאַרגעסן

אנחנו לא אשכחו

Rubin Roy Cobb
July 30, 2017

Rubin Roy Cobb

Geopolitical Information:

Brańsk, Poland is located at 52°44' North Latitude and 22°51' East Longitude

Alternate names for the town are: Brańsk [Polish], Braynsk [Yiddish], Bran'sk [Russian], Breinsk, Brainsk

	Town	District	Province	Country
Before WWI (c. 1900):	Bransk	Bielsk	Grodno	Russian Empire
Between the wars (c. 1930):	Brańsk	Bielsk	Białystok	Poland
After WWII (c. 1950):	Brańsk			Poland
Today (c. 2000):	Brańsk			

Jewish Population in 1900: 2,374 (in 1897), 2,165 (in 1921)

Notes: Russian: Браньск. Yiddish: בריינסק. Hebrew: בראנסק
30 miles SSW of Białystok, 15 miles W of Bielsk Podlaski.
[Not to be confused with Bryansk, Orel district, Russia.]

BALTIC SEA   LITHUANIA

RUSSIA   Vilnius ●

POLAND   **Bransk**   BELARUS

GERMANY

● Poznan   Warsaw ●

● Lodz

● Prague

CZECH REPUBLIC   UKRAINE

● Krakow

SLOVAKIA

250 miles

0

0   250 Km   500 Km

POLAND - **Current Borders**

Map of Bransk in Poland

Acknowledgements

Special thanks to the National Yiddish Book Center in Amherst, Massachusetts and the New York Public Library for supplying the high resolution images used in this book.

Notes to the Reader:

This is a translation of: *Bransk, sefer hazikaron* (Bransk, Book of Memories),
Editors: Alter Trus and Julius Cohen, Brainsker Relief Committee of New York,
Published: New York 1948 (Y 440 pages)

Within the text the reader will note "[34]" standing ahead of a paragraph. This indicates that the material translated below was on page 34 of the original book. However, when a paragraph was split between two pages in the original book, the marker is placed in this book after the end of the paragraph for ease of reading.

Also please note that all references within the text of the book to page numbers, refer to the page numbers of the original Yizkor Book.

The pdf of the original Yizkor book can be downloaded from the National Yiddish Book Center at:

   https://ia801904.us.archive.org/19/items/nybc313710/nybc313710.pdf

In order to obtain a list of all Shoah victims from Bransk, the reader should access the Yad Vashem web site listed below; one can also search for specific family names using family name option. These lists are continually updated by Yad Vashem, so it is worthwhile to periodically search these lists.

There is much valuable information available on this web site, including the Pages of Testimony, etc.

                http://yvng.yadvashem.org

A list of this book and all books available in the Yizkor-Book-In-Print Project along with prices is available at:

             http://www.jewishgen.org/Yizkor/ybip.html

Yiddish Title Page of Original Yizkor Book

בריינסק
ספר הזכרון

אַ באַשרייבונג פון אונזער היים, איהרע פאָלקס מענשען, איהרע
העלדען און פיהרער פון די רעליגיעזע, סאָציאַלע, פאָליטישע
און עקאָנאָמישע אינסטיטוטציעס. ווי אַזוי ברײנסק האָט
געלעבט אונטער די פאַרשידענע אָקופּאַציעס פון
בײדע וועלט מלחמות, איהר ענדליכער שוי־
דערליכער אומקום אלס אַ אידישע
קהילה

פון

אלטער טרוס און דזשוליוס קאהען

●

אַרויסגעגעבען פון

ברײנסקער רעליעף קאָמיטע אין ניו-יאָרק
אונטער דער אויפזיכט פון די ברײנסקער יאָנג מענס בענעוואָלענט אַססאָסיאיישאָן

1948

BRANSK

Book of Memories

by
Alter Trus and **Julius Cohen**

Published by
BRANSKER RELIEF COMMITTEE IN NEW YORK

Under the Sponsorship of
Bransker Young Men's Benevolent Ass'n

Proceeds of this book
for
Relief purposes for
Bransk

Coordinated by Not'e Kozlovsky

Printed in the United States of America by
The Shoulson Press, 227 W. 17th St., New York 11, N.Y.
Trades Council New York City 255

**Dedicated to the memory of my
deceased father Mordekhay–Abba
deceased mother Sheyne-Yente
my wife Sarah Trus
my children Ruven-Layzer and Nokhman-Aharon
my daughter Khanah
my sisters Zlatke, Bashe-Reyze and Tcheshe
my brother Maishe -Yosl, who fell on the front in
the Soviet military in the battle with the Nazi murderers
my honoured and deceased brother-in-law Khayim-Tsvi Branski
and my nearest who perished in the
gas chambers of the German beasts
Alter Trus**
Stockholm, Sweden

BRAINSK

Book of Memories

by

ALTER TRUS and JULIUS COHEN

Published by

Brainsker Relief Committee of New York

Under the auspices of

Brainsker Young Men's Benevolent Ass'n

Proceeds of this book
for
Relief purposes for
Brainsk survivors

צייכענונגען פון נאָסע קאָזלאָהסקי

Table of Contents

PART THREE

Footnotes (Mindle Crystal Gross)

1. This was a movement to protect the Polish language by teaching it to children who otherwise speak Russian.
2. The capture of young Jewish boys for 40 years of military service.
3. The Polish cardinal said that beating Jews was not allowed, but boycotting them was fine with him

Part One

Forward

Dear Landslayt[1]

I will introduce myself. I am Alter Trus, Motye-Aba the hat-maker's son. My mother was Sheyne-Yente. I am 50 years old, born and raised in Bransk. I am by trade a hat-maker. I have been employed in this trade my entire life.

What propelled me to write this book? Especially about our home Bransk and mostly for Branskers? To answer this question, I wrote this forward.

[Page 10]

In 1940 several Branskers and I, especially those who were interested in community work, and were elected representatives to the Bransk Town Council and in the Bransk community, were sent out of Bransk by the Soviet authority. This was a result of certain Bransk communist leaders, primarily those who began to become the leaders as soon as the Soviets took control of Bransk. They could not tolerate that any of the previous community leaders remained in Bransk.

My station there lasted until September 1941. I then enlisted in Shikorski's army. Because of the terrible anti-Semitism there, we Jews of the Bialystok,

Brisk and Rovner area entered the Russian army at the battle of the Lower Volga. I became ill. I was then sent to work in a pelt factory. When the war ended, I continued to work there as a civilian. Eventually, I gained the right as a Polish citizen to return home. On the eve of Passover, 1946, I arrived in Bialystok. I found about 40 Branskers there who had been forced to abandon Bransk because of the anti-Semitism in Bransk even though the war had already ended.

In Bialystok we establish anorganization to unite all the lonely Branskers who live there and who felt strange in the new unfamiliar surroundings.

At one of our gatherings, we made the decision to bring to the attention of the world the horrific events that the Bransk Jews experienced prior to the liberation of Bransk.

This work fell upon me. I immediately received personal descriptions from some of the 42 survivors about their experiences, as well as from some who were already in distant camps.

All of these descriptions were recorded in writing. Many of the events have not yet been confirmed because I was unable to locate the only surviving witnesses. Eventually, through my connections with such Branskers, I received from them written descriptions which shed light on our formerly collected facts.

[Page 11]

I received descriptions from Bransker Christians who witnessed certain events.

The most important assistant in assembling all the chapters that stretch from 1939 to the liberation was Moshe Yentchman. His intelligence was of great help to me in this matter.

Footnote (Rubin Roy Cobb)
[1] Countrymen or compatriots.

Moshe Oskart, Khaim-Velvl Pribut, Hershl Shpak, my son Leybl, Fishl Lyev, Khava Okon and the Alyentskys – were important contributors in the publication of this valuable material.

I am most especially grateful to the president of the Bialystok Committee Magistrate Turek, the second president Pesakh Burshteyn, the co-workers of the Bialystok Historical Committee, Mrs Fuks and Mrs Factor.

Magistrate Turek afforded me the possibility of contacting the court authorities through whom we later brought to justice many of the Bransk bandits who had participated in the murder of Jews. The Historical Commission gave me the possibility and aided me in receiving all materials connected with Bransk activity.

Many of the historical documents and copies of court-sworn descriptions were sent to Mr Julius Cohen of the New York Relief. He photographed them and sent the originals back to me. These will probably be printed in the book.

My activity became known to the Bransk Polish Christian bandit groups and I was forced to leave Bialystok and went to Stockholm, Sweden. It is here that I am free to send everything to New York to Mr Julius Cohen.

We also felt that the history of Bransk must be included as far as is possible to do so, from the first day of her existence as a Jewish town to her last days in order to give the book a complete portrayal of all the phases of her life, her strivings, her various activities, her society, her political parties, her various classes of people, who influenced Bransk during all the years of her existence.

[Page 12]

In order to detail this part of the book, I used the Bransk pinkas which I had studied for years. My activity in all matters relating to the Bransk Jewish community life, my 50 years of living in Bransk from my birth on, all of which helped me greatly.

At the same time I admit that I am neither a professional nor a writer. Working for my parents as a hat-maker from anearly age, I did not have the opportunity to become educated.

I compiled all the collected facts in accordance with my capabilities. Knowing that my literary knowledge is lacking, I turned the rest of the work over to the New York Relief Committee which agreed to print the book.

The work of publishing the book in a literary language, in a logical and readable format, will be done by everyone's beloved and honored landsman, Mr Julius Cohen.

I gave him the complete freedom not only to correct and edit, but also if necessary, to rewrite it properly and to expand my work.

I am certain that the Bransk Yizkor Book, after its reworking by Mr Julius Cohen will be recognized by all landslayt, in all parts of the world as animportant contribution to the history of our life, aspirations and eventual horrific demise.

I myself await with the greatest impatience for the publication of my book just as all of you await it as well.

Alter Trus
Stockholm, November 5th, 1947

[Page 13]

Forward

by Julius Cohen
Secretary of the Bransk Relief in New York

It became my destiny to help in ensuring that the Bransk Yizkor Book, compiled by our landsman Alter Trus, be published for the world to read.

I received from the writer, who resides in Stockholm, Sweden, the manuscript and almost 60 handwritten letters. Only now did I comprehend the great and important work ahead of me.

[Page 14]

The manuscript could not be completed in its original form. Alter Trus is not a professional writer. However, he was able to put together this book, which will surely occupy an important place when the history of European Jewry is written, and most especially about the destruction that occurred during the five years 1939-1944.

I took upon myself the responsibility of helping so that the Brank Yizkor Book would take its proper place in history.

This was not aneasy task. Alter Trus is in Sweden, I am in New York, and there was no possibility of working together. The writer turned his manuscript over to me. I approached this work responsibly, made an earnest effort to remain within the bounds of the given facts as far as they were known to me or confirmed by other surviving Branskers.

I must admit however, that I do not pretend to be a literary person or a writer. My talent in this matter is quite limited, and yet I promised to rework Alter's manuscript and bring it to you in accordance with my abilities.

The persons who are in the first part of the book are not familiar to me from my youth. Alter was yet a seven-year old boy when I already participated in Bransker culture and also in the revolutionary activity in 1905.

I had personal conversations with several Bransk landslayt in New York who clarified certain events for me from the end of the 18th century, and I include them in the chapters wherein they belong.

When I reworked the third part of the book, I included additional information that I received in New York about Bransk life from remaining witnesses as well as private letters I received from Poland from those who had lived through the horrifying events.

[Page 15]

I most especially made an effort to ensure that the Bransk Yizkor Book be the written as a memorial about our hometown, about our past and final heroes of religious, political and economic life in Bransk.

Another difficulty that I had to deal with was of a financial nature, to raise funds for the publication of the book. My appeal to all the landslayt to help make this possible brought the desired results. For this you can be grateful to the almost 60 persons who responded to my appeal who made possible that the proceeds of the book would be a significant one and will be used for relief purposes for Bransk refugees.

In general, I saw to it that the book should be written in simple Yiddish so that every Bransker, wherever he may be located, would find it easy to read and understand. Not being a professional writer, I believe however, that to a certain degree, I succeeded in popularizing the book.

When reading the Bransk Yizkor Book you will yourself experience the events of Bransk. You will shed tears at the fate of our dear loved ones as I did while writing the chapters. I cried and continued to write.

I am certain that every Bransker will hold this book dear and will read it at the very least, at every yearly memorial observance, just as we observe Tisha b'Av when the destruction of the Jewish temples are mentioned. May this book become the written memorial, the monument erected in our homes, the words engraved in our hearts.

As a representative of the Bransk Landsmanshaft[2] since 1918 until today, I did that work also with the same energy and devotion, (I believe) with which I fulfilled all the duties in the interest of the Bransk Relief work, and believing that you, honored landslayt, expect this from me. If this contribution of mine to the book will help to improve it, I will be grateful to the writer for the opportunity that was given me to work on the Bransk Yizkor Book.

[Page 16]

With this feeling I present to you, dear landslayt, the Bransk Yizkor Book, compiled by Alter Trus, corrected, enlarged and edited by me.

I am certain that you, like the writer, will understand that with my rewriting of the book, I did not seek any honour or credit for myself.

Julius Cohen
2060 Ocean Avenue,
Brooklyn 30, N.Y.

Footnote (Rubin Roy Cobb)
2 Countrymen's or compatriots' club or organization

[Page 19]

Bransk

Our home–town of Bransk, where we, our parents, and grandparents were born and raised.

Bransk is located in the former Russian Poland, Bielsk Circle (*district*), Grodno Guberniya *(State or Province)*, now known as Bransk, Bialystok.

Bransk is about 20 miles from Bielsk, and the same distance from Tchekhenoftse and 20 miles from Shepetove, the train station of the once Warsaw–Petersburg line. The town is connected by a paved road to Bielsk and muddy roads to Tchekhenoftse and Shepetove.

Bransk is located at the confluence of the Nuretz and Bronke Rivers. Bronke is a small village. Bransk is a town with a population of approximately 7,000. The Nuretz swallowed the Bronke River just as Bransk surpassed the village.

The Nuretz is the river that encircles Bransk on two sides. We called it the Bransk River. We drank water from this river and used it for making tea. We bathed there during the summer and skated on its frozen ice during the winter. Our mothers washed their laundry at its edges. The Nuretz provided Bransk with fresh fish for Shabbos and holidays. The river claimed many of our brave young people who dared to measure themselves against its hidden depths.

The Nuretz demanded and received its victims during Passover, when its waters spilled over all the roads and engulfed its travelers.

There is a mountain located on the second side of the river. The Poles call it the Shloss. This is a historic place, shaped like a circular fortress. The centre of the mountain is lower, level with the river bank. By whom and when this mountain was utilized as a fortress, we do not know. What we do know is that within the mountain a couple of thousand people could hide.

[Page 20]

There remained in Bransk three important historic buildings. They were specially built as fortified places or for military purposes. The buildings are situated opposite the river in strategic places. These are: Yosl Benye's brick house, the old synagogue and Boyike's brick house. The walls of these buildings are about six feet thick.

The old almost totally collapsed brick building that stands near Yankl Zavl's orchard is also historic. That was where the archives of the region were kept. All the documents of hundreds of years were kept there. At the end of the 18th century the important papers were transferred to Grodno. The rest remained uncared for, rotting from old age, from the rain and snow that poured through the broken walls. Kheder[1] boys never wanted to crawl in there because they were certain they would see devils.

The Kumant (?) is also an historic place, near that well and little bridge where there took place all the wars and battles during the times of the Swedish War up to the last war when Poland entirely lost her independence to Russia, Prussia and Austria and only Congress Poland remained as a remnant of her former greatness. Bransk is about 20 miles from the Bug River which remained the border with Russian Poland.

It is a known that until 1808 there were no Jews in Bransk. At the very least, there is no record of Jews in Bransk until that time. In the villages around Bransk there were Jews, those who worked for the lords as their "zhidkes."[2]

Bransk is famous for her market–days and fairs. Every Monday is a market–day. The annual fair sometimes lasted three days. The layout of the town, with its large square in the centre, is suitable for the markets. The market in the smaller market–place is known as the horse–market.

[Page 21]

In 1813, after the end of the Napoleonic Wars, when all of Poland was destroyed by the Russians, and the retreat of the French from Moscow, Bransk rebuilt. Jews were now to be found in Bransk, in a small number at the beginning. Later there was a larger number. Most probably Jews from the villages slowly moved into the town. The town records indicate a Jewish population in Bransk, but not of a Jewish community.

The following villages around Bransk had several Jewish families through whom later on the Jewish community in Bransk evolved:[3] Mien, Damanove, Alyentsk, Shvirir, Zaluske, Malyeshe, Bronke, Kalnitse, Kersnove, Atop, Karibovke, Lubine, Kashive, Alyekshen Zaminove, Dolabave, Planeve, Smurle, Pyetrosk, Poplov, Glinik, Potok, Lazefine, Kozlove, Zalyeshe, Mervin, and so forth. In all of these villages there were Jews who found favor with the nobles and lived peacefully, married off their children, and the son and sons–in–law of the village residents later moved into Bransk, because in the villages their fathers or fathers–in–law saw that there was no possibility of earning a living.[4]

There is a record in the Bransk pinkas of 1816 of a meeting. The names of those present are stated: Reb[5] Yankev bar Khaim or Reb Dov bar Yankev. Nobody knows who these people were. There is talk at this meeting about building or purchasing a building for a synagogue. This indicates that Bransk already had a minyan[6] or even more because previously Bransk Jews went to pray with the Poplov minyan. According to witness Motye–Leyb's[7] the glazier, born in 1822, his father went to the minyan in Poplov.

In the pinkas[8] of 1820 there is already mention made of money collected in the sum of 70 gildn for a small synagogue/house of study.

Footnotes (Rubin Roy Cobb)

1. Jewish elementary school.
2. Derogatory name for "Jews"
3. See Maps 2 I and II
4. I did the best I could with the names of the villages
5. Reb – Mister (Mr.) – not to be confused with H'Rav or HaRav or Rav being Rabbi
6. 10 males over the age of thirteen that are required in order to have public prayers
7. It was common to refer to someone by his first name and add his father's name without even referring to his surname. When Rubin Roy Cobb visited Bransk with Jack (Yankel) Rubin, his third cousin and a survivor, to make the PBS documentary "Shtetl" in November, 1991; kept on asking him if he knew where Welwl Alberter's home was, Jack insisted that he had never ever heard of him. Then Jack pointed out where Welwl Shammes's house was and described him as being tall, a carpenter, who had relocated to Africa (as South Africa was referred to in Bransk). immediately connected Welwl's son named Shamai as being named after his grandfather (Welwl's father) Shammes! Reference was also often made to the person's occupation such as Herschel der stoller (carpenter) or to a special feature that that particular person had such as a Keke (stutterer) Pisher (urinator) or Der Reite Hon (red rooster) because he had a large red nose.
8. Jewish records, chronicles, documents, files, minutes etc.

[Page 22]

Beginning of the Jewish Community

The cemetery was purchased in 1820. Up to that time, the deceased Jews of Bransk and the villages were laid to rest in Orla. Later on, an agreement was reached with the Jewish community of Bocki, and they were permitted to use their cemetery for the Bransk deceased.

The Bocki community placed great demands for this privilege. They demanded that Bransk pay a portion of their taxes. Many times they demanded no less than 100 gildn burial money. Later they demanded that the Bransk Jews supply recruits for Bocki in accordance with the proportion of one[a] recruit for 10 burials. They wanted these recruits in advance. Many times they could not agree on the same day and the deceased's body remained overnight in Bocki. There was no place to keep the deceased's body. The wagon that had brought the deceased's body to Bocki had to return to Bransk, so the Bransk Jews had to remain with the body all night.

This forced the Bransk Jewish community to search for a place for a Bransk Jewish cemetery.

Burial societies already existed at that time because they took the deceased's body to Bocki after they had ritually cleansed the body.

After an agreement with the town administration, the community either received or purchased the ground for the old cemetery.

This area was low, with lime and water. It belonged to the (*katuzski?*)–where once there were carried out death sentences. According to legend, Jews who had received death sentences during the time of the Polish Kingdom were buried there.

[Page 23]

According to the descriptions by the Bransk Polish writer Novitski, who in the diaries of Rutker–Bronye's, found various important historical facts about

Bransk. It is told there that in the area of the old cemetery, death sentences were carried out on young Jewish people on a particular Sunday, affording everyone from Bransk and Brezhenitse the opportunity to be present. The hangman was even praised for his good work. They were buried there where the old cemetery is now located.

Cited from the Pinkas

After the second death sentence had been carried out in the cemetery, the town was pleased. For a period of eight months there were no deaths. The first deceased was a young girl, the daughter of an organ–grinder. This only grave was guarded day and night because it is not permitted to leave the deceased's body alone on the cemetery. Nobody refused to do his duty. For eight months, this one grave was guarded until another deceased's body was buried there, and they were freed from their obligation.

Footnote (Mindle Crystal Gross)
a.   This was a movement to protect the Polish language by teaching it to children who otherwise would speak Russian

[Page 24]

Bransk during the time of the Polish Matyezh[a]

The first unsuccessful Polish uprising took place in 1831. There is a legend from that period that the Matyezhnikes hanged a Jew in the village of Sheklik. The Jew was a cantor and he traveled from town to town to pray on Shabbes. On his way from Bocki to Bransk, he was captured by the Matyezhnikes. They accused the Jew of espionage. The Jew defended himself, and not knowing how to say "cantor", he said he was a tailor. They put him to a test and he could not sew. He was hanged. The Sheklik Christians did not permit the deceased to be buried. They kept watch over him. The Bransk rabbi, R' Meir[1] Nekhe sent women Friday evening in order for them not to be suspected. The women brought the deceased's body to town and he was buried that same Friday evening.

About the second Matyezh in 1863, the following story is told: people were afraid to be out and about because they would be accused by Poles or Russians. But both of them took revenge in such matters. The Jews who lived in the villages were actively pursued, so 70 Jews from various villages moved into town. They felt more secure there.

In 1863, on a winter's night, a large horde of rebels entered Bransk. They found out that the commissar was in Dvora's brick house (Avrum Shkop's mother). They burst in, dragged the commissar out and hanged him from the tree near Dvora's brick house. They also hanged a soldier, Rozhitske. The following day Russian military, under the direction of General Manukin, entered Bransk. They immediately accused Dvora that she had betrayed the commissar. They demand of her that she give them the names of the Poles. Dvora was tortured and afraid of being jailed. It took a lot of money to obtain her freedom. The Poles knew that Dvora could have turned them in but did not want to and yet, when they came into town, they committed robberies. At the pastures they ate the cows. Jewish women even hid just to be safe.

[Page 25]

Cited from the Pinkas

A Terrible Act During the Matyezh

In the village of Tchane, eight kilometers from Bransk, an unfamiliar poor man arrived for Shabbes Khanuka in 1863. The peasants accused this poor man of espionage. Gutman Tchaner pleaded with the Poles to let this poor man live. It did not help. He was hanged. The Poles permitted the murdered victim to be taken to Bransk for burial. The deceased was buried in the poorhouse cemetery. The community sent the guard of the dead[2] to spend the night there. The following day Jews came to the poorhouse to say psalms and found the guard dead near the murdered victim. It is told that Moshe–ItslMendl's, dressed like a Russian officer, rode around with General Manukin to help capture the murderer of the Jew, and the robbers of Jewish possessions. Jews had to make larger contributions of payments than the Poles when the Matyezh was subdued.

Footnote (Mindle Crystal Gross)
1.   This was a movement to protect the Polish language by teaching it to children who otherwise would speak Russian

Footnotes (Rubin Roy Cobb)
1.   Rav or Rabbi
2.   Shomer hamet or wakhter

[Page 26]

Bransk During the Time of the Kantonistn[a]

There were already rumours that they would begin to take recruits. It was being said that they would not take anyone who was married, and there began a rash of weddings in Bransk in order to result in the birth of children.

Motke–Farber's (Taptchepski) told me when I was still a child, that his father, Velvl–Shaul's, was at that time a child of eleven years. He was playing with his friends at the Grutch ? when suddenly his father Shaul takes him and leads him to the khupah.[b] Little Velvl shed bitter tears. He felt ashamed before the children who ran after him, shouting "married, married."

Jews decided to fast and maybe this would hold off fate. Money was also collected for Grodno, i.e. the police chief of the guberniya.

The order from Nikolay the First[1] arrived, stating that all Jews must register in the Meshtchanske district books. The Jews of Alyekshener and Malyesher belonged to Bransk. This included 52 villages around Bransk.

Jews thought about where to register. They sought to register with such places where they had friends and community affairs leaders. Many Branskers registered in Orla, in Tchekhenoftse, but nobody registered in Bocki because of the disputes Bransk had had with Bocki about the Bransk burials of the deceased.

Very few Bransk community leaders registered boys in Bransk. The fewer registered– the fewer recruits. Eventually, the day arrived in 1827.

[Page 27]

The heads of the community are summoned and they are informed that they must supply 1 recruit for the year 1826, 1 recruit for 1827 and 1 recruit for old unpaid taxes.

Darkness engulfed the town. People flee from Bransk. Those registered to Orla flee to Orla and are immediately taken as recruits because Orla recognized them as strangers and not as regular town residents.

Bransk community leaders quietly assembled a list of the poorest tailors' boys who would be the first victims.

On a winter's night, Leyb–Tate's[2] shows up in Bransk. He was the Orla "catcher." He had come to Bransk to catch the Branskers who were registered in Orla.

The Bransk community engages Leyb–Tate's to be the Bransk catcher. His helper was someone whom no one knew. Later on, there were other "catchers."

It is unknown who the first caught recruits were, only that they were of the poorest working classes is a certainty. Ruven Katsev relates: "I was a child of eight. One night, Leyb–Tate's came to our house with his Bransk helpers and desyatnikes.[c] I was sleeping with my brother who was 13. The catchers ordered me to stand, measured me against my brother, and began to grab my brother. My mother begins to scream, to cry and wail. My brother and I become silent out of fear, cannot shout. The drunken catchers are stronger. The older brother is taken away from our house. We mourned and yearned for him, but little–by–little, we forgot him.

"40 years later, exactly on Tisha b'Av, my brother shows up in Bransk, dressed in the military clothes of a major. It turns out that he is no longer a Jew. He had been baptized. We put distance between us, and yet, he begged us, so we went with him to the cemetery, to our mother's grave. The entire town accompanied us. His heavy crying broke the hearts of all.

[Page 28]

His words were: "Mama, why did they tear me away from you? Why did they tear me away from my religion?" People point to a certain grave where one of the catchers is buried.

The Major Sashin trod and spit upon the grave, stuck his sword into the grave and spat again. Everyone who witnessed this felt fear. Major Sashin wanted to meet with HaRav Meir–Sholem Ha'koheyn,[3] who was the rabbi of Bransk at that time. Rabbi Meir–Sholem requested that he not be brought because he, the rabbi, is too weak. He would not be able to endure this. Major Sashin bids goodbye to his brothers Ruven Katsev[4] and Mordekhay Furman[5] and leaves. He sometimes writes a letter but no one answers him.

Ruven Katsev, age 95

When Ruven Katsev told this story, he was more than 80 years old, but he cried like a child.

Yankev–Yosl the tailor relates that they caught Mendikhe the tailor, locking him in the little community prayer house of the old small–synagogue/house–of–

study until he was sent to Bielsk. The tailors came to the old synagogue and vehemently protested: "Your children are at home. You are taking away from us the only ones to feed our poor families." The leader of the protest was Binyomin–Leyb the tailor. Reb[6] Dovid, the then community representative shouts: "Throw out this sheygetz.[d] " The people quickly implemented Reb Dovid's order. Binyomin–Leyb's the tailor receives a beating resulting in broken bones and is thrown out of the synagogue.

[Page 29]

The catchers were of the worst types and yet, the community heads were friendly with them when drinking a l'khaim. For a difficult job, they brought in Leyb–Tate's from Orla. He was a terrible sadist. He called his victims bastards. When a mother opposed him, he gave her a terrible beating.

Friday evenings were the best time for catching. The search began Shevuos–time right up to the holidays. Those who were caught at the beginning of the summer were imprisoned in the old synagogue/house of prayer in the little house with grates on the door and fortified with strong bars. Food was thrown in to them in the morning – bread and barley soup, and on Shabbos – a khale. The work of feeding the prisoners was the responsibility of the bath attendant who ensured that the bastards did not receive any food before praying. Shofar blowing was arranged specially for them. When they were taken to Bielsk, each received an arba–kanfes[e].

This is how those who were caught were kept in the Jewish jail that was a part of the old small synagogue/house–of–study. It was impossible to escape from there. They were guarded day and night, each time by different guards. Nobody demurred from this duty of guarding those who had been caught – (bastards according to Tate's designation.)

It happened that the guard was once Moshe–Aron's the hat maker. He was a calm person, so some good friends attacked Moshe–Aron's, placed a sack over his head and freed the boy.

[Page 30]

A terrible commotion erupted in Bransk. The community wants Maishe–Aron's. They want to get even with Maishe–Aron's for the boy, and his mother–in–law, Rokhl the midwife intervenes and she succeeds in getting her son–in–law freed.

Of those who succeeded in fleeing, most ran to the Galician border, to Brod, Austria. After the edict several returned home and they called them the Broder. This is how Berl Broder obtained his surname.

The community heads of Bransk had various methods of avoiding recruitment. First of all, they did not register their sons, but if they did they assigned them to other parents. Everyone knows that Yekhiel Leyb's second name is Zeyfman, so he registered his son Zelig to Leyzer Gevir's father. Everyone called this Zelig, Zelig Yekhiel–Leyb's and his surname was Hurvitz.

There were those who knew these things, could not tolerate these doings on the part of the Bransk community heads and informed the police chiefs when none was registered. One of them was Nakhum Shrayt who was a bone in the throat of the community heads. Something had to be done to stop this, so they caught Nokhum on a Shabbos night and put a sack over his head. To his good fortune, someone passed by and Nokhum Shrayt was saved. This worked and Nokhum remained silent.

In addition, the catching came to an end. General military service was begun.

Motye–Leyb's the glazier relates that his brother Avrum was caught, but he returned 45 years later, an educated person and finds his father Zalman the glazier still alive.

About the other returned Nikolayevski's[7] soldiers, there was Yenkl Royfe. He somehow was able to become a doctor. The other one was Alishke, who experienced great trouble at his return to Bransk. After forty years no one knew him or wanted to know him.

[Page 31]

The community felt sorry for Alishke and made him the sub–Beadle[8] of the Shlyakhetske small–synagogue/house of study[9].

Yaleshke heaped revenge on the Bransk children of the rich who came to the small–synagogue/house of study to fool around. He beat them. They are afraid of him and quickly run away to the other small–synagogues/houses–of–study.

This was Yaleshke's revenge upon the grandchildren of the people who were responsible for his 45 years as a solder.

Footnotes (Mindle Crystal Gross)
a. The capture of young Jewish boys for forty years of military service.
b. Wedding canopy
c. A group of men acting as corporals
d. A non–Jew or a Jew who dares to speak his mind in front of those in power.
e. A ritual four–cornered garment

1. Footnotes (Rubin Roy Cobb)
2. Russian Czar
3. Father
4. Priest – a Jew who is descended from Aaron the High Priest
5. Butcher
6. Wagon driver or coachman
7. Mr
8. Russian Czar
9. Jewish beadle – shames
10. Later called the third small–synagogue/house–of–study

[Page 32]

Bransk Synagogues, the Old–Small–Synagogue/House–Of–Study

When Napoleon's armies were chased from Russia by Poland, they usually burned everything as they retreated. Only sturdily built houses remained. In Bransk, there remained the stone structures already mentioned previously. The Russian government granted one building to Boyeken. He was a Russian lord. That is why it is named for him. The second was bought by Yosl Benye's family and that is why it is called Yosl Benye's stone structure. The third was sold to the community of Bransk as a small–synagogue/house–of–study. The community rebuilt it, added a second floor and the little rooms that later served as the rabbi's residence, Talmud Torah[1] and the jail for those children who were caught.

According to the pinkas, the small–synagogue/house–of–study was completed in 1821 and became known as the old small–synagogue/house–of–study.

In the 1832 pinkas, one year after the Polish uprising, there is another small–synagogue/house–of–study in Bransk. This was an old house purchased from a Bransk Christian by the name of Pavlovski. It got the name of the "new small–synagogue/house–of–study" twenty years later after it was beautifully rebuilt.

In the pinkas we find in the rabbinical writings of the second rabbi, Rabbi Yudl Kharif, that on the second day of Rosh Hashonah and the second day of other festivals, he is supposed to pray in the new small synagogue.

According to the names in the new small–synagogue/house–of–study, one can imagine that the rich or the newly–minted house–holders prayed there, because we find there Yosl Benyen, Yoken, R'Dovidn, Yerukhim Goldberg, Yekhiel–Leyb's, Nokhum Iteld, Yoske–Menukke's, Itskhak Shapira, Yoshe Libashitz, Shmuel Kotlovitsh. The simple folk remained in the old small–synagogue/house–of–study.

[Page 33]

Later on another group of well–to–do men organize: Yankev–Meir's Kharlop, the Gottliebs, and they found the third small–synagogue/house–of–study which was also called the Shlyakhetsker small–synagogue/house–of–study.

The shoemakers and butchers led by Avrum Vayner purchase Binyomin–Leyb's the tailor's old house and establish the fourth small–synagogue/house–of–study with the name Poale Tsedek. In 1908, they build a new building and it becomes one of the most beautiful small–synagogues/houses–of–study in town.

The Holy Ark with its carvings is a masterpiece. After the death of Avrum Vayner, the important work of Poale Tsedek is conducted by his son, Leybl Vayner.

The tailors were organized before the shoemakers. They had a minyan in the attic of the new small–synagogue/house–of–study. They were not their own bosses because the revenue from the donation–box belonged to the new small–synagogue/house of study. During the Days of Awe, they had to pray downstairs.

There were energetic leaders such as Khone Kashtan, Arye Krok, Sholem Krok, and with the help of Dovid–Hersh's Rubin[2] (his nickname is Shtsiyopke) undertook the work of building a tailors' small–synagogue/house–of–study. They had many disruptions. The authorities did not permit too many synagogues in Bransk. They opened the synagogue without permission and it actually happened that it was shut down by the authorities while they were in the middle of prayer.

At this point, Nosn Zelvin intervened. He was known as the Moscower, because he had lived in Moscow until the Jews were chased from there.

Nosn Zelvin was a remarkable type, very learned in Talmud. At the same time, he was very knowledgeable in Russian. His Russian speech was impeccable. His voice and his diction was that of one Russian born. In spite of the fact that he had been chased out of Moscow along with all the other Jews, he nevertheless remained a true Russian patriot, devoted to the Czar. In Bransk, Nosn Zelvin earned a living by writing petitions to every important official. Nosn Zelvin went to Petersburg, to Moscow – everywhere. When someone had a request to the higher–ups of the gubernya or the Russian district, even the capital city, Nosn Zelvin was able to have entry there. Whatever he undertook he accomplished.

[Page 34]

When the tailors' small–synagogue/house–of–study was closed by the authorities, Nosn Zelvin becomes very busy. He writes to Grodno, but it doesn't help. He writes to Petersburg appealing to the highest administration and receives permission to open the small–synagogue/house–of–study in the name of the young Czarevitch.[3]

Upon receiving such permission, Khronye Pototski sent all the wood needed for building a small–synagogue/house–of–study. At the end of 1909, the new beautiful Bransk tailors' small–synagogue/house–of–study opened.

The khasidim also built their own house of prayer. Mordekhay 's the teacher donated the place for this purpose. Up to that time, they always rented various places for prayer. Mordekhay–Hersh's earned a steady invitation as an ever–welcome guest at every khasidishe mlave malke's.[d]

These were the Bransk synagogues.

Footnotes (Rubin Roy Cobb)
1. School for instruction – higher elementary school
2. Family of Roy Cobb through his paternal grandmother
3. Prince
4. Evening meal marking the end of Shabbos.

[Page 35]

Bransk Rabbinate

Bransk was a fortunate town vis–à–vis its rabbis. All the Bransker rabbis were the greats of their generation. Many were famous not only in Poland, but throughout the entire world.

By 1822 the Bransk community is already organized. They now have their own cemetery. There arose the question of a rabbinate. By that time there had certainly taken place all kinds of disagreements among the Jewish residents of town and of the villages surrounding Bransk. There were arguments because of livelihood, leasing a farm from the nobleman or opening a tavern where there was not even enough income for the existing tavern owner. This led to

fighting and insults. What was missing was the tradition of generations, the Jewish authority who could delve into the details and bring about a resolution between the opponents. In a word, there was the need for a rabbi in the newly organized community of Bransk.

You understand that more than one meeting took place. There were enough candidates for the Bransk rabbinate. Many of the village residents were learned Jews, experts in the Torah. They had a strong influence in the choice of a rabbi for Bransk.

Rabbi Meir–Nekhe's

He was the first Bransk rabbi. Rabbi–Meir Nekhe's was a Bransk son–in–law. This woman, Nekhe, must have been an important personality for the rabbi to be called Rabbi Meir–Nekhe's after his mother–in–law. According to the pinkas of 1822 (5382). It was decided to grant a written rabbinical document to Rav Meir–Nekhe's. It is mentioned therein that he is a great expert in Torah and that there is no one equal to him in Bransk. In this written document he is called the first rabbi, Rabbi Meir, in the tradition of generations.

[Page 36]

The following points are found in the written document: paying him a salary of 27 gildn a week, providing him with living quarters and heating in one of the rooms of the old small–synagogue/house–of–study. It is mentioned that by Passover the poorhouse must become the responsibility of the community.

In honour of the holiday, or for reading from the Torah on Shabbos Hagodol and Shabbos Shuva, there is the addition of a bottle of wine, tea and sugar. The rebitsn[1] receives the right to sell Shabbos candles. She must give two–sixths of the profit to the community. Also included in his salary are monies earned from the sale of khometz[2] and the rendering judgments.

As a young man I saw the rabbi's apartment several times. It was like a jail.

The walls were wet and it was dark and damp. There was never a bit of sunshine there. Living there were Yenkl–Parifke's the crazy one and Moshe–Aron's the shadkhan.[3]

Rabbi Rabbi–Meir Nekhe's did not derive much joy from the Bransk rabbinate. The Kontanistn edict had been implemented. Little children were caught and held captive in one of the little rooms on the other side of the wall from his apartment. Jewish mothers were always wailing and crying there, banging their heads against the wall. The prisoners protested and cursed everyone. Rabbi Meir–Nekhes and his wife, good–hearted, could not tolerate the heart–rending cries of the unfortunate children and their mothers. His heart burst from pain.

The wet walls cried along with the rabbi, with the mothers from the other side of the wall until he died at a young age. This was the fate of the first Bransk rabbi, Rabbi Meir–Nekhes, of blessed memory.

Rabbi Yudl–Kharif's

He was hired as the second rabbi of Bransk to replace Rabbi MeirNekhe's. He was a great genius. Branskers used to say that the Divine Presence always shone upon his countenance.

Rabbi Yudl–Kharif's also dies at a young age. He is buried in the old cemetery near Rabbi Meir–Nekhe's.

[Page 37]

Old Meir–Itsl's wife used to speak with pride about the first two Bransk rabbis who were her relatives. She named her eldest son Yudl Meir after both Bransk rabbis.

Rabbi Shaul Regenbirger

He is chosen to fill the place of Rabbi Yudl Kharif's, of blessed memory, as the third rabbi of Bransk. Rabbi Regenbirger is not like the former rabbis . He protests. He does not like the wet apartment where the dampness creeps into the bones. He does not like the Bransk homeowners who have a desire to hire brilliant men as their rabbis and do not provide them with the most basic suitable conditions enabling them to live somewhat decently.

Rabbi Shaul Regenbirger decides to leave Bransk. He receives a written rabbinical document either in Lomzha or Pruzhene.

Many people gathered at his departure from Bransk and stop his wagon. Others lie down on the ground near the horses, not allowing him to move. They shout: "Rabbi, do not forsake us."

Rabbi Shaul Regenbirger stands up in the wagon and says to the crowd: "I must not be here. Here is not my place of death. It is anedict from above. You have insulted me. No good will result from my remaining here. I refuse and G–d will help you." This had an effect. With much crying, they all bid goodbye to Bransk's third rabbi, Rabbi Shaul Regenbirger. For a long time, especially by those in the crowd, there was talk about the farewell with their beloved rabbi of Bransk.

Rabbi Meir–Sholem's Ha'koheyn

He was the fourth rabbi of Bransk. He was hired in Bransk in 1870. He was a brilliant man. He came from a family of geniuses in Lithuania. He quickly became beloved in town. He was by nature a very endearing person. Bransk respected him very much and was very proud of him for his genius and for his good nature.

[Page 38]

The Bransk community heads did not understand how to properly value such a shining personality. His salary was minimal, barely enough for the necessities of life. His residence was the same wet, dark and damp little apartment. The simple folk virtually idolized him but did not have a say in influencing either the community heads or the leaders that they should make the rabbi's life more comfortable. Rabbi Meir–Sholem's Ha'koheyn while living in this apartment becomes ill. The bala bosim[4] do not take this seriously. His situation worsens. It is already too late to do something to save the life of this great genius.

Rabbi Meir–Sholem's Ha'koheyn, of blessed memory

Rabbi Meir–Sholem died in 1884 at the age of 43. He was buried on the old cemetery next to the earlier Bransk rabbis. The rebitsn is left with small children.

[Page 39]

It took much effort until she finally receives a couple of rubles to sustain herself and her family.

The following fact, related to Julius Cohen by his uncle Hertske Fuks, a man of 80, who has lived in New York for more than 60 years, will afford an understanding of the respect all the residents of Bransk, especially the simple folk, had for Rabbi Meir–Sholem Ha'koheyn.

In Bransk, as in all other towns, it was the style to have the wedding canopies set up in the street near the old small–synagogue/house–of–study, both winter and summer. On a certain winter day, the snow having just fallen, there takes place a wedding at the old small–synagogue/house–of–study. At these weddings, the youth would always make some mischief with the parents or with the groom, most especially if he was from another town.

Precisely as Rabbi Meir–Sholem performed the blessing over the wine, a large snowball hit him in the face. The goblet of wine tumbled to the snow.

The following day it became known in town that this mischief had been carried out by Berele–Manes's. Berele was a youth before whom the entire town trembled because he was capable of committing the worst things.

Rabbi Meir–Sholem sent for Berele. Berele came to the rabbi. He admitted he had thrown the snowball at others. Rabbi Meir–Sholem delivered two fiery slaps to Berele. "Do you know, you mischief–maker, what you did? Because of you I wasted a prayer."

Berele Manes's left the rabbi without saying a word. He left humiliated.

This clearly shows the great respect that all in Bransk had for their fourth rabbi, Rabbi Meir–Sholem Ha'koheyn, of blessed memory.

According to the Yizkor Book that was published in New York by Rabbi Borukh Cohen, from 5421 to 5430 (1861 to 1870) there had not been anyone chosen to be rabbi in Bransk, or even if there was a rabbi in Bransk during this period of nine years.

[Page 40]

Rabbi Shmaryahu Margolis

He is the fifth rabbi whom Bransk engages as its leader. We all still remember him. His patriarchal appearance, his silver–white beard, his proud, straight walk elicited respect and love from everyone. Rabbi Shmaryahu Margolis loved everyone as if they were his children and everyone returned his love in full measure.

Rabbi Shmaryahu Margolis, of blessed memory

It is also characteristic that Christians had the same respect for him. Christians willingly went to the Bransk rabbi to straighten out their disagreements with Jews.

[Page 41]

He lived in a nice, large and comfortable apartment, first at Leyzer–Smurtchik's and then at Shepsl–Katsev's in the brick house. He did not need much because he did not have children.

The rebitsn, Krayndl, had a wonderfully good nature. Her kitchen was always open for the hungry. She was always prepared to do charity for everyone. Julius Cohen remembers that as a young child he would go to the rabbi's house early Monday morning, entering through the back door. The rebitsn was already prepared with twenty rubles for charity for his mother Khane for the market, even though she had only requested ten rubles. Those who received charity at the market would always return the charity they had received [from the rebitsn].[5]

The rebitsn had a house–maid. She was there a long time. Later on they married her to Yeshaye. He is called the Afrikaner because he later went to Africa.[6] Everyone calls him Shaye the rabbi's son–in–law.

It is difficult to imagine the absolute authority Rabbi Shmaryahu Margolis had over the population of Bransk.

Rabbi Shmaryahu Margolis died on the fifth day of Av in 1906.

Rabbi Shimon–Yehuda's Ha'koheyn Shkop[7]

He was the sixth rabbi of Bransk. He comes from Maltch. Rabbi Shimon comes to Bransk with his large yeshiva. Bransk suddenly becomes famous because of its great rabbi and his large yeshiva. Hundreds of young men of Poland and Russia come to Bransk to study in the world–renowned yeshiva led by the Bransk rabbi, Rabbi Shimon Shkop.

Rabbi Shimon himself teaches a lesson twice a week. All the town students come to be present at these lessons. He brings with him the famous yeshiva head and ritual inspector[8] Rabbi Alsvang.

Bransk is proud of the rabbi, of the yeshiva. The community however, ignored his meager wages. Rabbi Shimon, a world–famous personality, did not receive a suitable amount which at the very least would enable him to live with the honour deserved by such a great person.

[Page 42]

Rabbi Shimon had a specific request – to dedicate his talents to increasing the study of Torah by the Jews. The town rabbinate required a lot of time, mainly about trivial town matters. Rabbi Shimon felt that he must free himself from the rabbinate so he could dedicate himself properly to his holy mission. Had his economic situation been sound he would probably not have wanted to leave Bransk.

The Bransk community heads did not understand their great rabbi, or did not want to understand. He did not receive a raise in salary. This resulted in Rabbi Shimon's decision to leave both Bransk and the rabbinate. Rabbi Shimon relocates his yeshiva to Grodno. The big Jewish manufacturer Shershefski gives him a large building for the yeshiva.

[Page 43]

The day of Rabbi Shimon's departure neared. Bransk begs Khaim Pentman, the gabai[9] to double the rabbi's salary. Pentman refuses.

Rabbi Shimon leaves Bransk in 1920. Goodbyes take place at the old small–synagogue/house–of–study. Children and adults cry bitter tears, wish much success to the world–famous and sixth rabbi of Bransk, Rabbi Shimon–Yehuda Ha'koheyn Shkop.

When Rabbi Shimon's son, the old gray, grizzled rabbi who is now in New York told the editor the details, he shed bitter tears, like a child, as he recalled that long–ago time.

Characteristics of Rabbi Shimon Shkop

In 1915 when the war front nears Bransk, there is word that the Cossacks burn all the towns. Tcherenovske was already burnt. Rabbi Shimon becomes very busy. He collects money, putting it in his pockets. He is going to meet the Cossacks who are already busy burning the town before the arrival of the Germans. Rabbi Shimon stands, hands out ten rubles to each Cossack. He notices a Cossack officer eyeing his gold watch. Rabbi Shimon, with no further thought, takes off his gold watch and gives it to the Cossack officer. Bransk was saved. Bransk was not burnt.

In 1918 the Germans are battling with the Poles. It was the third night of Khanuka. Germans attack Bransk, killing Jews and Poles and setting fires in all four sides of the town. Rabbi Shimon gathers young and old together and tells them to douse the fires. He appeals to the Germans for them to be allowed, at the very least, to put the fires out.

The drunk and wild Germans insult him and hit him in the head. Rabbi Shimon does not leave. He shouts loudly to all the Jews: "Put out the fires, Jews!" Rabbi Shimon died in Grodno in 1939 by which time World War Two had already begun. Bransk chose his great student, the current yeshiva head of Bransk, Rabbi Khaim–Leyb Lyev, to represent Bransk. This is how Rabbi

Khaim Leyb–Lyev's bid goodbye to his rabbi and the greatest rabbi of Bransk of all times, Rabbi Shimon–Yehuda's Ha'koheyn Shkop, of blessed memory.

[Page 44]

Left: Rabbi Khaim–Leyb's Lyev, of blessed memory, Rabbi Shimon's best student

Right: Rabbi Shimon–Yehuda Ha'koheyn Shkop, of blessed memory

The seventh rabbi of Bransk arrives in town in 1920 on Rabbi Shimon's recommendation. Rabbi Ziv is accepted without any arguments.

[Page 45]

Rabbi Itskhak Ziv

Left: Rabbi Itskhak Ziv, of blessed memory

Right: Rabbi Itskhak–Zev Tsukerman, of blessed memory

He did not derive much pleasure, as at that time the war between Poland and Russia was raging. The Poles drive the rabbi to hard labour, hauling wood to build bridges. Bransk Jews want to take over for the rabbi, to do their own work and that of the rabbi. Rabbi Itskhak Ziv does not permit this. He works along with everyone else. The rabbi was famous as a very active person and teacher. The leaders of the Bransk community ensures that he does not live in the Talmud Torah. They give him an apartment in Rubin's brick house.[10] They now realized the mistakes they had made earlier.

A tragedy occurs. Rabbi Itskhak Ziv becomes ill with heart problems. He is taken to Warsaw and it is there that he died. He is brought back to Bransk for burial. He is interred on the new cemetery near Rabbi Shmaryahu Margolis in the same (hut, booth, tent) where the ascetic Rabbi Leyb Margolis is interred.

[Page 46] .

Rabbi Avrum–Yankev Sekarevitz

He becomes the temporary and eighth rabbi of Bransk. After Rabbi Ziv died, his widow was left alone with two small children. It was too difficult to engage a permanent rabbi and also pay an allowance to the widow of the deceased Rabbi Itskhak Ziv.

The community decides that Rabbi Avrum–Yankev Sekrevitz should be the temporary rabbi of Bransk, until such time there would be a rabbi who would take over the Bransk rabbinate which was also famous in Poland.

Avrum–Yankev Sekrevitz accepts the temporary position. He receives only one–third of the salary. Two–thirds is paid by the town to the widow of the deceased Rabbi Itskhak Ziv.

Rabbi Itskhak–Zev Tsukerman

He is the 9th rabbi of Bransk. He is hired in Bransk one year after the death of Rabbi Itskhak–Zev, of blessed memory. Rabbi Itskhak–Zev Tsukerman was an outstanding student from the Volozhin yeshiva during the time when Rabbi Hirsh–Leyb's and Rabbi Khaim Brisker were the yeshiva heads in Volozhin.

In the rabbinical world he was well–known as Rabbi Itskhak–Lebedever or the Lebedever prodigy. At 21 he was the yeshiva head in Krementchug where he was known as the great. In 1908 doctors forbade him to teach a lesson. He is engaged as rabbi in Nove Ukrainka. In 1922 he and his family leave Russia and come to Poland. He is engaged as rabbi of Bransk.

The khasidic element was not pleased at the beginning that Rabbi Avrum – Yankev Sekerevitch, who was a khasid and prayed in the khasidic house of prayer did not become the town rabbi.

[Page 47]

However they quickly forgot this and recognized the greatness of Rabbi Itskhak Tsukerman.

The last rabbi of Bransk Rabbi Tsukerman received honour and respect in Bransk . Regrettably, difficult times engulfed him in Bransk.

The town suffered much from the anti–Semitism in Poland that had carried over from Hitler's Germany.

He saw how the economic situation of the town was worsening from day–to–day. There are still many letters held in the Bransk Relief in New York that Rabbi Tsukerman wrote, appealing to Bransk landslayt in America to help the community carry out many improvements for the benefit of the Jewish population in town that they themselves could not manage to accomplish.

[Page 48]

On June 25th, 1938, his wife Esther became ill. She is taken to a hospital in Bialystok. She dies the following day and is buried there.

Bransk sent a suitable delegation to her funeral: Leyb Rubinshteyn, President of the Jewish community, former President of the community Rabbi Khaim–Leyb Lyev, ritual slaughterer Yekhiel Kontchik and the gabay of the Talmud Torah Shmuel Levin who all went there to pay their respects to the deceased Bransk rebitsn.

His son–in–law Rabbi Binyomin Kagan was also famous in Bransk. He was involved in many town activities.

The situation grows much worse with the Soviet occupation of Bransk. The rabbinate is no longer valid. The youth looks at rabbis in general with disdainful eyes.

His grandchildren are forced to go to the secular schools. Regardless of their refusal to do so at the beginning, due to various threats they later were forced to go to classes on Shabbos.

This aggravated the old rabbi. There was nothing he could do about it.

In spite of all this he was the respected leader of the town under the most difficult conditions. He carried out his work in the ghetto during the Nazi occupation.

On November 7th, 1942, during the Shabbos of welcoming the month of Kislev, Rabbi Itskhak–Zev's Tsukerman along with the teacher Rabbi Avrum Yankel Sekarevitz were taken out of Bransk, where he (Rabbi Tsukerman), at the head of the entire community of Bransk come together as martyrs on November tenth, precisely at 4 p.m. in the gas chambers of Treblinka and then burnt in the lime–kilns that Hitler, may his name be blotted out, instituted as the modern inquisition of 1942.

The farewell speech of Rabbi Tsukerman at the liquidation of the ghetto is in later articles.

This was the end of the Bransk rabbis and the Brank rabbinate along with the entire European Jewry.

Footnotes (Rubin Roy Cobb)
1. Rabbi's wife
2. Not kosher for Passover
3. Matchmaker
4. Homeowners
5. Gmilos Khesed – interest–free loan to help make a living (as opposed to straight forward charity)
6. Those who emigrated to South Africa were commonly referred to as Afrikaners
7. Rabbi Shimon Shkop became the Rosh Yeshiva of RIETS (rabbinical school of Yeshiva University) in New York but   ed to become Rosh Yeshiva of Grodno where he died in 1939 after the Nazis attacked Poland. Grodno was placed in the Russian occupied zone of Poland

in terms of the Molotov – von Ribbentrop Agreement a few days prior to the joint German–Russian attack on Poland on September 1, 1939

8. Manager of synagogue affairs
9. Mashgyakh – inspector to ensure ritually correct slaughtering of animals and chickens and all other foods and drinks were strictly Kosher
10. Family of Rubin Roy Cobb through his paternal grandmother. Jack Rubin, the sole surviving son of the owner told that he had sold it after the war and it was converted to a clothing workshop. It was still there in 1998 when visited the town with his son Gavin Aryeh Cobb

[Page 49]

Town Meat Tax
and Management of Synagogue Affairs

Both of these institutions were associated with each other because the management and the meat–tax were inseparable.

Like all other towns, Bransk had its own Jewish town needs, such as paying the rabbi's salary, providing him with a residence and heating. Bransk also had to partially cover the expenses for the upkeep of the police – the commissar and the one policeman who received their salaries from the government. The Bransk community contributed to this indirectly. The amount was a thousand rubles a year which the community paid to Grodno.

In order to raise these monies they instituted the meat tax. This is a tax on meat and fowl. This tax had to be paid prior to the slaughter of the cow or the fowl by the shokhet[1] and a voucher had to be brought to him. The voucher was bought from the khukar.[2] He was the one who kept the meat–tax. Do you remember the voucher of Yenkl Khukar? If not, I will remind you. It was a piece of white paper on which was written "to slaughter some fowl" or "to slaughter a cow" and signed by the khukar. This had to be bought from the khukar and then the chicken or the calf taken to the shokhet and in addition, pay for the slaughtering.

In this way Bransk took in monies for the community fund. These monies had to cover all town expenses. Each week the khukar turned the money over to the gabay (manager) of the town. Nobody knows how the monies that came in were controlled. What is known is that the town leaders always complained that there is no money and we need other sources of income, like sale of salt. This was never successful. The town gabay or the chief treasurer were the decision–makers, even in town matters. They even called meetings many times of a number of businessmen, but nobody knew who had the honour of being invited to a meeting.

[Page 50]

The secret of who were so lucky was held by Shaike Broyda because it was he who summoned the businessmen to the meetings.

The meat–tax, being the only source of revenue in town was closely guarded. Should it ever occur that a butcher had something slaughtered by a shokhet from a neighbouring town and did not present the voucher, he suffered bad consequences. The rabbi immediately pronounced the pots in which the meat had been cooked as treyf[3] (unclean), even when the shokhet who had done this was G–d fearing and the slaughter had been kosher.

In this way there developed and revolved around the meat–tax the community leaders, the public and ordinary folk.

The first khukar that we remember is Yenkl Khukar. He was the khukar for decades. Then, through the intervention of Yoke Berlin**Error! Bookmark not defined.**, the meat–tax was turned over to Motl Rabinovitch. There were two brothers, Motl and Yankl Rabinovitch. They were big land–owners, celebrities, who rode into town behind four horses in tandem. In addition, they were very learned and very philanthropic. When they occupied the courtyard on Marvizne, Rabbi Shloyme Hersh, Julius Cohen's father, worked there as general manager because the Rabinovitchs had another business in forestry. Times changed. The two Jewish noblemen became poor plain people. Yankl Rabinovitch commits suicide in 1896 and Motl remains without livelihood and receives the meat–tax in Bransk.

However, Motl did not devote himself personally to the meat tax, so he hired strangers to take care of it. This resulted in the meat tax losing money and suffering a deficit. Bransk turns the meat tax over to Aron Khukar and then to others. However, Bransk purchased the vouchers and this brought money into the town coffers.

[Page 51]

The treasurer was Yitskhak Shapira, knowledgeable in Torah, but a very stingy Jew. He did not eat and could not tolerate others eating. Itche Shapira had a beer brewery and a little horse to transport the barrels of beer. Yenkl Fuks, the father of Hyman and Louis Fox, told me here in New York, that he worked for Shapira in 1880 or a little later, and he suffered a lot, not from the hard work but he could not tolerate how the little horse became skinnier and skinnier from day–to–day from hunger.

This Itche Shapira was the treasurer, so you can imagine how easy it was to pry out a few rubles for town necessities. He would say: It is a shame to spend money for foolish things.

Gaboyim and Community Leaders

These were influential Jews. The first was Reb Dovid Berman. His daughter was called Esther Reb Dovid's. Reb Dovid ruled with an iron hand.

During the time of the kontanistn , when Binyomin–Leyb the tailor came to complain about why the sons of poor Jewish tailors were being taken as recruits and leaving their own sons alone, Reb Dovid Berman threw Binyomin Leyb the tailor out of the old small–synagogue/house–of–study. Binyomin–Leyb was badly beaten up.

Reb Dovid was the Gabay of the Burial Society and of the old small–synagogue/house–of–study. He was replaced by Reb Yekhiel–Leyb Zeyfman, a businessman. He had a candle factory. He was a calm person. One could speak to him although it never did any good.

[Page 52]

Yoke Berlin, Reb Dovid's son–in–law, was a very stern community leader, precise but a dictator. Everyone was afraid of him. He had a position in the Bransk administration. Christians tipped their hats to him.

Later on, the position of Koziyanem[a] rabbi is instituted in Bransk. He becomes the first Koziyanem rabbi. He also becomes the accepted leader in all parts of Bransk town life. Following him as Koziyanem rabbi was Gedalye Berl Shloyme. This was a Jew of great strength, a hard-working small businessman. He could also sign his name in Russian so he became the Koziyanem rabbi.

It happened that someone forged a signature on a piece of paper. It turned out that this was a death certificate for someone who supposedly died in Bransk with a certain name. The person who had this name, however, was alive, but he was insured in Petersburg. So the insurance company forewarned by experience became interested. They came to Bransk looking for the deceased. Gedalye Berl Shloyme's finds out just in time and must flee to America where he suffered bitterly his entire life and died almost in his 90th year.

Velvl–Daniel's was one of the town leaders and as it happens, a democratic individual. He never prayed to the east[4] but instead he was always below at the table.[5] He was also gabay of the Burial Society and involved in all town affairs.

Ezra Goldberg takes his place. He was a big wholesale merchant. My mother, Khane Shloyme Hersh's bought barrels of herring from him to pickle. He was a very honest merchant and good–natured person.

For his daughter's wedding, which was held in his home, he prepared large tables with a wedding meal for hundreds of poor who came from surrounding villages and enjoyed the roasted meal. He conducted town business very strictly.

Itche–Gimpl's, called Grazhinski, was an uneducated Jew but clever. He worked his way up to a position in the administration. Christian petty bourgeoisie came to his tavern to enjoy themselves. Thus he was actually summoned to meetings because they had to. Itche–Gimple disliked the community leaders and they felt the same about him.

[Page 53]

Elye Gotlieb was the owner of a Bransk ironworks. He was not a gabay and did not want to be one. He was once a rude trustee and did not want this job. Nevertheless, he played an important role in town matters.

Itche Mr Dovid's Rozenboym was a handsome businessman and actually tried his hand at everything but did not have any luck.

Khaim Pentman, nicknamed Fyorn, was gabay of the Burial Society. He was an uneducated Jew with a big mouth, yelling and insulting. He had something to say about everything. He constantly irritated the butchers. He would demand payment for burial in an amount greater than one gave as a daughter's dowry, and insisted on dollars. He would pay the rabbi's salary in small change, throw it on the rabbi's table and saying: count, rabbi. In general, Khaim Pentman was not beloved by Bransk Jews because of his commonness.

Shaulke Farber was a Koziyanem rabbi, a very modest person, quiet and calm. The entire town respected him. He was rabbi in 1914, a very bitter time. Because of the war everybody was required to have a passport with a photograph. However, nobody was registered. How do you issue such certificates? Meir–Khaim Simyatitski came to his rescue. He was a brilliant Jew, a Kotsker khasid. He was very learned in world matters and in Torah. Meir–Khaim, in his entire life, never forgot a single thing. He remembered everything when someone was born even 50 years ago. Meir–Khaim helped Shaulken. He confirmed that so–and–so was born in Bransk on such a date. Shaulke was able to issue a certificate that was correct because Meir–Khaim was never wrong. In this way many Jews in Bransk were legalized, receiving official documents thanks to Meir–Khaim memory. Shaulke was a dyer , also made kvas, was a scribe, a prayer leader and remained poor from all these trades. Shaulke liked to do favours without charging any money.

[Page 54]

The Germans arrived in Bransk in 1915. Shaulke Farber (dyer) is no longer rabbi. He takes to earning a living, displeases the Germans and is sent to a

German prison. He returns to town a broken man, sick, and dies shortly thereafter.

The entire town accompanied this good–natured, truly honourable Shaulke Farber.

Yerukhim Goldberg becomes the rabbi after Shaulke Farber. He conducts all business properly. There are no complaints against him even though he was not lazy to make a couple of marks. The position of Koziyanem rabbi is outlawed with the decree of 1924.

In the old small–synagogue/house–of–study. Reb Dovid, Artche Yekhiel–Leyb's, Dovid Mishurek, Zalman Kotsk, Yudl Vulker, and the last Avrum Yentchman, the brother of Julius Cohen rebuilt the old small–synagogue/house–of–study which took on a different character.

The last gabay, Avrum Yentchman, is murdered by the Poles along with his wife Khaye Sore, shot the night of November 15th 1942 in the street near Artche Katsev's house.

In the new small–synagogue/house–of–study. : Mr Yekhiel–Leyb Zeyfman, Itche Shapira, Yoshe, Avraham Pulshanski, Fishl Spishiner, Motke Golde, Yoske–Menukhe's, Khaim Leybl Golding, Sanes son–in–law. The latter was taken to Treblinka on November 7th 1942.

In the third small–synagogue/house–of–study : Yakev Meir Kharlop, Elikh Gotlieb, Khone Vaynshteyn. The last was Meir Kestin[6] who was taken to Treblinka November 7th 1942.

In Poale Tsedek: Mr Avrum Viner, his son Mr Leyb–Viner's. Mr Leyb–Viner perishes along with 70 Bransk Jews because of the informant Ishaye Tsuker on November 14th 1942.

[Page 55]

In the Tailors' small–synagogue/house–of–study : founder Binyomke the tailor, Aryeh Krotz, Alter Kapelikhes. Alter Kapelikhes was taken from Bransk to Treblinka November 7th 1942.

Khaim–Leyb Golding and Leybl Viner, gabay of Poale Tsedek

Khasidim house–of–prayer: led by Velvl Sofer, Yankev Vilk, Shloyme – Hersh Yentchman, Sholem Itche Kalman Maishe Ginsberg the teacher. The last, Khaim Klode is shot along with 70 Jews on November 15th 1942 because of the informant Ishaye Tsuker.

These were Bransk community leaders and gaboyim.

Footnote (Mindle Crystal Gross)
a. In Czarist Russia a state–appointed rabbi

Footnotes (Rubin Roy Cobb)
1. Ritual slaughterer.
2. Examiner.
3. Not kosher, unclean.
4. At the front, that faced East towards Jerusalem, when prayers were held.
5. At the desk from where the Torah was recited or prayers were lead from.
6. Henry Cobb (Khlawne Kobylanski), the father of Rubin Roy Cobb worked for a Kestin in Bransk as a cabinet maker. A son of Kestin settled in Bulawayo, Southern Rhodesia (now Zimbabwe) before WWII and visited the Cobbs in Johannesburg in 1953.

[Page 56]

Bransk Scholars

We have learned from previous chapters that Bransk was fortunate in that its rabbis were exceptionally brilliant men of their generation. Bransk however, also had a significant number of scholars from the first years of the 18th century up to the end.

Among the first were Mr Dovid Berman the gabai, Mr Yosef Betsalel, his brother Maishe Khaim. This Maishe Khaim was a remarkable Jew, with the long white stockings. During the entire year he prayed at home with his minyan, and only during the Days of Awe did he come to the small house–of– prayer/house–of–study. The poresh[1] Reb Leyb Farbshteyn, The poresh of the new small–synagogue/house–of–study, Mr Avrum Yekutial, Binyomin the watchmaker, who was a patriarchal figure with his snow–white beard, Mr Yankev Meir Kharlop, Aron Yenkl Royfa**Error! Bookmark not defined.**, Mr Itskhak Shapira, Mr Meir Khaim Simyatitski, Mr Yankev–Mordekhay the khasid, Shloyme–Hersh the khasid, Fishele Bog, Aron Branski, Leybl Vein, Yoshe Liboshitz, the latter five were already interested in world matters, read Hebrew newspapers. Of the later scholars: Alter Vilk, Motel Kanopyate, Avrum Verpikhovski, Meir Kestin, Meir Khaim two famous sons–in–law, Avrum Yentchman, the last gabai of the old house–of–prayer/house–of–study, Rabbi Avrum–Yenkev S, temporary rabbi in Bransk, Rabbi Khaim Leyb Lyev, Hershl Stolyer's[2] son–in–law, best student of Rabbi Shimon Shkop's yeshiva, who later receives a recommendation from Rabbi Shimon Shkop, Rabbi Ben–Tsiyon Kagan, Diodke Maishe Gusikhe's son–in–law, who came from Bocki. The latter five taken to Treblinka on November 7th 1942. Avrum Yentchman falls victim to German bullets the night of November 15th during the fire in the empty ghetto.

[Page 57]

Of the latter group of gaonim[3] who left Bransk and settled in other towns, there must be included: Mr Shaul Yentchman, the eldest son of Mr Shloyme–

Hersh. He was called Shaul'ke. Even as a young boy he was called a prodigy according to the information from Rabbi Maishe Matmid in Brooklyn, married and settled in Parisov deep in Poland. He was one of the greatest privileged persons of the Gerer rabbi. Thousands of khasidim come to Ger and Shaul'ke is beloved as a gaon.[3]

The two Warsaw khasidishe millionaires Shaye Ayzenman and Mendl Bliaz engage Shaul'ke to be he who will learn Torah with their sons. remains with the Warsaw millionaires for more than twenty five years as their teacher of Torah. Even after the sons married Shaul'ke continued to study Torah with them.

During the last years, Shaul'ke lived in Parisov. When the ghetto there became surrounded Shaul'ke required that all Jews fast to the point of starvation so as not to perish in the lime kilns. The Jews laughed at him. Shaul'ke, in his late eighties, almost ninety years old, begins to fast. He succeeded. The Germans did not burn his body because he died of hunger of his own free will. He refused to leave the ghetto with his own children and grandchildren who saved themselves.

We must mention Reb Yankev Rukhamkin, Khaim Fishl Melamed's son, Itskhak Kashnik's brother. Yankev Rukhamkin married in Volozhin and became famous there as a great gaon * and had an iron business. All Volozhin loved and respected him as the most honoured businessman and great learner. He studied with other great men in Volozhin.

Mr Yankev Rukhamkin apparently also perished along with the Volozhin community.

[Page 58]

Rabbi Borukh Cohen

He is the son of the Bransk Rabbi Meir Sholem's Ha'koheyn. He was of the time of the great gaonim in town. As a child, I remember how Rabbi Borukh Cohen, or Borukh the Rabbi's as they called him in Bransk, gave a sermon in the new small–synagogue/house–of–study speaking about the Khovovey Tsiyon (Lovers of Zion).[4]

Rabbi Borukh Cohen, of blessed memory

Borukh Cohen could not accommodate himself to Bransk. He goes to America around 1901. In New York Rabbi Borukh Cohen is accepted with great friendship by all the landslayt. He becomes their spiritual leader. The landslayt, not having a synagogue, could not help their worthy rabbi. Rabbi Cohen obtains a position as ritual inspector of kashrus in a certain kosher salami factory. However, he cannot tolerate how his name is used for uncertain kashrus and he immediately resigned.

He lived quietly with his family, albeit it in poverty. The landslayt called upon him whenever it was possible to act as m'sader kedushin.[5] of which fact the writer of this article, Julius Cohen, is proud to this very day that Rabbi Borukh Cohen of Bransk was the m'sader kedushin at his wedding on November 12th, 1907 in Brownsville, in the home of the writer's uncle, Hertske Fuks.

[Page 59]

Rabbi Borukh Cohen later goes to Eretz Yisroel and settles there. He finally fulfilled his dream of Khovovey Tsiyon and turned it into a reality. He spent his last years in Eretz Yisroel.

Pesakh Filipovski, Alter Maishe Hitsl's son, was one of the great gaonim. He got married in Shavel, Lithuania. Later he was the head of the Slonim yeshiva. Pesakh is one of the Bransk great gaonim who disseminated Torah among the Jewish people. He did not want to make a career of the rabbinate for which he was qualified. Pesakh was taken from Slonim along with the entire Jewish population of the town and perishes as a martyr with everyone.

Maishe Leyzer's Vilk is the son of Gedalye Berl Shloyme, the Bransk Koziyaner rabbi. He was a great Torah learner and a student of the Slobodke yeshiva where he was one of the best students. He prepares for the rabbinate, but he is forced to go to his father in America where he works as a shokhet. For many years he lived in towns in the Catskill Mountains. He died in 1926 in Liberty, New York.

Worldly Educated and Maskilim (Followers of the Enlightenment)

Bransk did not have any ties with the big Lithuanian cities where Haskala (Enlightenment) first began.

There were sometimes to be found those people in whom the desire for education was strong, but they were quickly pushed out of Bransk. Bransk did not believe in too much education and was satisfied with the several subjects taught in town and wanted to keep the rest in an atmosphere of ignorance.

There was a story printed in "Moment" by the writer Tsitron in his series Apostates about a Bransker during the time of the Kontanistn.

It is a story about one *Khlavne*[6] Royzkele's. They lived in a house that was lately known as Itche Yenkl the tailor's house. This was Royzke's house.

[Page 60]

Khlavne, already a father of two children, was a great student, but could not find any friends in Bransk with whom to study, so one day he said goodbye to his wife and children and went to various strange places to study. He arrives in Kamenetz Podolsk where there were many students and maskilim. *Khlavne* quickly becomes well–known as very knowledgeable. There gather around him many young men who believe as he does. He is also interested in a worldly education. He and a friend of his, the son of a Degensburger activist arrive in Vilna where *Khlavne* prepares for the exam for higher education. Friends of the rabbi's synagogue help him. He becomes very popular with the Vilner scholars, maskilim and the rabbinical students and their parents.

His friendship with the Degensburger activist's son results in his becoming sent to Petersburg medical university. He is now certain with his future and his education as well.

Khlavne Royzke craves for his wife and children, he writes to them that they should come to him in Petersburg. They did not answer him. In Bransk he is already regarded as an apostate.

Khlavne returns to Bransk in order to convince his wife that he is a Jew, an educated Jew. Bransk greeted him with stone–throwing, with dirt. They ran after him in the street, shouting "apostate." He was forbidden to see his children because a rumour had been spread that he had come to take the children to convert them.

Khlavne Royzke, broken in spirit, without energy, leaves Bransk and returns to Russia where he converts.

His wife, through the courts, demanded a get[7] He insisted that the get should take place in the council offices of the church. There is no other way. The get took place in the office of the Grodno church council.

[Page 61]

This was the end of one who dared to leave his home to seek an education or enlightenment elsewhere in the world.

Only at the beginning of the 19th century did it become a necessity for every young boy who wanted somewhat to learn or achieve high grades in a worldly education to leave Bransk for other city yeshivas or just large cities in general where they received the possibility of an education.

Footnotes (Rubin Roy Cobb)

1. Recluse, one who devotes himself exclusively to the study of the sacred books.
2. Carpenter, cabinet maker.
3. Geniuses – plural; Gaon – genius singular.
4. The Zionist group that was established before Hertzl's Zionist Conference in Basel in 1897.
5. One who formalizes and makes official a Jewish wedding ceremony
6. The same very unusual first name of RCC's father. The Yiddish spelling of the name is the same and the only place where I could find the same name, besides in Bransk, was in Bialystok. The name is of Slavonic Czech origin that probably originated in Prague ca. 11th century and then spread from there to North–East Poland. The Hebrew name is Lapidut (or Lapidos) who was the husband of the prophetess Deborah (Judges 4:4).
7. Jewish religious divorce.
8. *[Page 62]*

Cantors and Ritual Slaughterers in Bransk

The first town shokhet who is remembered in Bransk is Mr Isakhar Shokhet.[1] My father would speak with great respect about Mr Isakhar. It is not known when he was in Bransk and when he died. According to what my father related, Reb Isakhar was very much loved in Bransk. All the elderly Jews who mention him are in agreement that he was animportant and respected personality in town.

Mr Eliyohu Shokhet hailed from Symyatitch . Mr Eliyohu was very well versed in Torah. He too, was much loved by the Bransk population, studied Torah with the people in the Poale Tsedek small–synagogue/house–of–study. The editor of this book still remembers Mr Eliyohu Shokhet very well. He remembers that Mr Eliyohu Shokhet was loved by the khasidic elements in town. On the other hand, the Bransk women had a heavy heart towards his wife. When a woman came to the shokhet with a fowl to be slaughtered for someone who was sick or had given birth, his wife always found an excuse: "Come tomorrow she said" the shokhet is not home, even when Mr Eliyohu was in the house, he is busy studying so his wife never wanted to disturb him. MCG It appears that his wife thought more about Mr Eliyohu's world to come than of the four groshn he would have earned from the slaughter of a fowl . Mr Eliyohu died at the age of eighty .

Mr Maishe–Matesyohu Heftman was the next shokhet after Mr Eliyohu. Whoever remembers Mr Maishe–Matesyohu knows that he was very learned, a

Jew with a beaming countenance and a welcoming face. People could not get over his goodness, his loving and jolly nature. In general, there were few such nice Jewish types.

[Page 63]

The butchers, who were usually very critical of a shokhet, most especially when he made a piece treyf[2], never had complaints of Mr Maishe Matesen that he, Mr Maishe–Mates, had made something treyf, and there was never a protest.

Mr Maishe Matesyohu , when he was not busy, spent time studying . Children could never engage in an argument with him. His good–nature always prevailed.

His wife was loved by all the Bransk women. When she went shopping everyone was eager to help her. Everybody knew that she did not have any time to waste. She begins to prepare for Shabbos on Wednesday and by Friday evening, she is barely finished.

We will speak in later articles about his son, Yosef Khaim, the town's writer and linguist.

Mr Yehoyshe Zelig Fraynd, Cantor and Shokhet

Following the death of Eliyohu Shokhet, Bransk engages a cantor[3] / shokhet. Bransk was fortunate with the first khazn /shokhet in the person of the friendly and clever Mr Yehoyshe –Zelig Fraynd.

The khazn, as he was later called, came from Vashlikove, from Amdur and Lahishen. His first performance in Bransk was during Khanuka. How well I remember his blessing over the Khanuka candles in the old small-synagogue/house–of–study. The synagogue was packed. The khazn appeared with a wonderful choir of specially chosen singers, young Bransk boys whom he had discovered during the short time he had been in Bransk. These were the Yangnikes, two dear, sweet little voices, Shmulik–Leyzer Tcheslyer**Error!**

Bookmark not defined., Yoel'ke the Benduger and the Ganer**Error! Bookmark not defined.**.

As soon as the khazn concluded the blessing of the candles, it became quickly well–known. For years the entire town sang the blessing of the candles. It was a great pleasure to see how the town was happy with their first khazn, Mr Yehoyshe Fraynd.

[Page 64]

The khazn quickly became famous in town not only for his cantorial ability, but for his ritual slaughtering. He was a capable and swift shokhet and butchers idolized him as an artist in this trade. Even the grandmother Bashe Royze loved him for his ability and swiftness as a moyel. "A light hand, no evil eye" should befall him, as she would say.

The khazn quickly accustomed himself to the general life of the town. He became known throughout the entire area surrounding the town. People liked to spend a couple of hours with him. Everybody said he was a wise man, a Jew, speaking thus of him.

His home quickly became the centre of various businessmen who loved to sit in the large, warm house, companionably drinking a glass of tea which was always present on the table. The samovar was always on. Everybody listened with pleasure to the clever words of the khazn.

When the khazn's children became a little older there developed a new friendship between them and their kheder[4] friends. They were always together there in the house, studying together, and learning about worldly matters.

The khazn's house became even more popular with all the Amerikanerkes. It was there that they brought the letters from their husbands in America to be read and to write a reply. The khazn's wife, Sore, always said to Leybl "Paste a stamp on the letter."

The khazn's house was virtually a centre for young and old. All found a warm, friendly atmosphere there. It is characteristic that Mr Zelig did not make any attempts to endear himself to the community leaders, was proud of himself, his ability and wit. He even expressed that he would rather be a worker on his own than the holy dish of the Bransk community.

The khazn always had enough meat. He himself would purchase a little sheep or a calf, slaughter it, sell the hide and the cost of the meat was minimal. The khazn's wife, Sore, ensured that poor women would benefit from this. She made up packages of meat and Leybl would distribute them to the needy and poor women.

[Page 65]

Bransk was rightly proud of its khazn–shokhet Mr Yehoyshe –Fraynd.

Mr Yehoyshe–Zelig's Fraynd, chazan

Mr Yisroel Sivavitch

The khazn's two sons, are in America. His eldest son, Leybl, is now also in New York. There is a special article in the book about him. His son Nekhemye is somewhere in Poland.

Mr Yisroel Sivavitch, Khazn /Shokhet

Mr Yisroel Sivavitch was an artist in all three trades. He was an extremely nice looking personality, conducted himself in a modern manner, clothed very neatly. He was a truly intelligent person. His children studied world matters in the Bialystok Gymnasium and were very hygiene conscious. After a slaughter, he always washed his hands with soap. Bransk Jews were not accustomed to this and behind his back held grudges against him. However, the people really liked him.

He later left for Vibarg, Finland, and was there for two years as a shokhet. He could not bring his family over to him, so he returned to Bransk. They no longer want him as their shokhet. The people are now interested in town affairs and force the businessmen to rehire Mr Yisroel Sivovitch as shokhet.

[Page 66]

He did not devote himself to being a khazn. He disliked the Bransk businessmen and did not want to sing for them.

Mr Yisroel Sivovitch decides to leave Bransk. Bialystok wants him as their shokhet. He makes the decision that it is better to go to America. Within a short time, he brings his family over. It was fated that Mr Yisroel Sivovitch should be saved and that he and his family live in freedom in the United States

Mr Yisroel Sivovitch is now a shokhet in New York. To this very day he cannot forget Bransk as a town that was one of those in Poland that recognized and loved its truly devoted leaders and community organizers.

Mr Yisroel Sivovitch specifically reminded the writer of this article in New York of the nice and noble behavior of Yankev Yentchman. He never argues with the shokhet. He always accepted his decisions with respect. When his wife (he is referring to Reb Yisroel's wife), MCG before she left for America, came to pay several rubles that were owed to him, Yankev Yentchman refused to take the money from her. He told her that she, going now to America, would sooner need it while travelling. There would be servant girls of the businessmen who were sent with their chickens to be slaughtered precisely prior to the holiday before the candle blessing and when he refused to slaughter so late because he was certain that they did not need it for the holiday, the businessmen became angry and ill treated him for his behaviour .

[Page 67]

Mr Avrum–Hersh Shokhet

He came from Ostrove, a khasidic Jew, wearing a yarmulke under his hat. He did not get along well with the butchers so he did not do well in Bransk. He had a large family. In addition, Khaim Pentman the gabay of the Burial Society always derided him, only as he, Khaim could do. Mr Avrum becomes the shokhet and the first to dare call a strike if they would not increase his salary. This lasted an entire week, but for Shabbos he slaughtered for himself. He could not decide whether to leave Bransk without any meat in honour of Shabbos. The simple folk actually were on his side but the community leaders hated Avrum Hersh.

At the end, he returned to Ostrove.

Khatskl Kontchik

He came from Trestine. He was a good shokhet and a good prayer leader. It was said in Bransk that he was "equal to gold", a human being to God and man. Anytime there was any disagreement, they went to Khatskl Kontchik, he would straighten things out and restore peace in the home. He is always recognized in town. He is sent to represent Bransk on various occasions. Within this person was embodied a world of goodness.

Khatskl Kontchik, along with everyone else in town, is taken to the gas chambers on November 7th 1942.

The shokhet's son is also taken to the gas chambers on November 7th 1942.

There were two more shokhtim in Bransk. They were the old shokhet/preacher who would go to the Jews in every village and do the slaughtering there, and the Vishinker shokhet who came to Bransk from Vishink when the Jews, because of the pogroms, were forced to leave the town. At the beginning, he was not permitted to do any slaughtering, but later when Vishinker Jews settled in Bransk, he was allowed to slaughter in the town.

[Page 68]

The Vishinker shokhet also perished in Treblinka with all the Bransk Jews.

Yenkl Hershl the shoemaker and Isser–Shepsl the Butcher's son learned how to be shokhtim, but they were not allowed to perform any slaughters because they were from Bransk. It was the custom from long ago that their own should not be permitted to be the shokhtim in town.

Footnotes (Rubin Roy Cobb)
1. Ritual slaughterer.
2. Non–kosher.
3. Khazn – cantor.
4. Kheder – traditional Jewish religious elementary school.

[Page 69]

Burial Society and Gravediggers

The Khevrah Kadisha[1] was established in 1820 even prior to Bransk having its own cemetery.

As you know, Bransk's deceased were driven or carried to Bocki for burial. The funeral service was held in Bransk.

It is difficult to know, who were the first members of the Khevra Kadisha, because in the pinkas they are called Mr Flugi son of Flugi. It is known however, that one of the first gaboyim was Mr Dovid Berlin, followed by Mr

Yekhiel–Leyb, and then Velvl–Daniel's, Mr Ezra Meir Kestin and the last, Khaim Pentman.

Not one from the general population was accepted into the khevra Kadisha . Only during the epidemic of (5520? [1860]), when the existing khevra could not by itself handle the difficult work, when simple folk were sought after to help them. Later, these temporary members became permanent members of the khevra. In this way, such Jews as Yosl Stoyler, (carpenter/cabinet–maker), Avrum Tevl, Nokhmen the hat maker, Zalman Yeshaye were included.

Like in all towns, the Bransk Khevra Kadisha in certain cases was very strict. They sought to receive a substantial amount of money from the family for the burial.

Their expenses were great. They have to pay a certain percent to the Bikur Kholim.[2] The Talmud Torah was also subsidized from the Khevra Kadisha money, as well as giving to the Ha'kneset Kala.[3] The fence around the cemetery had to be repaired constantly. There were fiery protests despite the fact that the Khevra Kadisha conducted itself like all the other societies in the Jewish towns of Poland and Russia and certainly no worse.

[Page 70]

In addition to the aforementioned gaboyim, there were many who never refused to come to a ritual washing the body of the deceased. Every generation had its Khevra –Kadisha members: Dovid–Gimple, Yankel –Meir's Kharlop, Shloyme Blok (?), Aryeh Krotz, Binyomke the tailor, Nokhum Trus , Motel Rimer, Avrum Rybke who was the official shroud–sewer, Tsalke Yosl Stoyler, Malshe Viner, Dovid Kopkes, Khaim Klade, Velvl–Shepsl Katsev, Diadke the locksmith, Leyzer–Fishl Spishiner, Yankel Patoker, Shmuel Kodlubofsky, Khaim–Leybl, Yudl Voylker, , Avrum Verpikhovsky, whose fate it was as the greatest hero during horrific conditions to carry out his activities, to provide the deceased with their final honour. More about this in later articles.

[Page 71]

The Khevra Kadisha had a custom of fasting on erev Shabbos,[4] before the new month, going to the holy place, to the old small–synagogue/house–of–study for minkha (afternoon prayers) to recite Yom Kippur Katan,[5] and then the seuda[6] would take place. Every gabay made an earnest effort to ensure that the seudas be better and nicer.

Avrum Rifke

Yankev Patoker

Various Khevra Kadisha types

If you went to the market on any cold winter's weekday and smelled all kinds of aromas of broiled geese, you then understood why today is the Khevra Kadisha seuda. The general population would be very angry as to why the Khevrah had to have such rich seudas. . They did not know of the great difficulties that were encountered at a ritual cleansing where many times it was necessary to sweep worms out of the deceased. Certainly they did not know and did not see nighttime funerals that took place in the hardest frosts and the deepest snows.

The ceremony for electing the gabayim took place at the Khevra every Lag B'omer,[7] at which time they arranged a ballot box. Through an indirect vote, the arbitrators were elected and they had the right to choose the gaboyim. Usually the same gaboyim would be elected from year to year.

After the election of the gaboyim a dairy seuda would take place, but there was no shortage of spirits at this dairy seuda. These Khevrah members wended their way home through the streets in quite a happy and jolly mood.

During Shmini Atseres[8] the Khevrah were given beer and apples, and at the end of Pesakh, wine and nuts.

The Jews would bring their young children and grandchildren to all the Khevrah Kadisha celebrations, so that they too could experience pleasure.

The Khevrah Kadisha always fulfilled its work. Nothing deterred them even under the most difficult and worst conditions. In the sealed ghetto, under a hail of bullets and war battles, the Khevrah Kadisha was prepared while endangering their own lives, to provide ritual cleansings and funerals with honour in accordance with Jewish law.

The Khevrah Kadisha ends along with all Jewish organizations, with the entire Jewish life in Poland on November 7th, 1942 after existing for 120 years. Officially, one Khevrah Kadisha member, on November 15 th, 1942, single-handedly fulfills the rights of 70 murdered Jews and falls dead into a mass grave. More about this in further chapters.

[Page 72]

Bransk Grave Diggers

The first who is familiar to the elderly Branskers is Itche Kutnik, the grave–digger. If you remember, there was a young married woman Kutnik in Bransk. Itche Kutnik was her father.

It is written in the pinkas that when Itche Kutnik went to open a grave at night as was then the custom, he took AvrumBer the beadle along with him to light his way with a lantern.

Water had already entirely overflowed the road between the bricks. They walked in water, feeling their way. They thought the water was not deep. There was still ice in several places. Itche Kutnik took a step and fell in. Avrum Ber, half–dead, barely made it back to town. The town mourned: "Such a tragedy!" Two days later they found Itche Kutnik's body and buried him. Then the community decided to hire someone else as grave–digger. He was called Antkhele bagreber,[9] a little man, a quiet man, he was half blind. They were always frightened of him. In the small–synagogue/house–of–study he prayed separated from the others, alone at the table. He never had anyone next to him. At a Khevrah Kadisha seuda Aantchele was very important. He was asked by everyone to : eat Antchele, drink Antchele. And Antchele did not need to be begged. He ate with appetite all the delicious broiled meat.

Antchele was a special type of grave–digger. It took him no time at all to open a grave. He always took with him a stick, a long one. When someone died, Antchele immediately came with his stick to take measurements, exactly as if someone would steal the work from him. In 1892, during the epidemic, he managed to open five or six graves every day. He did not release the work until he was paid his money because he had already been cheated a couple of times. Antchele died too. To take his place they chose Hershl Pantz. He is also very capable but not as good as Antchele. He is also sub–beadle in the old small synagogue.

[Page 73]

After his death, Yosl the porter is chosen to be the grave–digger and he too, is subordinate beadle in Poale Tsedek (small–synagogue/house–of–study).

Footnotes (Rubin Roy Cobb)
1. Burial Society
2. Visiting the sick
3. Aid for a poor bride
4. Sabbath eve
5. Wikipedia – "Minor Day of Atonement", a practice observed on the day preceding each Rosh Khodesh or New–Moon Day, the observance consisting of fasting and supplication, but much less rigorous than that of Yom Kippur proper
6. Festive meal
7. Wikipedia – Lag B'Omer – is a Jewish holiday celebrated on the 33rd day of the Counting of the Omer. It marks the hillula (celebration), interpreted by some as anniversary or death of Rabbi Shimon bar Yochai, a Mishnaic sage and leading disciple of Rabbi Akiva in the 2nd century CE
8. The eighth day of Succos (festival of Tabernacles) that merges with Simkhat Torah (ending and beginning of the usually annual cycling of the reading of the Five Books of Moses)
9. Gravedigger

[Page 74]

Bransk Prayer Leaders[1]

All the Jews were capable of praying at the[2] lectern. The title of prayer leader belonged to a few who could pray during the Days of Awe at the lectern.

There were many such in Bransk.

Avrum Ber the beadle had great strength for morning prayers : others had great strength for additional morning prayers. When more small–synagogues/houses–of–study were established in Bransk, it was necessary to pay leaders of prayers. Sholem–Itche the teacher was one of them. He had two good assistants, Khilye the baker and Hertzke Fuks who has lived in Brownsville for more than sixty years, and is well known as a good leader of prayers during the Days of Awe in Sholem–Itche's style. Today, at the age of eighty, he still performs at the Midwood Jewish Centre. He complains that the children don't let him pray at the lectern. In Spring Valley, where Hertzke Fuks spends the summers, they do not know that Hertzke Fuks' style stems from Sholem–Itche's, as long as they are satisfied with his praying the closing prayer of Yom Kippur.

Zalman Shames and Binyomke Melamed, Avrum–Ber's son were good leaders of prayers but with additional talents. Maishe–Yehuda the beadle was a man of great distinction. For all prayers he was outstanding with his pleasant voice and he could pray at the lectern for several days running. His assistants were the Shmultchikes. The last assistants were Khaim Hersh–Zalman Rutker, Khaim Oddeser. Binyomkes assistants were Mendl Toker and Leybl Stelman who later became a leader of prayers.

[Page 75]

Itche Alyarnik, was good at leading prayers, a very good weeping prayer leader. His praying virtually caused the congregation to melt into tears. The crying began in the women's section, carried over to the men's section and developed into a great plea. With deep sighs all those praying pleaded with He Who is in Heaven to be written into the Book of Life. He did not need any assistants. All those who were praying assisted him.

Shaul'ke Farber, was a quiet and heartfelt leader of prayers. His praying was so filled with sadness, filled with such a pleading that they must be accepted. A Jew such as Shaul'ke Farber could not be forgotten.

Hertzke Fuks, *Sholem–Itche's assistant*

Fishele Bog, of blessed memory, *leader of prayers*

Fishele Bog, was a wonderfully hearty leader of prayers, but he shouted and had to strain his voice. His assistants were Avigdor Katsev, and sometimes Avrum'ke Katsev.

Leybl Stelman kept to his rabbi's strict style. He was a good leader of prayers, slow and full of heart. The women liked his praying very much. His brother Mendl Toker was his assistant.

Mendl Toker, also Binyomkes assistant, was one of the truly excellent leaders of prayer. The youth most especially liked Mendl Toker's praying and filled the new small–synagogue/house–of–study when Mendl RC prayed. Mendl actually studied his prayers during the entire year while he was at work.

[Page 76]

Leybl, his brother also assisted him, and sometimes his son, Maishke. Maishe Viner, Elye Gotlieb, Khatskl the Ritual Slaughterer, Kadish the Ritual Slaughterer, Dovid–Ezriel's, Yudl Voylker, Nisl Lavitch, Hershl Zagel,[3] Aryeh Kratz, Alter Kapelikhes, Avrum Sussen,[4] Yekutial Morvinker, Hershl Platrat, Yoel'ke Platrat, Avigdor Katsev, were leaders of prayers.

Avrum Verpikhovski was a modern leader of prayers. Khaim–Leybl Golding, Sanes son–in–law, was also one of the good leaders of prayers, well–liked in town and a participant in all town activities. The latter two were taken to Treblinka November 7th, 1942.

Footnotes (Rubin Roy Cobb)
1. Ba'ali Tefilus (or Tefilos) – Leaders of Prayer
2. Davend far'n omed – pray at the lectern
3. Dov Berel Zagel (Segal, Chaggal) was married to Shaynste [Yaffa] Kobylanski, a sister of Rubin Roy Cobb's [] father Lapidut Khlawne Kobylanski [Henry Cobb – he can be seen on the right side of the middle row in the photo on page 417 of the Bransk Union in Johannesburg, South Africa; also two grandchildren of are named after him, viz. Ariel Deborah (the wife of Lapidut – Judges 4:4) Khlawne Frankel and Lapidut Khlawne Cobb]. They had a son Yossele. All three were gassed at Treblinka on November 7, 1942.
4. Two Sussen [Sussin] families live/lived in Johannesburg, South Africa. Berel Sussen [he can be seen on the third from the right side of the middle row in the photo on page 417 of the Bransk Union in Johannesburg, South Africa] lived to the age of 104 and almost to the end blew the shofar at the Pine Street Shul in Johannesburg, South Africa, on Rosh Hashanah and Yom Kippur

[Page 77]

Bransk Khasidim

Almost all the khasidim in Bransk were not born in Bransk but came from near and far Polish cities and towns.

In 1900 there were about two prayer quorums of ten male adults of khasidim from various khasidic dynasties. They had their own khasidic shtibl[1], and there they held their quorums of ten male adults on Shabbos and on holidays.

Itskhak Kashemakher and Shloyme–HershYentchman

Among the well–known are Mordekhe'le the Khasid of Nayshtot, Dovid Khazn of Tchekhenoftse, Abele of Volomin , Sholem–Itche Melamed of Sakole, Sholem Hitzl of Drogetshin, Zavl–Hersh of Sokole, Ben Tsiyon Melamed of the Shedlitser area, Meir–Khaim of Simyatchev, Shloyme Hersh of Sokolove, Khaim–Fishl Melamed of Orla, Kalman–Maishe of the Kobrin area. Only Yankev Mordekhay was born in Bransk.

[Page 78]

In this group were found Gerer, Radzeminer, Alleksandrer, 1 Kotsker, Kobriner and Slonimer, and yet all the khasidim lived peacefully among themselves.

The khasidim shtibl was the spiritual centre of all the Bransk khasidim. They congregated there on Shabbos for prayer and in the evening for the shalosh seudas[2] all the khasidim came together, each bringing with him a piece of khale.[3] There were about ninety small flasks in the khasidic shtibl and everybody sang Sabbath songs together, listened to the wonderful stories about good Jews which never seemed to run out. Visiting khasidim brought new khasidic thumping melodies which they heard from their rabbi and studied with the crowd. Kalman Maishe quickly adapted these thumping melodies. Dovid Khasid, with his strong voice, practiced the new style.

The large melave malke seudas[4] which always took place every year during the night of the first slikhos[5] was a big celebration. To this melave malke the khasidic wives prepared a good grits with a piece of goose. Little k5hasidic boys brought the hot food to the khasidic shtibl and for this were paid a kopek each. The khasidic youth gladly paid the kopek to the little boys because they themselves would have had to do this work.

The biggest celebration took place Passover eve at Shmuelke Aynbinder's when they baked the shmurah matzah.[6] The Zarember teacher kneaded the Passover dough, everyone rolled it out, but they had to have a redler.[7] When the matzah. was finished, they all began to pray, uttering praises and afterwards having a little taste of Passover brandy. It was necessary only for a few drops of spirits for all to become jolly. It was aninternal happiness that was felt at khasidic celebrations. Such celebrations helped them to get through the rest of the year in the terrible poverty that most of the khasidim experienced.

The enthusiasm of Simkhas Torah[8] is impossible to describe. The entire khasidic population went from the khasidic shtibl to the khasidic homeowners where they found tables already laden with what had been prepared earlier for the holiday. The good food quickly disappeared from the table and the khasidim disappeared from there as well, going to a second khasidic home, and so forth, until the evening. Then it was time for afternoon prayers and the khasidim were quite drunk as they marched to the khasidic shtibl, praying the afternoon prayers almost at dark. And then evening prayers in a week ending somber style. The arrival of autumn could already be felt, with the cold and rainy days. They had no wood, no warm clothing. After evening prayers little Mordekhayle would call out that all should carry up the summer garments to the attic and bring down the warm coats. Khasidim sighed heavily. The warm clothing was already long torn and had patches upon patches.

[Page 79]

Ginsberg the Teacher and Efraim the Teacher

Two Khasidic Jews

From time–to–time, the Kobrin or the Slonim rabbi would come as a guest. They would usually stay with Shloyme Hitzl in the brick house and hold their "tables" there. The entire town would come to witness the khasidic "tables". Only the most important people would be invited, but the most honoured would be the khasidim. They felt that the celebration was theirs. In general, the khasidim lived in a friendly fashion among themselves.

The little khasidic children on the festivals had a special complaint.

[Page 80]

This was when it was necessary to bring a pail of water from Elye Vatnik's well for the Levites[9] to place It before the Kohanim[10] to enable them to perform the priestly benedictions . Avrum–Zavl Hersh' was a Levite, already a youth of 18 or 19 and was embarrassed to carry the pail of water through the street. Therefore he paid a bribe to the little khasidic boys for bringing water from the well. There was no money permitted on a holiday, so Avreml had to give a package of cigarettes. After the holiday, he bought the cigarettes back for two kopeks.

The khasidic children later became interested in all community activities. They quickly became familiar with politics and put forth candidates for the town council and knew how to get these candidates elected.

Through the activities of the younger khasidim together with the new additions from neighbouring towns, they became active in various areas in "ha'shomer ha'Shabbos"[11] and carefully watched the rows of candidates to ensure that no one slipped in through the back door on Shabbos. Ben–Tsiyon the Zarember's was the one who took upon himself the duty of helping the One Who is in Heaven to keep watch over Jewish children to ensure they did not stray from the straight path and G–d forbid, have any Jewish concerts or theatre performances that is forbidden by the true God on Shabbos.

The situation has changed lately. New people appear in the khasidic ranks. Jews dress with a smaller hat and become khasidim, travel to Ger, return well educated in the Aguda[12] movement, they are no longer interested in any new khasidic melodies. They become interested in the daily Aguda Tzaitung newspaper and agitating for the elections. The political activities of the khasidim results in many in town being angry at them. Eastern (?) wall Jews and unaffiliated are united in their hatred towards the khasidic politicians, but they can do nothing. The khasidim already have their own khasidic shtibl which is the centre of their activities. They no longer have to worry about paying rent money.

[Page 81]

Among the politically astute khasidim were the four Konopyates brothers: Yisroel, Yankev, Mates and Aron Shmuel, Klodke, Itskhak Finkelshteyn, Alter Gotlieb, Ben–Tsiyon and others.

Shabsi Verpikhovski and wife

Ben–Tsiyon Zarember and wife

The khasidisher element did not want to mix with the mitnagdishen.[14] adherents in the ghetto. The khasidim, with all its followers in Bransk, ends with all other Jewish religious and free institutions on November 7th 1942 with the evacuation of Bransk residents to the gas chambers and ovens.

Footnotes (Rubin Roy Cobb)

1. Khasidic and Ultra–Orthodox House of Prayer and Study
2. Wikipedia – the "third meal" customarily eaten by Sabbath–observing Jews just before the end of Shabbos.
3. Wikipedia – a special Jewish braided bread eaten on the Sabbath and holidays (among South Africans, the majority being of "Litvak" stock refer to khallah as "kitke")
4. "The ushering out of the queen," the evening meal marking the conclusion of the Sabbath.
5. Prayers recited days preceding Rosh Hashannah, usually at midnight.
6. Smurah means "watched." And it is an apt description of this matzah, the ingredients of which (the flour and water) are guarded from the moment of harvesting and drawing.
7. One who makes punctures in the dough.
8. Wikipedia – Simkhas Torah – "Rejoicing of the Torah" is a celebration marking the conclusion of the annual cycle of public Torah readings, and the beginning of a new cycle.
9. From the tribe of Levi such as the brothers Moses and Aaron.
10. Priests in English, Kohen in Hebrew and Yiddish, Kaplan in Polish, Kagan in Russian, Kayhen in Lithuanian Yiddish, Cohen or Kohn as a surname.
11. Guardians of the Sabbath.
12. Agudath Yisroel Ultra–orthodox anti–Zionist movement commonly referred to today as "haredim".
13. This was a few houses away from the home of Rubin Roy Cobb's maternal grandparent's home, Akiva Skornik.
14. Wikipedia – Misnagedim is a Hebrew word meaning "opponents" (who are mainly from Lithuania or commonly referred to as "Litvaks" which most of Bransk Jewry identified with – the Litvaks originated from present day Lithuania, Latvia, North–Eastern Poland [Bransk], and West Belarus and commonly refers to opponents of khasidim

[Page 82]

Society for the Study of Talmud and Society for the Study of the Repetition of the "Oral Torah"[1]

The Khevra Shas (Society for the Study of Talmud) was founded during the time of Mr Shaul Regensburger, the third rabbi of Bransk. The facts are confirmed in writings in old books that were given to the Khevra Shas in the name of a deceased Jew in 1865.

The daf yomi[2] (page of the day) has lately become popular, when all cities and towns study the same page of gemora every day. All of Poland studied the same page on the same day. The siyum (conclusion) was carried out on the same day.

The teachers of the daily page of gemora were from the old small–synagogue/house–of–study Rabbi Tsukerman, from the new small–house–of–prayer/house–of–study Rabbi Khaim Leyb's Lyev, Hershl Stolyare's son–in–law from the third small–synagogue/house–of–study, Mr Meir Kestin, from the Poale Tsedek, Mr Shloyme Kontchik from the Khasidim Shtibl, Rabbi Avrum Yankev Sekerevitch. The "tisch" (table) were usually attended by scholarly Jews who derived pleasure from learning and from the teachers who were great scholars.

I remember that during the time of the first German occupation the Khevra Shas was led by Ezra and Khaim Stolyartshik. At the table tens of people would stand by to hear them. After the lesson, Aharon Velvl the baker would relate the news from the newspapers. Everyone paid attention. The scholars did not leave their seats. Aharon Velvl had a talent for telling the news although he would sometimes not be clear. Suddenly somebody said: "It is almost eight o'clock and we will not be allowed to be on the streets. It is time for evening prayers and we have to go home. " There were sometimes those who fell asleep during the lesson, but nobody ever slept during the conclusion. A shame to waste a drink.

[Page 83]

The Khevra Mishnayes now consisted of a different class of Jews. Here there were simple Jews who could not study by themselves, so they sat listening to the teachers. Many of them actually could do this and others not so. However, the audience was pleased.

The Khevra Mishnayes teachers were Mr Maishe Yehuda from the old–house–of–prayer/house–of–study, Khaim Pentman from the new house–of–prayer/house–of–study. It is unknown how he knew Torah. From the third house–of–prayer/house–of–study there was Mr Shmuel Kruk, and from the Poale Tsedek, house of–prayer/house–of–study, Yosl the porter. Avrum Meir Kanapyater was from the Khasidim shtibl. There was no Khevra in the tailors' house–of–study/house–of prayer, but you could encounter Khone Kashtan in the old house–of–prayer/house–of–study at the Khevra Shas. Mordekhay Askard was at the "tisch" of the Khevra Mishnayes also in the old house–of–prayer/house–of–study.

All of these khasidim were very popular. There was no one missing. It was a duty that each gladly fulfilled. The two Khevras were active during the German occupation and as well during the Soviet regime only in two houses–of–prayer/houses–of–study. In the gas chambers of Treblinka there perished all the Torah Jews and scholars. Not one of them was fortunate enough to survive.

Footnotes (Rubin Roy Cobb)
1. Wikipedia – The component of the Talmud comprising rabbinical analysis of and commentary after the Mishnah.
2. Wikipedia – is a daily regimen of learning the Oral Torah and its commentaries (also known as the Gemora), in which each of the 2,711 pages of the Babylonian Talmud are covered in sequence. Under this regimen, the entire Talmud is completed, one day at a time, in a cycle of seven and a half years [it still carries on to this day]. – Rabbi Meir Shapiro of Yeshivas Khakhmei Lublin, Poland inaugurated this on the first day of Rosh Hashanah 5684 (11 September 1923). The concept of Daf Yomi was initiated by the World Agudath Israel [anti–Zionist] movement in Vienna on 16 August 1923.

[Page 84]

Talmud Torah Of Bransk

There are lists in the pinkas of the Khevra Kadisha of subsidies for the Talmud Torah for the year 1861.

This clearly shows that there was a Talmud Torah in Bransk. It had lately been arranged that the Khevra Kadisha contribute 20 percent of its income to the town Talmud Torah. Usually the head gabay of the Khevra Kadisha was the one who was actually in charge of the Talmud Torah.

Like in all Polish towns, the little Jewish boy in Bransk received his education from private teachers. Every poor man paid tuition with the last grosz[1] of his money.

However, there were those who could not pay at all for a rabbi. The teachers themselves were very poor and could ill afford to teach these poor children. In order to prevent such poor children from not being able to read and pray, the Talmud Torah was established. This was the free schoolroom for poor children.

The parents of such children had to be satisfied with the Talmud Torah education they received and certainly did not have a say in the way the community school was run. Regardless of any displeasure they may have felt, they could not protest. Certainly no one would have paid them any attention. The Talmud Torah was located in one of the rooms of the old house–of–prayer/house–of–study, there where the rabbi's rooms were.

[Page 85]

The Talmud Torah teacher was the poorest of all the teachers. He endured the most trouble from his non–paying students. Most of them were orphans or had fathers who were poor and downtrodden, and were not interested in their childrens' education.

The boys felt free to play various tricks on the rabbi, and that is why the Talmud Torah teacher's work was so difficult. One thing was a certainty for him, he received his wages every week and did not have to wait for the boys to bring the rabbi his tuition fee.

The necessary money was collected at Purim, Khanuka, and Khol Hamoyd.[2] On erev Yom Kippur the pledge plate with a long list printed in the script of the Sefer Torah: Talmud Torah of Bransk – was prominently displayed on the table.

The name "Talmud Torah boy" was considered by the boys to be one of which to be ashamed. And yet, there was pity felt for the Talmud Torah boys because everyone knew that such a child suffers terrible slaps and beatings from the rabbi, and nobody defended them.

In 1911, a special modern building is erected in Bransk for the Talmud Torah. Yoske Menukhe's becomes the gabai of the Talmud Torah. The Khevra Kadisha gabai no longer has a say about the Talmud Torah. A sign is mounted on the building – Kheder Tsiburi,[3] no longer Talmud Torah. The entire Talmud Torah was an insult in Bransk to the parents and the children.

Several children from various groups could not be found in the Kheder Tsiburi. All were taught by one teacher.

One thing is certain, that during the time of the Kantonistn there was no Talmud Torah in Bransk because no mother would send her child to the Talmud Torah. He would surely have been taken away by the "catcher" to become a soldier for the Tsar Nikolay.

The Talmud Torah was founded after the time of the Kantonistn and continued during all times. In this way Bransk took care of its poor children, ensuring them of a somewhat Jewish education in accordance with the understanding of the time.

[Page 86]

During the last years, the Talmud Torah has taken on a folk character. Many Jewish children, poor and rich, studied there. They were taught by modern teachers and received a worldly education. Yosef Zeyfman, Hershl Vaser and Khaim Klodke were the Yiddish teachers. Rubinshteyn taught worldly subjects.

Then Bransk pointed its finger at such children: "These are Talmud Torah children."

In 1939, when the Soviet government comes to town, all the kheders and the Talmud Torah are disbanded. Modern schools are established for all the town's children.

Footnotes (Rubin Roy Cobb)
1. Wikipedia – In Poland a grosz (plural grosz or groszy, depending on the number) is 1/100 part of a Zloty.
2. Intermediary week–days between the first two and last days of the holiday – Passover (Pesakh) and Tabernacles (Succos)
3. Folk school.
[Page 87]

Acts of Benevolent Lodging and Visiting the Sick in Bransk

The Khevra was founded in 1893, during the intermediary days of Pesakh by Yankev–Meir Kharlop, Dovid Milner and Yosl Dubiner. Yosl was also called Yosl Kosovitski, or Yosl the Royfe[1] and Abele Khasid. There were many illnesses in town that year. The measures taken by the Khevra consisted of helping the sick to get a doctor, medicine, blood and paying a visit to them.

The income of the Khevra was made up of weekly collections from the homes in town. Shloyme Blok would go about with his pushke[2] wrapped in a white paper that read: "Linat Ha'tsedek" and "Bikur Kholim"[3] in Bransk.

Every kitchen had a pushke from the Khevra. Every woman, prior to candle lighting, would drop a coin into it. Erev Yom Kippur, a collection plate would be in the Synagogues. A pushke would also be set out at weddings and ritual circumcisions.

From this collected money, they had to take care of one who was sick and poor, and provide a doctor and medicine, or the barber–surgeon Prazhmen and sometimes also pay Bashe–Royzen the grandmother, for poor new mothers. They also had to prepare berry juice for sweating, instruments, tubs, bladders, odds and ends, etc.

When someone needed a doctor, he came to Dovid Milner for a voucher. He also gave a voucher. to the pharmacist. The instruments were kept at Abele's. He gave the instruments only when a pledge was given. The best pledge was for a Yom Kippur makhzor.[4] If the instruments were not returned in a timely fashion, then Shloymeh-Efrayim and Avrum Makofski would go into town together to bring them back to Abele. The berry juice was at Frumele's. When there was a benevolent lodging, the rich did not attend but instead hired somebody for this purpose. They mostly hired Shepsl the porter or Mikhalke the porter. This afforded these two poor men a small source of income.

[Page 88]

Shepsl the porter would spend a night sitting at the bedside of a sick person. Tired from a day of carrying heavy packs on his back, he would fall asleep. He would rise at five o'clock in the morning a kikhl[5] or an apple or have a sip of sweet tea, and on a good day wish the sick, clean the sick person up a bit and also clean off the table. He would drink the juice, nibble person a complete recovery. The sick person could not benefit too much from this, so the Khevra found a new solution, that one must himself attend a benevolent lodging and not hire anyone else. The members of the Khevra were almost all townsmen and women.

On Shabbos Parshe (chapter) V'ira,[6] the Khevra made a kiddush at Avrum Shkop's brick house. The rabbi would say a few words from the parsha, the attendees would partake of the good cake and drink the strong shnaps.[7] Mordekhay Hersh the teacher and Aryeh**Error! Bookmark not defined.** Krotz were specialists in eating the cake and drinking the brandy.

You understand that Friday prior to the kiddush they went to everyone to collect 20 groshen towards the kiddush.

On Purim or Khanuka Yankev–Meir Kharlop, Yerukhim Goldberg, with Dovid Podratchik would themselves go through town collecting a few rubles for the Visiting of the Poor Sick. Nevertheless there was always a deficit. On the first of every month, Prozhmer would bring about 50 vouchers for the seriously ill. Dr Tkashkevitsh would bring vouchers for the very sick. Bashe–

Reyze would bring several vouchers for women in childbirth and a few ritual circumcisions. The pharmacist would bring vouchers for castor oil, Chinese powders, black salve, (species of mushroom?) water, suppositories and spirits of camphor. Yosl Kosovitski would bring a couple of vouchers for twisted fingers, casting a broken leg or hand or for a couple of children's throats. Yosl was a specialist in such things. Nobody could clear a child's throat as well as Yosl the–barber–surgeon:

[Page 89]

Righteous Administration of the Benevolent Lodging in Bransk

Sign in front of the group reads:

Administration of the Poorhouse and Hospital for the Poor
Bottom row: **Ayzik Fakhter, Beynish Okon**
Second row: **Hersh Avol, Mordekhay Golde, Yankel Patoker, Khaim–Leyb Golde and Maishe Fatinke**
Third row: **Khaykl Rakhovin, Alyeh Yentchman, Alter Glik and Yankev Pribut**
Top row: **Zakhryh Oskart, Alter Saperstein, Shimon–Dovid Pribut and Elye Gershon Perlman**

[Page 90]

Yosl Dubiner was a wonderful human being. He had three names: Yosl Dubiner, Yosl Katavitski and Yosl the barber–surgeon. The work went on without complaints. The Bikur Kholim (Hospital for the Poor) C was a truly democratic institution.

In 1915, when the Germans occupied Bransk, sicknesses in Bransk increases 300 percent and income decreases. They call a meeting, new people show up, younger, Asher Nyman, Itskhak–Mordekhay Vaser, Hershl Hurwitz, Khone Schwartz, Mr Maishe–Mordekhay the son of Rabbi Shimon Shkop, and me (Julius Cohen). We decide to continue working in the Bikur Kholim but to increase the income through modern means, such as arranging spectacular shows, readings, concerts, with the participation of a Bialystok Jewish amateur troupe. Money is raised. Sickness increases in severity. It was the time of the German occupation, and there was little food, no wood for heating homes and the result was – hunger, typhus, diphtheria in increasing amounts in town.

In 1918 when the Germans leave the town, many have to flee Bransk because of political or other reasons. The rabbi's son goes to Grodno, new people join to work devotedly. The most active during the last years are Shabtay Chomski, the Kadolbafkar Rimer, Khaim**Error! Bookmark not defined.**–Leyb Golding, Mr Khaim–Leyb Lyev, Beynish Okon, Motye Aba the hat maker's son–in–law and Akiva (aka Kiva) Skornik.[8] The Khevra had various medicines and instruments. This was supplied by Shabtay Chomski, Dr Kaminyetski and his wife, both good doctors. The Khevra arranged lectures at which there was taught hygiene and cleanliness.

During the first air attack on Bransk on September 7th, 1939, all the instruments, books and medicines of the Poorhouse and Hospital for the Poor of Bransk are burned. And so ends the finest democratic institution after an existence of three years along with the demise of the entire Jewish community.

Footnotes (Roy Cobb)

1. Old–time physician, one not formally trained; bonesetter
2. Collection box.
3. Acts of "Benevolent Lodging" and "Visiting the Sick."
4. Festival Prayer Book.
5. A sugared rusk.
6. Parshat Vayera (Genesis 18:1 – 22:24) is the 4th weekly Torah portion in the annual Jewish cycle of Torah reading. The verses refer to the dramatic story of the Akedah – the binding of Isaac that is central to Jewish liturgy and thought. God told Abraham that He will make his descendants as numerous as the stars in the sky and as the sand on the seashore and through Abraham's offspring all the nations on earth will be blessed.
7. Alcoholic drink
8. The maternal grandfather of Rubin Roy Cobb

[Page 91]

Hospitality for Poor Guests[1]
– Aid for Poor Brides[2] – Loans Without Interest[3]

There were 2 houses for lodging poor visitors in Bransk: at Binyomke the teacher for special guests, such as a preacher or a courier of a yeshiva or an old–aged home[4] in Jerusalem. A guest such as this stayed at Binyomke the teacher where there was a special room with five beds with straw mattresses and warm quilts.

Binyomke did not rush headlong into inviting the guests, firstly, the guest had to be dressed properly, secondly he had to show his signature for who he was and that he was legal, and not God forbid one of those who had been caught up in socialism. He had to say definitively, when he will leave. When Binyomke was not at home, Khane Riva requested all the requirements be met or she would not permit them to enter the house. Most likely she must have already been chastised by Binyomke for not being careful. Yet Binyomke would complain: "Everyone comes to Bransk, only to Bransk, from all over the world they come only to Bransk." He earned one ruble per month.

The second house was for lodging poor visitors and was located in the Poorhouse and was for coarse Jews, wandering poor Jews who would beg from house to house and receive a prutah. Most of them were scruffy and filthy, for these people there was the hekdesh.[5] This was the domain of Antshl the assistant–beadle or the gravedigger. There they also had beds with mattresses but they were old and musty. When these poor men were finished with their work in a day or two, they were required to leave. If they did not do so, they would not receive a voucher from Maishe Yehuda for Shabbos. On Thursday, they would cash in the prutahs at Nokhman the hat–maker and receive a couple of zekserlekh[6] and continue on their way.

[Page 92]

The prutah was a Bransk coin, a little cardboard stamped "Prutah of Bransk." The poor man came to Nokhman the hat maker and received ninety prutahs for thirty groshen.[7] With this capital, the poor man went around to houses begging. A housewife would give a grosh and ask for two prutahs change. A rich housewife would ask for one prutah change. When such a poor man received a grosh and did not have to give any change, he was in seventh heaven.

However, it once happened that the prutahs of Bransk flooded the town. Poor men did not come to Nokhman the hat maker for prutahs because they had enough prutahs. The writer of this article (Julius Cohen) must now confess that he caused the inflation, because he, simply by virtue of being at his father Nokhman the hat maker's, got the stamp, stamped prutahs and gave them to poor men cheaply at the rate of ten for a groshen. I do not know who suffered from this damage because Nokhman the hat maker was beloved for his honesty. The community had to pay out to the poor men according to the official rate – three for a grosch. Nokhman complained, that someone was copying the prutahs. In case such poor men did not want to leave Bransk before Shabbos, there were those jokesters who copied Maishe Yehuda's vouchers for Shabbos. It so happened that at one homeowner there were two guests for Shabbos. One was the legitimate one and the other the false one. The homeowner was suspicious, how did they send two guests for Shabbos. Well, so be it. If Maishe–Yehuda sent, there are no complaints. Avrum–Maishe Bertche was the forger of Maishe–Yehuda's vouchers.

The hekdesh was the designated place for such guests. The gabai of the guest lodging was Avrum Vainer. The expenses were minor. To heat the hekdesh which was the taharah shtibl,[8] the poor went begging for a couple of pieces of wood. They went to the neighbors, to Beyle–Feygn, to Zislen, to Shames the Vatnik (?),[9] to Yankl Zavl or to Aron Velvelekhe, the bathhouse attendant.

[Page 93]

Others simply took apart fences or stole a couple of pieces of wood from the small–synagogues/houses–of–study, and this is how they slept in a warm hekdesh.

During the war years 1914 and beyond, there are no more guests, and the first–class guest lodging closed. Those who did come all looked as if they belonged to the second class of guests, and that is how the hekdesh continued. Later they arranged to have guest lodging for the better class at Yenkl Brezhnitser.

They found there a poor man with two small children who had perished and were never identified. And so ended the Bransk lodging for poor guests, two years before the entire Jewish population perished.

Aid for Poor Brides in Bransk[10]

Until this very day I do not know who were the gabayim or gabay'etes (women) of the aid for poor brides, only that if a poor bride was to be married, somebody made sure that she would not be shamed.

Gershon–Ber the shadkhan[11] had only to find a couple, and the rest was taken care of.

As a young boy I (Julius Cohen) noticed that Leybl Styelman, Dovid the shmid[12] or Tsivye the rimerke[13] and Rokhele from Bocki going around the town collecting for the expenses of a wedding for a poor bride. Rikl Beeber[14] and Yokhe Vayn, Khaye Yenkl Khukar with Stsyaptchikhe also went around collecting for this purpose. These sort of weddings took place at Itche the garbater,[15] Zalman, the rabbi's Antshl Bagreber's daughter. In order not to embarrass a poor bride, they collected linens/bedding. They hired klezmer and brought Shloyme Efrayim Badkhan to sing/talk about the bride. Shprintse the bathhouse attendant already knew with 40 years of experience, already knew whom to invite to such a wedding.

[Page 94]

When the Gutman Klezmer played at such a wedding, the fiddler spoke to everyone's heart, not only played but cried with tears.

The Khevra was a self–created one during the time of the plague in 1892. At that time the town married Itche the tanner[16] to the seamstress as a remedy to put an end to the plague. The aid for poor brides remained as a permanent institution.

The money that Gershon Ber earned for making such a match consisted of the right to be present at the wedding and enjoying a good wedding meal. Maishe Aron the the matchmaker was a strong competitor of Gershon Ber the matchmaker but he never could surpass him.

The proudest accomplishment of Gershon Ber's career was when he married off Khinke Brokh. This was a single woman of about 50, six feet tall. There was a big celebration at Khinke Brokh's wedding to a 22 year old groom from somewhere in the Kiev gubernya.[17] Tsivye Rimerke, Rokhl–Bashe – Sime's danced. Mordekhay –Hersh the teacher and all from Khanale Farber's family were invited. Everything was beautiful. Gershon–Ber felt himself to be a very important and successful matchmaker. Dowry was created. The groom received a new overcoat.

Regrettably, the celebration was short–lived, fell apart because the groom quickly disappeared along with the dowry and the new overcoat, and Khinke Brokh remains an eternal aguna.[18]

Free Loan Society of Bransk

This was the name of the Khevra dedicated in 1863 after the Polish matyezsh (uprising). The economic situation at that time was such that Jews began to open little stores. Artisans had to prepare wood, especially the turners. The turner industry was very well–developed. All the peasants needed wheels for spinning their flax.

[Page 95]

There was no place to obtain a free loan. Who would lend a poor man a couple of rubles, Then the community activists created such an institution where one could borrow money through a pledge. They would bring to Mr Dovid a pair of earrings, a ring, seven strands of pearls, necklaces or a good watch. They would receive a loan of five to ten rubles. The borrowers had to bring 30 groshen each week. This was a hardship. The poor people who borrowed were ashamed to go to the rabbi every week and Mr Dovid's sons did not want them as visitors every week. So they found a solution, that each could pay back the five rubles all at once and retrieve his pledge. This was even more difficult for the poor borrower. This resulted in the pledged item being held. Later, Ezra Goldberg became custodian for the pledges. When a child became sick and a couple of rubles were needed for the barber–surgeon, they once again came with a pledge. Mr Ezra looked the item over: "it is not worth much," he sighed, but he gave five rubles.

The money for this institution was raised from the pushke contributions, town gatherings, from the erev Yom Kippur bowl with the note "Gmilas Khesedim of Bransk." The Khevra Kadisha had to hand over a portion of its income for this purpose.

This institution was not very popular. People were embarrassed and ashamed to borrow. When someone's mortgage was held they felt very debased. Over the years there remained many items with the Khevra. During the First World War when the Germans entered Bransk, the Gmilas Khesed ended. The German soldiers took the pledged items for themselves. Nobody mentioned that it belonged to them. Everybody was ashamed. This was the end of the free loan society in Bransk.

There arises once again an institution, better organized and handled more efficiently. More about this in later chapters.

Footnotes (Rubin Roy Cobb)

1. Hakneset orkhim
2. Hakneset kalah
3. Gmilas khesedim
4. Mayshev Zkeinim
5. Hekdesh – filthy place –Poorhouse – hospital for the poor. A word borrowed from the Mishnah and the Talmud, in which it means "a coin of smaller value". It was an ancient copper Jewish coin worth about one thousandth of a pound.
6. Coin of six groshen
7. A small Polish coin.
8. Shed at a cemetery in which Jewish dead bodies are cleansed before burial
9. Garment maker
10. Hakneset kalah
11. Matchmaker
12. Blacksmith
13. Harness/saddle maker
14. Great–Aunt of Rubin Roy Cobb, family lives in Atlanta, GA USA
15. Tanner
16. Znaydektshikhen
17. Province or State
18. Wikipedia – Agunah – is a halakhic term for a Jewish woman who is "chained" to her marriage. The classic case of this is a man who has left on a journey and has not returned. For a divorce to be effective, Jewish law requires that a man grant his wife a get (divorce) of his own free will. Without a get no new marriage will be recognized.

[Page 96]

Psalms Society[1], Splendour of Young Men[2], Tailors[3], Brotherly Love[4], and Book Correction[5]

As we know from the previous article, the Bransk scholars had their Khevra Shas. The others, who were not so scholarly, had their Khevra Mishnayes.

The uneducated was not familiar with many things, and needed something of a spiritual nature. The Psalms Society fulfilled his desires. Here at the Psalms Society he felt equal to everyone else. He could read into the Psalms whatever he wanted. These were his prayers to G–d, his thanks for everything.

It is difficult to state with any certainty, when the Psalms Society was founded, but surely it has been in existence a long time. It is told, that the Psalms Society gifted the old house–of–prayer/house of study, with a candelabra of twenty four candles that burned from Friday's candle–blessing until daybreak on Shabbos morning. Then the second tier of candles would ignite by itself. In this way, early Shabbos in the winter was the best time to recite Psalms in the Synagogue near the large candelabra. Also the time for reciting Psalms was according to their rules on the 7th Adar, being Maishe Rabeinu's[6] yortsayt, Shavuos[7], Hashanah Raba[8] and summer Shabbosim in the evening before ashrei temimei derekh[9]. The Psalms Society came to a mourner's house to recite Psalms.

The teacher and gabai during our time was Avrum Portselaynik who was beloved by everyone for his baking of kasha kugels and potato kugels that tasted heavenly. [10]

[Page 97]

When he was gabai the Psalms Society carried out all the rules, carefully and precisely watched. He went to all the synagogues to see how the reciting of Psalms was progressing. It was determined, by whom and where the Psalms would be recited at the lectern.

He retained the old house of prayers/house–of–study for himself. Fishl Spishiner had the claim in the new small–house of prayer/house–of–study. Following him was Leyzer Filipovski, in the Merivinker in the third small–synagogue/house–of–prayers, the Shmultchikes, then Asher Tikatzki, in the Poale–Tsedek small house–of–prayers/house of studies, there was Yoel'ke Shuster; in the Tailors' small–house–of–prayers/house–of–studies, Binyomke or Kaprutke; for the Khasidim KalmanMaishe. There were synagogue gabayim like Leybl Stelman, Dovid Ezriel, Mordekhay Ayzik but Avrum Portzelaynik was the chief–gabai. After Passover, at the Psalms Society, there was wine, nuts, and at Shmini–Atzeres[11] – kvas[12] and apples.

When Avrum Portselaynik suggested choosing a new gabai, they answered: healthy may you be, and he was the gabai of the Psalms Society. A fine funeral was held for him after his death. Rabbi Avrum–Yankev Sekrevitz eulogized him. Lipe Portzelaynik, Avrum's son takes over the position of his father as gabai. He is a modern Jew, without a beard. In the market he is interested in displaying his knowledge about a horse, but he is a good gabai of the Psalms Society. He contributed some brandy for the holiday celebrations.

The Psalms Society also functioned during the war years. During the time of the Soviets, Lipe paid no attention and sent Jews to recite verses of Psalms. Lipe went with all the others to Treblinka's gas chambers, on November 7th 1942.

In the partisan detachment in the Bransk forest, Hershl Shpak, as the eldest, led the recital of Psalms. Quietly he mentioned the gabayim who had preceded him, Lipe and Avrum Portzelaynik.

Splendour of Young Men[13]

This was a Khevra of young men, the working youth. The founders were Avrum Broder, Khaim Odeser, Motl Shuster, Shaye the Afrikaner[14], Falek the tailor, Alter Maishe Gusiki, Alter– Maishe–Aron the butcher and other such young men. In 1890, the Tiferet Bakhurim[15] wrote its own Sefer–Torah. They have a minyan every Shabbos at various homes, at Binyomin Leyb the tailor, at Alter–Arkes, also at Maishe Susel, even prior to the time of Yankl–Zalman Avrum's.

[Page 98]

Every Shabbos a different young man prayed at the lectern. They later became good prayer leaders. There was not a Shabbos that did not have a minyan. Aron Tsheshlyer was the zmiros[16] singer, Abele Khasid had a great love for the Khevra. He never chastised them. He was friendly to the young men. They became accustomed to him. If someone wanted to make fun of Abele, he later felt very insulted because the young men punished the person for it. On a winter's Friday evening, summer's Shabbos afternoon, they studied the parshes[17]. It was the Salanter young man, a student from the yeshiva. The rabbi then was Rabbi Khaim Leyb Lyev. All the youth would come to listen to him.

The gabayim served up until their wedding. If a gabai got married, they had to elect another gabai. The number of young men for prayer reached 150. AvrumVerpikhovski is taken to be a soldier in 1913, so Alter Trus becomes gabai in his place. Then the World War erupts and the Psalms Society disbands. Within a short time, Verpikhovski returns from the military and the Psalms Society is revived. We organized evening–classes, in which the intelligentsia becomes interested. The courses are varied. Rabbi Olshvank teaches parshe, Rabbi Khaim Leyb Lyev teaches us Mishnah, Hershl Stolyer's son–in–law teaches Jewish history by Graetz[18], Tzimbol[19], Tanakh and world–history are taught by Mr Khaim Hersh Braynsk. We receive permission for courses through the effort of Rabbi Shimon Shkop.

However, the times were not favourable for such activity. The German occupation–authority seeks out more people for forced–labour. We are turned in. On a Shabbos during prayer, the house is surrounded. They want to take us to work. The gendarmes[20] were unsuccessful. We closed the doors and slip out through back ways. Nobody is caught. The gendarmes remained looking like fools at the empty house.

[Page 99]

This minyan was the last gathering of the Psalms Society of young men in Bransk.

Tailors' Society[21]

According to their pinkas, the Khevra was founded in 1858. Up until then, there were tailors in Bransk but not an organized Khevra.

You most certainly have heard, that long–ago tailors travelled to the villages taking with them their young boy apprentices. They would leave on Shabbos after Havdalah[22], carrying their packs, and return Friday before the candle–light[23] blessing.

There were those who arrived on Friday in farm carts, tailors to the rich, such as Elye–Dovid, Brishke, Zalman–Avrum. Elye–Dovid was an artist, he traveled from rich woman (landowner's wife) to rich woman and tolerated various demands from them. Bishke sewed for the rich and Catholic priests. Zalman–Avrum was also a tailor for the rich. These were the privileged tailors.

However, there were others: Vi Kokitze, Binyomke, Yankev–Yosl, Binyomin–Leyb, and the Shmultshukes. Later on there were Zushe,–Hersh Sane. They travelled on foot to the neighboring villages 20 kilometers distance from Bransk.

According to the decree of 1858, that master craftsmen with workman's rights may not be taken to be soldiers, a guild was created which received the right to punish all those who did not follow their rules. Since the tailors' boy apprentices were the first victims to be taken for service, the guild had a lot of power. When the guild confirmed that a boy apprentice–is a master craftsman, he could not be taken. The community became very angry because when they decided upon certain youths to serve in the place of their children, the guild destroyed their plans. Therefore, all the tailors and boy apprentices became good members of the guild. They established a minyan for prayer in the attic of the new small house–of–prayers/house–of–studies. The ten guild leaders led a wonderful life. Most of them would spend time resting in the tavern. The apprentice–boys were quiet in order to be protected from soldiering. They received little in the way of food and had to do all the work they were instructed to do. Among the first Branskers who traveled to America there were young master–craftsmen who simply could no longer tolerate the treatment they received from their guild–masters.

[Page 100]

In 1887 the guild is disbanded, but the Tailors' Society – this was the name of the guild – remained with the minyan. The Tailors' small–house–of–prayers/house–of–studies was a later result of this. Then the Khevra was no more. Binyomke the tailor took care of the pinkas by paying attention to and obeying with devotion the pinkas.

The Tailors' small house–of–prayers/house–of–studies, was the outgrowth of the Tailors Society, is burned on September 7th 1939 as the result of German bombs along with a large part of the town.

Society of Brotherly Love of Bransk[24]

This Khevra was founded in 1896 by a group of master craftsmen. Its purpose was to furnish help to a member in a time of illness or, God forbid, death.

The leaders were Mordekhay Askart, Mordekhay Furman, Khaim Odeser, Bertche the quilter[25], Aryeh Kratz, and Motl the shoemaker. Its first bookkeeper, usually unpaid, was Yosef Kasavitzki. that when a member becomes sick, his wife should receive three rubles a week from Their rules stated the Khevra. When a member dies, God forbid, each of his children under the age of 16 should receive half a ruble a week.

The income of the Khevra consisted of a weekly fee A zekser a week. The zekser would go to the members every week with a book in which he made a little circle for each zekser he received.

[Page 101]

The master–craftsmen would go about town to collect for the Khevrah. Aryeh, Mordekhay Furman, Khone Kashtan, Avruhmele's Broder in one day, strolled through town and collected some additional zekser.

Bertche the quilter and Mordekhay Furman

Founders of the Society of Brotherly Love

A Purim–play[26] was arranged for after the Purim seuda[27]. The performers consisted of such "famous" actors as Alter Kopiliekhe, Yankel Fidel, Khaim Obzak, Gavrilke the shoemaker. The performances took place in AvrumShkop's brick house or in Shtziopken's brick house. Aryeh and Mordekhay Furman spent an entire day selling tickets. There was room for 200 but they sold tickets for 300 or more so that the important people of the town would themselves come to the performances. Nobody ever dreamt of this. Well, so they actually did come for the sale of tickets of the Yosef's play. Don't ask what went on there. If the committee did not want to let any more people in, turmoil ensued. The actors who had invited their entire families refused to perform if their friends would not be admitted. When they finally settled the matter of the audience they were seated, then Khaike the butcher fainted. Once again a noise. It takes a long time until everything settles down. Now something else happens, a table upon which twenty five women were standing broke, once again screaming, once again fainting. The performance is finally presented and the audience is pleased.

[Page 102]

On the day of Purim these Purim–shpiler (players) went about town to various homes to sing a little and receive a zekserl. This money went to the Society of Brotherly Love. On Shabbos Purim, the Khevra prepared a Kiddush at Avrum Shkop's brick house. The guests to this Kiddush come in groups. First comes the group from the third small house–of–prayers/house–of–studies, then from the old small–synagogue/house–of study, and so forth. Brandy and cake disappear as soon as they are brought to the table. The following day they figure out the money. It does sometimes happen that the deficit resulting from the Kiddush is so large that they need to use a lot of zekserlekh to cover it.

Many of the young men in town became part of the large wave of emigration. The World–War in 1914, the German occupation destroyed all the Jewish Khevrahs.

Book Repair of Bransk[28]

This Khevrah had its own seal. Each book that left the bookbinder was stamped with the approval of the book repair Khevrah as well as to which small–synagogue/house–of–study the book belonged to.

The Khevrah took care to see that all the torn books of all the synagogues were repaired.

The income from this work consisted of a pushke[29] collection. Every Thursday Shloyme Blekh went around town with the pushke labeled "Book Repair of Bransk." It so happened that sometimes there was not enough money, so the gabayim added to it from their small–synagogues/houses–of–study funds. The gabayim of the Khevrah were: Yankev–Meir Kharlap, Khone Farber, Avrum Vainer, Avrum Pulshanski.

The repair of these books was the main source of income for the town's bookbinder. They were Shmuelke the bookbinder[30],

[Page 103]

Itche Garbater, a very good expert. Lately there was Mates Lys, bookbinder. Zarember the teacher's son–in–law. He was both the gabai of the Khevrah Book Repair and also mended the books. The gabayim of the small–synagogues/houses–of study assisted him.

This bookbinder, Mates Lys, was shot by the Germans along with his parents on 25th June 1941. This took place in the middle of the street, the purpose of which was to frighten the population.

After the demise of the Bransk Jewish population, all the Jewish books of the synagogues were burned in public in the market place.

This was the end of the Khevrah Book Repair.

Footnotes (Rubin Roy Cobb)

1. Khevras T'hilim
2. Tiferet Bakhurim
3. Khayotim (from Hebrew for tailors)
4. Ahavos Akhim
5. Tikun Sefarim
6. Moses is always referred to as Moshe, or Maishe (as pronounced by Lithuanian (Litvak) Jews – which group the majority of Bransk Jews were part of – Our Teacher. He died on the 7th of the Hebrew month of Adar, i.e. his yohrtzayt (anniversary of his death) which date is observed throughout the world by all Khevra Kadishot that come together and recite psalms.
7. Wikipedia – Feast of Weeks in English, Pentecost in Greek. Shavuot commemorates the anniversary of the day God gave the Torah to the entire nation of Israel at Mount Sinai. The holiday is one of the three Biblical pilgrimage festivals – the others being Succot and Passover. It marks the conclusion of the Counting of the Omer.
8. Wikipedia – The seventh day of the Jewish holiday of Sukkot. This day is marked by a special synagogue service, in which seven circuits are made by the worshippers with their lulav (from a palm tree) and etrog (lime).
9. Wikipedia – Psalm 119 – the opening words being Ashrei temimei derekh, which means "happy are those whose way is perfect". Specific verses are recited prior to the Shofar blowing on Rosh Hashanah, by the moyel at a brit milah, during the recital of the weekday Amidah
10. In the Yizkor Book it is referred to as gan eden – the Garden of Eden.
11. Wikipedia – "the Eighth [day] of Assembly" in the Diaspora an additional day is celebrated, the second day being separately referred to as Simkhat Torah.
12. Wikipedia – A fermented beverage made from black or regular rye bread. It is often flavoured with fruits such as strawberries and raisins, or with herbs such as mint.
13. Tiferet Bakhurim – Ahavos Akhim
14. Afrikaner referred to South Africa as Amerikaner referred to the U.S.A.
15. Splendour of Young Men
16. Wikipedia – Jewish hymns usually sung in the Hebrew or Aramaic languages, but sometime also in Yiddish. The best known zmiros are those sung around the table during Shabbat and Jewish holidays. Some of the Sabbath zmiros are specific to certain times of the day, such as those sung for the Friday evening meal, the Saturday noon meal, and the third Sabbath meal just before sundown on Saturday afternoon.
17. Wikipedia – Heinrich Graetz (died 1891) was amongst the first historians to write a comprehensive history of the Jewish people from a Jewish Perspective.
18. Wikipedia – "portion" or a section of a biblical book in the Torah.
19. YIVO Encyclopedia of Jews in Eastern Europe – The tsimbl (cimbalom) was played by Jews generally and was a general component of the klezmer band until the Holocaust (Shoah).
20. Wikipedia –"a soldier who is employed on police duties" per The Shorter Oxford English Dictionary.
21. Khayotim (from Hebrew for tailors)
22. Wikipedia – Havdalah is Hebrew for 'separation.' A Jewish religious ceremony that marks the symbolic end of Shabbat and Jewish holidays, and ushers in the new week. Shabbat ends on Saturday night after the appearance of three stars in the sky.
23. Wikipedia – Shabbat candles are lit on Friday nights, 18 minutes before sunset, to usher in the Jewish Sabbath. In Yiddish, lighting the candles is known as "licht bentschen."
24. Tiferet Bakhurim – Ahavos Akhim
25. Shteper
26. Shpil
27. Seuda
28. Book Correction in Bransk – Khevrah Tikun in Bransk
29. Alms box
30. Bookbinder

[Page 104]

Sextons[1] and Sub–Sextons

According to the Small–Synagogues/Houses–of–Studies[2] in Which They Held Their Positions:

Avrum–Ber the sexton, second name Vrone, he was the sexton in the new small–synagogue/house–of–prayer, and yet he was the official town sexton for the rabbi and the community.

If it was necessary to summon someone to a Jewish Religious Court[3], it was Avrum–Ber who would do it. If it was necessary to invite someone to a first Friday night[4] after the birth of a boy celebration or to a ritual circumcision[5], or to distribute invitations to a wedding Avrum Ber would do it. He knew who was to be invited to the celebration and who was not. He never made a mistake. When there was a yohrtsayt[6] Avrum Ber would indicate with his finger, where the grave was located. He would summon attendance in the synagogue every evening. He would stand in the middle of the market and in his thin, but ringing voice shout: "To the synagogue" and then continued on. Avrum Ber would accompany the rabbi to the synagogue well as to the bathhouse on Friday. He was the rabbi's consultant. He was a very clever person with a good sense of humour.

Shepsl Katsev came to the rabbi to complain, that Efraim–Kiva the butcher had beat him up. Avrum–Ber said to the rabbi: "Rabbi, we need to go see how Efraim–Kiva is." His wages were small, a sickly amount, he had other sources of income, he was a tombstone engraver.

Avrum–Ber's grandchildren and great–grandchildren live in America, Argentina and Palestine. Sam Baker, the most important active member of the Bransk Relief, who today lives in Atlanta, is Avrum–Bergrandchild.

[Page 105]

Following his death, the position in the new small–synagogue/house–of–study is filled by Markel, although he was not suited for the work, he probably had a good side. When he went to collect Khannukah gelt[7], he would spend hours in each house, so that he barely completed this until just before Pesakh. After his death, Mikhl Dovid Granitze follows as sexton. His distinction is, that he is Avrum Ber's son–in–law, but a too quiet Jew. He was a forest (timber) merchant, he could not ask for contributions. He felt remote from everyone, .and Bransk Jews do not give easily, if they are not strongly urged. After his death the position of sexton is filled by Reb Nakhum Skornik.[8] He too, was a former patron of the –saloonkeeper, not suited to being a sexton. However, he did have one good trait, he excelled with liquor. He simply had a delightful time at any celebration. The people would urge him on: Reb Nakhum, have some more liquor. He was assisted in his duties by Khaim Leybl Shayne's son–in–law. Reb Nakhum permitted him to do this.

These were the beadles of the new small–baiz Medresh.

In the old baiz–Medresh (small–house–of–prayers/house–of–studies):

Maishe–Yehuda the sexton. Who did not know him? And whom did he not know? He knew everyone's problems, all the death anniversaries. The day, the place, where, by whom each was buried and next to whom, Maishe Yehuda kept all this information in his head. He was the sexton for the Jewish Religious Court after Avrum–Ber's death. He did not curry favour from anyone. His summons to synagogue was also magnificent. He knew everyone, even a father's name. He never had to ask anyone. On Rosh Khodesh Elul[9] at the cemetery, Maishe Yehuda was a necessity. Women and many men, poor things, wailed over the graves of strangers. He made certain to pray El Male Rakhamim[10] for those deceased whose children were already in America, and he did not do this for the money. He was a wonderful prayer leader. And in addition a clever Jew. He had a smile for everyone. He was sexton for about 55 years. At a ritual circumcision he would quiten the assembled children, warning them that something would be done to them. They would run out hanging on to their pants. In 1937, the good–natured Maishe Yehuda was attacked by a band of Poles, beaten and battered. Maishe Yehuda was sick and suffered for a long time, going about with a bandaged head. Maishe Yehuda at the age of 87 and along with the rabbi and all the other Bransk Jews dies a martyr in the Treblinka gas ovens on November 7th, 1942.

[Page 106]

Sub–Sextons in the old small Beis Medresh were: Antchele Bagreber, followed by Hershl Pontz. They were both good at ritual circumcisions and weddings. They both kept careful track of the holiday–money and Khannukah gelt. They swept out the –bez Medresh every Friday, cleaned the lamps, and on Mondays, after the market swept around near the Beis Medresh. During the winter they heated the large oven. This they did very well because otherwise there would have been much criticism from the regular oven sitters, if ever they did not do this.

In the Third Beis Medresh:

Zalman the sexton, Avrum–Ber's son–in–law, was a great scholar and also a good prayer leader. He was not too well liked for his performance as a sexton by the rich leaders of the third Beis Medresh. Zalman the sexton died at a relatively young age.

Zalman sexton's place is taken by Maishe Aron Vasser. He did not depend solely on being a sexton. He was a teacher and also a *kliyektar*, that is, he sold tickets for the lotteries, and yet he was one of the poorest people. There were always scholars gathered around him. After his death, Shmuel Kruk, Pinye Shteper becomes the sexton. Shmuel Kruk was a preacher, calling himself Rabbi Shmuel of Bransk. He stooped down to the wealthy members of the third Beis Medresh. He was also not too poor. He had a family of eight children. He called them tartars He was a small, thin Jew wearing a stiff hat. He was liked in town. There were others who were angry at him because the town had to pay for his operation in the hospital where he remained for a couple of months.

In 1939, when the Soviets occupy Bransk, Shmuel Kruk finds himself without a roof over his head, nowhere to live. He leaves with his family and goes to Russia.

[Page 107]

To this very day, no one has heard from him.

The sub–sextons Yoel'ke the Nikolayevsker soldat (Tsar Nikolay's soldier) was an angry Jew, he never permitted any children to warm themselves even a little. He kept the Beis Medresh very clean. The lamps always shone. He did not have too much love for the Beis Medresh leaders. They called him the Russian. Following him Avrum Henekh the Kominyar [*chimney sweep* (?)] his family name was Katz, a very thin soldier from Denenburg. He was married in Bransk. He was a very good person. He kept the Beis Medresh clean. He had many stories to tell, was always looking for someone to tell them to. Everyone said: "Avrum–Henekh, we already heard the story." He was taken to the gas–chambers of Treblinka on November 7th, 1942.

Tailors' Beis Medresh:

The first was Maishe Velvl the sexton, Mushanski the sexton. He was quiet, sickly, a slow–moving Jew who lived in a room in the Beis Medresh. He had little work and even less income. When he dies, there is no sexton to take his place. Aryeh Kratz and later Alter Kopelikhe are both gaboyim and sextons.

Poale Tsedek Beis Medresh:

The first sexton was Maishe. He was Hershl the carpenter's father. His name was Maishe Ber Rutzki, According to what elderly Jews relate, this Maishe Ber was a very honest Jew. He did not benefit from being the sexton. All he had to do was sweep out the Beis Medresh every Friday.

Zelig the sexton used to be called Zelig Kutshmirer [*coachman* (?)] His family name was Kaplansky. Zelig was a Jew with a stately appearance. People said that Zelig Kutchmirer, years before, had travelled about the Volin area as a khasidic rebbe, writing good luck charms. His gabai was Leybe Alyentzke. The appearance of both of them was suited to this.

[Page 108]

He was perfectly suited for what was now called the shoemakers' Beis Medresh.

Zelig Kutshmirer was a good natured person. When those who were skating on the frozen river were chilled to the bone and looking for somewhere to warm themselves, all the Beis Medreshim were closed to them. However, not by Zelig. He went about his duties slowly, beginning mid–week. He had good bosses, good payers.

His sub–sexton was Yosl the porter. He was a good little Jew, kept the Beis Medreshim clean. After the death of Zelig Kutchmirer, Yosl the porter becomes the sexton in his place. It turns out that Yosl the porter's his family name is Kaplan, he is a good sexton, not lazy. He takes over the work of delivering invitations to weddings and ritual circumcisions. Yosl the porter's life ends in the gas–chambers of Treblinka along with all the other Bransk Jews on November 7th, 1942.

There were no sextons in the khasidic shtibl. Those who prayed there themselves did all the work of sextons and sub–sextons.

Footnotes (Rubin Roy Cobb)

1. shammes
2. Beis Medresh
3. Din Torah or Beis Din
4. Ben Zakhor
5. Bris
6. Anniversary of a death
7. Wikipedia – The tradition of giving money (Khannukah gelt) to children is of long standing. The custom had its origins in 17th–century practice of Polish Jewry to give money to their small children for distribution to their teachers. According to popular legend, it is linked to the miraculous victory of the Maccabees over the ancient Greeks. To celebrate their freedom, the Hasmoneans minted national coins. It may also have begun in 18th–century Eastern Europe As a token of gratitude toward religious teachers.
8. Akiva Skornik was the grandfather of Rubin Roy Cobb, perhaps this was his father, uncle, brother or cousin?
9. Wikipedia – The twelfth month of the Jewish civil year. During the month of Elul it is customary to blow the shofar every morning from Rosh Khodesh Elul (the first day of the month) until the day before Rosh Hashanah. Many Jews also visit the graves of loved ones throughout the month in order to remember and honour those people in our past who inspire us to live more fully in the future.
10. Wikipedia – God full of mercy. A funeral prayer used by the Ashkenazi Jewish community. The cantor recites it, for the ascension of the souls of the dead, during the funeral, going up to the grave of the departed, remembrance days, and other occasions on which the memory of the dead is recalled.

[Page 109]

Women Synagogue Wardens/Trustees

– Women Who Read Prayers in The Women's Section of the Synagogue, for Other Women to Repeat

These were special types of women, who did their work to help the poor families in town with anything they could. We must make the acquaintance of the women in order for the picture of all their activities to be understood. Most especially, these women are worthy of having their work on behalf of the poor be documented for future generations.

Frumele the gabai'ete, was the wife of Mr Noakh Berman. On Fridays, Frumele goes to the housewives to get from everyone a khale[1], a roll or several little cakes. Frumele does her work even during the worst frosts and storms. She collects Shabbos baked goods. In case Frumele comes a little late, the housewives know and they save a portion for her. Frumele has her steady customers. Without fanfare, she leaves the khales and rolls in the homes. She does this so skillfully that nobody notices where Frumele has been and to whom she gave her festive Shabbos baked goods. But you may be certain that in no house was there ever nothing for Shabbos because Frumele knew about everyone and everything. Frumele was also the gabai'ete of the Khevrah Kadisha. In the Shul[2] she was the main prayer leader as all the women listen to her and pray with her. Frumele was one of the true righteous women. She dies alone, childless. There is a virtuous funeral with a eulogy that she truly earned.

Khaye Esther the Gabai'ete/Trustee

Her husband was Nokhum the hat maker. She too, was the same sort of woman like Frumele. Whenever there was someone who was sick, hungry or barefoot, Khaye–Esther knew and immediately became interested. Many times Rabbi Itskhak Ziev or Rabbi Tsukerman would call her and make her aware of certain instances that required her help. Khaye –Esther always knew where to obtain a quarter chicken. She marches in to Aron Velvelikhen's bakery, Manye Goldvaser or to Reizl Blume Patinke, Sore the Baker or goes from house to house an says: "Poor thing, a poor, sick woman who just gave birth." She is given a couple of groshen and whatever is necessary. In case she falls ill and cannot go herself, it does not matter. She buys with her own money. She has trust in her steady customers that they will not do this. The housewives know that if Khaye–Esther needs money it must have been necessary. Therefore she pays no attention to anyone's protestations. If someone was not so religious, Khaye–Esther pretended not to notice: "It is a pity, poor thing, sick," she says. Her home was always open, whether it was for some to share a secret with Khaye–Esther about another or just to have a glass of tea. Peshke the crazy woman was well aware that at Khaye–Esther's she could always come in, have a glass of tea or lie down in her bed to take a nap. Khaye–Esther would only remark: "It is time to change the bed–linen." Zalman the 'Rabbi'. is a steady visitor to her house. He drinks a glass of tea and Khaye–Esther mends his pants and jacket. On Fridays, Zalman finds a fresh shirt and soap for him when he goes to the bathhouse.

[Page 110]

[Page 111]

Khaye Esther the Gabai'ete

Erev Shabbos, Khaye Esther, carrying a large basket, goes around from house to house for baked rolls. She now has enough food for an entire week for all her customers. She is also one of the gabai'etes of the Khevrah Kadisha, busy with work for a ritual cleansing of a body. She cleans the house and cooks something so the children when they come from a funeral, will have something warm to eat.

She is also the prayer leader in the synagogue. You will find Khaye–Esther wearing her spectacles and the women praying near the window of the women's section in the old bez Ha'medresh. Should she become ill, her only concern is who will now pray for the poor and sick? She was alone, Fayvl the shoemaker did not visit her often, but my (Alter Trus) father and mother did visit her often. When she died, the rabbi delivered a eulogy which she truly deserved.

Kalman–Maishke's takes over the work. She does her work with excellence, but she talks a little too much. She tells who gave her a burnt baked roll and to whom she gave the burnt baked rolls – certainly to one who doesn't pray. Khaike the butcher likes this a lot saying: "You did well, may you live a long time. However these "goyim[3] make their bed, so that they may sleep in it." She is very active at a ritual cleansing of a body, not only with the work but also with her mouth. She carries a terrible hatred towards those who do not pray. At a Khevrah Kadisha seuda she always finds someone to blame for not doing the work properly: "You stay at home during a ritual cleansing of a body but you come to a seuda. "

Kalman–Maishe's also dies alone. Her children and grandchildren are somewhere in Chicago.

The tall Feyge: She was not a collector of baked rolls. Her main work was as a prayer leader in the Shul. There are always a couple of dozen women gathered around her and Feyge causes them to cry with bitter tears. The tall Feyge is however, a very happy woman, has a wealth of sayings and jokes. There were whisperings that she only came to a ritual cleansing of a body of a distinguished woman, the first of the month of Elul[4], when the women come to the cemetery. The tall Feyge was at the cemetery directly after the first prayers. Without her, the women could not know where their dearest ones were buried. Feyge knew everything. She did not begin to pray without Maishe–Yehuda the shammes because he had to make the eulogy. After the eulogy the tall Feyge becomes overwhelmed with pleas and tears. She knew of everyone's problems, and in these pleas included them, asking exactly what the women wanted to ask. She knew who, poor thing, needs a complete recovery, who needs to marry off a daughter or whose son must report for conscription. It was not necessary to tell her anything. She knew everything.

[Page 112]

She was always prepared with a joke, when she saw a woman, not waiting for her, began meanwhile to weep over a grave. She would say to Maishe–Yehuda: "Just look, Maishe–Yehuda, how she cries over a stranger's grave." There was not a yohrtsayt at which the tall Feyge was not present.

Her source of income was from a brick house which was her inheritance. Asher Tikochski lived in this brick house. Instead of paying rent money, he gives her a list of expenses for repairs, and when she gets a bit angry, Asher says that the brick house is after all, Mendl– Hitzl, and she keeps quiet. She too, dies alone. Maishe–Yehuda provides a nice place and a fine funeral but without a eulogy.

The Bocki teacher collects baked goods for Shabbos, has her customers and does not participate in the Khevrah Kadisha work. She excelled in that during the summer she went about on market–day carrying cold water, giving everyone some to refresh themselves with a drink. She would remind the Jews only to make a reckoning.

The last two woman gabai'etes were Alterke the odishaver's (?) wife, and Frumke Yenkl Brezhnitzer's second wife. Poor strangers often spent the night at Frumke's. She never took money from them for this. Both participated in helping anyone who was in need, and also went about to collect baked rolls and had their customers to whom to distribute them. Both women were led to the gas chambers together with everyone on the 7th November 1942.

[Page 113]

There must still be mention made of the following women: Bayle Eyge, Hershl Shuster's wife. Her house was one from where anyone who was hungry would emerge completely satisfied. The Kadluvbovker rimerke's life ended along with her husband's and children's in the gas chambers together with all the other Jews.

There were other prayer leaders. The women's gabai'ete Rokhl Shloymeh Ma'aleskher who was not only a prayer leader, but a truly righteous woman. She helped with everything. However, she is turned in with seventy two Jews. She is shot on November 15th 1942, and is buried on the Bransk cemetery in an adjoining grave.

Zise'le Yenkl Zalman Avrum's and Rokhke from Bendige are also well-known as good prayer leaders. Women said pearls flowed from their lips.

Footnotes (Rubin Roy Cobb)
1. A twisted white bread eaten on the Sabbath and festivals
2. Synagogue
3. Non–Jews, gentiles – here in a derogatory sense.
4. Wikipedia – Elul, the 12th month in the Jewish calendar when the shofar is blown every morning from the first day of Elul until Rosh Hashanah (except on Shabbat).
5.

[Page 114]

Emigration

The reasons that propelled the Bransk Jews to emigrate were varied. Bransk was developing into a town with a significant Jewish population.

Yet there were always specific reasons that led Branskers to emigrate to faraway places.

The first thrust, that led to this was during the times of the Kontanistn edict. There were in Bransk young, courageous boys. They were very afraid of being caught to become Nikolayevske (Tsar) soldiers. In the main, they were poor youths with no protection. They were uncertain of their safety in town. So they simply tore themselves away from Bransk and fled.

Such youths dragged themselves on foot to Brisk[1]. Volin[2] merchants would come there with their horses and wagons. The youths would sign on as drivers in the hope that upon arriving somewhere in Volin they would be able to reach the Austrian border.

Brod[3] was then very popular as the border town between Russia and Austria. But not everyone was successful in carrying out their plans, because in Volin these strangers would be caught for their own town recruits, or these same merchants would turn them in to the catchers, thereby freeing their own young boys from conscription.

Others however, were successful in crossing the border and then, after much difficulty, arrived at the shores of America or other distant lands.

[Page 115]

In 1851, there was talk in Bransk that someone by the name Falik is in (I)stanbul, Turkey.

There were other reasons that pushed people to emigrate. In case certain people sinned before God and man, there was only one way open for them – emigration.

The following story will give you a sense of such emigrants.

In 1937, a delegate from the Warsaw –Palestine office arrives. He introduced himself as a judicial representative from the Palestinian legal inheritance office. He explained to the Bransk population that in 1930 a woman by the name of Liebe Adeser died in Jerusalem. She comes from Bransk. She left Bransk in 1861, had given birth to an illegitimate child. Her relatives then sent her to Palestine to cover their family's shame.

The woman died in an old–age home in Jerusalem. She had no survivors. She was a rich woman, had a large orchard. In her will she left everything to her relatives in Bransk, Grodno province.

He therefore came here to find the relatives of this Liebe Adeser. Nobody in Bransk in 1937 knew or remembered who she was or who her relatives were in Bransk or in other countries. There were those who did report for the inheritance, however without any positive documentation. For three days we in Bransk carried out an investigation, asked and asked again, most especially the older people in town.

The eldest in Bransk at that time was Liebe Silberstein, Yenkl the water-carrier's wife, 93 years old. The old Liebe however, was in no condition to remember such anoccurrence. She stammered, wrinkled her 93 year old forehead which was already wrinkled from age, but no definite conclusion could be reached as to who this woman was.

[Page 116]

After a thorough investigation the representative of the Palestinian legal inheritance office judicial administration left with nothing.

This shows that in 1861 they were already aware in Bransk of emigration and made use of it at various opportunities.

It is known that in 1867 the Milkhiger tailor's uncle left Bransk. Years later – in 1873 a letter arrived from him from America.

During the years of 1875 until 1880 many Branskers left for America. Shloymeh Bolbor had already brought over several of his relatives.

Avrume the hat–maker and Dovid Prager were among the Bransk emigrants at that time.

1880 is the beginning of a larger emigration, especially from the tailoring trade. Possibly times were not good for the tailoring trade.

Alter–Yokl Itshike's

A Bransk Immigrant in New York in Shabbos Clothes in the 1890s

[Page 117]

During this emigration we find Shimon Vilk, Yenkl Mordekhay the Khasid's brother, Avrume Yenkl Sanke's, Avrume Kartoflye, Alter Yokl Itchikhe's, Yashe Hersh Branski, the children of Zavl Fuks, Hertzke Fuks and his brother Yenkl Fuks. In the ten years up to 1890 there are in New York a large number of Bransker landslayt. There is already a Bransk colony somewhere on the east side of New York.

In 1894, there are now in New York two Bransk societies. The first is named the Old Bransker Society.

The number of emigrants who leave Bransk grows. New emigrants and families of earlier emigrants go to America to their men.

The character of the emigration up to 1905 was only an economic one. There was virtually no bread, so they set out for faraway lands and through hard work to earn a living for themselves and for their families.

Political emigration:–

A new stream of Bransk Jews leave their home, and not because of earning a living, but for political reasons.

It begins in 1904 when the Russo–Japanese War is at its peak and is followed by the Revolution of 1905.

Among the emigrants of 1905 we no longer find workers but young men from all classes, children of small merchants, intelligent, educated children for whom it becomes uncomfortable in Russia because of the political connections. Among these emigrants we find Alter the writer, Moshe–Hitzl Rose, Blume Mishurek, Yosl Mishlibovski, Khaim Baker, Shmuel Leyb Berl Leybishe's, Khaim Gold, Itche Rutker, Yudl Shloyme Hersh's, Binyomin Zelvin, the Moskver's son, Binyomke the protzenitzke's [percent?] and many others.

Even Borukh Cohen, Borukh the Rabbi's, is already in America at that time. In 1901. Children of the Maydener (?) leave and settle in Chicago.

In 1906 after the hopes for a free Russia were shattered, Bransk was almost empty.

[Page 118]

The youth had already left.

From 1906 until the First World War many Branskers left, especially the youth who having grown up in the interim, left Bransk in masses. Among them were William Cohen, Shaul'ke Kashtan, Avrum Moshe Bertche's, Yankl the cart man's [?] and his brother Alter Itskhak the cart man's [?] son. Several from Domenive, Shloyme Wolfke's two sons, Lazer the cantor's, the Plonever's two sons, Sam Verp and his brother Louis Verp.

The youth who arrived in New York during this period established the third Bransk group by the name Bransker Young Men's, and the previous group was now called the "Old." The very first Bransk group is now called "The Very Old."

The last emigration of Bransk Jews that took place after the First World War had now ended.

The emigration consisted mostly of relatives of American citizens[4], who obtained visas for them, because the opportunity for a large emigration was no longer available. Only certain privileged persons were then permitted to travel. Among the first were Nosn Zelvin, the Moskver, who came to his children, Yenkl Baker's, from the Shmultchike's two sons, Zaydl Zalefski, Noske Katsev's son, Shaye the harness maker children, Aryeh Leyb the hat maker's wife and children, Hershl the carpenter's son, Fishl Rutzki, Noakh Shtaynberg and many others. A number of these new arrivals brought their own relatives over shortly thereafter. Others helped their relatives to go to Argentina or Africa[5] where there was no quota. It must be mentioned that many of the emigrants did little to take their families out of Bransk. In this way many more would have been saved from the gas–chambers.

Others went to Johannesburg, Africa[5], where we find Hinde Sashin, Brakha Vainer, Khone Smurzshik, Jospa Skornik[6], Piekucki.[7]

In Buenos Aires, Argentina there are Khaim Kestin, Shmuelke Tsukhtlyer, Goldings, Zagel and Hershel Stolyer's children, the Rutski's and many other Branskers.

[Page 119]

In Cuba we find a few Branskers.

In Palestine there are many landslayt from Bransk. A large portion were from the Polish kibbutzim, where they prepared for pioneer work. Other older folk also went there. There we find Yosef Khaim Heftman, Ginsberg the teacher and his children, Khanna Kashan's daughter, Esther Yentchman and many others.

The emigration lasted eighteen years until the beginning of 1939. Branskers made use of every opportunity that was available for emigration. Little by–little all the possibilities were narrowed. The emigration to America became animpossibility. There also developed difficulties in leaving Poland, and yet there were landslayt who managed to get through and go to various countries.

By the beginning of the war all doors were closed to emigration.

There was only one door that remained open – the door that led to Treblinka to the gas–chambers, to the crematoriums, to the complete demise of everything and everyone that remained in Bransk.

Footnotes (Roy Cobb)
1. Brisk d'lita (Hebrew), until 1921 Brest–Litovsk; from 1921 until 1939 Brzesc nad Bugiem; after 1939 Brest – capital of Brest district, Belarus.
2. Wikipedia – Volin (Yiddish) is called Volin Oblast (province) in present day north–western Ukraine; it was adjacent to Galicia (Galysye in Yiddish), the largest and most populous, and northernmost province of the Austrian Empire, where it remained until the dissolution of Austria–Hungary at the end of World War I in 1918.
3. Wikipedia – Brod (Yiddish), Brody in Ukrainian. In 1869 there were 15,138 Jews out of a total population of 18,700 = 80.9%; 1880 15,316 / 20,000 = 76.3%; 1890 n.a. / n.a. = n.a.
4. The United States is referred to as America
5. South Africa is referred to as Africa.
6. Jospa Cobb (Kobylanski) (nee Skornik) is the mother of Rubin Roy Cobb. Her picture as well as of other Branskers in Johannesburg can be seen on page 417 – she is on the right of the second front row.
7. Shortened their name to Peck – cousins of Jospa Cobb

[Page 120]

Epidemics and Fires
in Bransk

Life in Bransk was very poor. The population lived in cramped conditions. Homes were not cleaned from Passover to Passover, so is it a wonder that from time–to–time there were epidemics? In 1844, in the month of Adar (March), an epidemic began. The largest number of victims were the young and grown children. Most children were kept hidden in their homes because of fear that they would be caught as recruits. They were actually the first to become victims. The community emptied out, the cemetery – filled in the six months until Elul–(September) time. The methods the town adopted in an attempt to stem the spread of the epidemic consisted of fasting, reciting Psalms, burning old names in the street and recital of hymns[1]. It is told that the waters of the river were halted by the sluice of the windmill and were responsible for the epidemic, but they did not allow the sluice gate to open because of the mills that would have to stop. Eventually they opened it, and the water flowed in the village of Karpye, but the epidemic arrived with the water in Tchekhenovtze. It is told that Rabbi Yudl Kharif announced on Yom Kippur at Kol Nidrey that nobody should fast this Yom Kippur because of the weakened condition of the population.

In 1852 an epidemic affected mostly small children. According to what is told, there was hunger. They ate corn mush. They did not know how to cook the flour, so they used it raw, resulting in many stomach ailments and many deaths. The epidemic lasted until 1854. There was then issued a warning in town not to eat corn mush. Understandably, the greatest number of child victims was from the poorer population. The more affluent had other food to eat, so they were in less danger from the epidemic. The first epidemic did not make much of a distinction between poor and rich. Everyone suffered equally from this.

[Page 121]

In 1852, due to the epidemic, it became necessary to purchase a second cemetery. And so the cemetery was purchased on Brezshnitzer Road from the Christian Marushevski. In 1892, another epidemic – diphtheria – arrived. They knew that any child who contacted diphtheria would die of this. It was terrifying. They conducted the funerals at night, not telling who had died. Sometime later, the epidemic carries over to older people. It became necessary to help the affected, to rub spirits on them.

The founders of this help group were Shay'ke and his brother Kesilke Mulyer. The Voluntary Burial Society then issues a manifest to include ordinary Jews to help do the work of burying the deceased. In this way just plain folk became part of the Voluntary Burial Society, remaining there as Burial Society members. A hospital[2] is set up in the new House of Study although no one ever leaves there alive. They cover the canals with starch (?) (or ?) crabs (or a misspelt Yiddish word ?). They opened the sluice gates everywhere, allowing the water to flow in Tchekhenoftse[3], in Symyatitch[4] and Botke[5].

The fourth epidemic occurred in 1915 when the German soldiers entered the town. Dead horses lay in the streets. Bloodied clothing from dead soldiers and dead bodies were everywhere. Flies and worms did their work. The word comes that there were already victims of the epidemic in Bielsk[6] The first victim in Bransk is a little girl, Yisroel'kales daughter. Alter, Leybl Styelmakh's son, Leyzer Godzshiber's wife, a mother of four children and tens of other people also died.

[Page 122]

The German fights; he isolates, gives no aid but he poisons the affected. No one says anything, they are afraid of the German soldiers with the poison. It becomes quiet in town. All these epidemics will remain in the memories of the Bransk Jews.

Fires:–

Of the largest fires in town we must mention the following: In 1868 during the month of Shevat (January), when everything was frozen solid, a fire broke out at Nokhum Iteld's, Alter Iteld's father. The fire wiped out the entire street up to the Poor House. There was no way to stop it as all the water was frozen, even the wells. The unfortunate people were somehow helped by the town. Many, over a period of several years, were able to recover. The local administration donated wood free of charge. Five years later, a fire broke out at Leyzer Gedalye Shnaider's. Blame fell upon the Kvites, an underworld group, because Leyzer Gedalye's had told that they had burned the houses of Nokhum Iteld because their brother was caught to be a soldier. The community collected signatures and the Kvites were sent to Siberia.

On Lag B'omer[7], precisely at 12 noon in 1876, a fire started at Mordekhay Fuhrman's in a shed. This small fire ignited the entire circle of houses up to Khaim Burak's house resulting in almost half the town being wiped out. Fortunately there were no human victims. Neighboring towns reacted warmly, bringing wagonloads of old clothing, bread and potatoes. They later helped all those who wanted to rebuild. Fights broke out during the rebuilding over the amount of ground and distance between houses.ke They would kill over a piece of ground. Day and night there were court cases brought to the rabbi. Avrum Ber the sexton became exhausted from summoning all the homeowners to the rabbi.

In 1909 Valkostovski's factory burnt down, and about three dozen young women become jobless. There was great fear at the fire at Yankl Shimon's house. The situation was serious. A row of wooden houses stood next to one another. There was danger that the town would be destroyed. Jews exhibited heroism, most especially Rabbi Shimon Shkop, who brings all of his yeshiva boys together and the danger is averted. In addition, there were already hoses at that time, although not everyone had the ability to pump, so they used pails of water.

[Page 123]

When there was a fire at Mendl Toker or at Itche Orlyarnik's, the hoses did not work somehow. It was said that anti–Semitism was already at work, but they did not depend entirely on the hoses.

On the 16th September 1939, Bransk is bombarded with fire–bombs dropped from German airplanes. All ends of the town are enveloped in fire. 32 people fell victim in these fires.

It is remarkable how the fire did not affect any Christian neighbourhoods, only the Jewish ones. This was the first indication of the fate of the Jewish population.

Footnotes (Rubin Roy Cobb)
1. Hoshayne – during Sukkot (Feast of Tabernacles); willow twig, one of the four species used in Sukkot ritual; willow twig that is beaten during the hymns of the seventh day of Sukkot.
2. In Polish Ciechanowiec
3. See map over page
4. in Polish Siemiatytze
5. In Polish Bocki – a shtetl near Bransk where the maternal grandfather of came from
6. In Polish Bielsk Podlaski . A shtetl near Bransk where the father of originated from.
7. Spring holiday on the 33rd day after Passover, celebrated with excursions to the countryside

[Page 124]

Bransk in 1905 – The Beginning of the Collapse of Tsarism

In 1905 there was already a revolution in Russia. In all the big towns there were significant workers' battles. Terrorist acts against autonomous police rule were carried out in the towns. The same fate was suffered by the governors, and even ministers like Stolypin were blown up by bombs. (I don't know if he is referring specifically to Stolypin being blows up or using him as an example, because Stolypin died in 1911.)[1]

In Bransk they learned about these happenings through the newspapers that were already being read by such as Avrum Pulshansky and Yoshe Liboshitz. Fishele Bag claimed to be the first to read "Hatsfira" (The Siren).[2] Everybody read the daily newspapers, in the Houses–of Prayer and Study, in the home, in the streets, on the open porches, and especially at Avrume Gold's, there were always groups of people, who read the newspapers. The newspapers circulated from hand–to–hand until they became tattered.

They read in them what was happening in the large towns. Strange news was reported there, about demonstrations against the state, about strikes in large factories. Bransk read the news and thought that this would not happen there. There are no factories in town. There are no workers in Bransk, only in Valkastavski's jacket factory. There only girls worked. The tailors, shoemakers and carpenters were mostly apprentice boys who worked for a specific period of time. In Yerukhim's tile factory there were only peasants who were employed. What do they know about such things? However, the tailors' employers somehow became aware that their boys were disappearing in the middle of the day and who knew where they went?

[Page 125]

Strikes are now happening in Bransk. Workers from the small flour (?) stop doing their work, want more money. They let them strike and do the work themselves, working all night to complete the work that had been started.

People become restless, approach the bosses threatening beatings and winning small amounts.

The intelligent youth arranged a library in Moshe (or Maishe) Hitzl Mendel's attic. Young boys and girls come there to take out books to read. The organizers of this library are Yosl Shimon Rimer's, Moshe (or Maishe) Hitzl, Khaim Baker, Shmuel Leyb Berl Leybishe's, Yudl the teacher, Itche the ru(o)tker(?), also a teacher, and mostly not workmen's children.

The Bund develops among the workers. Speakers from the big towns come to Bransk only to small clubs. At Bashe Sime's daughter, in the attic, there often take place small gatherings and secret meetings to which workers and intelligentsia come.

There is formed an anarchist circle led by Dovid–Yoke's – actually one of the rich children, Alter Snop, Shloymeh Ok's son, Meir Shlom Aharon Velvl's who are already well–known as anarchists. Hershl the weaver also joins the anarchists.

The Zionist movement was also significant. Yoshe Liboshitz, Alter–Itche Shapira's, Moshe Khaikin, Moshe (or Maishe) Hertzke were the most active Zionists, with some even becoming Uganda[3] patriots.

The various parties preach their ideals. The Bund group preaches cultural autonomy. (Such a strange word in Bransk.) Socialism preaches equal, secret and direct elections. There are class battles. The anarchists believe in expropriation. They do not preach, but they actually practice this. They are armed and attack and take what they can– this is called expropriation. The Bund says they should not be given a grosh because they do not believe in expropriation. The anarchists come, but always with weapons in their hands. If they are not given, they take it themselves. Scenes occur between the followers of both sides and grew in size.

A new and strange Yiddish newspaper makes an appearance – "Der Veker" (The Awakener).[4] – an odd language is used there. A strange language, not understandable to the Bransk Jews. It speaks of cultural Yiddish autonomy, of secret and direct elections. They wonder that the state permits such newspapers, yet they allow them to read the "Veker."

[Page 126]

The workers cannot wait for the "Veker." The intelligent youth read the "Veker" with interest, and teach the workers to understand the difficult words, the strange and new ideas.

Speakers come to secret venues. A while later, the workers take over the Poale Tsedek, lock the doors and there, in the house of study and prayer, hold a gathering. There are fiery speeches, boys and girls shout: "The Proletariat lives, the Russian Revolution lives." All demand the freeing of the working class, demanding an eight–hour workday. After the gathering, there is a demonstration in the street. New songs are sung in the street.

The following day, don't ask what went on in Bransk. Each person told a different story about what he had heard yesterday from the strange speakers in the black shirts.

Zelig Kuktshmirer, the sexton of Poale Tsedek, was accused by everyone that because he had not thrown these people out, trouble came to the town.

Yosl Stoyler shouts: "Eight sicknesses I will give them, not eight hours of work." Shaye Tsalke's the kvasnik[5] cannot sleep. His heart tells him no good will come of this. He would like to see these people get their correct lashing and then there would be an end to this new nuisance.

There is no end to the nuisance. The movement grows. The town is flooded with illegal literature, brochure–leaflets, proclamations, calls to strike, to battle against the Tsar, against reaction, for freedom, and equality, for eight–hours [a day] of work. The legal library is turned into an illegal one where there are supplies of books, brochures and even a revolver is hidden somewhere. Gatherings in the houses of study and prayers are arranged more often. There are big demonstrations, massive gatherings in the forest, at the Kumant (?), beneath the windmill. They begin to prepare self–defense. They raise money for this purpose. If people don't give voluntarily, they take it anyway. There are others who oppose this and they are beaten up or have their windows broken. There are those who receive a warning not to show themselves in the street – in a word, the revolution had reached Bransk. Twelve policemen with bayonets on their swords like nails make an appearance in Bransk. For this reason they named these policemen 'tshvekes'[6]. People run to the police to denounce them and they receive even worse beatings and are now afraid to speak. The reaction becomes stronger. They now hear about pogroms in Bialystok[7] and other cities.

[Page 127]

A new regional police superintendent[8] Andreyev comes to Bransk. They catch and arrest. A group of anarchists travels to Wishonk to do its work and someone reports them, and Dovid Yoke's, Hershl, the weaver, Meir Shlom, Aharon Velvl's, receive a prison sentence. The quiet Bransk streets are strongly watched by the 'tshvekes'.

The day of the famous constitution arrives. Everybody is happy. The older folk say that it will not end well. They were correct. The reaction worsens. There are masses of arrests. There is no alternative. They must pull back. Yosl Shimon the harness maker, Maishe the hot–headed, Alter Snop have already left. Nobody wants to remain. There begins a mass emigration. Visas are not necessary. Also no affidavits. They speak with Sannen or Fishl Spishiner's. They bake sucares (?) dipped in beer. The old mothers, red–eyed, beg their children: 'At least write a letter once in a while.'

The revolutionary enthusiasts soften at their mothers' tears and their throats constrict and with a tear in their eyes they leave. Very soon they send for their friends. At the end of 1906, Bransk is emptied. There is no longer any youth presence. There is no more the lively and joyous youth. Bransk yearns for its children. The library closes as there is no one who would read a book. People like Shepsl Katsev and Shaye Tsalke's are happy. They and others like them are now free.

[Page 128]

However, this did not last long. Avrum Baker was right: "It is like an illness. It will have to come. We cannot avoid it."

Among the well–known youth in the movement were the following: the Moskver's children, Khane Shayne, Noske Katsev's daughter , Khaye Yentitshike's, Avrum Beker's son, the Markanerker's son, Noske, Kalman – Maishe's son, Gavriyel'ke the blacksmith, Shepsl–Itche Alyarnik's, Fraiche Shaye Mulyer's, Avrum Kratz, the chatterbox, Burake's two sons, Belke Alte Katsev's, Keyle Mordekhay Fuhrman's, BerlAryeh's son, Count Keller's son, Alter Kapelikhe's, Kolyendik's, Shaulke Patoker and many others, whom I find difficult to remember.

Footnotes (Rubin Roy Cobb)

1. Wikipedia – Pyotr Arkadyecvich Stolypin served as Prime Minister and leader of the third Duma, from 1906 to 1911. His tenure was marked by efforts to counter revolutionary groups and by the implementation of noteworthy agrarian reforms. Stolypin's reforms aimed to stem peasant unrest by creating a class of market–oriented smallholding landowners. He is considered one of the last major statesmen of Imperial Russia with clearly defined public policies and the determination to undertake major reforms. In 1889 Stolypin was elected Marshall of the Kovno Governorate. In n1902 Stolypin was appointed governor of Grodno (where Bransk is located). He became known for suppressing the peasant unrest in 1905.He was the first governor to use effective police methods. In 1911 Stolypin was assassinated by Dmitri Bogrov (born Mordekhai Gershkovich). In a 2008 television poll to select "the greatest Russian", Stolypin placed second, behind Alexander Nevsky and followed by Joseph Stalin.
2. Jewishgen – Yizkor Book – Dabrowa – "Hatsfira" [The Siren} was a newspaper established by Zionists that was read openly by some while others surreptitiously
3. Wikipedia – The Uganda Scheme was a plan in the early 1900s to give a portion of British East Africa to the Jewish people as a homeland. It drew support from prominent Zionist Theodor Herzl as a temporary means of refuge for Russian Jews facing anti–Semitism. The idea was brought to the Zionist Congress at its sixth meeting in 1903 in Basel. Before the vote on the matter, the Russian (where Bransk was located at the time) delegation stormed out in opposition. It was ultimately defeated.
4. YIVO – A. Litvak (Khaim Yankl Helfand) wrote regularly for the Bund's legal daily press: Der Veker (1905–1906).
5. Kvass maker – a drink made by fermenting rye and barley on sour fruits
6. Nails
7. See map overleaf
8. Prystav – so called in tsarist Russia

[Page 129]

Jewish Employment in Bransk
Up to the First World War

Up to the time of the Polish uprising, and a little beyond that, there was a significant number of Jewish families living in the villages around Bransk. These village residents earned a living from the land–owners. They held leases as shepherds and innkeepers. These Jews were beholden to the land–owner because for the smallest infraction the land–owner could throw the Jewish lessee out, leaving him without means of earning a living.

The Jews, in order to hang on to their employment, had to be subservient to the land–owner, always trying to please him and suffering various foolish and wild tricks. They were what was called Mayofes Jews (';how fair thou art', title of a Sabbath hymn sung on Friday nights – fig., cringe, be servile)[1]. This is the reason they received various favors from the land–owner.

Mele from Alekshon was especially loved by the Hodishaver priest "Burte", so he received from him his worn–out long coats. Meli'khe narrowed the priest's wide coat– sleeves and Mele, proud of this beautiful priestly coat, wore the clothes every Sabbath.

Many had employment from the innkeepers and trades and lived quietly. They hired teachers to teach their children Jewishness[2], married off children, gave good dowries such as did Nosn Leyzer from Zaluske, Itzel Daminover, Yakutia Marvinker, the Myenier, (?) Elye Nosn Glazer. When the families grew larger its new members no longer had possibilities for employment and they moved into Bransk. They began to work at various ways of earning a living. This is how innkeepers came to Bransk. Menukhe's, Dvora's, Leyzer Sotnik, Velvl's Bier breweries, Yosl Benye, Marem Leye, Yekhiel Leyb's tannery, Leyzer Shepsl's watermill, Dovid Gimpl's vyetrak[?]. Hershl Iteld opened a dry–goods store. Of the workers there were tailors: Bishke, Binyomin the tailor, Yankev Yosl, Alye. [?] Dovid the ladies' tailor, Shimon Dovid the carpenter. Later on there were more tailors, shoemakers, carpenters, glaziers. Most of them were young folk who had learned the work as former apprentices and who became independent workers working for themselves.

[Page 130]

There were some who took up trade, earning a living from markets every Monday when peasants brought various village products for sale. Others did not wait until the peasant brought these products to the market. They always went to the villages and there bought the products from the peasants. Workers also went to the villages and there got work from the richer peasants. For their work they received products as payment which they brought back to town and sold. The number of stores increased. There was a store everywhere. There are now dry–goods stores, hardware stores – Velvl–Daniel's and Gotlieb's. There are wholesale merchants like Ezra Goldberg factory and cotton by Elye Vatnik.

The tailors, shoemakers, carpenters, turners, blacksmiths, hat makers make their articles for the entire area around Bransk. They carry the merchandise to the fairs of other towns. It was usual to notice how the workers packed clothes, shoes, little wheels, tables and wheels for wagons to take to the fairs.

The painting business had grown in Bransk. This way of earning a living was handed down from father to children. Motke Farber, Alter Farber, Shimon Farber, Yenkl Shimon's, Khan'le Farber, Avrum Meir, Elke Riva, Ayzikl from Benduge.

There were kasha makers, Khaim Fishl Melamed and later his son Yitskhak Kashnik and Motye. Remarkably, both Kashnikes of Bransk also had the necessary implements for baking matzo for Passover.

[Page 131]

Later on, when the trains were built, it was necessary to provide the entrepreneurs with blocks of wood that were to be placed beneath the rails. They were called "voyitkes" and a business developed – Itche Rozenboym, Shmuelke Sloyve's, Shloyme Hitzl Rose. Bentsl the shoemaker also took to dealing with voyitkes. He would always ride carry in his pocket a folded pocket–knife and conducted business. This business suddenly crashed. Bentsl deserts the voyitkes and goes to America. The others cannot pay their debts.

There were those who earned a living by walking or riding to the villages. Shloyme Makher, his son Moshe Yosl. There are others like Berl Zavl's, Shloyme Wolfke's who buy everything in the village and bring it to town to sell.

Earlier on there were also women who walked to the villages, leaving at dawn, on foot, walking about ten kilometers. They would return at night, bringing something to sell. Other women would set up small tables in the market. Early in the morning these tables would already be covered with various types of merchandise. They sold soap, kerchiefs and even earthen pots.

The danger for these village–walkers and riders was great. Many times such Jews, while riding from the villages or from fairs, would be attacked by bandits who robbed and murdered them. This is how Dovid Khasid, who used to carry handkerchiefs, combs, laces and needles to the villages was near the village of Kurtshin was robbed and murdered.

Elber Shuster was robbed and murdered riding from the fair in Petchanke; Gutman Katsev is murdered and robbed on a back road in 1901. Shame Vatnik is murdered early in the morning coming back from Bialystok through the Pyetkever forest. Notche Kalnitser during this same attack becomes a permanent cripple.

Orchard workers – the first in Bransk, Yeshaye Patz, buys the entire fruit crop of the orchard of the land owners, pays for it at the beginning of summer and waits for it to be successful. In addition, he himself must keep watch over the ripe fruit so that no one will steal it at night.

[Page 132]

Hentche rents the gardens and sells a little bit of radishes in town, but the cucumbers vanish during the night.

Manufacturing – There was a small number of factories in Bransk. However, they did not call themselves factories. They were recognized as such, even though they were large, sending their merchandise throughout all of Russia.

Khane Zabludofsky had a weaving factory in Avrum Shkop's attic. She employed several workers there in addition to her own family. Hershl the weaver, was the master craftsman there in the factory. In 1905 Hershl Vever the weaver carried out a large strike in this factory. Why did the factory carry a woman's name? I don't know, but Khane was in charge along with her daughter who had returned from England and was called *The English Horse.*

Leybl, the belt–maker, that is what they called him in Bransk. There was a large factory in his big house where they manufactured leather belts. The belts Pasikmakher were sent throughout Russia. All the children were employed there. His brother, Lazer the belt–maker, was in charge of this business. Leybl, a decent merchant and a clever Jew, did not enter into town affairs, even though everyone sought his advice. He was, however, always busy riding around.

Later on, when Leybl's children became older, were learned and intelligent, they helped in running the business. Lazer opens his own business and there are now in Bransk two belt manufacturers. Laser's sons, especially Yosl, a very capable young man, helped in his father's business. Yosl was already a modern young man, interested in town affairs. He later pays for his activities with his life.

[Page 133]

Volkostafsky's jacket factory. Niske Broyde, (Niske with the embroidering frame) married off a daughter, brought his son–in–law Alter into Bransk. Alter brings a machine for manufacturing jackets or warm shirts. Bransk runs to look through the windows where they see a machine covered in what looks like a long shirt, spinning but remaining in the same spot, but the shirt becomes larger and larger.

Little–by–little, Alter Volkostafsky brings more machines. The demand for the merchandise is great. The place at Leyzer Katsev becomes too small for this undertaking. He opens up an entire building where there are employed 30 or 40 young women. They earn good wages, are pleased that they do not have to serve somewhere far from their home, which most would have had to do. Moshe Hertzke becomes the bookkeeper.

Alter Volkostafsky now becomes known in Bransk as the manufacturer. His business is recognized as a factory. However, the factory is totally burned down and forty lose their ability to earn a few rubles. This adds to the worsening of the Jewish economic situation.

There was a tile factory in Bransk. Yerukhim Kokhlyarnik was the owner of the factory. He employed Christians there, and only one worker was a Jew, this was Khaim– Gershon's son. He had to go to America, presumably because he had not met with too much success working for Yerukhim Kokhlyarnik.

Commerce – It is known that there was a store in every house. However, a permit was needed to have a store. There was no money for a permit, so no one had one. They either did not buy one or they bought a permit for a small store when they really needed a permit for a larger business.

These Bransk storekeepers sustained much trouble relative to these permits. From time–to–time Grodno sent someone to check on the permit situation. He was called the examiner. When the examiner was still ion his way to Bransk, the entire town already knew that he was coming. Shopkeepers would hide their merchandise under their neighbors' beds.

[Page 134]

Binyomke Melamed had an English scale. One needed a permit to have such a scale. I don't know why Binyomke Melamed needed a scale like this. When the examiner was coming to Bransk, the boys that attended the traditional Jewish school took the English scale on its wheels and hid it in the bath–house.

The examiner is accompanied by the town administrator and Zalman–Yeshaye as supervisor, along with Avrum Hershken the flour merchant as merchandise expert. Permits were to be bought at Avrum– Hersh'ke's from which sales he realized a certain percentage.

Avrum Hershke, God forbid, never did anyone any harm. When the examiner would shout that the merchandise is woolen and a more expensive permit was required, Avrum Hershke, with his Yiddish–Russian, would demonstrate that this is cotton cloth of low quality. The storekeeper, Zalman Yeshaye and Avrum Hershke stood before the examiner without a hat in great fear. The town administrator did not say a word because they had spoken with him earlier...

There were certain families who were characteristic of the **Following Means Of Earning A Living**: selling fish, raising and slaughtering geese, selling the meat, the fat rendered for Passover and sold, pickling herring, buying up all kinds of grain in the market and selling it to the largest merchants. After the market all the beans that had been bought from the peasants had to be picked through and separated by type. On Monday night all the children in the house did this work, because if Zalman Kots the merchant, God forbid found the beans mixed up, he no longer wanted to pay the full price. However, all of this did not afford enough of a living for the large family, so Khane Shloyme Hershl's, Julius Cohen's mother, baked bread, every day a bread, kneading the dough herself, and poor Yudl had to bring a large loaf of bread to the teacher Khaim Gershon in order to pay him, because there was no other way of paying the teacher. Beer Stores – There were several such stores. Little–by–little there were more of these stores than drinkers. The storekeepers especially suffered from the inspectors (?) who always looked to see if liquor was sold in the beer stores.

[Page 135]

Teachers – There were a significant number of teachers whose profession was teaching.

A certain number of young men or Bransk sons–in–law who, in the first couple of years had used up the dowry and their fathers–in–law could not or would not give them a second dowry, had nothing to do. They were not artisans, were not suited for business, so these young men found a solution, ten young boys got together, forming a traditional Jewish school and teaching, and in this way became permanent teachers.

Almost all the teachers were poor. Teaching did not offer them enough to sustain a family, so their wives stepped in and helped out with whatever they could in order to earn a couple of groschen. These wives, conducted business in the market, standing behind their tables, making candies.

None of these teachers were suited to their calling. Most of them were embittered, burdened with worries about making a living. In addition, the women nagged the men, calling them ne'er–do–wells. The children of such parents suffered a lot because the teachers were only able to pour their bitter hearts out to the younger children. The children learned to suffer, to receive blows, to become debased and to keep silent because protestations did not help. The parents always considered the teacher[3] right.

Possibly, thanks to such an education, Jews had the ability and the strength to survive so much trouble, so much debasement and silence, carrying the burden from generation to generation.

Raising Geese – This was a means of earning a living that only a few people could realize a wage. The business with geese consisted of buying out the flock that the peasants had brought to Monday's market or gathering the geese from the villages and chasing the flocks across town. One little Christian boy chased a flock of hundreds of geese that were later taken to Warsaw to provide the Warsaw taverns with the delicious geese and navels. This all belonged to one family and possibly was a trust. The head of the trust was Itche Rashke's. When his sons grew up, they carried on this business together. They were assured an honour on the Festival of the Torah[4] because when they sold the right to conclude the reading of the Torah[5] or the right to begin the reading of the Torah[6] no one could buy these honours from Itche Roshke's. His sons, Hershl, Yosl and Maishe Aron threw themselves into the business and played a significant role in it. Later Shtsiyopke became a big competitor. The end of this business came when Itche Roshke's sons emigrated to America.

[Page 136]

There were a couple of families who *lent money* to small land–owners so they could pay their peasants for working the entire winter and summer until the grain was harvested and sold.

Most of the poor but well–connected land–owners however, when the grain was sold, did not use the money to pay the debts that they had incurred. The Jews were forced to take grain or other field products in payment for these debts.

At the New Year, the proud Pan or Panye (Mr or Mrs) would come to the Jews for new notes, go to Warsaw or abroad and spend it.

Meir Khilikhe's and his family were such financiers to the land–owners. About their end – see the last chapters.

Carpentry/Cabinet Making – Carpentry in Bransk was taken to be a decent trade. This trade consisted of custom and ready–made work. Yosl Stoyler worked mostly for fairs. Within a short time Yosl Stoyler completed tables and on Monday was already in the market with them or was taking them to the fairs.

[Page 137]

Hershl Stoyler was the artist of this trade. He took orders to make a couple of beds or a chest of draws. He only began to dry the oak boards after receiving such an order. When three years later, Hershl was asked when the beds would be finished. He would answer that the boards were still wet. They waited until Hershl completed the work. Therefore, when a customer finally received his piece of furniture from Hershl, this furniture lived forever. So Hershl was actually very poor. His family was large, so Henye took part in the work herself and touted the best furniture and went about with a little box of glass to install a window somewhere, because Hershl could not drag any heavy weight.

The apprentice boys who had studied the work with Hershl themselves became good mechanics. Later on when his boys became bigger, they helped and Hershl felt a little less burdened. His children quickly took to this trade.

Now they are spread throughout the world, three in Argentina where one of them is a well–known furniture manufacturer whose work is sent over all of South America. One is in New York and his firm is known as the best in New York.

It is characteristic that Hershl's children in Argentina are interested and active in all the Bransk relief happenings. Hershl's two sons–in–law in Bransk were famous for their activity in town. Rabbi Khaim Leyb Lyev as the orthodox social worker in town and Elye Yentchman as the well–known Poale Tsiyon leader in town. About Elye's activities, his flight from the gas–chambers, his life in the forest and later demise – in subsequent chapters.

When the emigration to America grew, other means of earning a living emerged – **Agents**. Sane, Nyome, Froytche, Shmulye, Pyetrasker, were all agents. They would escort emigrants across the Prussian border, mostly through waters and mud. Sometimes they were captured at the border mostly because of a coincidence or someone turning them in. Then the agents and their passengers had great trouble until it was smoothed over.

[Page 138]

Pesakh the storekeeper – This was a special institution in Bransk. The New York five and dime stores apparently knew about this Bransk store and about its famous Pesakh the storekeeper. Pesakh's store measured four feet by four feet and yet one could buy anything one wanted. It was virtually a wonder how Pesakh was able to remember all of the merchandise that was to be found there in his store. One could buy there several different items for a total cost of a groshen.

When Pesakh made a sale that amounted to two groshen, Pesakh'shikhe was also involved in helping her husband with the big wealth. Pesakh would cut a pencil into four parts, each one the same size. The best customer for these pencil pieces at Pesakh the storekeeper was the editor of this book. For a grosh, he would also receive two or three other items along with the pencil pieces.

Horse Traders – This was a large business in Bransk. Several families made a living from this business that was carried out mostly with notes. The merchant needed to ask G–d that the peasant should have be successful to be able to pay off the note, or he had to ask G–d for the horse not to die, G–d forbid before the note would be paid.

Land–Owner Stores – Menukh'ke Gotlieb –near her store one would always see a land–owner's carriage with four horses in tandem. A land–owner was shopping in Menukh'ke's store. Menukh'ke's "excuse me please" had a special ring to it. These stores slowly weakened because the land–owners did not have the money or did not want to pay their debts.

Turners – Binyomin the turner. Yankev–Itskhak the turner, Mendel Toker,

[Page 139]

Yudl Toker, Alter–Maishe Gusikhes. This was a means of earning a living at the market and fairs. If the season was not a good one, they remained in debt until the next year.

Wagon Drivers – Pinye Gale's, Yosl Gales, Mordekhay Furman, Fishke Furman, Sholem Smurzhik, Leybl Furman, Yenkl Zavl's, Khaim Glaser.

This means of earning a living was divided. Some traveled to Bielsk, others to Shepetove to the train. There were those who went to Tchekhenoftse and still others to Bialystok or to the fairs. There were some who transported freight to the neighbouring towns.

These were the main means of earning a living in Bransk. More storekeepers were added all the time, more artisans who devoted themselves to work. The competition among them was strong and constantly grew.

In 1910 the police chief Sosnovski chased out almost all the Jews from the villages around Bransk. There remained only several in Rutke, Alyekshin, Kalnitser, etc. These new additional village residents settled into the town, built houses, now in the Christian quarters of the towns Benduge and Pshetmyesta. The competition became even more fierce. There were six wagon driver businesses in Bransk, 9 hat makers, 40 shoemakers, nine blacksmiths, five carpenters, 17 bakers, four cutters of linens for comforters, four glaziers, four wheelwrights, fourteen painters, 5 kvass–makers, butchers in every home. Food stores in every second house, six dry goods stores, hardware stores, one large and three smaller ones, five village riders and a number of village walkers, dealers in the market – every Jew and Jewish woman.

This resulted in many being pushed out and emigrating. According to the trades emigration, the following turners – Binyomin Toker's children, Yudl Toker, Yankev–Itskhok's children, of the hat makers, Maishe the blind's children, Motke the hat maker, RR Aryeh Leyb, Nokhman the hat maker's children. Motye Abe was also in America, but he came back.

Of the **Shoemakers**, Maishe –Yudl, Khaim Yoels, Aryeh Shuster's children, Berl Aryeh's children, Avrum Broder and his children. Of the Tailors, Shmini, Yenkl Kartoflye, Meir, Yenkl Meir's, Shrait, Dovid–Yosl, the Shmultchikes, Bere Leybishe's children, Alter Yokl Itchikhe's and many others. Of the Tailors there emigrated Noakh Shnaider's children, Kopke's children, Hershl Schmidt's children, Pesakh Stoyler. Of the **bakers**, Penzer the baker, the American baker Itchke, Aron–Velvl's. Of the **butchers**, Shloyme'le Shepsl Katsev's, Arke Katsev's children. Of the Painters, Motke Farber, Itchke–Shaul'ke Farber's, Alter Farber's children, Tchopke About the people without trades or small storekeepers who left we cannot write because they consisted of a large number.

[Page 140]

The only solution for all of these was emigration. Why? Because there was no institution in Bransk to help the Jews, such as a folks–bank or interest–free loan bank, If they did not sell their merchandise at the fair or in the store or at the market, they had to come to the usury lender in order to be able to sustain life. They received from him twenty or twenty five rubles to be paid back in weekly installments.

There were two such in Bransk. The first Shmuel Kestale. He was also called Shmuel B'. The second Khaim Leyb Golding. He was called the "the white head."

Shmuel B' would lend twenty rubles to be paid back one ruble and forty groshen a week. One had to wait for ten days until Shmuel B' completed his investigation as to whether the borrower would be able to repay. They had to bring something as collateral. He accepted items of gold, and in addition they had to sign a note with two witnesses. But Shmuel B' was afraid of G–d and the next world, so he demanded a contract. In this way, Shmuel B' was certain of this world and the world to come. On the other hand, Khaim Leybl was a more liberal lender, but Bransk Jews already had enough troubles. The only solution was to emigrate. This is what they actually did, leaving everything that was dear and beloved, wife and children, mother and father, sister and brother and left for America.

In 1910, things lightened a bit because all the small tradesmen, tailors and others, began to do business in notes. They no longer needed money. They signed a note and received merchandise. The notes were held in Tsuker's bank in Bielsk. In 1912, during the world crisis, Bransk becomes the equal of all the other towns. Credit came to an end. Notes fly back, contested. Bransk notes are also contested. We must declare that Bransk small business and artisans, with their last groshens, did not pay their debts. It was actually the bigger merchants and businessmen who did not do this.

[Page 141]

This is how the economic life of Bransk looked at the time of the First World War in 1914.

Footnotes (Rubin Roy Cobb)
1. Mayo'fsenik – person, especially a Jew, showing servility towards non–Jews.
2. Yiddishkayt.
3. Rebbe – also meaning a teacher as does Melamed
4. Simkhas Torah
5. Khosn Torah
6. Khosn Breyshis

[Page 142]

Political Life in Bransk
up to the Outbreak Of War in 1914

In general, it can be said that Jews did not participate nor were they interested in politics, but suffered from politics in all eras.

This was born out following the political uprising, when Russia placed mandatory contributions on the Polish towns as a punishment for rebelling against Russia. Bransk's contribution was 900 rubles. The Christian population promptly placed a large portion of this upon the Jews, even though they had certainly not participated in the uprising. They promptly accused the Jews of supporting Russia. When the time came to pay the contribution, they demanded it from the Jews. Fortunately, Maishe –Hitzl Mendel's was successful in having this punishment discharged due to his friendship with the officials.

In 1888 there were already monthly newspapers and then dailies, e.g. "Hatsofe" from Petersburg. Yosl Benye and Yoke were of the first to receive newspapers. By 1897 there were already daily newspapers at Leybl Vayn's and Yoshe Bashitz's. In 1902 there were now Yiddish newspapers with many readers. However, they were not interested in any community matters and worldly politics was foreign to them.

There were several licensed community workers such as Lamshl Yoke, Elye Gotlieb, Itche Gimpel's, Avrume Beker. They knew that the time had come to be active and to do something for the town.

[Page 143]

In 1905 as a result of the political developments, Bransk Jews became more politically astute.

The youth developed political parties, and then the older people made use of the political growth, most especially by the time of the elections to the first

"Duma"[1]. The electoral district was in Bielsk. Approximately sixty people in Bransk had voting rights. They had to travel to Bielsk to vote. Fifty four Jews did so, going to Bielsk to vote, with the remaining six staying at home. It is possible they were afraid of this new system, developed cold feet and did not go, although the transportation by wagon was free, arranged by Elye Khomsky, Yoshe Lybshitz, Yerukhim Goldberg, Itche Rozenboym and others, understandably Jews. The Bielsker banker, Tsuker, was elected. When the voters returned to Bransk, Aharon Velvl the baker reported about everything.

At the elections for the last Duma, the Warsaw Jews elected Yagelo, a bit of an Anti–Semite. Because of the politics which divided the Warsaw Jews, there was later a boycott and Jews already felt that they were becoming political victims. In this way, Bransk Jews learned the meaning of politics.

Footnote (Rubin Roy Cobb)
1. Parliament

[Page 144]

The Cultural Life in Bransk up to the First World War and the Accomplishments of Bransk Children Through Self–Education

Concerning culture, Bransk was backward. There were no educational institutions. Most of the children spent their entire day with the teacher, learning from the Hebrew a, b, and c to the five books of the Torah and the bible. Poor children had to leave the traditional Jewish school at the age of 13, or even earlier, because they had to help their parents who worked hard in their own workshops from early morning until late at night.

The only education a boy had was what he had learned with his teacher. The teacher taught him writing, beginning with the Hebrew a, b, and c and concluding with how to write a letter, mostly by copying a letter from a letter–writer.

Only those children of the more affluent continued on in the traditional Jewish school after becoming a bar–mitzvah. Children of those parents who paid with their last groshens continued in the traditional Jewish school to age fifteen or later.

Considering those circumstances, we must admire the Jewish youth who actually did accomplish something. It is true that if someone received a letter from America, he went to one of only a few people who could read it. Not everybody could do this.

Around 1900 teachers made an appearance in Bransk who devoted themselves to teaching Jewish boys and girls how to write Yiddish, Russian and arithmetic. It became stylish for children to study writing with regular teachers and not with religious teachers.

[Page 145]

The first teachers in Bransk – Alter the writer, Hershl Shuster's son. He was well–known for his calligraphy, a wonderful handwriting.

Left: Alter the Schreiber at 79 in America

Right: Leybl the Teacher at 17 in 1905 Bransk

Alter the writer did not earn much from teaching. He was forced to find a way to earn a living, so he taught himself photography. Within a short time he opened the first photography studio in Bransk.

His residence was in the courtyard of Yoshe Mulyer. Attached to the wall was a box with a glass window in which there were exhibited all his photographs, pictures of Bransk Jewish men and women who had allowed themselves to be photographed so they could send their pictures to their children in America who sent money back for this purpose. When you noticed a Bransk couple dressed in their Shabbos clothes with a prayer book in hand, you could be certain they were going to Alter the writer to be photographed.

I don't know if Alter made a living from these two trades. Alter was forced to go to America. He settled in Atlanta and surrounding states where he lived to a ripe old age.

[Page 146]

There was a teacher in Bransk by the name of Piker. This was a teacher whose name nobody remembers because he was known by the nickname of "the summer horse."

The supervisor of a group of construction workers was a shoemaker, a Bransk son–in–law. He did not make a living from his shoemaker's trade. He was not a great expert in this work. He had a pretty handwriting, so he began to teach. He had many girl students and was a popular person. However, this did not afford him a living. Being a shoemaker and a teacher were not sufficient for earning a living, so he became the in Bransk. He was known only as Yosl the supervisor of a group of construction workers. There was no other name for him.

There was a teacher – Binyomin – for higher education for boy and girl students. However, there were few such students.

There were intelligent young men in Bransk who themselves became educated in various Russian cities and yeshivas. Their parents sent them to these cities to study Torah. When they returned home several years later, they were not only highly educated, but also worldly educated people. These young people became teachers. Itche Rutker was one of them.

Yudl the teacher, Shloyme–Hersh's son, was very well–known. In 1905 and part of 1906, he taught Jewish boys and girls to write Yiddish, Hebrew and Russian and arithmetic. His students were from both classes – poor and rich. In Leyzer Shane's house he taught Russian sentence structure (?) With Leyzer Cheslyer's girls, he taught Yiddish writing. At Binyomin Toker's he taught Yiddish writing and a little Russian with the boys and girls. Binyomin Toker himself was not interested in what the children were learning, but Bashe begged the children to learn how to write Yiddish. She was ashamed to ask strangers to write an address for her.

Yudl the Teacher addressed secret gatherings at the Kumant in the forest several times. There Yudl would interpret for the workers world events in the light of the Socialist spirit. Khaim Baker was not in agreement with the popular interpretations. They should be taught Marx's more worthwhile theory which is more important than everything. And yet, the youth were pleased with Yudl's popular talks.

[Page 147]

The gatherings were all secret, but when Yudl came to synagogue at end of the Sabbath for afternoon prayers following such a secret forest gathering, the Bransk rabbi, Rabbi Shmariyahu Margolis immediately approached him and said: "It is not suitable for you and your family to be friendly with such people." With his usual friendly nature, he asked Yudl not to be involved with such people.

All the Bransk teachers are responsible for the little bit of worldly education the youth received during the first five years of the 19th century. They were all true to their mission.

Bransk Library

In 1905 a library was set up in the attic of Maishe Hitsl's house. There were many Yiddish books – Mendele Mokher Sforim and Sholem Aleykhem were very popular. Jewish girls were frequent visitors and good readers of the popular Yiddish books. No longer did the story books they had previously borrowed from the book seller satisfy them. We must explain here the institution that was called the book seller. This was a tall thin Jew with a short beard who used to come to Bransk every few weeks, stop in at the old house of prayer and study where he would spread out his entire stock of books, the books of the Torah, prayer books and calendars upon a table. The Jews in the synagogue would stand at this table and read, undisturbed, all that was laid out there. This was a sort of free library. Sometimes someone bought a book. This book seller however, had a secret stash of Yiddish storybooks to sell or lend. When everyone had left, the book–seller took out this pack of storybooks (he already had his customers) and sold or loaned them out until his next visit. Somehow he earned a couple of groshen from the sale of these books. You understand, that also in secret, he had Hebrew books of the kind that could not be seen in the synagogue on the book seller's long table. He kept them hidden for select individuals.

[Page 148]

When the library was opened, all the book sellers' and workers' children came to take out books. Among the Hebrew books there were widely known two books – "Amusing Ways of Life" (?) and "Lovers of Zion." that were the most popular. Little–by–little, the library was enlarged with books of various kinds for all classes of readers.

The chief initiative for the library came from Yosl Mishlibofsky, Maishe Hitzl, Rose, Khaim Baker, Shmuel–Leyb, Berl Leybishe's son, Blume Mishurek and Yudl the teacher.

Yudl Libofsky

Khaim Baker, may he rest in peace

Founders of the first library

Several idealistic young people paid the most attention to the library and finding books. The library grew in popularity. Others saw it as a destructive tragedy that would lead to apostasy.

[Page 149]

Illegal literature now begins to make an appearance, usually in secret and is distributed to selected individuals.

By the end of 1906, when the greatest number of youth were no longer in Bransk, Avrum Maishe Smurzhik. The books were now kept in secret. Khone remembers who has a book as no records are kept. The books are hidden in secret places that only Khone knows about.

In 1910 the library becomes popular once again. Books from the library can be found in every house. There is a strong desire for education. The books released their thirst to read, to study.

In 1917 the library is refreshed by the various parties that then existed in Bransk under the nose of the Germans who occupied the town at that time.

Thanks to the fact that the books had been carefully tended to all those years through the devotion of young boys and girls, there was founded in 1905 a library by the Bransk youth who are now spread throughout the world.

Zalman Yeshaye the mailman was a very interesting type. I do not know how Bransk came to have a Jewish mailman.

Zalman Yeshaye was the mailman for many years. He was an elderly Jew who could not read or write Yiddish nor most certainly, Russian. Yet he conducted his responsibility as mailman with the greatest efficiency. He never mixed anything up. When he took a letter into his hand, he knew immediately to whom the letter belonged. He must have had a sixth sense that never failed him.

When the Bransk youth learned how to write somewhat, it became stylish to go on the mail coach, i.e. waiting for the wagon that brought the letters from Bielsk. The youth now took their own letters. Zalman Yeshaye always received the kopek from them for a letter that they took themselves.

Zalman Yeshaye also had e second means of earning a living. He distributed the warrants s since Bransk did not concern itself with worldly matters and did not have any trials that was a rarity.

[Page 150]

Of course, Zalman Yeshaye was a poor Jew and had to do a little bit of tailoring work in order to earn something for the necessities of life.

Theatre was unknown of in Bransk. The Purim players of whom several, especially those from the various gr5oups of friends, performed from house to house during Purim, and this was enough for Bransk.

During the years from 1910 there were in Bransk young people who dared with their own talents to present a theatre performance at Avrum Shkop's brick house. Shloyme Efraim was the most talented of this troupe and himself played five roles in the presentation of "Shmendrikunye." He pleased everyone. In general Shloyme Efraim was a very talented boy.

There was a gramophone in Bransk. It was at Shayke's son–in–law's. This was a box with a large horn. During the summer evenings the Bransk women would gather at the window, listening to the hearty Yiddish songs which had never been heard in town.

Mothers whose children were somewhere in America wiped their eyes with their aprons upon hearing such songs as "A Brievele der Mamen Zolstu Nit Fargesn."

There were no children's schools in Bransk. Later, church schools made an appearance in Bransk.

Some Jewish children already left Bransk, went to study in the gymnasiums.[1] These were usually from the more affluent.

There was a large number of Bransker who through self–education, attained much and among whom we must mention:

[Page 151]

Yosef–Khaim Heftman

The famous poet and articular linguist. Even as a child he exhibited a great talent for writing. He studied at that time with his rabbi and wrote something about him. . This fell into the hands of the religious teacher. The rabbi took this composition to Maishe . Mate's the ritual slaughterer. . Yosef Khaim's father. All of Bransk waited for the blows Yosef–Khaim would receive for writing in such a joking . manner about his own rabbi, in order to teach other boys not to go down such a path that is suitable for a Mendele Mokher Sforim and not for a Bransk boy. Rabbi Maishe. Mate's, the gray and grizzled elder read it and said: "What do you know of this child? Everything that he wrote is God forbid, not a lie."

Yosef Khaim Heftman

Yosef–Khaim had a special talent in being able to learn foreign languages. Within several months, he was writing and reading English and French.

The writer of this article, Julius Cohen, spent much time with Yosef–Khaim, studied with him. His poet's soul was possibly an inheritance from his great father, Rabbi Maishe Mates.

[Page 152]

He wrote as an articulate linguist and much poetry. Here I present several of his poetic creations and how they were created.

I was with Yosef–Khaim in the new house of prayer and study for afternoon prayers where he was supposed to say the mourning prayers (kaddish) for his father. He stands for the eighteen benedictions said in the three daily prayers (shmoyne esray) for a very long time. Then he says to me: "Do you know Yudl, what I wrote standing shmoyne esray? And he sings it to me in a quiet voice:

No, I do not pray now with intent

Cannot now shed any more tears

Because the moon is shining through the window

And the stars are telling me something.

I remind myself of the childhood years

The night is telling me a story

And in my heart there are born

Songs and new meanings.

Motifs, a beginning, an end

Melodies that ring from afar

The night tells me a legend

Of long ago old times.

When the Revolutionary movement was in full swing by the end of 1905, Yosef–Khaim Heftman wrote:

Canons are thundering

A flash of holy blood

Masses with flags

Brothers. Do not shed your blood.

At the beginning of 1906, when many arrests were made, thousands of young men were already incarcerated in the prisons, Yosef–Khaim wrote the following as a consolation for the many arrestees:

[Page 153]

"Give me your hand through the bars of the windows

I squeeze your fingers to my heart and I swear

Soon the courageous fighters are coming again

Returning with the old and mighty weapons."

On one particular Shabbos evening, I was at Yosef Khaim's house. Darkness had already descended. His mother did not yet want to turn on the lights, wanted to be certain to keep the holy Shabbos until the last minute. Yosef–Khaim says to his mother:

Take the Havdalah[2] candle

Light a fire already

Say now the God of Abraham

Shabbos has gone

The worries return

Abele is lighting up his store.

Abele was a religious Khasidic Jew. If his little store opened, one knew it was certainly permissible to turn on lights Shabbos evening.

All of the above were cited from my memory. I never rewrote them. (Editor)

Yosef–Khaim goes to Brisk (Brest–Litovsk)[3] –where he is contacted by certain people who are interested in his talents. He becomes the editor of newspapers in Warsaw. He is now in Palestine and the president of the writers' union in Eretz Yisroel[4]

He is also the president of Irgun Yossi of Bransk in Tel Aviv that is active in helping Bransk survivors to settle in Eretz Yisroel.

[Page 154]

Leyb Yankev Fraynd the Khazn's Son

Studied in the yeshivas of Brisk, Minsk and Vilna where he receives his ordination from the brilliant (Ha'gaon) Rabbi Khaim Oyzer Gradzhensky in the presence of Rabbi Sholem Dovid Rabinowitz, author of the book "Questions of Peace." After he receives his ordination, he begins to educate himself in general worldly matters. Simultaneously, he enrolls in the Czarist Russian

Conservatory in Vilna where he studies music, theory and singing. At this same time he is a co–worker in the Hebrew newspaper "Hazman" (The Time).

Even as a child Leybl had a bent towards astronomy. While in Vilna, he becomes active in this, conducting a scientific correspondence with the director of the Petersburg University observatory, Professor Sergei Pavlovich from Glazenap. The professor becomes interested in the young Leybl's talents and he presents Leybl's astronomy work before the administration of the Russian Czar's astronomy organization. The organization elects him as member–correspondent. Leybl Fraynd sends to the Czar's Scientific Academy a report in which he establishes scientifically – "The reason for positive and negative in the Vinkl movement in the trigonometric functions."

Professor Glazenap read the aforementioned paper at the meeting of the basic (?) mathematics division of the Czar's Academy of Science. As a result Leybl is elected as correspondent of the Nikolayever head physical conservatory in Petersburg.

Leybl's striving for more education leads to him being a student at the Royal Academy of Technology High School of Dresden. He graduates from the technical school with a degree in engineering. He leaves Dresden. He arrives in France to engage in further studies. While he was in Toulouse for one year, the First World War erupts. He arrives in Bransk. When the Germans invade Poland, he goes to Harbin[5] in the Far East and from there to Shanghai where he becomes active as an engineer, and then he takes to business.

[Page 155]

In Shanghai Leybl finds limitless opportunities for community activities. He becomes friendly with the Sephardic Jews. Later he organizes anAshkenazi community, a Zionist organization, a literary and musical society.

According to the announcements of the central committee of Zionist organizations, Jewish communities in the Far East. He organizes in Shanghai the printing of Yiddish books, Russian and Hebrew dictionaries for those Jews in the Far East who have not had any books or religious books because of the war.

In 1923 he meets Professor Albert Einstein with whom he spends a scientifically orientated three days. Professor Einstein gives him an autograph in which he calls Leybl a colleague.

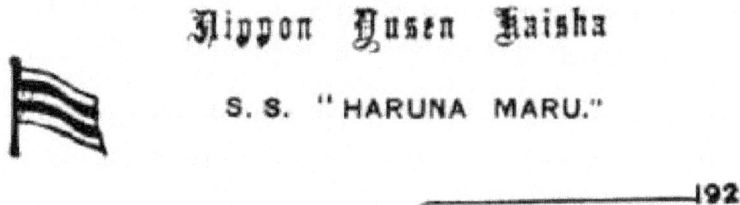

Nippon Yusen Kaisha

S. S. " HARUNA MARU."

———————————192

Professor Einstein's letter to Leybl the khazn's son written on the Japanese ship

[Page 156]

With the help of engineer Novomysky, he who had received the concession (for minerals) of the Dead Sea, he sends hundreds of pioneers (khalutsim) from Russia to Eretz Yisroel. He organizes the first Jewish (synagogue) chorus in Shanghai, opens two synagogues there. He writes Hebrew prayers for special fiery prayer services at which ambassadors, ministers and other officials are present. At this same time he writes scientific articles for the local English press. Leybl helps all artists who used to arrive in Shanghai on their way from Russia to other countries. Aron Levediev, Mr and Mrs Arke, Mr and Mrs Bodkin, Bulman, the artistic ensemble "Zmira" is helped with everything possible.

As honourary representative of HIAS (Hebrew Sheltering and Immigration Aid Society) in the Far East, he helps hundreds to receive visas to travel to

America, Palestine and other countries, making use of his personal friendship with English and American diplomats.

Because of Hitler's horrors, there arrived in Shanghai 23,000 Jewish refugees. They are helped by him with everything possible. Many, through his initiative became self–sufficient in Shanghai.

In 1940, when Lithuania, half of Poland and Latvia are occupied by the Soviets, Leybl became aware that in Kovno (Kaunas) there are many Jews who would have had the possibility to emigrate if they received transit visas from any country that had good relations with the Soviets.

Leybl consulted a friend of his, a Japanese admiral in Shanghai who asks the Japanese ambassador to give the Japanese consul in Kovno permission to issue transit visas to travel through Shanghai. With these visas, which were issued in the thousands, all the yeshiva boys and rabbis and heads of yeshivas were saved from a certain death by Hitler. Many in 1941 arrived in Shanghai and Japan thanks to the visas from Kovno. Two boys from the Bransk yeshiva were among those who benefitted from the efforts of their landsman (fellow–countryman) Zelig, the son of Leybl Fraynd, the Bransker Khazn's son.

However, fate intervened and this great scholar, he who helped all unfortunates himself became a refugee.

[Page 157]

1 month prior to Pearl Harbor, Leybl Fraynd arrived for business in Manila in the Philippine Islands. He remained in Manila as a refugee throughout the entire time of the Japanese occupation there. He suffered from hunger, without a roof over his head in concentration camps and looked death in the eyes more than once.

When the victorious American army marched back into Manila, Leyblimmediately became active. He organized the prayer service to which thousands of Jewish soldiers from the States came.

During the war, Leybl composed a prayer of victory for the allied armies. He sends it to President Truman and is honoured with a thank you letter from the State Department in Washington.

At the end of 1947, Leybl the khazn's son and his daughter Balfora come to America where he hopes to receive permission to make it home.

This is the record of the boys who attained everything by themselves through self–education.

Personal Biographical Sketch of Leybl Fraynd

Avrum Branski is famous in Soviet Russia as an artist/painter of the first rank. He too received his education through his own courage and his own efforts.

Maishe Zalusker, surname Pasinkofsky, now famous in Boston as an important lawyer with the name M. Parsons, is also of the same category – self–educated in spite of the fact that he has distanced himself from all activities of the Bransk landsmanshaft.

Hershl the Recluse's Son

Was greatly educated. Studied together with Yosef Khaim Heftman. He was proficient in languages. His education took place in very difficult conditions and he suffered mostly from hunger.

[Page 158]

There was never so much as a piece of bread in his house, and yet, with the greatest danger to his life, devoted himself to education. During the Revolutionary years he was drawn into Warsaw in a central office. He constantly comes under the scrutiny of the Russian police and is arrested and sent to Siberia for a long time.

He returns home a broken and quiet man.

Hershl the Recluse's   Leybl Fraynd the Khazn's

[Page 159]

Visible on him is the fact that life in Siberia had broken him. The young, intelligent and gentle person cannot recover. His every move is spied upon. He can no longer accommodate himself to any kind of work. He becomes ill and dies at a young age, never having been married.

Rabbi Avrum Yitskhak Edelman

This is Yenkl Ginsburg's son. He studied with his father and with the best Bransk teachers. He was a student of such famous Branskers as Yankev Mordekhay the Khasid and Binyomin the watchmaker.

At the age of 11 Avrum'tche comes to Visoke Mazavitsk. He studies there until he becomes a bar mitzvah. He then arrives in the Makaver Yeshiva and stays for two years. At the age of fifteen he is already in Trestine and is studying by himself. From there he come to Volozhin to the famous Torah–center of Russia which is led by Rabbi Rafayl Shapira.

Rabbi Avrum Yitskhak Edelman

The Volozhiner Yeshiva together with its leader arrives in Minsk at the outbreak of the First World War. The older boys together with Avrum'tche are advised by Rabbi Shapira to go to the southern Russian gubernyes (provinces).

[Page 160]

Avrum YItskhak was already at that time ordained as a rabbi and goes with several other youths to Yekaterinoslaver. The local rabbis, Harav Gelman and Harav Shnayerson welcomed these Lithuanian youths.

In the southern Russian provinces there were at that time many Lithuanian Jews who had been sent out from the Russian–German border towns. Schools were arranged in the provinces for the Jewish children.

Avrum Yitskhak Edelman is hired by the Yekaterinoslaver rabbis as the head mashgiakh (supervisor of Jewish dietary laws) and director of these schools and yeshivas.

Sometime later he is sent to the smaller towns of Yekaterinrslayer and Bersoner provinces for the purpose of establishing evening courses in those towns for young working people by the name Tiferes Bokhurim.

In 1917, when the Czarist government fell and the Kerensky regime ruled, the organization called "Traditon in Freedom" was allowed to function. Avrum-YItskhak is sent to organize such groups in Rostov, Kavkaz where there were large Jewish communities. From Rostov he went to Kislovodsk where there were many thousands of Jews who had come from the war zones.

Avrum–Yitskhak Edelman makes an effort to organize a group from the Jewish community in Kisklavadsk. He receives from the district tribunal of Vladikavkan permission for this. Through Avrum Yitskhak's efforts, Dr. Asherovski gave a large building as a gift. All the Jewish activities were concentrated in this building. There was a synagogue, a place for visiting guests and an interest–free loan society. In this way, the Russian health/cure-town Kislavadsk became the first Jewish center for all Jewish activities In Kavkaz at that time the battle between the Bolsheviks and the Imperial armies was raging in Kavkaz. As a result, all the Jewish leaders were arrested.

[Page 161]

Avrum Yitskhak Edelman and a couple of Georgian Jews set out on foot through the Kavkazer mountains to the town of Petrovsk, a port on the Caspian Sea. From there they arrive in Baku, then in Tiflis (Stalin's birthplace). They then go to Batum via the Black Sea to Constantinople, Turkey, then to Greece, Italy, Spain and from Spain to New York.

After he had been in New York for two months, Worcester, Massachusetts hired Rabbi Avrum Yitskhak Edelman as the rabbi of their large synagogue, Sha'arei Torah.

Six years later, Rabbi Avrum Yitskhak Edelman comes to New York to head the seat of the rabbinate in the Yagustaver synagogue in Harlem on 118th Street. However, the neighborhood changes and is no longer a Jewish quarter. Rabbi Avrum Yitskhak Edelman becomes the rabbi in the Makhziki synagogue, 808 College Avenue, where he holds this position to this day.

Rabbi Edelman learns through the newspapers about an event being held by the Bransk landslayt. He and his wife came to this gathering. He met there friends of his youth and landslayt. He enrolls in the Bransker Young Mens' and becomes active in all landsmanshaften work.

When the Bransk Relief begins its renewed activities in New York, Rabbi Avrum–Yitskhak Edelman is one of the most important and active of the Bransk Relief. He devotes much of his time for this holy mission to help the remnants of refugees in spite of the fact that he is very involved with Jewish community activities.

It is important to mention that his wife is also a devoted worker for all important activities. Their home is a gathering–place where many come to express their feelings, ask for advice or when they need to have someone to turn to for various religious institutions. They know of all the needy in the neighborhood and do much to help the poor. They help not only directly, but create much help through other means. The residence of Rabbi AvrumYitskhak Edelman is not only a house of wisdom, but a place of help and support and consolation for many downtrodden and poor in the neighborhood.

[Page 162]

In the summer of 1947, Rabbi Edelman travels to Palestine to visit his father. He meets with the Bransk landslayt there, becomes interested in their lives – building and establishing. He returns to New York, speaks before many well attended gatherings about his impressions, about the new and proud life that is being built fearlessly in Palestine, with certainty and hopes that eventually they will be successful in fulfilling the generations long awaited dream of the people of Israel in Eretz Yisroel.

Bransk should be proud of such children who attained much through their own energy, through their will in spite of the greatest poverty.

This was Bransk, its leaders, its khevras, institutions, children, religious and liberated, its most joyous and most sad moments up until 1914 then the entire world trembled from a shot fired in the Balkan half–island that reverberated throughout Europe and resulted in the war of 1914 which we now call the First World War.

Footnotes (Rubin Roy Cobb)
2. Private schools.
3. The ceremony performed at the close of the Shabbos
4. City from where the Kobylanskis originated from.
5. The Land of Israel
6. Wikipedia: Harbin – in 1898 the construction of the Chinese Eastern Railway, an extension of the Trans–Siberian railroad by Russia commenced. Many Jews arrived fleeing the pogroms and persecution of Czarist Russia.

[Page 165]

PART TWO

War 1914

On August 1st, 1914 there appeared mobilization notices on every house in Bransk.

These notices thrust fear into everyone, and most especially into the Jewish population of the town.

A couple of days later, sad scenes play out in town. Women accompany their husbands, mothers cry for their sons and little children stand in stony silence when their fathers bid everyone goodbye before they leave for service. Their hearts tell them that not everyone will return.

Very soon reports begin to arrive from the front, reports about the fallen:

Berl Koze, Meir, Yankl Meir's, Maishe Pesakh the miller's son, Khaim Libetchke's son, Mele Alyiekshener, Pinye Glazer, Anshel the grave–digger's son, Zavl the carpenter's son Khone and many others.

Many wounded arrive from the front: Maishe Gershon Ber's, Mordekhay the barber, Khaye Motelikhe's husband and others. They become aware of many who were captured and their relatives are happy.

The town is overflowing with many homeless Jews who had fled the towns that were near the border.

In Bransk temporary housing is created for these refugees either with acquaintances or with distant relatives and even with Jews who gave up space in their homes.

The Bransk youth sets up a committee for the homeless whose duty it is to supply everything possible for the refugee Jews in town.

In order to raise money for this work, they arrange a show and also readings of works by certain writers.

[Page 166]

The initiators of this undertaking were Ezra's daughter, Nakh Pentman, Leybl Bransky, Lahke the cantor's, Nekhman Goldberg, Levitt, a woman dentist. They did much to help the homeless get settled.

Bransk is filled with Russian military among whom are many Jews, most of them from deep Poland, Jews with beards. A kosher kitchen is established in the Khasidic house–of–prayer and study where Bayle the Malyesherke cooks for forty Jewish soldiers.

The general mood is a constricted one. There is word of false accusatory stories against Jews in other towns that are near the front.

The commandant at that time in Bransk, a true pogrom'tchik (instigator of pogroms) warns the Jewish population about sabotage. He threatens severe punishment.

A provocation occurs. A wagon with homeless Jews was traveling from Ostralenke to Bielsk. The soldiers who were guarding the highway cut the telephone wires and halt the wagon of Jews and accuse them of sabotage. It is almost at the point of a field–trial. They are faced with certain death when Rabbi Shimon Shkop intervenes. He convinces them of the innocence of the detainees. They are released.

A second incident occurs. Hershl Benduger becomes virtually insane, cuts the telephone wires. Dr. Domansky confirms that this person is insane. Even Rabbi Shimon cannot help. He is detained. There are already rumors that Hershl Benduger has been shot. They saw how they had led him to the Christian magistrate. Five years later, Hershl returns to Bransk, released through the revolution. He had left Bransk as a confused person and returned home completely insane.

The population is divided in two camps. A portion agrees with the Germans and is happy with their victories; a second part is for the Russians and are happy with German losses. There are always debates in the synagogue between these two camps.

[Page 167]

Aron Velvl Beker is thrilled with Russian defeats and Itsl Vartovnik shouts: "You will yet yearn for the Russians."

Only in the new house–of–prayer and study were there no debates, because Notn Zelvin the Moskver, a true patriot, was there. Mr Notn Zelvin saw to it that the congregation should rise up. He was very happy when he stood up in the "Hanutn Tshueh." (?) He was pleased when he read in the Novaya Vremya newspaper that the Russians had occupied Lemberg in Galicia. But the Moskver suffered much from the Russian defeats at the Mazure Ozyeres in Tanenberg in Prussia.

Bransk Jews became very familiar with geography, knew of all the important points of the Carpathian Mountains up to the Baltic Sea. They became well–acquainted with the names of all the generals who were heading the commands.

And so time played out in this fashion. Every month there was a new conscription. All of the youth is enrolled in the army. There are those who hide, waiting for the day the Germans would enter Bransk and they would become free people.

More homeless fill the town. In addition, Bransk becomes a military camp. There are soldiers to be found in every house. There can already be seen from afar how the fires light up the sky. The front comes closer to Bransk. Bransk begins to pack up in preparation to fleeing deep into Russia. However, their number is small because there no horses or wagons available. Many flee to Orla. They had convinced themselves that the town of Orla, according to their understanding, was not in danger. Those who come there quickly find out that their understanding was false because Orla is soon bombed. Three Bransk Jews become victims there: Berl the blacksmith's wife and a daughter and Hershl Yudl – Hoyever's wife.

Notn Zelvin the Moskver runs away on foot from Bransk. He has a single ruble with him, throws it into the charity box and sets out without a groshen, with nothing, not to fall into German hands.

Suddenly there is news: Tchekhenovtse is burning. Bransk is filled with those fleeing from Tchekhenoftse. Cossacks appear in the streets. They immediately begin to burn Bransk. Rabbi Shimon Shkop collects money and gives it to the Cossacks. One of the Cossack officers notices Rabbi Shimon's watch. Rabbi Shimon Shkop takes it out and gives it to the officer. Bransk is not burnt.

[Page 168]

An unanticipated fire breaks out on Mill Street. The bridges burn. The army retreats. The town is left by itself. There are no longer any Russians. Some time later they hear: mazel tov, mazel tov. A woman shouts that she had seen German troops coming. After a few minutes, there appear in the streets of Bransk Germans with murderous eyes and fat red mouths.

Young Jewish youths, dressed in civilian clothes who all had thought were no longer alive, make anappearance. Whether it was worthwhile to wish mazel tov when the Germans entered, we will see.

[Page 169]

38 Months of German Occupation in Bransk

On September 14th, at 6 a.m., the Germans enter Bransk. They immediately begin to grab people to build bridges. They behave brutally towards those whom they caught. Two people are forced to carry a heavy log. This is physically impossible and they receive a bad beating.

Horseback riders guard the side positions near Kalnitse. Bransk is filled with German wounded. It immediately becomes a garbage heap.

The following day the Germans begin to bring order into the town. The commandant requisitions the flour from all the flour merchants, as well as all other food articles. A plague breaks out in town. They hide the sick from the Germans because they poison them. They do not offer any medicinal aid.

A gathering is called and a town committee is formed. Who? You guessed it – Yerukhim Goldberg, Elye Gotlieb and Yitskhak Rozenboym become the representatives of the town administration. A militia is organized from the revolutionary elements of the town. A cultural group is organized – a community. The chairman of the community is Ezra's son–in–law, Auerbukh with the nickname Katshinskale.

Bransk Jews feel the taste of the German occupation. It becomes forbidden to be in the street after 7 p.m. They sit in the house in darkness. Lights are not permitted. They grab people from the streets to go to work. They grab them from their homes, from synagogue. You finish the work and are going home and then you are caught again. There are beatings at work, there is less food. There is hunger in many homes. There is no work available for anybody. Those who had merchandise to take to other towns are forbidden to travel. There is no raw material. The shopkeepers remain in their empty stores.

[Page 170]

They distribute bread cards, flour cards. The flour is mixed with something that gave the bread a bitter taste. People die from eating this bread. Certain deaths – the limping tinsmith's wife – are confirmed by the doctor as having been a result of the bread.

Women organize a demonstration to the magistrate with the bread in hand. The Jewish representatives shout to them: Go home. It appears that they have not eaten the bread. The majority of the Jewish population suffers from the cold. No Christian would bring any wood into town. And nobody had anything with which to make a purchase. There was wood lying on the highway that the Germans were taking to the train, so they would take a chance with their lives and go out at night to get a few pieces of wood so as not to freeze in their homes. This is how Khaim Odesser was shot, while trying to take a couple of pieces of wood.

Typhus showed up in town. The doctor immediately informed the occupying power. The people are removed to the hospital and quickly these patients die. This happened to Binyomke the baker, Avreml the barber and Kutikhe's daughter.

The deaths resulting from hunger, cold and illness were many; old and young.

The winter of 1916 was a terrible one in Bransk. The occupying power demands workers to be sent to the front lines as protective trench diggers. Our representatives at the magistrates and the culture groups make a list of whom to send for work. It is the poor and helpless who are usually chosen for the work. When there are protests the answer is: What Is the difference? You work here as well, so you will work there. The first group of workers who were sent to Baranovitch were, for the most part, from boys without families in town. They returned, having run away, with frozen hands and feet, broken. The Dzeshenikels boy, Yisroel Yehuda, did not return. He died somewhere out.

[Page 171]

The second part that was sent to Gainofke (Russian) [Hainovka – Polish][1] was also comprised of such poor worker boys. My brother Shloym'ke and I were included in this group. When they needed more, they took those who were married. Then they took women whose husbands were in the army. They gave them twenty marks and sent them away. Those who were once runaways did not receive the twenty marks. Deserters were also called. The more affluent did not go to any work because they were or were declared to be rabbinical students, or they were firemen. Poor people were not accepted as firemen, only the upper class. The firemen were used to help catch workers. Later, it was ordered that the firemen should be used to drive trucks, so the magistrate people invited the poor boys to enroll as firemen. They actually declined this honor to now become firemen.

Because the population of the town was too dense, the administration of the power ordered a portion of the people be sent to the village. Once again, these were people who had dared to protest against the community providers. I remember that Zushe the tailor, Yankl Brezhnitser, Maishe, Shmuelke Slove's, Shnebele and others, were part of those who had been sent out.

Others flee. Those who had been sent out are stricken from the bread list. Of these, only the deceased were brought back to Bransk for burial.

[Page 172]

People now went to work. The bitter bread now became sweet. A new means of earning a living develops – smuggling, i.e. bringing either food or merchandise into town. Smuggling was forbidden and yet, smugglers were mostly from the richer that made "protection" possible.

Yoske Leyzer Katsev's was in Bransk. He had strong protection from the Zshandar. He was a small man with an officer's jacket, officer's boots. Rabbi Shimon Shkop used to call him Mr Yosef. This Yoske was actually not a bad sort, a good brother. When Hershl Zager loses a wagonload of flour, Yoske gets it back – really a good brother.

At the beginning of 1917, new winds begin to blow. Political organizations spring up of their own accord: "Bund", "Zionist." The organizations are founded in secret so that the Germans should not take notice. The Zionist organization is founded in Yerukhim Vigodski's house, and in Gedalye Kozidovtche's, the "Bund", – both in secret. Speakers come from Lodz for joint gatherings. The battle between the parties is a lively one. Speaking for the Zionists was Shneyer, Rabbi Shimon Shkop's nephew and for the Bund – Shloym'ke Trus.

Proclamations against the occupation make an appearance in town. There are protests against eliminating bread and fat (grease). After a twelve–year silence, the old political parties come to life under the nose of the occupying. power.

The protests gain strength against the town cultural group which sends workers to the Germans for forced labor. The protests work. They no longer send anybody for forced labor. Rumors of a revolution in Russia begin to circulate.

Secret agents come from Bielsk to investigate what is happening in Bransk. Bielsker friends inform us beforehand. The occupation agents receive a warning to leave town within one hour. It works.

The hidden books of the library are brought out. The youth wants to learn. Newspapers arrive from Warsaw with Jewish train officials because the mail delivery did not include newspapers.

[Page 173]

Group of BUND in 1917, under nose of the German might

[Page 174]

The administration of Linat Ha'tsedek organizes a theatre performance – the "Wild Human" by Yankev Gordon. Several town boys and girls perform the roles. In secret there is brought from Bialystok the Jewish theatre group. They are couplets:

The German will give everything

For Shabbos fish and khales.[a]

There are now those giving information to the Germans who want to know the meaning of the song, and orders the artists to leave Bransk.

The Linat Ha'tsedek (? righteous) and Visiting of the Sick are active. They help with medicines for the sick to aid in their recovery.

Everyone is now aware that the Germans are stuck at the Marne in France. There is a feeling that the Germans will leave very soon.

During the night of November 11, 1918, the Germans pack up and depart the town. They leave behind their belongings. The German occupation has ended.

There are new sufferings for the Bransk Jews under the Polish government.

Footnote (Rubin Roy Cobb)
1. The town now on the Polish Belarus border where Rubin Roy Cobb's paternal uncle Shimon Kobylanski lived with his wife Tzvia Stern Kobylanski lived. They had no children and were deported to Auschwitz in January/February 1942.

Footnote (Mindle Crystal Gross)
a. It rhymes in Yiddish

[Page 175]

Bransk at the Beginning of the Polish Government

The Germans departed Bransk during the night, and a temporary citizens' committee is organized as well as a citizens' militia. Jews are part of both the committee and the militia.

The citizens' committee takes over the warehouses with various foods and military articles that the Germans in their haste, had left. The militia guards the magazines that were located in the church. Yakh'ke the shopkeeper constantly goes to Alter and warns him: "Alter, be careful with the rifle."

Once again, the town finds itself in a constricted mood. They already know which power will command. In place of the brutal Germans there will soon arrive fanatics, the legionnaires. They are afraid of the Poles.

The following day, the 12th two drunken Poles ride into town. Kuzshmes a son of Lubyeshtch, and a manager of the Rutkerestates around whom the Polish youth congregate. Their speech is brief: "People, we now have our own Poland. Now we will fight the Bolsheviks. Whoever will not follow will go to the gallows."[1]

They left quickly because there were still Germans who have wandered from Tchekhenovtse to Bielsk.

Doctor Domanski and the Christian pharmacist calm the town, but the Jews are frightened.

The Jewish legionnaire Hershl Sheyne's along with Polish legionnaires are caught by the Germans and dragged along to Bielsk where they suffer terrible beatings and are disarmed. The Germans quickly return to Bransk. On the 2nd day of Khannukah, at 1 p.m., a Polish military group arrives, disarm the Germans. The gendarme Lemkin is shot. The Germans are chased out with nothing. The following day Bransk is filled with returning Germans. The battle lasts the entire day. In the evening, Germans once again force their way in. They see their dead comrade, become enraged, murder and burn. There are victims. The miller with the nickname of Tchatche, the son of the Polyeteler shepherd, his wife and partner, a Sokol Jew, are burned when their house is set on fire. The Alientsker shoemaker's brother, who had just returned from the war, is shot. Bransk is burning on all four sides.

[Page 176]

Rabbi ShimonShkop immediately organizes a relief action. He is insulted by the Germans. A German by the name of Herman who had remained in Bransk stands up for the rabbi. Rabbi Shimon Shkop gets away with no more than fright. Then there was an uncertain situation – one day, the Germans and one day, the Poles; in town Germans and outside of town Poles. Jews are caught on the road or in the villages. They are robbed and relieved of their weapons. These captured Jews are taken to Lapy or to the village of Pyetkeve where they are beaten.

This will be corroborated by Sender Chomsky who received 25 blows. Revisions are made. My brother Shloym'ke Trus is arrested for having the Bundist archive. The legionnaire Shtaynman intervenes and for two litres of brandy my brother is freed. Five litres of brandy bought permission to open a Bundist club.

Some modicum of order is restored. There is a magistrate. Khaim Gotlieb is vice–chairman. A couple of Jews become community administration members.

It is not quiet. People are afraid to travel by train. Beards are being cut off. There appear in Bransk the Holyartchikes. Their first act is: upon encountering Binyom'ke the tailor in the street, they begin to cut his beard. However they receive blows because Lipe Portselaynik, Froytche Sane's fight back, and even the Christian Zogar helps them. There is no further attempt to cut Jewish beards in Bransk.

[Page 177]

It is very dangerous to ride on the roads behind Bransk. Bransk Jews travel to Shepetove and are attacked, beaten and robbed. The attackers are identified but it does not help.

It slowly becomes a little quieter. There is the beginning of some kind of normal life. Once again, political parties spring to life and there are gatherings, the library opens, there are many newspapers. Every couple of days there are presentations by various parties with their own talents. Decorations are painted by Avreml Bransky.

They organize a folk–school with good teachers: Khaim Tsvi Bransky and Avreml Branski as head teacher and Shvartz from Trestine. Children from all parties study in these schools, even from Mizrakhi[2] because the school administration is comprised of representatives from all parties.

A Mizrakhi[3] cooperative store becomes active in Bransk, managed by Yerukhim Goldberg, Leybl Vayner and Motl Shuster. Food was sold there only to a member of the cooperative.

In 1919 there is a gathering of all Jewish communities. This gathering takes place in Bialystok. The Bransk community has to elect a delegation. A big election battle takes place in regard to this gathering, and five parties are chosen. The "Bund" wins.

Later on administration members from various parties are elected. Elected are: Ratmener Epshteyn, Hershl Bransky from the Bund, Khaim Kestin and Yenkl Pribut from the Poale Tsiyon, ** Khaim Hershl Bransky, Yosl Mishurek from the Zionists, Maishe Smurzik and Berish Kagan from Mizrakhi, a Communist, Katchmarsky becomes the arbitrator (?). Later he runs away to Russian with the Soviets.

The magistrate decides to designate May 1ˢᵗ as a workers' holiday. In general, all the parties had representatives, responsible people. They worked together in all town matters.

[Page 179]

Yiddish Folk School, some of the Teachers

Left: Yosl Mishurek Murdered near Vishkov
Right: Khaim–Hersh Branski taken when 25 years old. Died in New York in 1947

The year 1920 sees the beginning of mobilizations. The war between Poland and Russia is in full swing. The youth as well as older people are called to military service. A movement is created that argues that Bransk does not belong to Poland and therefore, does not have to participate in military service. There are others, whoever, who are against this movement.

There are no proper records listing Bransk Jews. The magistrate with the aid of Christians say: Itchka Mordka are the same age as my Stazhek and therefore, do military service.

The war comes closer to us. Poland has already fled Kiev. Pilsudski's war plans fall through. Bransk is now filled with Polish military. Jews are grabbed for the trenches. Everything around Bransk is burning – the danger increases. Shooting can now be heard. The Polish military leaves Bransk. A folk–militia is organized. Jews are a part of this militia. On July 26th, 1920, all the Poles flee, and now unfamiliar soldiers arrive and rob the town. Screams are heard from Jewish houses, from the helpless Jewish women. Jewish daughters are raped. The Poznatchikes and Halyartchikes do their work. There is no protection.

[Page 180]

On July 27th there is a battle between the Polish and Russian military. Mordekhay Fuhrman is lightly wounded when he goes out for water. The Poles flee, leaving their captured comrades in the Bransk streets. They pay a second visit which fails. The first Red Army soldiers make an appearance in the streets of Bransk. The following day, July 28th, 1920 it was finally quiet.

Footnotes (Rubin Roy Cobb)
2. Tali – another word for gallows.
3. Religious Zionists
4. Workers of Zion (Labour Party)

[Page 181]

Polish–Soviet War

(20 days of the Soviet Power in Bransk)

New troubles begin. The shops are empty, the merchandise robbed. That which remained the Soviet soldiers bought out with their Soviet money that was worthless. There was no way to earn a living, no work.

The first Soviet commissar of the workers' military revolutionary committee makes an appearance in town. His name is Tsiganov. It doesn't take very long before Bransk figures out that Tsiganov is a Jew who comes from the Poltaver region. Tsiganov was a jolly person, full of Jewish jokes and songs. By trade he was an actor with the Jewish drama group in Odessa.

He arranges gatherings. He makes speeches. He answers questions, almost always with a joke.

A Poplover Christian asks a serious question at a gathering. "Good," says the Christian, "we will sell our bread and our products to the power. The money is worthless. There is nothing for us to buy. There is no merchandise here." Tsiganov answers him in Russian: "This will lead to difficult trouble too." Whether the Poplover Christian was satisfied, I do not know.

Two Bransk Jewish girls also ask a question: "We do not have a cow and the rich peasants have two cows. Is this justice?" Tsiganov asked the girls: "Did you ever have a cow?" "No," the girls answer. Tsiganov says: "So then you will continue to not have a cow." They had plenty of jokes, but in truth, there was nothing.

[Page 182]

Jews take positions in the militia. Epstein becomes the manager of the militia, Khaim Kestin chairman of the community. Alter Trus receives the post in Kalnitser courtyard as community leader, and other such work.

Various clubs are founded in Bransk; Yevsekishe[1], Poale Tsiyon and Bund. The Soviet power is now in effect in Bransk.

Now came the Tsherzvitshaayke spies. They stab through everybody with their piercing eyes. Arrests begin. Jews and Christians are arrested.

The Tsherzvitshaayke find documents in the cellar of Avrume Shkop's brick house. These spies find many items that people had hidden there. Among these were lists of Zionist leaders. They arrested Yosl Mishurek and Yisroel Shapira, 2 prominent Zionists. The front continued on further to Poland, and these two were dragged along to Vishkov. Later, when the Russians returned, they were found in Vishkov near Warsaw – murdered.

There is a noticeable dissatisfaction with the new Soviet rulers, even among the sympathizers, most especially with the military communists who were very strict during wartime. In addition at that time there crept into the main committees unwanted elements. Some of them used to check the ovens to see if the bakers had used them, others searched for no particular reason on the off–chance that they would find something or someone breaking the law, making themselves into big–shots. They would not have lasted long.

Suddenly there appear in Bransk large military divisions. Panic erupts. The Russians retreat.

Whoever can flee, does, and not only the officials but any Jews. Everybody runs. They already knew what this was about. The Poles (in Yiddish Polaks) are returning to Bransk. The front up to Warsaw has been broken. The Poles called it the "divorce" at the Vaysl. To this very day, many of those who had fled remained in Russia: Shloym'ke Trus, Avrum'tsye Kritz, Hershl Bransky, Avruml Bransky, Itche Albayter, Tsolke Shrait, Nomke Blayman, Berl the Beder's, Itche Gorokhovsky, Khaye–Dina and her husband and others. Others returned to Bransk later on.

[Page 183]

On August 18th, the Poles come to Bransk. There are no longer any Soviets present. The Poles now begin to take Jews for forced labour. They chase all the young and old to build the bridge, throw people into the lake. The rabbi, Rabbi Itskhak Ziv, is assigned to drag heavy logs and other difficult work. Sholem Krotz is tied to a horse and dragged through the streets. They do the same thing to Maishe Elye Dovid's. They steal whatever they find. They catch Jews to herd horses and cows.

Tchekhenover[2] Jews, brothers with the name London, are murdered by the Poles, as well as their sister's groom.

An unknown Jew is also murdered. To this very day, no one knows who he was.

The war did not last long. Peace is arranged in accordance with the Riga Tractate. A little bit of normal life begins in Bransk, filled with renewed hopes for better times. Poland becomes a free country.

Footnotes (Rubin Roy Cobb)

1. A leftist East European political organization
2. After the fall of the Tsar in October 1917, a secret political police force is established called the *Cheka*.

[Page 184]

Bransk in the New Poland

At the beginning of 1921 they began to believe that finally, a normal way of life would take hold. Bransk Jews make an attempt to rebuild the destroyed economic life. This was very difficult. The houses had no windows, the stores had no merchandise, because during the war years, everything had been burned or stolen. Workers have no work. There is no new material. Everyone's clothes are patched.

The first aid comes from America from the Bransk Relief of New York, from relatives, from friends. This mostly is used to begin building. Shopkeepers stock their stores with merchandise. Workers have work and there is raw material, dry goods, wood, iron and even thread that can now be obtained as long as there is money.

There are still many bandits remaining from the war years. They are in the woods, rob and steal. In the month of March, a group of merchants from

Shepetove, while traveling is attacked by a masked band in the Vilyener forest and are robbed. Murdered are Itskhak Mordekhay Vaser, Maishe Zilbeshteyn, Leybl Furman's son, Hershl and AyzikHurvitz, Beznazik's son and others. Yoske Bransky's son pretended to be dead and thus, was saved. Traveling by train was terrible. People were thrown out as it was moving. Little by little, it calmed down. Many Branskers left for America or other areas. Others did not have to whom to go to nor did they have the means with which to go.

Bransk slowly rebuilt, enlarged the businesses and adding many new stores. Workers of various trades worked for the markets and fairs. Others worked for the home front. There were new producers of kvass who take their brew to fairs in other areas. They are dubbed "zakazne."[1] Wheelwright and blacksmith businesses strongly developed while other trades, such as painting went under. The most important fairs were in Bielsk, Gainovke (Hanovka), Visoki, Mazavyetski, Sokole, Lapy, Tchizhev and Tchekhenovtse.

[Page 185]

There were many Jews who were village–travelers. They sold various small articles. There were also a large number of women village–travelers. However, later on, they ceased to be. There were many "table–merchants" who exhibited their wares on small tables in the market. Like in days gone by there was Gotshekhe Malke. They were called "the sitters" and there is no longer even a remnant of them. However, in their memory, there is one who still carries on this same business, like Notshikhe. (?) This is Yenkl Treger's wife, an aged woman. She sells apples, cherries, pears, red and black berries, beets and gooseberries in the street. I noticed her and her little table in the market in 1938. It reminded me of my childhood years when I sometimes would get a groshen from my mother. I would run to the table to buy the fresh berries, go home and make a shehekheyanu (thanking God). My mother and father would be so proud, wiping their damp eyes and wishing to live another year. I remember that I loved to buy from Malke the sitter. She would give a full spoonful of berries and then add five more. First she would ask me whose little boy I was – Sheyne Yente's son? So come here, a few more berries. Gotshekhe never gave away anything for nothing. She put the berries in a little paper, never giving any extra. She was a "berye" – (a woman capable of doing everything), a good businesswoman. I still remember the "krokhmales"[2], sort of little dolls, arms and legs outstretched, painted red and blue. These would be purchased by the Christian girls on their way home from church on Sunday.

From today's table–merchants – they were called "straganes", one could buy manufactured items: men and women's underwear, such as from Khanele's daughter and Perl's Ariel's and the candy–maker. The tin smith sat with her lanterns, graters, funnels and bunyes (?). The Poplover's table was covered with all kinds of combs, pins, laces, needles and thread. Khaye Esther specialized in selling paint. Shinke Bloyshteyn, Khanah, Shloyme Itche Yoske's and Dovid Litvak's wife had various items displayed. Slowly business grew. The Jewish artisans also had the means of earning a living. This is how it was until 1923.

[Page 186]

Taxes now make an appearance. There are taxes for both the present and past years. If one could not pay the taxes their belongings would be sold at auction. One cannot realize much from an auction, so once again, they owe taxes. The houses are now empty, everything has been taken and taxes still have to be paid.

Jews notice that the poorer shopkeepers or artisans pay higher taxes than the rich merchants resulting in scandals. They come to synagogue on Shabbos and they don't permit prayer. Why should this be? They did not have those representatives who could properly evaluate the worth of their businesses. The prominent merchants of the town were those who did the evaluation. One who had an income of 5,000 zlotys a year was valued at 100,000 zlotys. The tax collector comes to town on Monday and he does not know that prayer on Shabbos had not been permitted. He auctions and removes the property in his wagon. This was called Grobski's wagon.

This led to the creation of unions, a merchants' union and an artisans' union. These unions represented the interests of their members, and in the main, made sure that the taxes were completely just.

As a result, there arose many various and important organizations and institutions, credit–establishments under the new Polish government. We will describe them in further articles.

Footnotes (Rubin Roy Cobb)
1. Prohibition
2. Starch

[Page 187]

Merchants' and Artisans' Fareynm (Union)[1]

On a rainy day at the beginning of the summer of 1923, a gathering of all Bransk merchants took place in the third house of prayer and study. The merchants' union is founded under the leadership of Khaim Gotlieb, Elye Nosn Glazer, Motke Golde, Hershl Zagel, Havol, Leyzer Rubin[2], *Avrume Yentchman and Shloyme Lazer.

The big merchants, such as: Elye Gotlieb, Khash'ke Menukhe's and others kept their distance. It is possible that they did not see any worth in such an institution. They could fend for themselves.

An office is set up in Rubin's brick house. Two writers are hired – Berish Kagan and Itskhak Finkelshteyn. However, there was no great harmony in the union. To a certain extent they did good work. They created certain branches that had good representatives. They were: manufacturing, men's wear, wood merchants, iron, shopkeepers, traveling merchants and others.

The artisans were also members of the merchants' union.

The tax issue, which was the most important and affected everyone, could not be resolved easily and all at once to the satisfaction of everyone, and so the poor had to pay higher amounts. This created dissatisfaction. There were complaints that the interests of the poor merchants are not being properly represented, and to a certain degree, this was true.

[Page 188]

Eventually, this led to the formation of the small merchants' union, led by Bentsiyon the Zarember's. Berish Kagan was the secretary of both unions. The merchants' union is disbanded and Berish Kagan carries on with the work from his home. Prices for merchandise are set. They buy the licenses for the members. They write various requests for them because individuals are not permitted to write requests relating to any business matters.

In general, the merchants had where to go for advice, but no longer to the merchants' union, rather to Berish Kagan.

The union had no particular meaning in Bransk Jewish life due to the jealous character of certain members. In addition, each was concerned with his own business, with the usual daily worries. Polish competition became stronger and shopkeepers are finally forced to close. Trayne Yankev Meir's store closes, as well as Perl Shafran's, Yosef Batslalikhe's, Akiva Skornik's[3], Khantche Galise's, Yakhe Vayns, Pinye Kruks, Khaye Khazn's, Heni Esther Maishe Khaim's.

And thus, slowly, little–by–little, various small and large establishments folded. They were unable to sustain business in the face of the fierce competition of the Christians and the high taxes. The ability to receive credit was strongly regulated, so they were forced to shut their doors.

The Artisans' Union Bransk

It was a Shabbos evening in 1923, prior to the first slikhos[4], at Gedalye Aynemer's home that there was established the Bransk artisans' union.

The first members were the following: Gedalye Aynemer, Khone Kashtan, Sholem Kukofke, Berl Sussin, Hershl Platrat, Alter Okras, Sholem Krotz, Khaim Patiker, Khaim Rypke, Maishe Mendl Toker's, Alter Trus, Tsolke Yosl Stolyer's, Mordekhay Oskart, Hershl Shpak, Avrum'ke Sussin. Mendel Toker,

Berl Bobele's, Iitche–Meir Piekucki[5], Zelig and Antchel, Alter Radishover and others.

[Page 189]

They create their statute. They choose a presidium of five: Gedalye Aynemer, Sholem Kukofske, Alter Trus, Berl Sussin and Khone Kashtan.

The first important work has to be or is to take care of the dues of the members, and to see that they be just. This meant there should be a good representation in the evaluation committee.

Gedalye Aynemer was chosen to represent everyone. He was unable to carry out this activity. He was not familiar with all the trades and their special needs. The number of workshops was then 315. Regardless of his best efforts, he still was unable to represent the various trades. Naturally, there immediately developed dissatisfaction among the members.

It is then decided that the representatives at the evaluation committee should be only those from their own trade. In this way, carpenters would not represent tailors or the other way around. Only those of the same trade who knew about their own business would evaluate the tax and the activities of their fellow workers. This satisfied all the members.

It happened that Tsolke Yosl Stolyer's opened his mouth to one of his competitors, and they pulled him out of the committee. During my time in the evaluation committee, the artisans breathed a sigh of relief. It happened many times that the tax collectors sold their items, as in the case of Maishe Susel, when they sold his sewing machine. They sold Motl the Rimher's possessions, Leybl Stelmakh's wood – all for the purpose of tax revenue. Now all of this came to an end. The taxes were established according to the abilities of the members. There was no political involvement with these people. This naturally, led to the artisans' fareyn becoming the most popular folks–organization for everyone. The gatherings were interesting.

[Page 190]

Hershl Platrat always told jokes, the Bielsker tinsmith always made a little soda, Maishe Susel wants to make long speeches. However, he stutters, and yet wants to complete his speech.

At these meetings, the tradesmen were able to talk about what bothered them. They complain about the unpleasant atmosphere at work: at the smithy's – the axes, at the carpenters – the wood is always wet. The custom tailors complain about their situation regarding Barebare and Tchekhenoftser Mikalay fairs change place on the same day. The same is true of the Sakoler and Tchizhever fairs taking place on the same day. 'Go dance at two weddings at the same time.' To the barbers they would say wild man, and to the rimers – it smells from. The ladies' tailor would talk about bridal clothes.

The artisans' union broadens its activities, establishing the folks' bank and a no interest loan bank. When the time came for the town elections, the artisans' union puts forth its own list of candidates and wins.

In 1927, the law of artisans is accepted in industry. This leads to all workers needing to have either diplomas or artisans' cards. We all take exams, we long–time apprentice boys. The Bransk artisans' union is led so well that we receive the right from the government to examine workers and issue cards and diplomas to those workers who took the exams. We appoint for every trade special tradesmen to oversee the exams:

Tailors – Sholem Kratz and KhoneKashtan;

Hatmakers – Alter Truss and Itskhak Krinski;

Carpenters– Hershl Rutsky, Maishe Mann and Tsolke Tchakhnovetsky;

Wheelwrights – Maishe Matus Tshikhtlyer, Simkha Oyshpeter;

Butchers – Yankev Yentchman and Avrum Sassin;

Bakers – Yekhiel Leyb Piekucki[6], Berl Rozen and Fishl Kaplan;

[Page 191]

Shoemakers – Hershl Platrat, Mordekhay Ayzik Perlman and Shaye Zabludafski;

Quilters – Avrum Verpikhovsky and Leybl Vainer;

Turners – Mendl Toker and Avrum Abba Toker;

Blacksmiths – Antshl Rozen and Alter Lievartafski.

The artisans' fareyn joins the general central union of Jewish artisans. Nisl Levitch becomes the secretary. His house turns into a club where there are always people coming for information. Nisl Levitch's work is recognized by the government for his masterful activity on behalf of the artisans' union and he receives a medal for this from the government.

Every year – until the First World War – the union held a lively celebration.

The five–year celebration takes place at the first slikhos in Nisl Levitche's home. There was a holiday mood. The Polish flag and the Jewish flag fluttered on high, and between them flew the flag of the union upon which were inscribed the words of the artisans union. "Labour ? because ? how good is your lot!"

The firemen's orchestra played the Polish national anthem and the "Hatikva". The funeral march is played in memory of the deceased members. The gathering is opened with greetings from Burmish and Khaim Gotlieb. Khaim Leyb Lyev and Rabbi Avrum Yankev Sekerevitch represent the community. Greetings arrive from all parties. There are speeches given by several members. Many cry from happiness. The heart says – who knows? May this not be ruined. Representative from Bielsk and Tchekhenoftser artisans' unions also came.

The tables were full, the audience celebrated until daylight. No one was in a hurry to leave. The time for slikhos approached and little–by–little, each left for his synagogue to attend slikhos.

The artisans' union becomes a bona–fide folks institution. Old khasidim and Communists – there is no party, just a nice folk movement.

[Page 192]

The cultural status rose through the culture group of the union. There were theatre performances, one of which presented the play "The Rumanian Wedding." Dobtche Melamed and Riebtche Pietlak performed in the major roles. There are weekly presentations and lectures. They receive newspapers and books. The youth division is led by Itche Lievin, Shmuelke Beker's son, Aryeh Kratz and Yankev Kashtan, Khone's son. No longer are there any young apprentice boys.

There are attempts to establish a Bundishen artisans' union but their efforts are unsuccessful. The existing union is beloved by everyone. There is no way they can be dissuaded from the Bransk artisans' union.

The union functioned in secret during the Soviet power and in the ghetto.

Of the 315 members of the artisans' union there remained three living members: I (Alter Truss) in Russia and Hershl Shpak and Yokheved Golde in the partisans' division in the forest.

On September 7th, 1939, as Bransk was burning, the result of the German fire–bombs, the artisans' locale with its entire archive burns as well.

And so ends the existence of beautiful and true folks–institution that had dedicated itself to the needs and desires of the Bransk people – the artisans' union of Bransk.

Footnotes (Rubin Roy Cobb)
1. Fareyn
2. Related to Rubin Roy Cobb's paternal grandmother, Gelie Rokhel Rubin–Kobylanski.
3. Maternal grandfather of Rubin Roy Cobb
4. One of the morning prayers recited before and during the High Holydays and fast days
5. Maternal great uncle of Rubin Roy Cobb – abbreviated name to Peck when came to Johannesburg, South Africa in late 1920s.
6. Maternal relative of Rubin Roy Cobb

[Page 193]

The People's–Bank[1] in Bransk

Bransk was in need of a financial institution or bank. Trade and the growing need for raw material for the artisans, material that has to be purchased from other larger Polish towns, were bought on credit. Bransk merchants and artisans easily received this credit because the reputation of Bransk small and large tradesmen was good.

However, there was one difficulty that had to be overcome. Normally, this type of credit would only be extended when a note was signed by the purchaser. This note required a place such as a bank where the payments could be made. Bransk did not have such a bank. Bielsk[2] did have a bank like this. This meant that Bransk merchants and artisans had to travel to Bielsk and pay the note in the local bank there. This was a difficult matter. Many times they simply did not have the time to travel to Bielsk, or they had to lose too much time. Most of these merchants need to work themselves in their workshops, and so it was a great loss for them.

The artisans' union, having become a peoples' –institution, recognized the difficulty of their members and decided to do something to improve the situation, and in general, make the members more credit capable. They decided to organize a peoples' –bank in Bransk.

In March, 1924, at a gathering at the artisans' union at the artisans' locale at Nisl Lavitch's, the bank was established. The rules and regulations of the institution are put in place.

[Page 194]

An administration is elected: Alter Trus, President, Avrum Verpikhovsky, Vice–President, Gedalye Aynemer**Error! Bookmark not defined.**, Treasurer, Khone Kashstan, Itskhak Meir Piekucki[3] and Antchl Rozen.

An oversight committee is chosen: Mordekhay Oskart as President, Maishe Susel, Motele Konopyate, Avrum Pulshansky and Itskhak Finklshteyn as bookkeeper.

Everything is ready for a bank, but there is still one small item missing – capital.

We now begin the work of raising the capital for the bank, because a bank without capital is something that cannot survive too long.

We take subscriptions (pledges). The first to step up to the plate is Motye Abba Trus, followed by many others who brought in their pledges. Then

Mordekhay Oskart brings $500.00 without interest. This influenced others to bring in capital and the bank began to function, issuing small amounts of credit at the beginning.

The bank grows from day–to–day. Branskers bring their savings into the bank. The Peoples' –Bank becomes a true cooperative community. The central bank in Warsaw extend credit to the Bransk bank. The capital reaches the sum of 70,000 zlotys.

There is a significant improvement among the small merchants and artisans. The bank does not recall any notes. They already know who has had a bad market day and they had to wait a little longer [for payment].

The bank satisfies the needs of the population. Bransk receives a good name in the business world. Very few notes are contested.

The bank is run in a true peoples' character – there is no political favouritism, only the credit capabilities are evaluated.

Little by little, party battles develop in the bank. Various parties seek to control the peoples' –institution, but their effort is unsuccessful. The greater majority is in favour of the impartial character of the bank.

[Page 195]

After five years, the leadership falls into party hands: Bundists, Zionists, Mizrakhi, Agudanikes and artisan merchants. Credit is given not to the credit-capable but instead, to the sponsoring party people. Each party had its own sponsors who received large amounts of credit.

The year 1930 brings a crisis. The leadership does not take the times into consideration and does not reduce the credit of its sponsors – their good brothers. The result of this was that no one paid. Those people who had their savings in the bank demand their money be returned. The Peoples' –Bank is no longer capable of extending credit.

Financiers such as Alter Vilk are drawn in to help make the bank healthy again, but instead of curing the situation, they act for their own benefit. Itskhak Finklshteyn, Alter Aynemer and Alter Vilk are speculators. They profit if the value goes up. If there are losses, the bank loses. They deal with flour and for bank money, they take away Rekhl Zagen's mill. They carry on personal business and they think that no one knows. However, Bransk does know what is going on with their money. There is a run on the bank to withdraw their savings.

There is a group that warns that the party people must give up their control. In 1936, a bookkeeper arrives from Warsaw. Finklshteyn is sent away. Trust is renewed.

The Peoples' –Bank now has competitors from the gmilas khesadim bank that lends money without interest. Yet, in 1939, the bank holdings were intact.

On October 22nd, 1939, the Soviet power enters and nationalizes the Peoples' –Bank. Regrettably, the poor suffer because it was the poor small artisans who banked money that was nationalized.

They begged the bookkeeper Pyetrovski to cover their money with notes which they would little by little most likely have repaid. Pyetrovski refused to do this.

[Page 196]

And, so ended another nice peoples' institution that had served the Bransk population for 15 years.

It ended on April 4th, 1940 through the Soviet power in Bransk.

Footnotes (Rubin Roy Cobb)
1. The Folks Bank.
2. Birthplace of Rubin Roy Cobb's father, Henry [Lapidut Khlawne Kobylanski (Cobb)] some 16 miles east of Bransk. The County capital.
3. Maternal great–uncle of Rubin Roy Cobb

[Page 197]

The Folks–Bank in Bransk

Standing from the right: Itskhak Finklshteyn, Antshel Royzen, Pesakh Yerosalimsky, Itche Meir Piekucki, Alter Kokalikhe's and Shloyme Vaser the errand boy

Second row seated from the right: Avrum Verpikhovsky, Khaim Laznik, Alter Trus, Mordekhay Oskart, Sholem Kukafker, Rosencrantz, Motl Kanopyate and Hersh Awol

[Page 198]

The Interest–Free Loan Bank[1]
in the Name of Sholem Dovid Vayn of Chicago

Bransk had in various times interest–free banks from which the poor received small loans, usually without interest.

The first interest–free loan bank was at Ezra's, i.e. it was a town institution. It was run by Ezra. That means that it is a town institution, It was administered by Ezra Goldberg. We have already written about this in the first section of the book. There one had to leave an object of value as security. This institution ended in 1915 when the Russians retreated from Bransk. All these objects that had been left as security were stolen and the town interest–free loan bank was but a memory.

The second interest–free loan bank was established by the Bransk Relief in New York in 1919 when the delegates brought a large sum of money and the businessmen in town used this money to organize an interest–free loan bank for the poor.

The administration was in the hands of a few who denigrated the poor when they came to get an interest–free loan. If the poor man had children who were not such good religious Jews or were socialists, he could be certain he would not receive any interest–free loan. And yet, a large portion of Bransk did receive such interest–free loans. However, the times were not favourable. The inflation that everyday lowered the value of money wiped out the entire invested capital and nothing remained of the interest–free loan banks.

[Page 199]

The third interest–free loan bank was founded in 1926 in the artisans' union. However, they did not have much money, with their entire capital consisting of 600 zlotys. Therefore, one could not receive more than 20 zlotys.

On a Passover evening in 1928 in Rabbi Itskhak Vayn's home, a gathering took place, composed of activists whose purpose it was to found a loan–bank that would virtually be capable of lending substantial help to those who needed it.

Sholem–Dovid Vayn was the son of the Maydaner (?) who had the maydan (?) near Rutke which is the tar/pitch works. He had already been in America for the past 35 years, and yet he had not forgotten his hometown. With a generous heart he came to help with a quite large contribution to establish an interest–free loan bank in Bransk.

This bank became known in Bransk as Vayn's interest–free loan bank. This bank turned out to be a lifesaver for many community merchants and workers. The loan had to be repaid within sixteen weeks. Bransk Jews showed that they recognized this good and important institution. They paid promptly. One could get an interest–free loan of 500 zlotys from Vayn's bank, approximately 90 dollars at that time.

The number of borrowers eventually totaled more than 600. The bank was run wonderfully well. The central [bank] in Warsaw gave the interest–free loan bank more money because they saw the good results of the bank which enabled the people to get on their feet and give them the opportunity to earn a living.

The total funds of Vayn's no–interest loan bank consisted of 96,000 zlotys – a huge sum. The Joint[2] considered the Bransk bank as the best in the entire Bialystok area.

Herr (Mr) Vayn's contribution to the bank was 36,000 zlotys. Atlanta sent 4,000 zlotys, New York sent support to be distributed directly to the poor. Bransk itself raised 12,000 zlotys. The balance was what the Joint invested.

[Page 200]

The heads of the bank were Khaim Laznik, bookkeeper the younger Reuven Laznik was the treasurer. Their leadership was outstanding. The bank had its own office in the community offices. The bookkeeping was tightly controlled. There were always people in its office, some bringing in their payments while others applied for loans. It was a bank institution.

Hersh Avol was the President. He was very decent and devoted to the institution. In addition, he was a very talented individual. The administration members were Elye Perlman, Alter Kapilikhe's, Ben Tziyon Zarember, Velvl Branski, the Kadluvofker Rihmer, Zakhria Oskart, Simkha Oshpeter.

Sholem Dovid Vayn of Chicago
Founder of the interest–free–loan–bank

[Page 201]

The Revisionist[3] committee were Mr Khaim Layb Live, Rabbi Ben Tziyon Kagan and Shmuelke Beker.

In 1935, when the community elections in Bransk takes place, the administration decides to play politics. They put forth their own list of candidates. They receive only 12 votes. At the following yearly gathering, the administration is a different one: the President is Shabtai Chomsky, Avrum Verpikhovsky is the treasurer and members Maishe Ratnshteyn and the Kadlubafker rhymer.

The review committee: Rabbi Ben Tziyon Kagan, Alter Trus, Alter Sapershteyn and Yosef Zeyfman.

In 1937 the Polish boycott movement was in full swing. Bransk Jews cannot travel to any markets or fairs. There are Christian stores everywhere. It becomes difficult to earn anything. The interest–free loan bank in the name of

Vayn is the only place that can mitigate the terrible situation. Its relief work is substantial. The money from the good–hearted Mr Vayn of Chicago is limitless. People are virtually rescued in the time of their greatest need. The Peoples' – Bank which was a business institution and not a philanthropic one charged interest. Here loans [Vayn's] were given interest–free.

Bransk was one of the fortunate towns, having such a beautiful institution, the interest–free bank in the name of Vayn of Chicago. In 1946 Julius Cohen was in the main office of the Joint in New York. They showed him the records of the Bransk loan bank in the name of Vayn of Chicago as the premier organization in the entire Bialystok area.

During the eleventh or twelfth years of its existence, the interest–free loan–bank accomplished wonderfully good work. Bransk was proud and rightly so with the institution that was founded by the esteemed landsman, Mr Sholem Dovid Vayn of Chicago. When the 10th anniversary of its existence was celebrated, Mr. Sholem Dovid Vayn was unanimously elected as honourary President. See "Bransk Life" [*later on – newspaper*].

[Page 202]

We thank you, dear and esteemed friend, Sholem Dovid Vayn, for your beautiful and heartfelt gift to the Bransk community of the interest–free loan–bank that you founded there. It functioned beautifully, conducted itself masterfully, with its relief work always at the ready. Regretfully, it ended tragically, as did the entire Jewish life end tragically and horrifically. On September 7th, 1939, when Bransk was bombarded with Nazi fire–bombs, the town was consumed in flames, the locale, the archives, the notes and all documents were turned into ash. The fiery tongues of flames destroyed everything, the entire Jewish presence in Poland, Bransk included, and her finest institution, Sholem Dovid Vayn's loan–bank remains as a memorial for history. You may be proud, friend Vayn, with your accomplishment. History will evaluate your magnificent work, as is deserved.

Footnotes (Rubin Roy Cobb)
1. Gmilas Khesedim.
2. Wikipedia – "the Joint" or JDC is a worldwide Jewish relief organization headquartered in New York. It was established in 1914 and is active in more than 70 countries.
3. Followers of Ze'ev Vladimir Jabotinsky (now Likud in Israel).

Page 203]

Political Activity of Bransk Jews

In order to form a complete picture of all sides of Jewish life in Bransk, we must acquaint you with the political activity of Bransk.

Poland, at least on paper, became a free republic. Everyone had equal political rights and general town rights.

When the citizens of Bransk, especially the Jews, went to the polls, they became totally confused by the many parties that had submitted their lists of candidates. The parties were the following.

Before I acquaint you with the parties, I want to tell you that each party had under its wing many smaller parties. These hangers–on created more tumult than anything else. Naturally, the youth did not have voting rights, and yet all the parties made the effort to keep youth organizations connected with them.

THE BUND – The oldest Jewish party since 1905 and later under the Germans, the Bund figures as a political party. The number of members in Bransk is unknown.

The leaders of the "Bund" were: Alter Sapershteyn, Itzel the Vartavnik's son, Zaydl Tsivyatshekhe's, Ayzik Motl Shuster, Alter Kapelikhe's eldest son, Alter Susel, Shloyme Efraim Kvasnik's son and Sroyt's girl.

The "Bund's" first vikhovank (?) was the youth Bund, which was called "Tsukunft" (future). The leaders of "Tsukunft" were: Peshe Susel, Shloyme Efraim's girl, Leyzer Susel, Shloyme Efraim's son Menakhem Rifke. It must be said about Peshe Susel that she was a well–educated girl. The "Bund's" second vikhovank (?) was an artistic division by the name of "Skif", which was led by

Gedalye Susel, Shloyme Efraim's son, who was also a talented youth. It was said in Bransk that Gedalye is the most talented boy in town.

[Page 204]

The Bund in 1920

As you see, this Shloyme Efraim the kvasnik[1] was a fortunate person. His sons and boys and girls worked for the "Bund". There was also a sport division called "Morgnshtern" (morning–star). I do not remember who its leaders were.

THE LEFT POALE TSIYON – the second important party. The organization was in existence from the time of the German occupation. Its leaders were: Yankl Pribut, Elye Yentchman and another Yentchman, Tseplinsky the rope-maker, Rozke Glezer, Itche Levin, Elye Kratz, Bomtche, Elye Dovid Pribut and Nakhke Glik. Nokhke was also a thoughtful, calm and well–informed worker.

The left Poale Tsiyon had a youth division called "Borukhovtses." The leaders were: Itche Levin, Shmuel'ke Beker's son. This Itche was a genius. One seldom encounters such boys. He was very polite and had a great desire for physical work, and Alter Kopelikhe's youngest son – small and a great comedian. His comic roles in a theatre performance were loved by Bransk, and Maishe Khaim Dambravske.

The left Poale Tsiyon also had a sport division with the name of "Shtern" (star). The leaders of the Shtern group are no longer familiar to me.

RIGHT POALE TSIYON – This was the third political party in Bransk. Its leaders were decent Jews: Yankev Gotlieb, Yeshaye**Error! Bookmark not defined.** Tsuker, Yekhiel Don, Beynish Okon, Bishke Safran, Khone Sokolovitch and Fradl Hurvitz.

Their divisions were: "HA'KHALUTZ", whose leaders were: Mann, Elye Goldfarb, Sender Shafran, Hodes Susel, Keyle Smurztchik, Bertche Vilkansky and Minke Levortafskil.

[Page 206]

People's fraktsya (wing of a party) Tseirey Tsiyon (Young Zionists) in Bransk

Centre sign says: **Eretz Yisroel L'am Yisroel (the Land of Israel to the People of Israel)**

Right–hand sign says: **Ha'avoda Hi Khayinu! (Work is Our Life!)**

Left–hand sign says: **Arad, Arbeit, Fraihait! (Forward [?], Work, Freedom!)**

Their sport organization was the "HAGANA." The right Poale Tsiyon also had a workers' group called "HAOVED" (the work), which was intended to show the world that they also have workers included in their party.

[Page 207]

At a gathering the left Poale Tsiyon or "Bund" would shout to them: Where are your workers? With pride, the right Poale Tsiyon would point to Gershon Kopke's, the single worker.

MIZRAKHI – This was the 4th political party in Bransk, led by the rabbi's son–in–law, Rabbi Ben Tsiyon Kagan. I do not know much about who the Mizrakhi members were. Two of them are known: Maishe Piekucki[2] and Khaninah Khafetz.

THE AGUDA – The 5th political party led by Ben Tsiyon Zarember. Its members were known as being khasidim and other participants. They were in charge of the Beis Yakov School.

BETAR – The 6th political party led by Yosef–Betzalel Kestin, the Betar had a division called "Brit Ha'khayal" (the soldiers alliance). Yosef–Meir Skolke was their commander. His adjutant was Pinye Pontchke, the corporal was Gutman, Tchane's son–in–law, and the greatest wise man in town.

COMMUNISTS – They were not legal. It was then common knowledge that Praysl the Blacksmith's children were all red. Khaim Mann, Velvl Pulshansky, Rivtche Kofke's, Broyzman, Pesakh Malkhle's, the glazier, Dovid Tsuker and Benye Fayvl Shuster's were also known to be Communists.

Their youth division was called "Komsamol." Another division of theirs was "Mapar" (?), led by Libe the Redl's. Their sport organization was "VITZ".

These are the political parties in Bransk – six legal, and illegal, totaling with their branches more than fifteen.

It begs the question – what did all these parties do in Bransk? Of what did their major activity consist? Only of one thing – to fight among themselves. If this was their main goal, then they were very successful.

[Page 208]

When any one party arranged a gathering, all the followers of the other parties came as a united front, not to hear something but to cause a disturbance and undermine their opponents. Naturally, such tactics result in fights, fights to the blood. Then the fights would flow out into the street, mostly on Shabbos or holidays. There was not a Shabbos or holiday without party fights. When Jewish passers by asked questions about why they were killing each other, they did not have an answer. Really, why?

Most serious was when the fathers inserted themselves, and then it would virtually result in scandals.

There was a gathering in 1936 on a Shabbos at four o'clock. The speaker was Doctor Tal of Warsaw. Those who were causing trouble were busy handing out blows and the fight erupted into the street. Yenkl Voytek becomes aware that his frightened children were being beaten and quickly, he runs there, becomes enraged, and blood flows.

Velvele Sehpsl Katsev's also hands out blows on another occasion when his children were insulted. The following day – the children all discuss these same questions again among themselves and the fathers remain enemies.

Bransk was a very important centre for political agitation. There came here speakers from the higher ranks: Wasserman, Mikhailovich, Himelfarb and Yankev Pat from the "Bund," Zrubvel, Lyev from the Left Poale Tsiyon, accredited doctors from the Right Poale Tsiyon. Jabotinsky was the only one who did not come to Bransk.

Bransk businessmen ask why here in Bransk? Why are they all coming to Bransk, so that we should all beat up each other. It was bad when several youths from one home were members of different parties. The father of such a 'lucky' family was not to be envied. Babtche was blessed with four sons – two Right Poale Tsiyon, one Left and one a Betarnik. Friday evening, Yekhiel Leybl and Babtche want to rest a little after a hard week of work, and there develops a fight among the members of the three parties at the Shabbos table. The result was that the hot noodles flew overhead. "Unhappy," shouts Babtche, "join together in one party and do not disturb the Shabbosim." The following day, Shabbos, the town knew about what had happened in the house. Babtche's sons went about with bandaged heads.

[Page 209]

As a contrast, it was known that at the candy–maker's all the children were of one party and it was always quiet and peace in the house.

In 1935, there took place a large political debate about a united peoples' front of all the parties. This now interested the adults as well. The gathering took place at Avrume Makofske on the front porch there was a Polish crowd. One would always encounter there Aryeh Leybl Adesnik, Pesakh Malkale's, Khone Sakalovitch, Menasha Levin, Zagel's son–in–law, Leybl Poliak, Leybl Krinsky, Yenkl Shnobl, Pesakh Shloyme Valfke's son–in–law, and the Kanival. (?) Everyone discussed the peoples' front. Some said that if the "Bund" does not join the peoples' front it will not happen, and the "Bund" does not want to be with the Communists because it doesn't want to lose its legal status. Kanival shouts 'Tshemnotcha.' (?) They will never unite. Pesakh Shloyme Volfke's says the "Bund" "Zobatovtchiki,"[3] (?) Leybl Poliak says right at the beginning that nothing will come of the peoples' front and nothing did develop.

The decision is made to hold a peoples' meeting and demonstration on the First of May. The day before the First of May, the "Bund" informs the other parties that it is pulling out of a joint demonstration. The Left Poale Tsiyon states that they don't believe in a First of May demonstration in the Diaspora. The leftists are afraid for their parents and they too, are pulling out. The Communists certainly cannot demonstrate by themselves. After all, they are illegal, and so the entire plan disintegrates.

In 1937 the "Bund" organized its own demonstration. Approximately 40 schoolchildren and transports participated. They barely made it to the locale at Zaydl Tsivatchike's house.

There was only a single occasion when in Bransk there took place a joint demonstration on the First of May. On that First of May I (Alter Trus) heard Peshe, Shloyme Efraim's daughter speak. She made a good impression on everyone. Rivtche, Dovid Kafkev's was also one of the speakers. This was the one and only time that the parties in Bransk did anything in a united fashion.

[Page 210]

The activity of the Communists consisted of disseminating flyers and hanging up Russian banners (with inscriptions) and collecting money for the "Mapar." They were arrested many times and were sent to prison for a term of three to eight years. Broyzman, Shepsl Treger's grandchild, served five years, Benye Fayvl Shuster three years, Velvl Yosef Khaim's eight years, Rivtche Pitlak 6 years, Dovid Tsuker 5 years, Berl Praysl's 5 years, Khaim Mann 3 years. Others suffered prison time for their Communist activities in Bransk.

The "HAKHALUTZ" used to send its members to the kibbutz so they could immigrate to Palestine. The MIZRACHI sold shekels.

The AGUDAH was one of the aggressive parties. They were active in every election, never missing a political action.

The "BETAR" was satisfied with the members dressing up in brown shirts decorated with emblems, mostly Jabotinsky's picture.

ELECTIONS – By 1939 there were taking place about fifteen elections in Bransk. Magistrate elections took place three times every seven years, community council elections also every seven years, Parliament elections every seven years, for the Linat Ha'tsedek, Interest–Free Loan Bank, Peoples'–Bank, all town institutions made use of the elections system to elect their officials. There were no longer any permanent community activists or community representatives for generations.

At these elections, Bransk Jews learned the political game. They knew very well what they wanted to have passed at the elections.

In 1926 the first elections for magistrate took place. The Jewish parties went as a united bloc together with all the people. The Christians united, and the result was – two parties. The Jews win seven and the Christians five to the town council. Khaim Gotlieb becomes the mayor's representative and Berish Kagan a city councilman. The Jews have a total of nine representatives in the town council and the Christians have seven. The elected were: Mordekhay Askart, Alter Trus, Zaydl Varaftig, Itchke Tchigelsky, Yankl Pribut, Yankl Gotlieb and Shabtay Chomski. The Jewish majority decides to name the "Beys Hamedresh Street "the "I.L. Peretz Street."

[Page 211]

At this same time, houses and streets receive electricity. The streets, are paved with asphalt. At the second town council elections in 1933, the Jewish parties are unable to unite. Luckily, the Christian parties as well are unable to unite. At that time the representatives of the authority consist of six Jews and six Christians. The Jewish representatives were: Khanina Khafetz of the Merchants and Zionists, Mr Khaim Leyb Lyev of the Mizrakhi, Alter Trus, Avrum Verpikhovske and Gedalyeh Aynemer of the Artisans' Union, Avrum Yentchman and Itskhak Finklshteyn of the Small Merchants' Union is elected burmishtsh. (?)

Finklshteyn is not like Khaim Gotlieb. Khaim Gotlieb would take the part of the Jews. He demanded and received the right for the Jews whom he had not represented. Most importantly, he was a true people's representative, but some of his wealthier friends accused him of having certain personal benefits from his position. They went to the police and prosecutor. Khaim Gotlieb is in prison for two months. He is freed without any blame. Khaim is no longer the same person. This had affected him deeply and he dies, six months later his father, Itche Gotlieb passes away.

In 1939 the elections take place for the third time for the town council. This election battle was a very bitter one. All the parties desired to represent the Artisans' Union which had its own list. The Artisans' Union demanded two spots at a unification so they refused. The result of these elections was that three were elected from the Artisans' Union: Alter Trus as calendar keeper, Avrume Verpikhovsky and Motl Rihmer as councilmen, one from the "Bund," one from "Betar". Three combined Zionist groups lose.

[Page 212]

It is a characteristic fact that the Jews who lived on the "Untershter" Street did not have any voting rights. Due to certain regulations they were included in the Christian election circles.

KEHILA ELECTIONS – These elections were for all the town representatives to the community. The Jewish community in Poland was recognized as one with the full rights to devote itself to special interests regarding the Jewish community life in town.

The times when the Jewish community activists inherited the right to be the leaders of the town in all Jewish undertakings vanished. There had to be official elections for the Jewish community.

The first election took place in 1925. The election battle was a bitter one. Twelve lists were submitted. The following were elected: from the Artisans' Union three, Alter Trus, Nisl Lavitch and Motl Kanapiate, from the "Bund" one, Alter Sapershteyn, Right and Left Poale Tsiyon one, Khone Sokalovitch, Agudah one, Khaim Leyb Lyev, Businessmen Class one, Elye Gotlieb, Beys Ha'medresh Poale Tsedek one, Shloyme Kantchik and also the rabbi.

The second community elections in 1930 elected two from the Artisans – Alter Trus and Berl Rozen, Right Poale Tsiyon – one, Yekhiel Dan, Left Poale Tsiyon, Yankl Pribut, Khasidim, Motl Kanapyete, Agudah, Khaim Leyb Lyev, the Old Beys Ha'medresh, Avrum Yentchman and Merchants Khanina Khafetz.

In 1935 the third community elections takes place. The Artisans win three, Alter Trus, Maishe Rotenshteyn and Motl Rihmer, "Bund" one, Alter Sapershshteyn: Right Poale Tsiyon, Yeshay Tsuker, Merchants, Khanina Khafetz, Khasidim, Ben Tsiyon Zarember, "Betar", Yakov Meir Kharlap's son-in-law.

[Page 213]

In the elections for the Interest–Free Linat Bank the majority elected was always from the Artisans' Union.

At the elections of the Linat Ha'tsedek all the parties were always represented.

There were elections in 1929 for the Peoples' Bank. The Artisans were defeated by the Merchants in all the parties.

There were elections to the Zionist Congresses. There were always fights at these elections. Warnings had no effect. There were always hot–heads who fomented fights.

At the elections for the Polish Parliament there were also big election battles and although the Bransk area never had any Parliament deputies the activities never stopped.

At the elections to the Senate, Rabbi Rubinshteyn was elected from our area in spite of the agitation by various parties against voting for him.

This is how the political life in Bransk looked during the time of the Free Polish Republic.

The arrival of the Soviets in Bransk changes the entire political picture.

Footnote (Rubin Roy Cobb)
1. Manufacturer of kvass, drink made by fermenting rye and barley or sour fruits.
2. Related to Rubin Roy Cobb's maternal grandmother.
3. The nearest that I could find was in the "Slavic Review" Vol. 49, No, 3 (Autumn, 1990), pp. 427–445 by Robert Weinberg – 'The Politicization of Labor in n1905': The Case of Odessa Salesclerks. "One remarkable feature of the 1905 Russian Revolution was the efflorescence of labor organizations that occurred throughout the urban regions of the empire. Many workers throughout the empire demonstrated their resolve to promote and defend their interests in an organized and rational manner."

[Page 214]

The Cultural Condition in Bransk
after the First World War

A great change took place in Bransk with regard to the cultural condition of the population. In the years following the war, Poland was a free Republic. Government schools for children are recognized. In addition, parties are legal, with the exception of the Communist party. All the other parties were legal.

Every party in Bransk had for itself and its members its own library. In actuality, these party libraries were cliques. There were a few books there, but mostly there was party literature. This was very important for the existing parties. No party wanted its followers to go to other parties to look for books to read. They could, God forbid, become confused with strange ideals. That is why there were special little libraries at each party.

The Bransk youth had by now grown up. They were not satisfied with the few books that they had already read many times. They wanted new books, more reading material, the classics, not party brochures. Among these young people were Yisroelik Mek, Hershele Rubin[1], Ruven Ayzik Trus, Avruml the cake baker's, Kayla Smurzhik, Ruven Kazak, Khaim Ravak.

[Page 215]

The group that consistently lost at the elections never abandoned its cultural work. They, using their few groshens, established a library in Bransk that could be a source of pride everywhere. All the Jewish classics were there. They quickly purchased the newest works for the library. Regardless of foolish people bothering them, enlarged and made their library nicer. When I sometimes came for a book from the library, Itchele Levin, with pride, brought it to me. I remember a particular book that first now has been praised. The Bransk library had seven copies of this book.

The accomplishments of the Left Poale Tsiyon in raising the cultural spirit in Bransk were very great. They virtually devoted themselves to this mission with respect, in comparison to all the other parties, like the Bundists, Zionists and the Communists, who wore their party emblem on their lapels but did not take into earnest consideration any cultural questions.

The library was the actual cultural centre of every unaffiliated, or even affiliated who sought to quench their thirst for education and literature. Thanks to the earnest efforts of the Left Poale Tsiyon Bransk was the recipient of the written word.

THEATRE – The youth was very interested in the Yiddish theatre as a spiritual pleasure. They made an effort to make use of their own talents, carefully studying the best theatre productions: "The Dybuk", "The Puste Kretchme (the empty tavern), "Der Dorfsyung" (the village youth), "Sergeant Grishe." For difficult presentation, special theatre directors would come to Bransk. The youth was interested in earnest in theatre art. A large number participated in the performances: Ruven Kazak, Banish Okon, Elye Yentchman, Maishe Khaim Kapale, Leyzer Oskart, Khaim Raibak, Datche Melamed, Rikl Oyshpeter and Yankel Susel.

[Page 216]

Their performances were well–attended. The Bransk population valued the young amateurs because they knew that it was treated as a serious matter and the town–folk really had pleasure from the performances.

Sometimes they brought other artists in for concerts or to help direct. In Bransk there was Zjak Levi, Kurt Kotch, Turkov, Zabludofsky, Grinhoyt and others.

There were also recitations read by Ruven Kazak and Company. There were frequent lectures about various subjects. Doctor Kaminetsky would lecture about sanitary methods. There were party lectures and evening courses which the Bransk youth enjoyed and where they received their education.

Many concerts and dances were arranged, mostly by the Jewish National Fund. Mayofes (?) would take place out–of–town.

All these various undertakings were well–attended. The population was very interested in learning, in listening to good music. Bransk was not a backward town.

Bransk also liked the older preachers who would come to town to give sermons in the synagogues. Everyone came when there were good preachers, even the youth, filling all the seats. Bransk had its own town preacher, Shmuelke Pinye's. His surname was Kruk. Shmuelke Kruk was a good preacher.

The Bialystok[2] preacher, Rappaport, came to Bransk. The entire town awaited his first sermon which turned out to be a great success. The youth filled the synagogue every evening when Rappaport spoke. There was nothing that could deter them from these sermons. For ten days, the Bialystok preacher brought full attendance.

However, it happens that Rappaport lost his prestige in Bransk because of an event which is worth mentioning. He possibly underestimated his listeners, who were mostly plain folk. Itche–Yankl the Shnayder died in 1921 in Bransk. He had no children. Years earlier, Itche Yankl the Shnayder had made a will stating that after his death, his house should revert to the community to serve as a rabbi's residence. The community said the Bialystok preacher should give the eulogy for the deceased Itche Yankl. They did not want the Bransk rabbi to give the eulogy. The ordinary person did not like this, but kept silent.

[Page 217]

The Bialystok preacher begins his eulogy with the following topic: "From plain ragezje (?) one makes silk." (I believe this is the equivalent of making something from nothing) MGM This immediately upset everyone. Itche Yankl was not an ignorant man. If the Bialystok preacher thought a tailor is uneducated, Bransk thought differently about its shoemakers, tailors and other workers.

Now no one in Bransk came to hear Rappaport's sermons. His appearances remained unattended. He quickly left Bransk. This is how Bransk taught the Bialystok preacher a lesson.

CHILDREN'S SCHOOLS – The question of the education of Jewish children was a very painful one. Poland was divided into various parties. Each party wanted the education of Jewish children to be in accordance with their party program. Yiddishists, Hebraists, Bundists and Poale Tsiyon, The parties had central headquarters in Warsaw to which the province paid money and they fought among themselves about the responsibility for Jewish children's schools.

The Agudaniks did not give it much thought and opened a school in Bransk for girls called Beis Yaakov. The Aguda school quickly became popular in Bransk. Girls of all classes and parties recognized the school as being the best.

The Aguda is completely entitled to receive credit for their accomplishment in the education of Jewish girls.

The private kheders and Talmud Torahs were not sufficient to satisfy the population.

There were a number of older boys who studied with Mr Khaim Leyb**Error! Bookmark not defined.** Lyev and Rabbi Avrum–Yankev Sekerevitch. The boys enjoyed the reputation of being good students.

[Page 218]

SANITARY CONDITIONS – The sanitary conditions in Bransk were much better than in earlier times, despite it being very crowded in the houses because of the population growth in town, and therefore, much attention was paid to the sanitary conditions. The houses were cleaned more often, not only for Shabbos every couple of weeks. Even the courtyards were cleaned more often.

In addition, the authorities paid strict attention, ensuring that the courtyard cleanliness would not be neglected, as well as the streets and houses.

The Linat Ha'tsedek helped the poorer population with medicine needs. This helped much in the general improvement of the sanitary conditions in Bransk.

CLOTHING – Bransk was not any more backward in this respect than any large city. The latest styles, the newest outfits quickly arrived in Bransk. All the workers of the wealthier elements quickly began to wear the new styles. The older folk also quickly paid attention to their mode of dress, keeping themselves neat and clean.

Women were still wearing shaytls (wigs), but styled in the latest fashion. However, many gave up their shaytls altogether, even women from religious homes.

It was a special pleasure to look at the Bransk youth on their Shabbos strolls. No longer quiet and solemn, their faces were happy – proud Jewish children who took their walks. The older people as well looked different. It felt like a new life was developing in the free Polish Republic for everyone.

CONSTRUCTION – Bransk began to build houses. There is no room to spread out, so they added a second story, a second floor and added more rooms.

Lazer Broyde, who was the architect, the engineer and builder at the same time, was the one who knew where one could build or enlarge the house. Lazer Broyde was very busy because Bransk was building.

[Page 219]

Overall, the town had a nicer appearance. New sidewalks were laid, the river was straightened, a modern slaughterhouse was built, as well as an electric plant that produced power for the entire town. The streets of Bransk were bright with electric lights.

The town's wells were cleaned. A new building was built with a modern tiled mikva. A special building is constructed for the Bransk courthouse with new offices. The marketplace is paved, new roads built to Lapy, Tchekhenoftse, Drogetchin and Symyatitch.

People are buying new furniture for their homes – modern with closets and mirrors. The stores have large display windows.

The nicknames with which every Bransk person is familiar are no longer used. Surnames are now in use. No longer do they say: Maishke Yankl

Zalman's Avrum but Maishe Susel, etc. Other sorts of surnames arise, translated names – a "Bundist" is called Medem, a Communist is called the Moscow preacher, Mussolini, Goebbels, Fashist, Zrubbl, Jabotinsky. These were now mostly nicknames that became popular.

The little stores also had a different appearance and character. What now attracted the customers was a large billiard table where there were almost always to be found about 30 people playing billiards. Avrume Makofski had such a table.

It was even worse at the candy stores where they arranged back–rooms where they played cards. The card playing was in full swing at Makofsky's, Shnebl's and Burak's. Various types of people would be at the card tables – Jews and Christians. It developed that each place had its own customers – at one, semi–intelligentsia, at a second – just plain young men for whom cards were most important and at others, just plain drunks.

[Page 220]

We must mention that the youth was not involved in such things. They were more interested in education, in reading, but nevertheless, there were those who did participate in card playing.

Jednodniówka   פרײַ 1 גראָשן   „DOS BRAŃSKIER LEBEN"

=== דאָס ===

בריינסקער לעבן

| Brańsk, dn. 25 września | 1 9 3 6 | בריינסק, פרייטיק פון י"ב תשר"י |

לשנה טובה תכתבו

לשנה טובה תכתבו

Serdeczne Życzenia
Noworoczne
składa
IZRAELSTWO BRUK
Warszawa
P. LERMAN, Brańsk.

Jednodniowka	Price 15 Groshen	"The Bransker Life"

===THE===

BRANSKER LIFE

Bransk dn. 25 wrzesnle	1936	Bransk, Friday Yom Kippur eve 5697
A Happy New Year [Heb] A Happy Year, Healthy and Prosperity We Wish All Our Brother Members of the "Bransker Union", the President Mr Rosenthal and Mr Cohen Shloyme. Rabbi Yitzkhak Ze'ev Zukerman Greetings from Gmilas Khesed [Heb] Bransk Secondary District Committee . . . Bureau Personnel		A Happy New Year [Heb] A Happy, Healthy and Prosperous New Year We Wish All the Leaders of the Loan Interest–Free Society [Eng] in Bransk, Sholem–Dovid Vain and Family, Chicago Rabbi Yitzkhak Zukerman Management of the Gmilas Khesed [Heb] in Bransk Secondary District Committee. . . . Tzyoro Perfogal (?)

To the Head of Betar **Ze'ev Jabotinsky** With Blessings and Affection For the year 5697 The Commander and Unit of Betar Bransk "The Group (?)" Bransk	To All Our Friends and Good Friends in Chicago, Local and Overseas, May You All Be Inscribed in the Book of Life Khaim Lasik and Family from Bransk The President and Executive of the Jewish Community in Bransk Wish All A Good Year Khaim Lasik and Family	To My Potential (?) Students From Their Elder I Wish You All Be Inscribed in the Book of Life Yosef Zeyfman An Easy Study (?)
I The President, Executive of the Gmilas Khesed Treasury in Bransk and District I Committee Wish All I A Good Year I Khaim Lazik and Family		

[Page 221]

New Year Greetings to Branskers All Over the World

In 1935, Bransk published a holiday newspaper called "Bransker Life."
Yosl Zeyfman was the editor and the co–workers were: Yosef–Betsalel Kestin,
Fayvl Shapira and Velvl Rosenblum.

A Happy New Year
We wish our daughter
Yospe Kobylanski husband and children
Yossele, Khone, Ruven
Johannesburg
Akiva Skornik and Wife

Bransk

[Page 222]

אויף דע

צום געזעלשאפטליכן משפט!

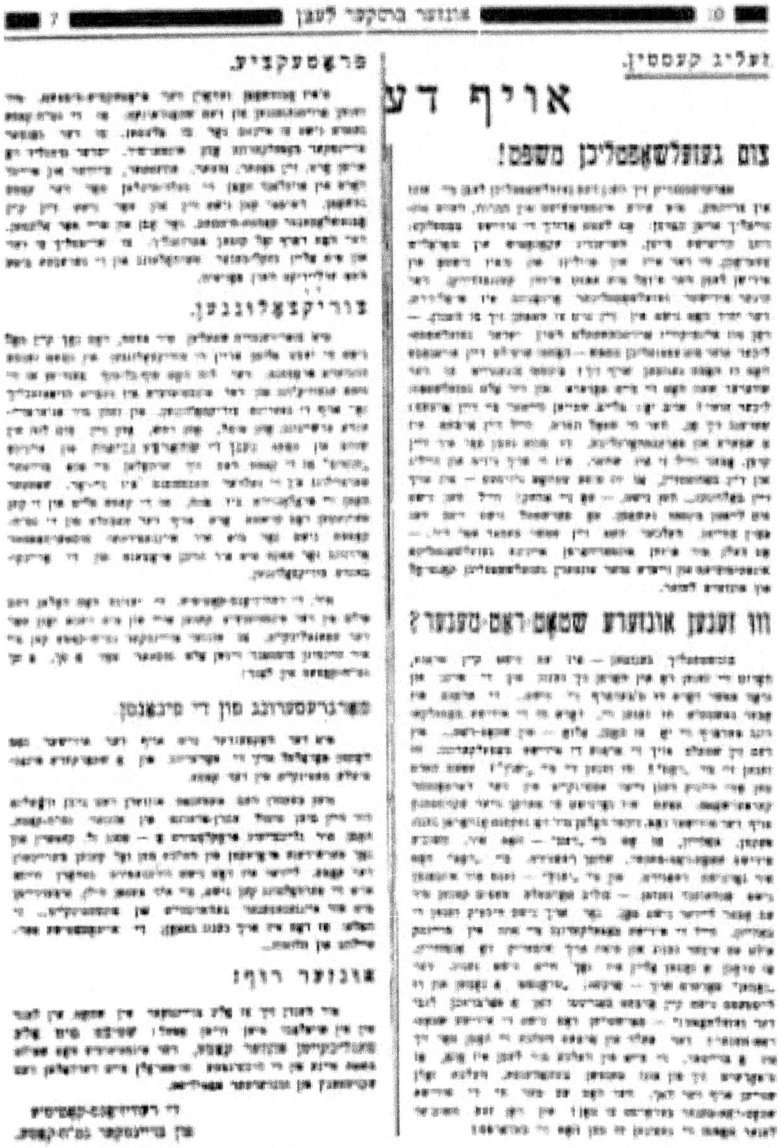

Critical articles about Bransk institutions – "Bransk Life"

Reports about institutions, town news and critiques would be reported in "Bransker Life." The newspaper had a good healthy humour. There remains no copy of the newspaper.

The "Bransker Life" was published every holiday until 1939. The twelfth issue of "Bransker Life" was ready to print. Regretfully, it did not make it because of Hitler who in September made certain that not only should a single Jewish word not be printed, but that no Jew should live through the horrific elimination campaign that he was then carrying out.

[Page 223]

When the book was already at the printer, I (Julius Cohen) received from Chicago, from Yosl Artche's daughter two of the examples of the Bransker newspaper. I have photographed three different pages for you – the first page and a second page with greetings from many landslayt to their families and relatives throughout the world. Perhaps this is the first time in your lives that you have seen these greetings. Very few of those who sent the greetings are alive today. I reproduced two articles that cover in a broad fashion Bransk's important institutions.

We express hearty appreciation to you, Esther Margolios, for the opportunity you gave us to acquaint ourselves with the "Bransker Life", edited by your father, Yosef Zeyfman.

Footnotes (Rubin Roy Cobb)
1. Related to Rubin Roy Cobb's paternal grandmother
2. Birthplace of the maternal great–grandparents of Rubin Roy Cobb's wife Renee Davidoff–Cobb.

[Page 224]

Professional (Trade) Movements in Bransk

There were three functioning professional or class unions in Bransk: 1. The Needle Trades Union; 2. The Carpenters' Union; 3. The Leather Workers' Union.

These unions had the responsibility of improving the material and cultural conditions of the workers.

The workers in the professional (trade) unions suffered a great deal from the political parties that sought to obtain influence in the unions. There were instances when the Needle Union agitated for a raise in the amount of loans. The party that had no influence in the union destroyed the agitation attempt. Strikes happened in the unions and members of other parties in the same union agitated in favour of going to work. The "Bund" had the upper hand in the Tailors' Union, the Left and Right Poale Tsiyon were the driving forces for the Carpenters' Union.

In the Leather Union, it was the Communists who had the power. All these parties sought to bring their control into the unions. Each party, however, wanted to rule the professional (trade) unions as well, so you can imagine that there were plenty of arguments and the workers of all the unions suffered from them. There was no question now about competitive cultural work. It was political work, but in very cultural activities. It was a shame in the times when the working class throughout the world was already so aware and understanding of their economic interests to defend in the best manner. There continued to be in Bransk a struggle between politics which did not permit the workers to receive improvements to which they were entitled.

[Page 225]

Eventually, the workers came to the realization that they were suffering from the parties, and they freed themselves from the party bosses and became independent. The Bund was quickly sidelined by the professionals (trades).

The united professional (trade) federation then began to be active on the right path for the workers.

The eight–hour workday is instituted. According to position, each worker had to ensure that at his workplace the proper loan increases be carried out – that they received the appropriate increased amount. They regulated the subject of the apprentice–boys. They completely controlled the matzah products. There were several modern matzah bakeries that immediately exchanged the old *shavalnyes* (?) that were found at Itskhok, the puree maker Shakhnikhe's, Noakh Shmid, Partselaiknik, Smuelke Ainbynder, Yosl Firshkhrler's and Yankitchke. There were now modern matzah bakeries: Ayzik Zaifman, Menakhem Rifke and Yekhiel Don, Layzer Kapeloyzh and Rivka Motl's bakery, Henye Hershl Stolyer's bakery, Bobbe Gershon Ber's bakery.

The head of the united professional (trade) movement was Itche Levin. Everyone had full trust in Itche. His impartial leadership led to a substantial improvement in the material and cultural situation of the Bransk workers in all trades.

The Physical Condition of Jews in Bransk

During this period, the physical well–being of Bransk also greatly improved.

Right after the war when people were suffering from hunger and living in broken houses, it was inevitable that the health condition of the Jewish population was at its lowest ebb. Slowly, the situation began to improve.

[Page 226]

The Jewish population in Bransk grew. Newspapers now became available. In 1928 there were 2,700 Jews. At the census of 1933, the count was 3,762. These are the official census reports. During the last years, the numbers increased. There were almost no incidents of child deaths. The death rate of the elderly was within a normal range. Life was normal. The population now ate meat every day. Salad ingredients were available year–round. Everything was available for purchase at the marketplace – and people did buy. Their diet was now a balanced one. People no longer had to make do with a diet of grits and fat to last the day. This exerted influence on the health condition of the Jewish population. Children were freer, allowed to participate in various sports and their bodies developed.

The different sports groups that the parties had: e.g. "Skif", "Shtern", "Morgenshtern", "Haguda" – all attracted the older boys and girls. There were specific times for exercise, football, rowing, motorcycling and swimming. Swimming became very popular. There were always competitions among the various sports organizations. Military exercises carried out by the "Brit Ha'khayal." In addition, the volunteer firefighters in Bransk were young men who participated in exercise.

The conscripts[1] – This was an institution in existence from long–ago when the young boys would fast entire days and at night, recite psalms in the synagogue and not sleeping. This had a physical effect on their bodies, breaking them down, so that they had the appearance of being victims of torture their entire lives. At the present time, the conscripts were always active but no longer fasting. They wandered about at night and horse around, doing various kinds of mischief. They would take the sign off the pig butcher shop and hang it above Jewish food–stores.

[Page 227]

The conscripts would bring all the wagons and place them in the middle of the street. On the following morning, their owners had the job of disentangling their wagons from the circle. Usually, they could buy their way out from such punishment which cost them a kilo of seeds. By paying this price to the conscripts, one could sleep. It also happened that much damage was done at night. The trees that had been planted along the streets were uprooted. The conscripts accused their admirers. Then an order was issued stating that their admirers should not be permitted, with only the conscripts being allowed to spend the nights in the streets. The police now paid attention. On one particular night the conscripts took the cleansing board from the cemetery and placed it near the door of Kaddish the ritual slaughterer. They brought the wagon/hearse to Itchkale. Just imagine what transpired in the morning when they found these tools of death near their houses. They happened to be very afraid of death.

The conscripts brought much amusement to Bransk. They no longer feared military service as they had once been even though the anti–Semites in the Polish army made trouble, laughing at Jews because of their Polish speech. And yet, Jews studied the Torah and it was not detrimental when in six months they became corporals. The six weeks of exercise did not frighten anyone. Remember the fact that when Aron Kagan, Merimke's grandchild left for the service, he looked like victim of tuberculosis. He returned on furlough and nobody recognized him. He was filled out and his posture was straight.

Physical work – Nobody was any longer afraid of this in Bransk. The time had passed when one had to hire a Christian to saw a pood or pud (Russian weight of approximately 36 lbs) of wood. Jews did it themselves, and actually by many young boys.

[Page 228]

The desire to work was great in the Jewish youth. Every boy went from one boss to the next, asking him to be taken on as an apprentice to learn a trade. Every year there were more requests for apprentice boys in the trades. The anti–Semites searched for any remaining possibilities to escape from Jewish hands.

In 1924 there were 36 apprentices in Bransk, and in 1937, there were 122 at the 315 Jewish artisan workshops in Bransk. The apprentice boys did not have to spend more than three or four years until they became fully certified in their trades because they had the will for it, had the necessary education during their school years. Therefore there were many boys who quickly received diplomas as artisans.

The facts will give an understanding of the desire in Bransk to work. Aizik Zaifman's grandchild, Yosl Zaifman's child, Maishe Aron Vasser's son all quickly became fully competent in carpentry. Avreme Sushin's son was a tailor, and a good one at that. Yankl Vaitek's son who had studied to be a wheelwright became the best wheelwright. His wheels fetched the highest prices. He gave up his father's trade of buying horses: "Let the horses die," he said.

Bertche Vilkanski was also a boy from parents who were storekeepers. If it had ever been said to his father that he would have a son who was a worker, he would not have believed you. This Bertche quickly became proficient in carpentry.

Emigration: The yearning to emigrate was great, but this was out of the question. America's doors were closed. The only way was to go to a kibbutz, learn and then be able to immigrate to Palestine.

There were many kibbutzim, free and religious and they were all full. Branskers joined these kibbutzim. There were no luxuries in the kibbutzim. They had to work hard. This did not scare anyone. There were boys and girls in the kibbutzim. There were many marriages, both true and fictitious, because a kibbutznik could bring with him his wife as well to Palestine.

[Page 229]

Many times, these fictitious marriages resulted in real marriages. This was the case with Motl Rimer's daughter and a strange youth, Elye Nosn's grandchild with Zhamele's son.

This was the physical life in Bransk until 1939.

Footnote (Rubin Roy Cobb)
1. Prizivnykes – In Czarist Russia; hum. modern) military conscription; conscription draftee, conscript.

[Page 230]

Shattered Jewish Hopes for a Better Life

This is how Bransk lived during the period of the new Polish Republic, slowly recovering from the war years, from the wounds that the war had brought from 1914–1918.

Bransk Jews, along with all the other Polish Jews, worked and conducted business, helping to rebuild the entire economy of Polish life.

Regretfully, this period did not endure long. Slowly, Poland began to veer off in other directions which very much frightened the Jews. Laws forbidding Jews to participate in various forms of Polish life were established. Little–by–little the laws became harsher. Their goal was to sideline the Jews from everything that enabled them to earn a nice living through work and trade.

In 1933, with the uprising in Germany and Hitler agitating to kill Jews, it is noticeable in Poland that Hitler's agitation has taken root there. A new era comes to Poland. There is new talk, new anti–Semitic rants at Parliament meetings. Poland wants to surpass Hitler in restrictive laws against Jews.

There slowly begins agitation to boycott Jewish stores, Jewish small merchants and Jewish professionals. Agitation now comes out into the open, out of the secret meetings. The boycott against Jews later becomes the official government policy, shameless before the eyes of the world, which pleases Hitler's Germany.

[Page 231]

Poland becomes blind, does not see that its neighbour Germany, will make it the first victim of its war machine. Poland believed that it would ingratiate itself with Hitler with its strict laws against Jews in Poland.

At the same time that Poland was clamoring for national defense, for strengthening its army, its air force, she choked the only group that would have been able to make Poland strong and capable of defending itself.

The politics of Poland severely affected Polish–Jewish life. We will return to Bransk and see how Bransk lived through the times of the Polish anti–Semitic politics, politics that destroyed all Jewish hopes for a better future, politics that made Hitler more daring upon seeing how his hatred towards Jews quickly becomes part of the Polish population.

[Page 232]

The Allowed (Ovshem) Anti–Semitic Politics

Jews Expelled From All Economic Positions; Pogrom in Bransk

About the beginning of 1935, there is a substantially noticeable change in Jewish life in Bransk.

A Polish bakery opens in Bransk. Written on the sign are the words: "one's own to one's own." Clothing manufacturers make an appearance, food shops with large Polish signs with the same content: "one's own to one's own".

The markets and fairs in Bransk and neighboring towns are filled with Polish merchants. Christian tailors, blacksmiths, carpenters, hat–makers are now in Bransk. Poles go to Jewish homes, asking to rent their stores. They are not successful. The Polish cooperative opens a business in the centre of town, near Yankl Khukar.

There are not enough stores for the Poles. The Polish majority of the Bransk Magisterial District decides to build a merchants' *halye* (?) in the marketplace. They want to make an inroad in town for this undertaking. This requires an Agreement Decision by the Magistry. The Jewish representatives in the Magistry do not want to agree to this project. They sabotage the meetings and the market shops are not built.

On one particular Sunday in 1936, the Vice–Administrator of Bielsk, Doctor Mesayev, comes to Bransk. He summons the Jewish council members of the Bransk Town Council to a meeting, at which I (Alter Trus) was present as a councilman.

[Page 233]

The Administrator informs us if we will not agree to the budget for the failing shops, he does not guarantee that Bransk will not burn. He warned us that we should keep the fact of burning with which he threatened us, a secret. Aware that several towns have already suffered from fires, we agreed. The Council stores were built with Jewish credit.

At the beginning of 1937, Christian sellers displayed their merchandise out by the windows, but they don't sell anything. They have no customers. Only the Jewish shops have customers.

The decision is made that it is necessary that the village Christians must be chased with sticks to the Polish stores. At this same time an announcement appeared in the anti–Semitic Polish press: "Let us start to push the Jewish small merchant out of business."

Now there were Bransk youth, hired by the stall merchants who, armed with sticks, chased the Polish Christians from the Jewish shops to the Christian businesses. Many Jews were beaten. They question the Interior Minister, Skaladkofski. His response: "boycotts yes, beatings no." This meant boycotts, why not? This how the word *ovshem* 1 became popular. Those who did the beating were crowned with the name of *pickets*. Now begins the era of picketing. We become aware that in Tchizshev, Vysoke, Sakole, Lapy and Tchekhenoftse pickets stand at the doors of shops and chase the Christians away from the Jewish businesses.

Bransk Jews who travel to the above–mentioned town fairs are met with a hail of stones. The pickets do not permit anybody near them. There are instances of attacks upon Jews. At a fair in Sakole, there is a pogrom. Merchandise is stolen from the Bransk Jewish tailors, shoemakers and turners. They abandon their merchandise and come running to Bransk, barely escaping with their lives. Jews return to Bransk from the Vysoke annual fair. They come with bandaged heads. Mordekhay Fuhrman's grandchild, Zelig Yellin is murdered in the Tchyzev marketplace.

[Page 234]

The anti–Semitic hooligan attackers come closer to Bransk. The traveling Bransk village merchants can no longer go to many villages. They are showered with stones.

In Pyetrosk, Smurle, Prushanke there appear words written at entrances: "Jews are not permitted to enter."

Bransk is in a panic, most especially after the pogrom in Pshitek where they arrested not the perpetrators, but the Jews who defended themselves. There are enough capable youths in Bransk to fight back. The Bransk leadership depended on the police commandant who, each week, received his salary in order to be on the alert and not permitting any unrest in Bransk.

Vishank is a little town, much older than Bransk where there were about 30 Jewish families, mostly artisans and several shopkeepers. The pogrom–mongers had a free hand there. Every several days, Vishank telephoned: "Bransk Jews, rescue us." We were attacked, robbed and beaten in the middle of the day.

Many times Bransk sent paid policemen to help or wagons to bring their possessions to Bransk. They now knew that there was no hope for Vishank. They must abandon Vishank. However, it is not easy to leave from the place where you were brought up. This day was destined to come because Bransk found out that preparations were being made for a big attack on the Jews in Vishank on a Friday evening. The Bransk defense committee called the Bialystok police chief and he agreed and did send police. This led to a battle with the pogrom "heroes". Some of them died and others were wounded, but Vishank Jews abandoned the town and arrived in Bransk.

[Page 235]

Pogrom in Bransk

During the summer of 1937, groups of nore–layt (ignorant–people) {*scumbags*} [pogrom–heroes] appeared on market day in Bransk. They stand at the Jewish shops and do not permit any Polish customers to enter. They do not allow the Jewish merchants to unpack their merchandise. Bransk Jews carry out their merchandise by sheer force, at least in small amounts in the market, so as not to admit they are subservient. Finally, the Bransk police assured them that no unrest would be permitted.

About 2 p.m. the town siren announces a fire alarm. They look around, there is no sign of a fire. There are rumours that there is a fire burning on Bendige. The firefighters and police rush away to Bendige. Suddenly the scumbags appeared. They attack passersby, Jewish heads are split. Sounds of windows breaking are heard. The tables of Jewish merchants are overturned. The merchandise is stolen. Jews are suddenly defenseless. The police are at the fire. It turned out that it was a false alarm in order to draw the police away from the centre of town. When the police came back, the pogrom was already in full swing. The streets were strewn with Jewish possessions, many covered with broken glass from the windows. This was the first Monday in Bransk. In the middle of the week there once again appear in Bransk pickets. They keep watch, not allowing the Christians to buy from Jews.

The Christian population understand now that they must make their purchases from non–Jews. The actual fact is that the police kept an eye on the pickets to prevent them from being beaten up because the pickets became sure of themselves due to Skladofski's interpretation of the Polish law.

Bransk is now under the scumbags' control. There now opens a scumbag club. Jews are insulted, and now know they must not try to defend themselves. It is permitted to beat them.

Sometimes Jews went to Otposten with kvas and baked goods, so they (the scumbags) confiscated all the bottles and broke them. The baked goods were stamped upon in the street and they (the Jews) were chased away.

Jews rented orchards around Bransk. They paid in advance for the fruit. These orchard–renters were Maishe Piekucki[1] , Tchaner, Elye Yentchman and Leybl Poliak. All were ruined because the scumbags did not allow them in their orchards. They themselves tore off the fruit for which the Jews had paid to the Christians. Several weeks later on a market–day, the same story again.

This time came to Bransk thousands of scumbags. Jews now did not display their wares. They already see the danger. Bransk Jews asked that the market be closed. For them market–day is only a pain. The police chief refuses to close the market. He assures them that there it will be quiet. He was wrong.

[Page 236]

The leaders, two Brezhnietzer Christians show the scumbags which homes are Jewish, that they need to rob. They work undisturbed. The policemen did nothing to stop the pogrom because they had not been instructed to stop the work.

The bandits 'painted the town red' for a long time in the streets. They (the Jews) wanted to summon more help, but to go to the post was impossible, so they made telephone calls. Yosef–Betsalel Kestin, connected via the telephone with the Jewish National Council, as well as with the interior minister in Warsaw. He also, via telephone, reported the events to the Jewish Telegraph Agency, asking help from everywhere. There was a German officer present at the pogroms who taught the Poles the correct methods. He took photographs of the scenes. In the evening police and secret agents came from somewhere, investigated whether Jews acted defensively.

Results following the pogrom – 80 wounded Jews of whom 20 suffered serious wounds. Some were taken to the Bialystok hospital. Among the severely injured were Maishe Yehuda the beadle, Khaim Hersh Kartoflye, Meir Brenner, Yosl Gakes, Bergerman from Rutker Tertak. There were 1500 broken windows and one house was totally destroyed. At Zalman Sane's they tore apart the bedding and the street was full of feathers. They threw children out of their carriages. The lightly wounded were too many to list. The following day everybody went around bandaged. At 1 a.m., the Bielsk police chief came to check on the wounded and view the destroyed town. I was awakened in the middle of the night because I was a community activist to go with the police chief and show him the seriously wounded. There was not a single unbroken window in the Third Synagogue. The police chief asks not to make a tumult, but the opposite happened. When the Jewish Telegraph Agency in America received the news of the pogrom, then immediately on Tuesday morning there were cables from New York Jews, Bransk fellow–townsmen, to Feyge Reizl the watchmaker and to Bobtche. The cables inquired whether they were alive. The cables made a commotion in the Polish ministry. The world now knew about everything. Poland did not like this. On Wednesday two Jewish deputies of Parliament arrived in Bransk, Rubinshteyn and Zamershteyn. They saw the destruction with their own eyes and issued protests in the Parliament. Representatives of the Professional/Trade Class Union show up. Mr Goldman distributes money to fix the broken windows.

[Page 237]

Khatskl Shokhet, Alter Kamshin and Velvl ShepslKatsev's rebuilt Rivke Motl's house because it had been virtually torn apart during the pogrom. The situation worsens. No one has the means of earning a living. Stores are shattered, there is no merchandise. Now the tax collector comes to Bransk and begins his work, precisely at this critical time to collect all taxes, present and past, although no one has a single groshn. This is how the Polish anti–Semitism works to break economically the entire Jewish existence.

[Page 238]

Poverty increases and the no–interest gmilas khesedim banks already have about 600 borrowers. There are those who advise Jews to flee from Poland. Emigration is difficult. They run to the hakshara farms (preparation for life on the kibbutzim) in order to be able to emigrate to Eretz Yisroel.

Help comes this winter from the Bransk societies in New York. The number of those requesting help grows. 250 Jews ask for help for Passover. Help comes from the Bransk Relief for Passover.

The end took place in the central court. You understand that nobody is punished because beating Jews is now in Poland the fashion according to Hitler's plans.

There was another Monday of unrest, but this time it was against the power, and at that time the police chief used weapons and made the Nore Party illegal. It then became calmer. There were no longer any Jewish merchants, merchants going to the villages, no Jewish orchard managers. Everything was no longer in Jewish hands. It was no longer necessary to stimulate any pogroms. The Jews are now ruined.

The year 1939 arrives. Jews are approached for money for everything. Bransk Jews are taxed 69,000 zlotys for the Polish air force. The Bransk Christian merchant class is taxed 6,000 zlotys. This was the Polish math.

This is how Bransk looked until the war in 1939.

Footnote (Rubin Roy Cobb)
1. The great grandfather of Rubin Roy Cobb. His daughter was Henye Rivka (Anni) Piekucki–Skornik, mother of Jospa Skornik–Cobb (Kobylanski) mother of Rubin Roy Cobb. Dr Gold of Chicago (born in Bransk) told that he remembered when he was a boy of about 6 Maishe Piekucki gave him an apple from his orchard

[Page 241]

PART THREE

Start of the Second World War

In the spring of 1939, Bransk is in fear of war. Hitler is now strong and his demands are slowly acquiesced to by the European countries, the very same countries that could have smashed Hitler like a worm at his first daring foray into mobilizing the Rhineland (on March 7, 1936)[1], and did nothing because of their narrow small political interests. Eventually they could not tolerate that France should become a strong power in Europe and this led to and helped to strengthen the Nazi monster.

Now England is terrified of the Frankenstein that it itself had helped to rise to this level of power. Giving in to fear, it hands Hitler everything that he demands.

Poland, so quickly taking on the Nazi teachings to destroy the Jews; thought to find favour * with Hitler, and now finds itself in deadly fear. It knows that Poland will become the first battlefield in the approaching war. Poland is partially mobilized. War preparations ramp up. The greater portion of Bransk youth is now in the Polish army.

Bransk, in the past quarter–century, had lived through various government regimes. With each change, the Jewish population paid the greatest price. The Czarist government changes to German occupation, the Poles chase back the Germans and they themselves are thrown out by the Soviets. Eventually – the Polish government that had begun with much hope for Jews to finally become freed from all of their life's troubles and equal to all as recognized citizens, took an anti–Semitic turn.

[Page 242]

Bransk was already accustomed to living in Poland under all the new restrictions, against workers, against businessmen.

This was on a Friday, September 1st, about 4 a.m., when the majority of the Jewish population was wrapped in deep sleep and many artisans had shortly before returned from the fair in Bielsk having just ended their work of unpacking the left–over merchandise and figuring out their receipts from the fair.

Several women were awake, those who had already prepared for Shabbos.

The quiet of the early morning is suddenly shattered. The sound of heavy thunder is heard from afar, a long rolling thunder. However, the noise continues to get stronger and nearer. No, it is not thunder, it is airplanes. They fly closer to Bransk. Now they are above the town and with a terrible roar they disappear in the direction of Bielsk. People run into the street, raise their eyes to the sky. Whose are these airplanes? Are they Polish on maneuvers? A second airplane squadron flies past the town and disappears in the same direction to Bielsk. Hearts said that it is war. Mouths however, did not utter the word. Children in the fire positions – who knows? Bransk did not know that the airplanes had already destroyed all Polish trains and all military installations, deeper into Poland to the east.

This is how the several early dawn hours stretched into morning. No one had a definite opinion and yet, everyone knew, felt in their blood and their bones that the war had begun.

[Page 243]

At 9 a.m. the radio announced that Germany had attacked Poland with no declaration of war having been issued.

The Jewish population reacts to this news with heavy hearts. Although calm they are full of fear but outwardly calm.

And so, several days passed. The mobilization increases. New groups are called and inducted into the army. At this same time, there are many earlier inductees who are returning. There are not enough clothes for the enlarged army, no weapons for teaching. And yet, new groups are called up. The farewell scenes are awful. Mothers accompany their children. Wives go with their husbands. Children cling to their fathers. Everyone is crying, everyone is bemoaning the fate of the mobilized who are leaving Bransk.

During these same several days Bransk receives reports of the first victims: Motke Olyentsky, Yankl Vaitek's son, Khaye Kaplansky's younger son, Elye Friedman's son and others.

These same reports notify that the Nazis are marching forward, destroying every attempt at self–defense.

The number of Bransk Jews at the front is already in the tens.

The airplanes fly over the town every day, fly over Bransk on the way to Bielsk or to the east.

The special militia chases the residents into their houses. The firefighters' siren warns the population to seek shelter quickly when the fiery airplanes come. They get used to the firefighters' warning.

On September 6th, a squadron of enemy flyers makes an appearance. The streets are quickly emptied. The people hide. Suddenly, there are heard heavy explosions. Bransk, especially the Jewish houses, are enveloped in flames. The town is showered with incendiary bombs. The flames spread everywhere. There is no longer talk of any possibility of escaping the town. All corners are burning. New fires begin every minute. From Sane up to Itche Gimpel's, from the Third Synagogue up to Yobzakn, both sides of the street, from the horse-market to Shtiopken – everything was surrounded by the fiery tongues.

[Page 244]

People are running around in the street, in choking smoke between the flames, searching for children. No one can tell where there is a house or a street. The smoke is thick, choking everyone, and yet they search.

There are already dead in the streets: Shaye Mulyer's daughter, 22, Khaye Atiper's daughter, 18, Shloyme Platrat, 26, Hershl Shuster's son. All are lying burned beneath the rubble of Sholem Kratz's burning brick house.

Beneath the burning and collapsed walls of Shloyme Hitsl's house, there lay a stranger, a wandering indigent man with two children aged about 10, also Aron Pribut's son, 17.

Near Sane there lay a Kolnyer woman of about 55, shot. Wounded: Dintche Zeyfman, Itche Orlyarnik, Kotente's wife, Fidl the shoemaker, Zlatke Marvinker's daughter aged 10. All of them die as a result of their wounds.

Shloyme Raibak, Fishl Lyev, heavily wounded and many more.

Victims of a second air–raid are: Simkhah Oyshpeter's daughter aged 22. Yankl Mann's daughter is severely wounded.

Not a single Christian house was damaged by the German air–raids. It was only the Jewish streets that were burned and destroyed.

People run from the hellish fire, from choking smoke, set out into the open fields and forests, naked, hungry.

On September 11th, German tanks tear into town, finding Bransk already destroyed, in ruins and the population demoralized.

An issue is ordered stating that the entire male population is to gather at the market. About 500 Jews are held in the Polish theatre (?). The following day they are all taken to Germany. I (Alter Trus) was among the captured. We suffer hunger, cold, beatings. Our clothes are taken away and given to Christians. Then the Christians themselves take our remaining clothing. Our mood is terrible. Five days later there is another tragedy. Incidents of death: Enoch Sivak, Bashe Sime's grandchild, and many others are seriously ill.

[Page 245]

We are later freed thanks to the intervention of the Soviet power. On their return, falling victim to hunger, cold and beatings: Khaim Laznik, Zshelye the shoemaker, Zagel's son–in–law Liakhiver, the old watchmaker's grandchild. The Germans chased them all out of their camp near Vlodove, and then opened fire on these Jews. Moshe Vayner's eldest son falls from a shot through his back near Vladave.

The Germans were not in Bransk long, only 14 days. The agreement between the Germans and the Soviets was meanwhile implemented. Bransk was to belong to the Soviet power.

On September 25th, the Nazis withdrew from Bransk. Their final act was to burn the Old Synagogue which had not long before been rebuilt.

That same day the Soviets make their appearance in Bransk.

Branskers hope for a little rest and wish each other happiness.

Footnote (Rubin Roy Cobb)
1. Date of Birth of Rubin Roy Cobb.
    [Page 246]

Bransk Under the Soviet Regime

(According to Maishe Yentchman's Account)

The Red Army entered Bransk on September 25th, 1939.

There was deadly silence in town – only women, children and the elderly, hungry, homeless. The air was thick with the choking smell of the burned houses. The dead bodies of people and cows lay about, poisoning one's breath, not yet having been removed from the streets.

Maishe Yentchman and wife
Most important aide to Alter Trus

[Page 247]

A number of young people who had either fled or hidden returned.

Attempts began to have the Soviets intervene with the Nazis to free the Bransk Jews whom they had earlier chased away. It worked. The Germans freed all the prisoners from the Bialystok prison. Bialystok had officially become a part of the Soviet regime. Several returned, many died in the camps.

Soviet order is set up in Bransk. The first order from the new Soviet regime is a very painful one.

Like all periods of change this one too, was difficult to adjust to – new rules, new privileged classes which now arose in Bransk. People who looked at each little store as if it was a middle–class store that must be destroyed.

The big–wigs are now Velvl Pulshansky, Benye, Faivl Shuster's, Ryvtshe Pytlak, good communists from before. and Shepsl Praisel's and Khaim Mann. They immediately begin the work of nationalizing the Bransk middle–class stores. Shops are nationalized and their merchandise is taken away. However, they look for money, jewelry and other expensive belongings and line their own pockets with them as a reward for the holy nationalization work. There must, after all, remain a remembrance of this. Better merchandise is also given to good friends in order to sell these themselves at a later date.

Such a job was done to Elye Gotlieb's iron business, to Leyzer Rubin's[1] stepson's manufacturing business, carried out by Velvl Pulshansky and his wife Rikhtche.

Shepsl Praisels and Khaim Mann did this job on Motele Kanapyate. The Kanapyates later proved that he should not have been nationalized and they would have to return his possessions, but there was no longer anything to return. The merchandise had already disappeared. Whoever had good relationships with Shepsl Praysels or Pulshansky became the big–shot in Bransk.

[Page 248]

The new community activists, it appears, could not divide anything equally because they fought like dogs among themselves.

Their behavior towards the Jewish workers was no better. They are forced to work in cooperatives. There is a punishment of 50,000 rubles (no small matter) for non–compliance or they are threatened with Siberia.

At a time when they were going to send some of the Poles to Russia, there come together about ten youths with rifles, throw the Christian belongings onto a wagon, and terrorize the neighbors. Hatred towards all Jews increased. They now start on all the former community activists, prominent people, Zionists, former councilmen of the Bransk community, and they are all arrested, sent with the procession of prisoners under escort to Russia. The process lasted for many more than a year. To their good fortune, this enabled them to remain alive. Alter Trus was also among those arrested and sent out. It appears that his fate was to be responsible for the publication of this book.

Slowly, they became adjusted to the new order. They appealed to those who assigned work to give them employment.

Rabbi Ben Tsiyon Kagan, the Bransk rabbi's son–in–law came to ask for work as a bookkeeper. Gavrilke the shoemaker's daughter, laughing, responded: "Let the rabbi openly declare himself a freethinker and we will permit him to work." Rabbi Kagan categorically refuses. He turns to the higher level of the party. They order that such behavior to the population must immediately be stopped. Rabbi Kagan receives work as a bookkeeper and does not have to work on Shabbos.

For such Communist leaders that Bransk had during the first days of the Soviet regime there was good medicine in Russia – Siberia. It has now been 25 years that their bones have been resting there. Upon their graves have now grown large trees.[2]

Slowly these people were sidelined. Life became more settled under the Soviet rulers. Bransk Jews find work in the *emptei*(?). Shopkeepers receive permission. Ribah Layah Tcheslyak, Itskhak Kashnik's daughter, Rokhl–Dvora Dinah's, Mordekhay Fraiman – in the manufacturing trade, Yankl Bransky and Mates Kanapyate. Velvl Pulshansky's uncle becomes the pelt purchaser. There is a great shortage of homes. The population increases. Jews from towns on the other side of the Bug River, where the Germans were still in occupation, fled and came to Bransk. Bransk, not being far from the border, about 30 kilometres, is flooded with Russian military. Through Jewish Red [Army] commandants and soldiers, contact is established with Russian Jewry. Trade developed, even though the larger part is not legal, because the Soviet law forbids private trade and exerts strong punishment measures. A large portion of Jews are now at state jobs, something that was impossible under Polish rule. Former private shopkeepers became employed in state stores. Most of the workers, i.e. tailors, shoemakers and carpenters formed cooperatives and worked together. A certain portion worked at manual labour. Many of the former wealthier element were represented in the militia. Bookkeepers were needed, so many learned bookkeeping, taking special courses. Khane Kashtan's daughter, Yankev Mann's son who had a limp.

[Page 249]

There were two synagogues open, the Poale Tsedek and the New Synagogue, led by Rabbi Tsukerman and Rabbi Sekarevitch.

The system of traditional Jewish school/classes that had existed up–to–now is no more. Children learn in the Jewish school or in the Russian. The Jewish community institutions ceased to exist, such as the Interest–Free Loan Charitable Society, Visiting the Sick. There developed a desire for education. Adults begin to take evening courses.

A town chorus is founded as well as a drama circle. Movies are shown twice a week. There is now a town park and a dance area that was built on the foundation of the Tailors' Synagogue. Many dance evenings took place there affording the youth great enjoyment.

[Page 250]

A certain number of Bransk yeshiva boys left Bransk and came to Vilna, and later made their way through visas from Lithuania to reach Harbin[3] where they remained.

Naturally, not everyone could become accustomed to the new order, to the new laws, of not being traders. People such as these were arrested. At this same time, former community activists such as Alter Trus, Yosef–Betsalel Kestin, the Kantchik family, Lyev. All became poor. The complaint against such people was counter–revolutionary. The fault for the arrests falls directly on several Branskers who sought to get rid of the former activists of the former regime. This was lucky for the arrestees because most of them, regardless of the difficulties they had experienced in the Russian army or other armies, remained alive.

It was worse for the former merchants, big merchants who were forced to leave their businesses and become manual labourers.

All of the youth are drawn into the Soviet order, most especially from 1917, 1918 and 1919, experiencing the war in the ranks of the Red Army. Regretfully, not one of them was saved, almost all fell in battle against the Germans bandits, or perished in Nazi prisoner camps.

There were only a few who fought in the ranks until the victory was reached.

The 21 months under Soviet rule Bransk generally lived satisfactorily. The fear of common militant Russians, *endekes* (?) and other crazy Poles, who gave the Jews no respite during the last several years, now disappeared and they felt free and equal in every respect to all the other citizens.

However, calm did not last long. On September 22nd, 1941, Germany attacked the Soviet Union.

A new chapter begins for Bransk, the final chapter of Jewish existence, the beginning of the destruction of Bransk.

Footnotes (Rubin Roy Cobb)
1. Related to Rubin Roy Cobb through his paternal grandmother being Gelie (Genia) Rokhel Rubin– Kobylanski.
2. This must refer to the Jewish communists of Bransk who were killed during the Bolshevik Revolution of 1917 – 25 years earlier from 1942.
3. Wikipedia – Between 1899 when first Russian Jews settled in Harbin, and 1985, when the last Jew in Harbin passed away, altogether more than 20,000 Jews spent their lives at one time or another in Harbin, on the Trans–Siberian railway line in China, just over 480 kilometres away from Vladivostok, Russia.

[Page 251]

Hitler's Attack on Soviet–Russia

Whether or not Bransk expected attack by Hitler cannot be determined. The Soviet economy continued in Bransk as usual. Wagonloads of grain fly by every day on their way to Germany, grain that Russian sent to Germany. At the same time it became noticeable that Bransk was becoming more and more crowded. Various Soviet military are now in Bransk. The town is almost like a military camp. Bransk is only approximately 28 kilometres from the border at the Bug River.

Poles predicted today or tomorrow Russia would be attacked.

The youth, on this particular Shabbos evening, were enjoying the dancing that had been arranged there where there had once been the Tailors' Synagogue. That evening there was noticed a large number of nice young people, dressed in Soviet uniforms, and who later turned out to be German spies. No one even dreamed that the fire which would destroy everything was already in Bransk.

Heavy shooting of faraway German artillery was heard about three o'clock in the morning. The population became very frightened, did not believe that the war had begun and Bransk was being attacked. Even for the Red Army commandants this was a puzzle. With daylight, everything was confirmed. Parts of exploded bombs of German origin and many wounded in the street –. Gitl Gurske, Sarah and daughter Shmuelke Bekker's. Many houses were already shattered by the cannons. No one could imagine that on this same day the Germans would already be near Bransk.

[Page 252]

Many Jews fled the town but few reached their goal and the rest were either killed by the Nazi bombs or fell victim from the German cannons.

The battle in Bransk lasted a couple of days. During this time others again fled to Russia: Motl Noske Katsev's daughter and her two–year old child,

Yankev Mann's son, Shaye Tsalke's stepson and wife and four children. Gitl Gursker's 16–year old daughter, and Berl Pukhalsky die along the way.

During the couple of days of the battle in Bransk many Red Army soldiers distinguished themselves with the greatest of heroic deeds. They defended the town like lions. Some of them exploded along with the tanks so as not to fall into the hands of the Nazis. The situation changed every couple of hours. The Nazis entered and immediately they were pushed out.

The section of town from Kopken to the bridge was totally destroyed during these couple of days. During this time Khone Kashtan and his wife were run over by a panzer (tank). Whether this was a Russian or German tank cannot be confirmed.

Khone Kashtan and wife

On June 25th, the Nazis finally broke into town. Their first murderous act was to shoot Khone Rutsky, Hershl Stolyer's boy, Yankev Mann, Mates Lees and his 20–year old son and the Zarember teacher's son–in–law, Elyt – Gershon Perlman.

[Page 253]

Khone Rutsky   **Khone Kashtan's son**

The Jews of Bransk now became aware of what awaited them. Many of those who had fled to the forests returned to town because the positions of the enemy neared to the forests, and many of the Germans returned to Bransk.

Every day captured Soviets are marched through Bransk. Recognizable among them are Bransk young men, Niske –Avrum, Abe the Toker's, the red–haired Mordish'es son and others. The Germans immediately began to rob and beat. At the same time they established a Polish militia led by the bandit Pyetushak. Everything is dragged from homes, from underwear, clothing, pieces of merchandise. No one dares to oppose them.

The well–known pogrom'tchik Dr. Dambrovski who had participated in all the Polish pogroms during the Polish regime, is appointed by the German to be the mayor. Dr. Dambrovski immediately terrorizes the Jewish population He struts around with his rubber truncheon. Everyone had already experienced Dambrovski's truncheon. He seeks revenge upon Jews.

[Page 254]

He especially orders that 30 Jews, mostly elderly, to dismantle the Lenin monument and take it away to the river. He makes use at that time of his truncheon to murder all those who participate in this work. He forces Jews to do the worst work. Jews are made fun of, spat upon and made jest of. He demands large contributions in dollars. He gives them 30 minutes under the threat of death to raise the money. In general, he is vengeful to the Jews who only three days before had been citizens on a par with everybody, with Jewish children studying in schools along with everybody, with Jews holding government jobs. He forces Jews to clean the streets with their bare hands.

Khaim Mann, a former Communist community activist, is arrested. Dambrovski demands that he be shot. Remarkably, a Judenrat member acts on his behalf and Yankev Gotlieb, who does not forget the days when Mann participated in his nationalization, does not want to mix in. Eventually, he succeeded in rescuing Khaim Mann who is released.

Dambrovski considered himself the permanent ruler of the Jews. He probably believed in his future as a Polish boss. The Germans had other ideas.

Little–by–little, they sidelined Dambrovski and eventually he fled. That is why the Gestapo appeared in Bransk as well as gendarmes. They begin to establish order in town.

This was the beginning of the new order the Gestapo instituted. This will later be a ghetto, a Judenrat, Jewish police, yellow patches and Jews doing the worst and filthiest work.

[Page 255]

The Yellow Patch

One of the Nazi demands in Bransk was that all Jews must wear yellow patches. They called it the 'mark of shame.' The patch was to be worn on the chest and the back.

The gendarmes, the Polish police and the Jewish police together with the Judenrat[1], paid strict attention in ensuring that the yellow patch is worn by everyone. The older Jews quickly became accustomed to the law and wore the yellow patch.

The youth opposed this. They did not obey the law. In order to wiggle out of hard punishment, they figured out a patent. They tied two yellow cards made like one of the four tassels on the ritual undergarment worn by males. If they saw a policeman from afar or a Judenrat'nik, they quickly tugged the string on their necks and the yellow patch was then in place.

Many Jews paid dearly because of this trick, receiving blows and beatings. The youth felt it was better to be beaten than to wear the yellow patch. Terrible scenes played out in the ghetto with gendarmes, Polish police and Jewish police all beating them for not wearing the yellow patch.

In the bulletin issued by the Bialystok Jewish Committee about life in the Bransk ghetto one finds the following story about the frightening scene.

[Page 256]

Itche Broyde, Lazer Broyde's son, a clever boy, did not wear the yellow patch. Itche is approached by the Jewish policeman, Itskhak Vasser and his rubber truncheon who speaks only German and no longer any Yiddish. Itskhak Vasser says to little Itche'le: "You little trouble maker." Where is your shield of shame? Itche replies: "If I don't wear the yellow patch you cannot stand it?" The tall Vasser says no more. He hits Itche with the truncheon ten times. Itche falls into a pool of blood. People in the ghetto come running. Yosl Broyde, who later becomes a partisan hero, comes running. He asks why the tall Vasser hit because of a patch? "Jews, all of you, throw away your patches." The youths obeys, throwing away the yellow patches and tearing them off the others who are present. Yosl Broyde grabs the truncheon from Vasser's hand and gives him a good beating.

The rest of the Jewish policemen come to Vasser's aid: Pinye Kaplovitch, Manes Shliep, Tatkale and Faynsor, beating with their truncheons anyone they can. Leyzer Vrone, Ayzik Benduger's son, Rubin, Yosl Tchap's son, join together as brothers. And now the truncheons are in the hands of the youth. The policemen receive broken bones and flee. They are whistled at and called: "Jewish Gestapo."

Vasser and the other policemen complain to the gendarmerie. The result was that Yosl Broyde and Leyzer Vrone each receive 80 lashes, barely remaining alive.

I (Alter Trus) could not believe this. Three and a half years later, I could still see the scars and the heavy marks of the lashes Yoslen had received. I did not see Leyzer Vrone. He is somewhere in Austria. I imagine that he too, was beaten like this for the great sin of insulting the Bransk Jewish police. Shame on the Jews who beat other Jews, respect for the Jewish heroes.

Occasionally, the policemen did not beat, but made arrests for breaking the law. They would sentence them in the ghetto court that had been established in Bransk.

[Page 257]

Finklshteyn, the Judenrat'nik saw Maishe Yentchman without his yellow patch. Maishe did not hide. He thought that since Finklshteyn was a Judenrat'nik and not a policeman, he would pretend not to notice. The following day, Maishe Yentchman was brought by the Jewish police to the Judenrat. Finklshteyn fined him ten marks because this had been his first offense.

The same happened to Khaim Velvl Pribut and Khaye Okon and others.

Maishe Yentchman told me most of the facts that had to do with ghetto-life, Jewish police, Judenrat and forced labour. While relating the above mentioned facts he was very depressed, not because of the monetary fine but for the shameless manner in which this Jewish policeman had behaved.

The youth did not give in. They all endured like heroes and exhibited pride in being Jewish. They did not try to court the gendarmes' favor and did not hold their personal interests above everyone.

As heroes they later came together with the partisans, fell as heroes, did not surrender.

Hershl Rubin[2] and other youths never ever wore the yellow patches in the ghetto.

Heroic Jewish children, may their names be for a blessing by all!

Footnotes (Rubin Roy Cobb)

1. *Wikipedia* The Nazis systematically sought to weaken the resistance potential and
    opportunities of the Jews of Eastern Europe. The early Judenräte (plural of Judenrat) were
    foremost to report numbers of their Jewish populations, clear residences and turn them
    over, present workers for forced labour, confiscate valuables, and collect tribute and turn
    these over. Failure to comply would incur the risk of collective punishments or other
    measures. Later tasks of the Judenräte included turning over community members for
    deportation.

    Through these occupation measures, and the simultaneous prevention of government
    services, the Jewish communities suffered serious shortages. For this reason, early
    Judenräte attempted to establish replacement service institutions of their own. They tried to
    organize food distribution, aid stations, old age homes, orphanages and schools. At the
    same time, given their restricted circumstances and remaining options, they attempted to
    work against the occupier's forced measures and to win time. One way was to delay transfer
    and implementation of orders and to try playing conflicting demands of competing German
    interests against each other. They presented their efforts as indispensable for the Germans
    in managing the Jewish community, in order to improve the resources of the Jews and to
    move the Germans to repeal collective punishments.

    This had, however, very limited positive results. The generally–difficult situations presented
    often led to perceived unfair actions, such as personality preferences, servility and
    protectionism of a few over the rest of the community. Thus, the members of the community
    quickly became highly critical of, or even outright opposed their Judenrat.

2. Family of Rubin Roy Cobb through his paternal grandmother Gelie (Genia) Anni Rokhel
    Rubin–Kobylanski.

[Page 258]

Forced Labour in Bransk

Two weeks after Bransk was occupied by the Germans, the Polish policemen issued an order in the name of the German command demanding all Jews from the age of twelve and older to report to the magistrate the following day at 11 o'clock in the morning. Punishment for not reporting will be death.

The Jews interpreted this order as being the end now. Is this the end? Everyone asked.

At the precise time, all the Jews appeared at the magistrate, old and young. They expected this would now end in their deaths. Rabbi Itskhak Zev Tsukerman was the head of the entire population, along with Rabbi [moyre-hoyro'e][1] Avrum Yankev Sekerevitch.

Everyone's heart was pounding. Why do they need us? What is our further fate?

The Germans finally made an appearance, accompanied by their Polish lackeys. They read out loud an order stating that all the Jews must work. The result of trying to get out of working will be death.

The Jews were now able to breathe a little easier as long as they would be permitted to live.

From that day on, Bransk Jews were chased to work. They worked on the highway. In Pyetkeve digging the turf, cleaning the fish in the pond standing in cold water up to their necks. In the village of Semini the Jews worked at building a palace for the Germans who were in charge of the Rutker forests. Jews were sent to the forest to chop wood. They would collect the weapons from the battlefields and transport it to the train. The lower streets, where it was always swampy, were made dry by Jewish hands. Canals were dug. Plantings were made. Jews, with their bare hands, cleaned the steps of Polish houses and villages. They were sent to Lapy where the work was filthy.

[Page 259]

They endured everything. All the Jews of Tchizsheve were shot. All the Jews of Gajnovka[2] were shot. This results is the Jews of Bransk working more quickly. With good work, with speedier work, maybe they would live. They established a factory of suitcases in the ghetto. The work there was hard and bitter. Bransk shoemakers supplied leather for the suitcase factory. They did everything, gave the Germans everything they demanded as long as they would be allowed to work and remain in Bransk.

If only the division of labour were distributed in an equitable fashion it would have been more tolerable and the denigration would not hurt as much. Regretfully, we cannot say it was so. Bransk Jews remember that Rabbi Zev himself worked at filthy work and did not permit anyone else to work for him, which is what many voluntarily offered to do.

The need for workers came to the Judenrat. The Judenrat chose a committee to decide who should go to work and where to go. This work committee consisted of Itskhak Finklshteyn, Yosl Levin and Bentsiyon Levin.

Now, under Nazi rule, there was another sort of spirit, not a friendly one. The Jewish officers suddenly conceived the idea that they were honored individuals and they are the policemen of the Jews. They did not feel enslaved as were all the other Jews, but somehow above them and who can act as they will, and did not take anyone else into account.

[Page 260]

Those who were the poorest and most down–trodden people were dispatched for the worst work, and those with a quiet nature who took everything upon themselves, suffered silently without protesting.

Protection was very popular – protection from friends, party people, acquaintances of the Judenrat'nikes. Monetary bribery played an important role. So who had to do all this work for one's self, for the officials, for the good, devoted party members of the officials? It was usually those of the lonely souls who had no friends, no sides. They did not have protection.

Pinye Katlavitch would tell them: "Bolshevikes, today you are not special, go to work."

The worst insult was for those people who worked in town. The German and Polish police with truncheons stood watch over the workers. The most privileged would stroll through town. Those who were working saw them and understood why the 'special' people are not working. Can you imagine the pain, the spiritual pain of these people? They return home after a day's work and then they find a new order from the Judenrat to once again go to work on the next day. Some people become anxious so they don't go to work. The Judenrat sends the Jewish police to make arrests. They put people in the Judenrat jail. The Judenrat orders beatings. The Jewish policemen administer beatings to those who rebelled.

Velvl Yerusalymsky, the scribe's grandson used to earn money to work in the place of others so as to have a couple of marks to help his sick father and five children. The Judenrat says: "Velvl must work for himself." He begs: "My father, mother and children are dying of hunger." It does no good. Velvl becomes stubborn. He is place in the ghetto jail of the Judenrat. They do not allow him to be fed. He becomes wild, bangs on the door of the jail: "Let me out." He berates the "holy" policemen Pontchken, Manes Shlyepn and Motkalen. His punishment is – 60 lashes, and he was actually beaten by these same Jewish policemen. He holds them off. The policemen, strong, well–fed youths are stronger than he. The town Jews gathered when they heard the shouting. The police disperse the crowd, keeping order and Velvl receives his lashes.

[Page 261]

Meles' grandchild was in Bransk. His name was actually Mele. The boy would also rent himself out to work in the place of others. He was hiding at Shloymeh Ephraim the maker of kvass[3] who was from Symyatitch. The Judenrat decided that Mele should go to work for them, for the protection without money. He is taken to work without payment. Shloymeh Ephraim begs to have the boy earn some money for a pair of shoes. He goes about barefoot. He is a quiet boy, a decent boy. He asks for pity from Finklshteyn. They put him in jail and he received only 50 lashes. The Jewish policemen were those administering the beating. They were always drunk, with no human feelings.

It was even worse when the forced labor workers were sent to other places. Where they simply died of hunger. The Judenrat was supposed to supply food for these workers. However it did not do this. The money was spent for enjoyment in the ghetto taverns. They had money for this purpose but no money for the poor who worked in Pyetkeve at the fish pond in the cold water up to their necks. Nobody worried about them because who were they, not one of their own. Such a boy did indeed perish, the Vishinker ritual slaughterer's fine boy, who could not endure the cold and hunger. His parents could not send him any food. They had 9 children. He had no income from slaughtering work in the ghetto.

There is another order that they need workers in Lapy, at the railway line. It was known that going to Lapy meant starving in Lapy. The work there consisted of two people having to carry a rail. Two people must fill a wagon in 20 minutes, and digging a canal without food with truncheons hovering over their heads. This is what Lapy meant. Whom did they send to Lapy? They sent the very same sort of people that my (Alter Trus) son, Nakhman, experienced there, where they promised to make an exchange in four weeks and to send food every week for those who were working in Lapy.

[Page 262]

Regretfully, they forgot about them. When the time came to send the workers all the Jewish policemen ran to the houses, chasing: "Faster, faster!"

Tatkale was at that time no longer a policeman but rather a Gestapo co–worker. He would usually not be sent because in addition, his uncle Epes Finklshteyn is involved with sending the Jewish workers to Lapy. He shouts: "Faster, Faster." His eyes burn with fury. There is no longer anything to lose. Hundreds of hands with truncheons attack the bandit Tatkele, taking revenge on their bitter situation. They beat this crook. The families of the Polish workers shout encouragement: "Hit the bastard again." He screams for the police but the fury of the people was so great that they were not afraid anymore of the police. The 'heroic' policemen are overcome with fear and scatter like mice. Is it possible that a little bit of conscience awakened in them? It is not believable. Maishe Yentchman exhibited happiness when he told me this story.

It is a known fact, that the most popular work for which Jews wanted to go was at cleaning the steps because there were no German gendarmes with truncheons standing by and no strolling Bransk elite there either.

This is how the forced labour work continued in the Bransk ghetto.

Footnotes (Rubin Roy Cobb)
1. Rabbi, one competent to decide matters of Rabbinical law
2. Russian pronunciation – in Polish it is Hajnovka. Rubin Roy Cobb's father's elder brother Shimeon Kobylanski and his wife Tzvia Shtern (from neighboring Bielsk–Podlaski) lived there. They had no children. Unlike Bransk Jews who were gassed in Treblinka in November, 1942, they were probably sent to Auschwitz at the end of January, 1943 or the beginning of February, 1943. However this was not known at the time that this Yizkor Book was written in 1947.
3. Drink made by fermenting rye and barley or sour fruits.
4.

[Page 263]

The Judenrat in Bransk

When the Nazis entered Bransk in the summer of 1941, they demanded that a Judenrat be formed in town.

This meant that the Jews in town should choose representatives whose duties would be to carry out German orders about various monetary contributions and to make certain that the contributions that were required from every resident had been made, and in addition to send the necessary number of Jews for forced labour and in general, be the instrument through which they, the Nazis, should be able, without difficulty, to keep the population in a state of fear.

It is understandable that Bransk Jews did not have any desire to become a Nazi tool. No one wanted to join in the Judenrat, to become a partner in overseeing the Jews in Bransk.

Finally, there volunteered Itskhak Finklshteyn, Avikhe's grandchild and others. The president of the Judenrat was Alter Yamshin. This was a person who could do no harm to anyone. Little–by–little, three Judenrat'nikes came to the fore. They were dubbed the 'troika.' They were Itskhak Finklshteyn, Yankev Gotlieb and Maishe Tikochski. The Judenrat consisted of twelve people.

Their work began with carrying out Nazi orders, collecting contributions of money, sending Jews to forced labour, establishing living quarters for the Jews in the ghetto, supplying food in accordance with the bread card, as well as creating a Jewish police force to help see that the work is done and ensuring that the yellow patch is worn by everyone.

[Page 264]

You can imagine that the Judenrat as a rule had the opportunity to take for itself and its relatives or other good comrades, many privileges. They used this opportunity quite well. They became the privileged people of the town. If someone did not have a Judenrat'nik in one's family or a party friend, he was defenseless. The Judenrat made use of its full power against such poor and defeated workers and especially against those who had a Soviet record. The privileged were usually freer, able to move about more. This resulted in terrible bitterness among the Jewish population, most especially in those who were most needy.

However, we must establish that the Bransk Judenrat was in comparison to other Judenrat'nikes of other towns, a righteous group. It was Bransk's luck to have as head Nazi gendarme a person with a certain amount of decency. He would warn the Bransk Jewish community not to go out on the street when gendarmes from Tchekhenofche were to pass by so as to be certain of their lives.

Zavl Rubinshteyn confirmed that the Bransk ghetto Jews, because of bribery, usually had various business opportunities, bringing food and merchandise to and from other ghettos. The Bialystok ghetto was grateful to the Bransk ghetto Jews for the food and merchandise that the Bransker brought them.

For these favors, the Judenrat'nikes received recognition. They earned money as well.

Avrum'tsye Top, Hershl Platrat's son–in–law would say: "You hear, Jews, if we survive the war, we will have a Judenrat because there is money to be made."

The sort of things that happened in the Tchekhenoftser Judenrat did not occur in Bransk. The Bransk Judenrat never turned anyone in when it had to do with endangering one's life.

[Page 265]

The Tchekhenoftser Judenrat would come to Bransk to capture those Jews who had fled from their ghetto. With the help of the Polish police, they would send them back to Tchekhenoftse, and turn them over to the gendarmes There they awaited death through various inquisition methods. Their horrific screams did not soften the hearts of the Judenrat'nikes who shared a brandy with the gendarmes. They continued with their work.

Two Bransk sons–in–law, the candy maker's and the Poplover's sons were in Bransk in hiding, and were captured by the Tchekhenoftser Judenrat bandits and sent to such a death.

It is well–known that approximately 600 Jews encountered their terrible death because of the deeds of the Judenrat'nikes in Tchekhenoftse.

Now we will present you with the description of the Bransk Judenrat.

Maishe Tikotchski – chief leader and decision–maker in the Judenrat, his work was to raise money. Because with money they could accomplish something. He was smart, never argued with anyone. His adjutants did the work for him.

It must be mentioned that in many cases when the life of the Bransk Jews was in jeopardy, Maishe Tikotchski endangered his own life to save these people.

Yankl Rubin[1], and Maishe Kamen had run away from the Lublin concentration camp, coming to Bransk. The Lublin gendarmerie sent a request to the Bielsker gendarmerie that these two Jews must, under any circumstances be brought back to Lublin. This meant certain death for the two Bransk Jews. Everyone in town knew they were in Bransk. Maishe Tikotchski was supposed to do this. It would have meant certain death for tens of Bransk Jews if the request would not be complied with. He did not become frightened and went to Shumanski and said, that they will not turn over any Jews regardless of any danger to themselves.

[Page 266]

Because of the human feelings that Shumanski possessed and the clever and tactful behavior of MaisheTikotchski who in no uncertain terms declared before the entire gendarmerie that the two Jews were not in Bransk which was corroborated by other Bransk Jews, they were rescued from a certain death. They survived the war. This cost a lot of money because Shumanski allowed himself to be well paid for such favors.

The brothers Alyentski, along with Bertche Yentchman, were arrested for breaking the law about taking food to another ghetto town. Their lives were in jeopardy because this was not the first time. The punishment was death. Maishe Tikotchski did not hesitate in the face of danger. He negotiated their freedom through Shumanski and refused to take money from those whom he had freed.

Itskhak Finklshteyn, a foolish Jew from whom no one ever received a favour. He sought ways of making money, and that is why he called Bentsl Rubin "Sir Rubin," because Sir Rubin was a source of income. Bentsl Rubin was never sent for work. For Bentsl, Itskhak Finkelshteyn was a good Judenrat'nik. This is told by Yankel Rubin the red rooster's[2] son.[3]

Yankev Gotlieb, In Bransk he was called "Gotlieb the helpful person." He was not an especially good man. Possibly he was bitter because the Communists had nationalized his father's business. He was a town councilman from the Poalei Tsiyon party. How did someone like this become a Judenrat'nik?

Bentsiyon Zarember, supplies commissar in the ghetto. He argued with everyone, fought with everyone. He was perfectly suited for the work.

Levin the Rutker, Khaim Yosl Shapira's son–in–law. He was the labour division commissar. Itskhak Finklshteyn was the one who led and controlled him. They compiled work lists, composed mostly of the poor and lonely youths. They paid strict attention to ensuring that none of the friends of the Judenrat'nikes should God forbid, be taken for work.

[Page 267]

Yekhiel Don, Yashe Krinsky, Yankev Dovid Kass were those who compiled the lists for the taxes.

Avrum Nadobrotsky, KhaimYosl Shapira, Ayzik Zeyfman, Motl Rihmer, Faivel Shapira, Khanina Khofetz, Meir Voltishnsky were Judenrat'nikes.

There were always those who hung around the Judenrat looking for favours for themselves, for acquaintances and party people.

Yeshaye Tsuker, Shloyme Kantchik's son–in–law. This man, Tsuker, had a special talent to always become the big shot. When the Soviet power took over Bransk, and the Bransk Communists were the chief rulers he then became one of the Communist activists, the official in charge to see that Jews turn over all their merchandise to the Soviets and receiving for it a few paltry groshens. Zavl Rubinshteyn[4], one of the rescued Jews is now in New York, and tells of his experiences at that time with Yeshaye Tsuker as head of the Soviet regime. When the Russian chief official saw Tsuker's over–the–top devotion to the Soviets, he dismissed him despite the fact that Yeshaye Tsuker insisted that he, Zavl needs to be punished for the great infraction he had committed when buying several skins that he had used in his work as a leather worker.

And now, in the Judenrat, Yeshaye Tsuker is once again active in various positions and is also the one who urged Yankev Gotlieb on. He saw that those who should be sent to work would only be those of other parties. His last position as police commandant led to the terrible deed of turning in Jews hiding in secret cellars of the ghetto.

These were the Bransk Judenrat'nikes. They were interested in making capital and did not notice the towns around Bransk were already cleansed of Jews (this according to Maishe Yentchman's statement).

[Page 268]

It is sad that the Bransk ghetto Jews were proud of their Nazi mayor and spoke badly of the Bransk Judenrat. To say the Judenrat always behaved in an honorable and loyal fashion is also not possible. In many cases they used their power in sending people to work and also in collecting taxes.

Footnotes (Rubin Roy Cobb)
1. Related to Rubin Roy Cobb through his paternal grandmother Gelie (Gelia) Rokhel Rubin–Kobylanski. I met him in Melbourne, Australia in the 1990s to where he had moved to from Bialystok in 1967. His son is an accountant in Melbourne and during July, 2014 told me that he had just ed from the funeral of the last remaining Bransk survivor in Melbourne. Yankl's His first name in English was John. His cousin Yankl from Baltimore was called Jack.
2. See page 265.
3. It was customary to add a feature of the person to his name, thus a small person was called "klein" [small], a dark person 'Schwartz' [black] etc. 'Red rooster' refers to a large nose with a large red swelling in the front of it.
4. Cynthia Rubinstein of Baltimore is his daughter. When he passed away his wife married Yankel (Jack) Rubin who was related to Rubin Roy Cobb through 's paternal grandmother Gelie (Gelia) Rokhel Rubin–Kobylanski. accompanied Yankel (Jack) Rubin to Bransk in October 11, 1991 for the production of the PBS documentary. "Shtetl". At that time did a walking tour with him videoing, recording and noting where most, if not all, of the 2,700 Jews of Bransk lived immediately prior to the liquidation of the Ghetto on November 2, 1942.

[Page 269]

The Bransk Jewish Police

The police in Bransk was comprised first-of-all, of the official's representative Lieutenant Shumanski and his seven gendarmes. If one of the gendarmes as much as looked at a Jew, one's blood ran cold.

The Polish police, who helped the gendarmes, consisted of all underworld people, former pogrom'tchikes. Their commandant was Pyeshakh. He was never without his truncheon in hand. He specialized in beating Jewish women with his truncheon. My [Alter Trus] sister, Tcheshe and Tsviye Yenkl Voytek's wife and many others know the meaning of being the recipient of beatings from Pyeshakh's truncheon. The aide-commandant was a Pole, Falikovsky, an underworld type and a Jew-beater. The children of Sjevoytsken, pogrom'tchikes for many years, another Markofske of Shaier Street. This Markofske has on his conscience, at the very least, 50 victims. There was also a Mikhal Panashuk, an uneducated Christian.

In addition to these gendarmes and Polish police, there were Jewish police, also recruited mostly from tainted elements. The commandant of the Jewish police was Itskhak Vasser (the tall Vasser), a very unsympathetic individual, also always carrying his truncheon. He spoke only German. The tall Vaser paid strict attention to seeing that Jews in the ghetto wore the yellow patch.

His assistant commandant, Yeshaye Tsuker a Judenrat'nik. He later became the police commandant. He managed to wiggle his way into the good graces of the Gestapo by bringing them to the hidden underground spaces resulting in 70 Jews being shot.

[Page 270]

Pinye Kotolovitch. Always kept an eye on those Jews who would sometimes smuggle something into the ghetto, food or other articles, Pinye was always looking for money, his livelihood. He was an ugly type, friendly with the Polish policemen, drinking l'khaim with them.

Tatkale Avikhe's grandchild, the most devoted policeman to the Germans, their official informer. He was the one who supplied workers. It was very difficult to woo him away from the police. His uncle Finklshteyn, the Judenrat'nik, always protected him. Yet he was sidelined for his deeds. During the liquidation Tatkale voluntarily presented himself to the German gendarmes. He helped to shove the Jews into the wagons. He probably wanted to remain on good terms with the Germans. They fooled him, pushing him into the wagon right along with all the Bransk Jews - it is true that he was the last one pushed in.

Belke, Alter Katsev's son, second name Faynsod, always with his truncheon, beating Mele's grandchild for not going to work. He was the policeman of the ghetto jail, and also expected to survive.

Manes Skavronek nickname of Shlyep. A very tall wagon–driver, a very crude young man. He fled during the liquidation. He did not depend on the good–heartedness of the gendarmes, did not want to go to Treblinka. He later arrived in Potok. I [Alter Trus] filed a complaint in the court against his murderer because this same person also murdered Yenkl Shvirider and Manes's father.

Velvl Halperen, Inditchke's grandchild, Ayzik Shuster Samikhodnik, Simkha Pam, Kopke's grandchild, Velvl Rozenblum, Leyb Shapiro, Meir Vishnevitz, Kopke's grandchild, Radzinke a Semyatisher, were also Jewish policemen.

Bransk Jews did not derive much pleasure from their Jewish police. They thought that if they listened to them, and went to work, they would perhaps remain alive. Regretfully, only a few of those who had fled lived. Several of the police such as Simkhah Pam, Velvel Halperen and Leybke Shapiro were later devoted partisans in the forest. They fought like heroes along with everyone else.

[Page 271]

In general however, the Jewish police were on a very low level. After every action that was carried out, e.g. chasing Jews to work or taking from the Jews pelts or bedding, the Jewish policemen came together to create a business. Nobody was held accountable. Each was for himself and did not want to know of anyone else. They considered their work to be la legitimate source of income. If anyone made any reference to their behavior their answer was, "Bolshevik, the time of your power is past. We are now the power and you must listen to us."

Yes, the Jewish policemen had the power and they used the power quite well. They were very well–suited to this tragic time.

At the end, the tall Vasser was sidelined. He felt mightier than the Judenrat, and he was replaced. Yeshaye Tsuker takes over the position of police commandant. The duties of the Jewish policemen consisted mainly of taking people for work. If they did not go willingly they were taken by force. The police also had to ensure that the taxes were brought in. If they did not pay, their belongings were taken away.

You understand the more the Judenrat increased the taxes, the more the Jewish police had to make revisions of the last bedding and clothing they could get.

[Page 272]

Bransk Ghetto

As soon as the Germans entered Bransk, they ordered a ghetto to be established.

The mayor at that time was an older German by the name of Shturman. According to MaisheYentchman's description, Shturman was a good person. Bransk Jews, Maishe writes, were pleased with Shturman than of their own Judenrat'nikes. It is true that Shturman was well paid for the favours, but yet he was friendly and not a beast. He always postponed any orders for the ghetto. When Shturman had to go away, a German by the name of Barvinsky took his place. Barvinsky caused the greatest trouble during the couple of days the time he ruled in place of Shturman. He squeezed everything possible from the Jews. There were also gendarmes. The Jewish population had to supply them with the best clothing and food. When any one of them went home on furlough he could never have enough things to take with him. They had to be given everything for their families at home. They were supplied with the very last that was left.

This cost the town much money. To raise the money, the Judenrat increased everyone's taxes. Finally, Shturman forced the establishment of a ghetto. He probably could no longer receive any more bribery money from the Jews, but he was forced to do this by the higher officials.

[Page 273]

He permitted the town to select which area of the town to designate as the ghetto. Arguments developed because both sides of the town wanted its side to become the ghetto. The ghetto was established on the left side of town coming from the bridges[1], from Sane to Yenkitchke's house[2], and the back street from the hospital to Dzjezjinshtchikh'es house. From Shayer Alleyway to Plonever.

There were not too many houses on that street any more. Most of the houses had burned.[3] There was not enough room to stuff the entire Jewish population into the few remaining houses. Shturman permitted the street from Yekhiel–Leyb to Leyzer Katsev[4] to become a part of the ghetto. This was called the small ghetto. The Christians who found themselves in the ghetto had to move out, and all the Jewish families were shoved into the ghetto.

Terrible scenes took place when the time came to move into the ghetto. HershlPlatrat lay down in his house with his feet pointing at the door and did not want to leave. He said: 'I know that no one will live to leave the ghetto.' The houses that were removed from the Jews were quickly occupied by Christians.

They had waited for this and finally Dambravski had already divided the houses among the Christians who deserved them. Poles, with arrogance settled themselves in the Jewish houses, took from Jewish shops stocked with Jewish belongings.

The ghetto became terribly crowded – four and five families to one room, all having to cook in the same kitchen. So there were always arguments. They couldn't even stand themselves. The Germans derived pleasure from this situation. They used to say that Jews could even live in a little sealed bottle.

The bread cards were reduced to 125 grams per day. Cows or chickens were not permitted in the ghetto. The Christians already made sure these would remain in their hands.

[Page 274]

Hunger increased. People sought ways to get a little food, so they took chances with their lives, sneaking out of the ghetto and bringing leather goods from Bialystok to sell. Workers sneaked out to work for Christians to earn a little bread. If someone was caught, he paid with his life. And the gendarmes, policemen and the Judenrat'nikes received their monetary bribes. The population suffered from hunger, so they took chances with their lives and went out. Some left on foot, got a few provisions and brought them to the ghetto. Jewish butchers would sometimes smuggle in a cow, slaughter it in secret and sell the meat for Shabbos. In secret they baked matzo for Passover made from cornmeal.

The Germans opened a factory to manufacture suitcases, so the shoemakers had to provide leather they had for making shoes to produce the suitcases.[5]

The ghetto was not yet locked. Jews were permitted to visit the small ghetto and those from the small ghetto visited the large one. All of this was thanks to Shturman who, compared to other mayors, was a good man. Bransk Jews called the 'zeyde.'[6]

Sometimes a German newspaper "Der Folkisher Beovakhter"[7], would make an appearance in the ghetto. On a non–workday, the Jews of the ghetto would assemble to read "Der Folkisher Beovakhter," most especially reading between the lines. When the newspaper wrote that the Germans had crossed 50 miles into the Russian front, it was actually understood that it was two miles.[8] There was a jail in the ghetto for those who had to be arrested for not going to work or not paying taxes. There was also a courthouse in which to settle.

It is understandable that when they saw a German or Polish policeman or a Judenrat'nik they would hurry into their houses. Various disagreements occurred between Jews. Advocate (Barrister) Volkovitch was the judge. Attending would be Rabbi Sekarevitch, and sometimes Rabbi Kagan, Mordekhay Golde and others. The Jewish police would have to carry out the judge's decision.

[Page 275]

At the beginning the Judenrat's quarters were at Rubin's[9] hotel and later moved into the New Synagogue.[10]

The Jews were forbidden to walk on the sidewalk. They had to walk in the middle of the street with the cows and horses. The cramped conditions in the ghetto worsened because many Jews from liquidated towns had escaped and arrived in Bransk. Rooms for these refugees to sleep were prepared. Food was also supplied by 'esn teg.'[11] Each person would feed a different person from another ghetto every day.

Hershl Platrat was caught outside the ghetto by a German while carrying a quart of milk. The German asks Hershl what he is carrying: "Milk," Hershl answers with pride. Hershl is beaten badly. As he left, Hershl says to the German: 'I am already sixty years old and you will not live to see so many years.'

Jewish tailors, shoemakers and workers of other trades take risks and go to the villages to work. You understand that if a German caught someone, he got the death penalty. But one had to live and pay the taxes to the Judenrat, so they had to take risks. Taxes were constantly raised and the Jewish police became more active.

In general, ghetto life consisted of working, working and paying taxes, suffering and keeping quiet as long as they remained alive.

The situation in the ghetto constantly worsened until the ghetto closed.

Footnotes (Rubin Roy Cobb)

1. Refer to Map # III
2. Refer to Main Map drawn up by Rubin Roy Cobb on November, 2011
3. Refer to Main Map drawn up by Rubin Roy Cobb on November, 2011. The areas marked by a double line are those that were destroyed by the bombing raid in September 1939 which was most of the Jewish quarters.
4. Refer to Main Map drawn up by Rubin Roy Cobb on November, 2011. The main ghetto is north of the main street Sienkiewicza and the small ghetto is north of the Nurzec River. Both ghettos are marked with Xs.
5. This sentence was omitted by the translator {MGC}
6. Grandfather
7. The People's Observer [MCG]
8. This corrects the Yiddish sentence as it appears in the book.
9. Related to . The original owner of the hotel was the father of 's paternal grandmother Gelie (Genia) Rokhel Rubin– Kobylanski.
10. See Map #15 page 3/3 drawn up by on November, 2011. It is believed (but cannot be confirmed) that my maternal grandfather Akiva Skornik Ha'koheyn prayed at this synagogue as per Yankl (Jack) Rubin of Baltimore.
11. Outside Yeshiva students were fed regularly at the homes of local families. This phrase (eating day) is a reference to that custom.

[Page 276]

The Ghetto is Sealed

At the beginning of the summer of 1942 Shturman delivered the news that the Gestapo had ordered that the ghetto is to be sealed, surrounded with a fence erected with the use of Jewish money. It was to be four meters in height, and constructed of boards.

A short time later, Shturman is replaced by an official by the name of Schmidt. Schmidt was not pleased with the fence because there were spaces through which to crawl out of the ghetto. He immediately ordered that between every second board another board was to be inserted in order to make it impossible to crawl out of the small spaces.

The Jewish population of the ghetto now understands that this is somewhat tragic. They are aware that the towns on the opposite side of the Bug River are already cleansed of Jews. The fate of the Bransk Jews is now no longer in doubt.

In secret hidden openings are made in the fence. Certain boards could be removed and replaced, with only a few selected people knowing about these secret openings.

The fenced–in ghetto has now taken on the appearance of a large camp. There are only two gates open through which to enter the ghetto. They are at Itche Gimpel's and opposite Khaim Pentman.[1] The gates are usually heavily guarded.

It is remarkable that in the sealed ghetto Jews felt a little freer. In the open ghetto, Jews were not permitted to venture out of their houses, receiving beatings for such a transgression. In the sealed ghetto, they felt as if they were in their own homes, or at the very least, the Jews felt free to go outside and to go between houses.

[Page 277]

From time–to–time they came together in the street and discussed their situation among themselves and talked about the war. The news about the war would come to them through the German newspaper "Der Folkisher Beovakhter" that someone would bring in.

Khatskel the ritual slaughterer, good–natured and good–hearted, was recognized as a good interpreter of the latest news. He comforted everyone. He already saw between the lines of the newspaper that the Germans would soon suffer their downfall. Everyone was happy with Khatskl and his heartfelt comforting words. These were so necessary for the unfortunates in the ghetto.

Sholem Kratz's grandchild was in the ghetto, Motl's son with the nickname "ikh drey zikh."[2] He always told the same news in a sad tone. The news as he saw it was always black, dark. The ghetto Jews hated him because of his interpretation and did not want to listen to him.

Often times ghetto Jews gathered at Kukafke the watchmaker in the small ghetto to hear the news from those who read the newspaper that had been smuggled in. There were different sides who interpreted the news in various ways.

Christians would come into the sealed ghetto looking for work at the Jewish artisans. Others came to buy Jewish things, usually paying with a little food.

The religious feeling greatly strengthened in the ghetto. Jews always came together in the ghetto houses for prayer, and even those who were known to be free –thinkers came to make up the quorum of ten men required for communal prayer.

The khasidim arranged their shtibel in Yenkl Yentchman's house. That is where the khasidim came to pray.

In the greatest secrecy some Jews began to dig deep holes beneath the cellars of the ghetto houses. This was one of the biggest secrets. They were wary of their neighbors, the Judenrat'nikes and the Jewish police.

[Page 278]

The cramped conditions in the ghetto were horrible with 5–6 families in a room, so they built huts in the ghetto. These were such little huts where a couple of families were lucky to have had a kind of roof over their heads.

There were plenty of jokesters in the ghetto. From time–to–time they laughed heartily, cracked jokes about their own troubles. Most especially the Jews laughed at the story about Hershl Benduger. Hershl was crazy. Hershl never wore any yellow patches. He came face–to–face one time with a German gendarme who knew that Hershl was a little crazy, so he asked him: Why don't you wear the mark of shame?" Hershl does not give this much thought and answered the gendarme: "It is already not fashionable to wear the yellow patch." The gendarme burst into laughter and lets Hershl be. For weeks they laughed in the ghetto about Hershl's clever answer. He was a crazy person and gave such a clever retort.

A terrible impression was made on all in the ghetto, young and old, orthodox and free–thinkers, when it became known in the ghetto that the Old Synagogue that had been burned by the Germans 1939 as they retreated and turned Bransk over to the Soviets, was now being dismantled, brick–by–brick, and that these bricks were to be used to build a soap production factory. Their hearts told them that something terrible was happening. A factory to make soap! Could they even imagine that the soap would be made from the fat of Jewish bodies? And the bricks of the Old Synagogue that had served the Bransk population for 130 years as a holy place would be used.

The younger people in the ghetto established a movement to obtain weapons and move them to the forest. This was done in the greatest secrecy because they were afraid to mention it. No one trusted anybody.

Hershl Rubin[3], Yenkl Shimon's grandchild, clever, skinny but very energetic, becomes friendly with a German soldier, with Communist leanings and a liberal individual. This German brings weapons to Hershl, usually in secret. Regretfully, Hershele told someone about this. Itskhak Finklshteyn, the Judenrat'nik, comes to Hershl and demands to be given the weapons. Hershl, very frightened by Itskhak's truncheon, has no alternative and gives the revolver to the Judenrat'nik. Finklshteyn weapons. Now he knew of whom to be careful. His lips were sealed.

[Page 279]

The youth do not have time to plan because they are chased to work. Few listened to the agitation to move to the forest.

Those who occupied themselves with smuggling also have no time. They need to work, they need to earn. The older folk certainly do not want to hear about such plans. They have hope. They hope God will have pity on them, send salvation through a miracle. Regretfully, no miracles occurred nor was there salvation. Cold death looked out between the boards of the fenced–in Jewish ghetto.

The Judenrat'nikes and the Jewish police are in power and rule the ghetto with a strong hand. They ignored the fact that the entire population of many of the neighboring Jewish towns had been taken to Maydajnek[4] or Treblinka.[5] They do not see that the liquidation of Bransk Jews is approaching.[6]

The entire Jewish population is in a dream–like state. They think this is all something of a terrible nightmare and not a reality. Somewhere deep in their hearts, there glows a spark of hope. One wants to lie down in the weak straw that was already burning from both sides.

Only Hershele Rubin did not dream. He gathers weapons little–by–little, telling no one and keeping his distance.

Something else happens that throws more terrible fright into everyone. All the Jews who were in the small ghetto near the river are brought into the ghetto. They are brought only with the clothes on their backs, nothing more.

The crowded conditions in the ghetto are now unbearable. Death is approaching.

[Page 280]

Their spirits are heavier. An unfamiliar hand squeezes and creeps in closer to their necks.

What does this mean? The ghetto is suddenly lit at night with electric beacons. They throw a strong light around the ghetto and a frightening darkness into the Jews in the ghetto. What does this mean? What does this mean? They ask one another.

The policemen and Judenrat'nikes shout: "Don't create panic, don't create panic." And they begin to establish hiding places for themselves and their families.

Footnotes (Rubin Roy Cobb)
1.   Refer to Map # 4 page 3/3 and/or # 6 page2/2 and/or # 14 page 1/1
2.   I wander around.
3.   Related to Rubin Roy Cobb through his paternal grandmother Gelie (Genia) Rokhel Rubin–Kobylanski.
4.   Death Camp in Lublin south–east of Bransk.
5.   Death Camp west of Bransk where most of the Jews in the Warsaw Ghetto were gassed as well as from the Bialystok region including Bransk.
6.   Jack Rubin told that a boy of about 15 who had walked from Lithuania (approximately 80 miles north of Bransk) had told them of the mass killings of Jews but everyone thought that he was crazy and did not believe him.

[Page 281]

Liquidation of the Bransk Jews
November 2nd 1942

The second of November is the day of sorrow and pain. This is the Tisha b'Av[1] of the destruction of Bransk. This is the day the decree was issued by the Nazi murderers to annihilate the Jews of the Bialystok area and was implemented with the accursed German precision.

The Jews in the Bransk ghetto already felt the impending approach of the terrible storm. They felt death in the cold oncoming winds of Autumn, and yet, they could not believe that in a few days all would end.

On the first of November, Yerukhm Don[2] of Bialystok arrived. He was involved in the smuggling business. He brings us the news that of rumours circulating in Bialystok that the Jewish population of the Bialystok area will be liquidated.

He was insulted by those in the ghetto because he brings such reports, and yet no one slept that night. Many left the ghetto to hide with Christian acquaintances. No one knows to whom and where they are going because no one tells anyone. They trusted no one. They sought only to save themselves and their families.

All the terrible expectations were realized that same night. At four o'clock in the morning heavy shooting is heard around the ghetto. Those seeking to escape the ghetto now fall victim. They become aware that the ghetto is now surrounded. There is now no way to get out of the ghetto.

[Page 282]

The electric beams cast a bright light everywhere. There is destruction in the houses. Everywhere there is crying, mothers pressing their little children to their hearts. Even the young now understand they must die because they are Jews.

The desire to rescue one's self is strong. They want to escape the ghetto. They know every unsuccessful attempt will end in death. This does not deter the people. They jump over the high fence, try to slip out through the secret openings that had been arranged during the construction of the ghetto's fence. Shots ring out from every side. Victims fall and yet, they still make attempts to escape.

Mirke Noske Katsev's

Khaim–Ruven Rypke[3]

Death no longer frightened anyone. Esther Hurvitz, with her child in her arms falls dead. The child remains alive in the arms of the dead mother. Aharon Pulshansky's wife, the pharmacist's daughter, Khaim Ruven Rypke all dead together on the sidewalk near Maishke Bakker's, and near the lake, while running, Yoel Oyslender, Motl's son–in–law and his two children fall.

[Page 283]

Many others drag themselves around, wounded and bloody. They drag themselves further using their last bit of strength, further from the beleaguered ghetto. Poor unfortunates, they do not know that death hovers over them from everywhere, that their fate is already sealed. Among those who had been wounded were: Itskhak Rekhlzon, BerlYatz. There is no longer any talk about running away, and yet a couple of hundred had fled the ghetto through various means. Many tore through the hail of bullets.

They ran to the forests. Not one of the Christians wanted to let Jews in. Signs made an appearance in the villages: 'For sheltering or helping Jews there will be the punishment of death.'

The ghetto is heavily guarded by SS troops, Ukrainian, Lithuanian and Polish police bandits.

In subsequent days many more Jews escaped the ghetto, a total of approximately 800 Jews, fleeing to the forests or to villages. Many of those who fled do not find where to hide. Christians do not take them in. Having nowhere to go they return to the ghetto.

The Paplover[4] Christians had already captured their first victim – Yankev Kashtan, Khone Kashtan's youngest son. He had hidden there and the Christians captured him, bound him and brought him to the gendarmes. Yankev Kashtan receives a terrible beating from the gendarmes.

Khone Sokolovitch, Dovid Gimpel's grandchild, throws his five year old son Berele, over the fence. The child survives. Then Khone Sokolovitch grabs a pail and goes supposedly to fetch water from the hospital, thinking that he would in this way be able to get a chance to slip out of the ghetto. A guard stands at the gate, a Jewish policeman. He notices Khone and says to his German gendarme, pointing at Khone: "This Jew is trying to leave." Khone is taken into custody to the mountain where he is shot.

[Page 284]

Velvl Golde Motke's writes from Germany on 11th August, 1947. He describes the liquidation of the Bransk ghetto. Velvel was in the underground hiding–place in the centre of the ghetto for 11 days. He is the only living witness of the betrayal committed by Shaiye Tsuker. But there is a special chapter regarding this. Velvel writes the following: "On the 2nd of November at about 5 o'clock in the morning footsteps of the military are heard in the ghetto. People are frightened. Some say they are going out hunting in the Rutker forest.[5] It turns out that the hunt was on for Bransk Jews.

About 800 Jews have already fled the ghetto. The ghetto was surrounded until Shabbos the 7th of November. There is no longer any possibility of flight.

The security watch is increased as were the electric projectors in the towers making sure no one could run away.

They are thinking of underground hiding–places. This too, was in secrecy. I notice Hershl Pipke carrying water and I understand he is carrying the water to the hiding–place. I ask him and receive permission to hide with them in the hiding–place beneath Khaye Yenkl Khukar's house.

During the past few days, people walk about like shadows. No one is eating and no one is sleeping. They are thinking of how to get out of the ghetto. Monday night the Jews of the small ghetto near the lake[6] are brought to the large ghetto without any of their belongings.

On Friday the 6th, Itskhak Finklshteyn, the Judenrat'nik goes to pay the weekly contribution to the gendarmerie. They take the money from him. A Polish teacher, an official, informs Tsuker that preparations for 500 wagons belonging to the neighboring villages are under way to remove the Jews early the next day, Shabbos.

On Friday rumors are spread that the security watch is being removed from the ghetto. The women are preparing for Shabbos. The gendarmes appear when it is time to light the candles and report that on Shabbos morning at seven o'clock everyone must report as families at the entrance of the ghetto. There must be no missing members. They are told to bring only bread and water.

[Page 285]

There is terrible crying in the ghetto. Crying coming from all the Jewish homes, they cry about themselves and the children, people go to say goodbye to the to the rabbinical teacher. We lived in Kashtan's brick house. We all gathered together at Isser Shepsl Katsev's son. I will never forget how Isser 'took this bundle of troubles and his stick in his hand,' and began to describe in what kind of situation we were all in. Early the following morning we all have to abandon the houses and die as martyrs. Then he made kiddush.[7] Each of his words trembled. The crying was horrible.

My father and I then went into our house. My father also made kiddush. Once again, we began to cry. As we entered the courtyard people came over to ask me how to save themselves. I answered that no one should report early tomorrow but hide instead wherever they can find a place.

I went to the hiding–place later. I ask my father to go with me, but he says: 'No my child, I want to die together with all the Bransk Jews!' I parted from him for all eternity."[8]

This is what Velvel Motke–Slove's writes:

"The happiness and driving force of life and death are not unconnected."[9] Many people, under this order did not want to part from their nearest and went to their death together.

Beynish Okan had the opportunity to flee. He did not want to. His wife, Tsheshe and her two beautiful children Dvoshe and Shoshana also did not want to perish without him. He decides to die with them. He goes to Treblinka with them.

Maishe Feldman, Alye Gershon's only son, has a wife, Reizl who is sick with typhus and already knows her fate. He decides to die. He does not run away. Mirke Noske Katsev's and her daughter of about fifteen years old run away. Her husband Menakhem does not want to flee. Then Mirke returns with her daughter to die together with her nearest. They die with everyone else.

[Page 286]

Sender Friedman, known in Bransk as the Dombrofker[10] linen merchant, can also not run away. His wife is sick, paralyzed. She does not want to nor can she flee. Sender decided to die together with his wife.

Hershl Shpak, Alter Orke's son, hid in the ghetto in an underground hiding–place. Several days after the liquidation, he describes the following: "During the first days of the ghetto, when it was surrounded, Hershl Stolyer, or as the elderly Jews called him: Hershl–Maishe 's, died in the ghetto.

Hershl Stolyer and wife Henye

Sarah's two daughters

Khaitche and Rivka

Their two daughters Sarah and Dvorke

[Page 287]

Everyone envied him dying a natural death, although he was not allowed to have a proper Jewish burial. He was buried near a Jewish house in the ghetto. The Germans did not permit exiting the ghetto, not even dead Jews." Hershl Shpak relates further: "Friday evening while they were saying their goodbyes, they broke everything in the house. They tore the clothing, even tore the money. They poured kerosene over leftover food. They did not want to leave anything to those who were waiting for these things.

Hiding–places were prepared with friendly Christians, but no one wanted to use them. They were going to their deaths along with everyone else. There was a prepared hiding–place with Skavronski the Christian shoemaker for Khaim Leyb Lyev, Hershl Stolyer's son–in–law and others. Khaim Leyb becomes aware of this accidentally and calls his wife and children to be with him, but no one of his family wants to go into hiding. He then goes to the attic by himself and can run away to the forest from there. There was enough food there for three months. However, Khaim Leyb returns to die with his family.

Early Shabbos morning everyone is herded to the exit. 500 wagons wait at the gate of the ghetto. The Bransk rabbi, Rabbi Yitzkhak Zev Tsukerman, says goodbye to the Bransk Jews and the Bransk community. His words are heart–wrenching: "It is ordained from heaven, we must die. I wish for those who will remain alive to be worthy of this, and to tell the world about our suffering." I was told that the Bransk rabbi's son–in–law, Rabbi Bentsiyon Kagan had hidden a bottle containing certain documents somewhere in the ghetto. The only one who knew this secret was Elye Yentchman. Regretfully, he too fell and no one knows what was contained therein and where it is.

Rabbi Yitskhak Zev Tsukerman did not console anyone, nor did anyone comfort him either. Everyone looked to heaven for revenge. Levin of the Judenrat informs everyone that they were only being taken for work. He admits that he had been told to say this."

[Page 288]

It is now time to leave their homes and their town where for 150 years they had lived a Jewish life.

A signal is given and all the wagons drive away on the road to Bielsk.[11]

At the same time, they remove the sick from the hospital together with Doctor Kaminetsky, Reizl Gotlieb's and Tsivye Alentsker. They all perish in Bielsk.

A notice in Polish and German appears in Bransk: 'Bransk is Judenrein.'[12]

The Jews are held in Bielsk for two days. Dovid Grinshpan, Lazer the beltmaker's son–in–law, an electrical technician, electrocutes his wife and two children and slits his own throat with a knife.

Things are being controlled in Bielsk. The Nazis discover that there are 800 missing Bransk Jews. Demand is made to the Judenrat'nikes to produce those who had fled. They promise them that they and their families would be saved. Yankev Gotlieb categorically refuses to turn them in. Other Judenrat'nikes also refuse. Yeshaye Tsuker did not answer the question, but more about this in another chapter.

Leybele Rose, Shloyme Hitsl's grandchild

Leybele Rose, Shloyme Hitsl the khasid's grandchild, fled from Bielsk. According to what he tells, all the clothing everyone had brought with them was taken away. They were divided into three groups, men, women and children separated. There is terrible crying when they are seated in the wagons. Families are divided and no longer together. They are beaten with sticks, with rubber poles, with rifle butts. Christians stand by and shout: 'stupid zhidkes[13] , why are you carrying packages, give them to us.' Little Leybele however, perished in the village of Alyekshin. More about this in another chapter.

Elye Yentchman, Dovid the candy–maker's son, Shloyme Hersh the khasid's grandchild, about 45 years old said that there were already dead Bransk Jews in the wagons together with Jews from other neighboring towns. They were now practically begging for death. Regretfully, Elye also did not survive. His death occurred during the attack in the Rutker forest.

On the 9th of November the Bransk Jews are taken through Bialystok to Treblinka[14] near Malkin. [14]

On the 10th everyone is already in Treblinka. According to the evidence the Jews who worked there and also from Koptchiven who had fled from there, all the Bransk Jews, men and women separately, breathed their last in the Treblinka gas chambers on the 10th of November, 1942 at four o'clock in the afternoon. Their bodies were burned in the crematorium in Treblinka.

And this is how our elders, sisters and brothers of Bransk came to the end of their lives. This is how 150 years of the lives and striving of the Bransk community ended.

There will be more in further chapters about those who fled and those who hid.

Footnotes (Rubin Roy Cobb)

1. Wikipedia – Tisha B'Av [lit. in Hebrew "the ninth of Av"], is an annual fast day in Judaism which commemorates the destruction of the First and Second Temples in Jerusalem and subsequent exile of the Jews from the Land of Israel.... (It) is regarded as the saddest day in the Jewish calendar and a day which is destined for tragedy...Many religious communities use Tisha B'Av to mourn the 6,000,000 Jews who perished in the Shoah.
2. Yankel (Jack) Rubin of Baltimore, [related to Rubin Roy Cobb through his paternal grandmother Gelie (Genia) Rokhel Rubin–Kobylanski], told on a flight from New York to Warsaw to film the documentary 'Shtetl' for PBS on 10/11/1991 that the person who reported that Friday night, November1, 1942 that the ghetto was to be surrounded, was a Pole. Was this person Yerukhm Don and the Pole the same person?
3. Related to Khaim and Khanah Rypka and also Reizl Albiter (Rypka) [mother of Anne Barber (Alberts) of Los Angeles] from Johannesburg [see photo on page 417].
4. See Map Section 2, Number II.
5. See Map Section 2, Number II.
6. See Map drawn by Rubin Roy Cobb on November, 2011,
7. Proclamation of the holiness of the Sabbath recited with blessing over the wine.
8. Yankel (Jack) Rubin of Baltimore, [related to Rubin Roy Cobb through his paternal grandmother Gelie (Gelia) Rokhel Rubin–Kobylanski], told on a flight from New York to Warsaw to film the documentary 'Shtetl' for PBS on 10/11/1991 that he begged his mother and father to accompany him and his brother and his brother's wife and children, but they refused and his mother gave him all the money that they had saved because they would not need it to where they were going. He tearfully (then 78 years old) told me that this was the last time that he saw his parents.
9. A Hebrew phrase, probably Talmudic.
10. See Map Section 2, Number III.
11. See Map Section 2, Numbers I and III.
12. Cleansed of Jews.
13. Derogatory word for Jews
14. See Map Section 2, Numbers I and IV.

[Page 290]

The Tsuker Story

Deep beneath the houses of the ghetto Jews, in the greatest secrecy, arranged hiding places. In hiding places such as these, there were hidden 100 Bransk Jews. Their hope was that little–by–little they would have the opportunity to flee the ghetto to seek sanctuary and safety somewhere.

The one hundred Jews spent eight days in the cellars. After all the Jews in the ghetto had been removed, they did not have an opportunity to emerge because the police kept strict watch at the gates. Other Germans or Christians would sneak into the empty houses looking and searching hoping to find something of value.

We can imagine what the hidden Jews were experiencing during this week. The fear and angst, as they listened to every footfall. They heard the laughter, the whistling of the police and guards. They were able to come out at night and crawl like worms to find a little water. The food they had prepared for themselves consisted only of bread. There was less and less bread, although on Monday and Thursday, they developed as fast days and did not taste any bread.

There were 15 Jews in Khaim Klode's cellar. The rest were in other hiding places. It is believed there were eight or seven such underground hiding places. There was no communication between any of them. One did not know of the other.

Sunday, the 15th of November, promptly at three o'clock in the afternoon the Gestapo came to their hideout, breaking open the doors and demanding they emerge. They hear them shout : 'Come out Jews.' How terrible their situation when the voice calling them was that of Yeshaye Tsuker along with the Gestapo agents. 13 of those hidden come out and two remain inside. The two died at another time.

[Page 291]

The 13 people are inspected, lined up in rows and taken to Avrume Makofsky's courtyard in the ghetto where they find more Jews who had also been removed from their hiding places, for a total of 71 people. Everyone tells the same story: Yeshaye Tsuker came with Germans and took them out of their hiding places. Yeshaye Tsuker stands there alongside the Gestapo and Polish police. Isser Shepsl Katsev's insults him, Tsuker, calling him various names, also in Polish 'Zdrajca – Zdrajca'[1] The Germans remove Tsuker from the courtyard and take him somewhere else.

All of these Jews are later taken to jail, locked up overnight. The following day, promptly at twelve o'clock noon, they are taken in farmers' wagons to the Jewish cemetery. Many of the Christian population are forced to witness this scene. They [the Jews] are all shot there after having been ordered to undress naked.

The list of people shot, with the exception of the 13 who were at Khaim Klade's, was later compiled by Christian acquaintances who had been there and possibly knew everyone personally. And yet, the list is incomplete, with several names missing because it was not possible to find them out.

The only survivor of this horrific blood bath episode also cannot remember all 70 who were there. The total number of seventy is confirmed regardless of there being only 46 names recorded.

This was the fate of 70 Jews who had hidden in the ghetto.

[Page 292]

Before we present the written story of the living witnesses about the entire tragic episode, I (Julius Cohen) will record the opinions of remaining Branskers, of those with whom I spoke to in New York and of those who wrote to me.

Maishe Yentchman asked me to write in the book that Tsuker was forced by the Gestapo in Bielsk, with abuse and torture to disclose the whereabouts of the hidden Jews. At the same time he admits that Yankev Gotlieb, the Judenrat'nik, did not want to hear about turning in the Jews.

The protocols that are now located in the Jewish Historical Commission of the Bialystok Provincial Committee are based on the eye witness account and written statement of MaisheYentchman, and therefore I will not note them once again.

During a personal conversation I had in New York with Sonya Rubinshteyn[2], the Deaf Maishe Hirsh's grandchild, despite the fact that her mother, Beyle, and her brother Shloymewere victims of the incident, she expressed her opinion that Tsuker thought the people were being taken for work, although why they needed between two and five year old children or men and women between 65 and seventy years old for work, she did not know.

On the other hand, her husband, Zavl Rubinshteyn, says Tsuker was far from being a naǞve person. He did this in order to save himself. While being in Bielsk, he saw that there was no longer anyone left of the Bielsk Jewish ghetto. The Bielsk ghetto was already empty. The Bransk Jews occupied the Bielsk Jewish ghetto houses for the two days that they were there.

We do not presume to pass judgment on the memory of those people who are no longer among the living because, as it is said: 'You should not judge your friend until you yourself will be in the same position as he whom you want to judge.' (*paraphrased* MGC).

The following is the letter, better said, the two letters sent, Velvl Golde, Shmuel'ke Slove's grandchild, the sole surviving Jew of the 70 individuals who so horrifically perished during this action. I have these letters with me in New York. I requested and received them from Alter Trus because the letters had been sent to him.

[Page 293]

Word for–word these letters are from Velvl Golde. The originals are with Julius Cohen.

"I noticed how Sholem Kratz's son–in–law of Wysokie Mazowieckie[3] carries water, and I immediately understood that he was taking it to an underground hiding–place. I saw him carrying the water in to my relative Kloden. I went in and asked if I and my father could also go into the hiding–place. They told us to come. My father did not want to go to the hiding place, so I had to part from my father for all eternity. Isser Bransky, and Yankev Kashtan went along with me. We only took bread and water with us and not even much of that. This is how we were out of touch with the world. Shabbos morning we prayed with the minyan.[4] There was a Torah. We bless the new month of Kislev. We arranged a fast schedule for Monday and Thursday.[5] When the food ran out we opened the baker's oven where there was a kholent[6] from nine days earlier. We ate this with great relish as if it was the best meal. We brought potatoes and other food into the hiding–place. We reentered the hiding place temporarily because in the evening we had to go to the courtyard for water.

This was the second Sunday that there were no Jews in the ghetto.

At three o'clock in the afternoon Yeshaye Tsuker and the Gestapo came to our underground hiding–place, tore it open and shined in light with flashlights. They order us to emerge from the hiding–place.

Tsuker calls for us to come out. We hear Tsuker's voice and this made a terrible impression on us. How does Tsuker come to do this? And how do they know of our hiding–place?

They ask us how many we are, so we said13. There were 15 people with us:
[Page 294]

Avrume Verpikhovsky and his wife Sorah, Khaye Klade and three children, Isser Bransky, Shloyme Lazer, Yankev Kashtan, Sorah Rubinshteyn, Hershl Shroyt and Rivka Bialistotsky, and two remained inside, Yoske Smurzhik and Kratze's son–in–law (they later left the hiding–place and fell victims under other circumstances.

I took food with me when I left the hiding–place and Tsuker says to me: 'Why do you need this? It's not necessary.' Then they inspected us and stood us in rows and then took us all to Makofski's courtyard where the well was.

We found more people there who have been taken out of other hiding places. The people of other hiding places ask us how we had been discovered, so we told them that Tsuker had brought Germans to our hiding place. They said Tsuker had also brought Germans to their hiding places. We were surrounded. There were more Germans than us. Fleeing was impossible. Then I thought to myself: the world is so large and for us it is so small.

I make a decision to go into the well. Perhaps they will not notice. Without giving it much thought I went into the well. The Germans did not notice. The water was already slightly frozen and it was dark in there. I had matches with me which gave a little light. I notice in a corner there lay a basket with sacks of items. I was in water up to my neck. I got to the corner and hid among the sacks. I lay there five hours. It was already night. It is quiet in the courtyard. Being there is not my end goal. I removed two shirts from the sacks and I carefully came into the courtyard. I notice the ghetto patrol walking about. They are whistling and singing on our account.

There already was snow on the ground, so I put a shirt on over my jacket and the second on my head so that it would be like a mask. I dragged myself across the snow to the fence that surrounds the ghetto. I remained lying at the fence for about fifteen minutes. As I lay there, I heard someone coughing on the other side of the fence, indicating that a guard was standing there. I dragged myself to the fence that separates the Christian hospital. It was light in the hospital because of the electricity. Getting out through the fence was not possible. A board could be torn off but that would certainly be heard. I dragged myself to Okonyen's house, took out a gutter with a basket, crept over to the fence, joined together the gutter and the basket like a ladder and threw it over the fence. When I found myself in the field I breathed easier.

[Page 295]

When I checked myself, I myself got frightened. I looked like the living dead. I took off the clothing mask. I ask myself where do I go now? I went on Pshedmyetar to a Christian who used to haul wood for us. His name is Nikadim Mishkevitch. I knock on the door, and the wife opens. When she saw me she screamed: 'Jesus!' The husband heard the shout and he became frightened. He immediately covered the windows and turned on lights. He asks me from where did I come now? I told them I was hidden between the wooden boards, but I don't have any food. That is why I came. I did not tell them the episode with the hiding places from where I had fled. I did not want to frighten them to think there would soon be attacks. They consoled me saying they would hide me. They gave me food. I could not eat, but I did eat in order not to arouse any suspicion. Then they took me to the stable, hid me in the straw. He went back to his house to sleep. The following day he brought me breakfast and asked me how I liked the accommodations. I told him that I liked them a lot and I was then the luckiest person in the world.

About 12 o'clock, I heard shooting from the side of the cemetery. I became frightened. I think that maybe they are shooting the people who yesterday were taken out of the hiding places. Two hours later, the Christian brought me lunch. He was frightened, telling me the entire story. He tells me that yesterday Tsuker came from Bielsk with Gestapo, indicating underground hiding places. They took seventy people out of the hiding places, overnight they placed them in Gotslyevski's prison. Today they take all to the cemetery and shot all seventy together with two Poles, and tells me all their names. I act surprised. I pretend not to know about anything, but in my heart, I know better than him, I was there. When he went away I began to cry.

[Page 296]

After the liberation I met a Jew from Simyatitch[7] and he told me that the Bransk Jews were taken to the Bielsk ghetto and then taken away from there. They convinced them that in Bielsk there would be a work camp and they would remain there. So they sent Tsuker to Bransk with the Gestapo. Tsuker gave the addresses of the hiding–places to bring them to Bielsk. This is how they fooled people."

(This is the letter from Velvl Golde, precisely related.)

Tsuker, under unknown circumstances was later shot. The details are unknown.

This is the history and facts about the Tsuker story.

Footnotes (Rubin Roy Cobb)
1. Traitor
2. She lived in Baltimore. After her husband passed away she married Jack (Yankel) Rubin. Jack, Cynthia and I together with Hymie (Howard) Shapiro (whose parents were also survivors from Bransk) travelled together to Bransk in November 1991 to film the documentary 'Shtetl' about Bransk for PBS.
3. See Map Sheet 2 Number III.
4. Jewish quorum of ten adult men meeting in prayer, the minimum required for public worship.
5. The Torah is read three times a week — on Monday, Thursday and Saturday.
6. Sabbath dish of meat, potatoes and beans, prepared on Friday and kept warm out of respect for the prohibition of cooking on the Sabbath.
7. See Map Sheet 2 Number I.

[Page 297]

The Heroism of Avrume Verpikhovsky

Jewish history is rich with our heroes and holy men who did not lose themselves under the most dangerous circumstances. The greater the danger, the greater was the courage exhibited by our martyrs.

Avrume Verpikhovsky[1]

[Page 298]

With bowed heads and a feeling of our smallness, we stand at the memory of Bransk's greatest hero of all times. His name should be immortalized for all time by Branskers throughout the world with a suitable memorial.

This is a man of the people, a worker who was acknowledged in Bransk by the various organizations, who was vice–president of the Bransk People's Bank (Folksbank), which was a folk institution and on many occasions represented the working man.

Avrume Verpikhovsky did not accept anything as having no importance, and employed his talents and dedication to everything in which he participated. He was one of Bransk's Khevra Kadisha (Jewish Burial Society).

As a member of the Khevra Kadisha he rose to the level of the greatest Bransk folk–hero. This was at the horrific scene when the seventy Bransk Jews who were removed from the cellars of the ghetto with Tsuker's help and were taken to the cemetery to be murdered by Nazi bullets.

Avrume was fifty years old, a cutter and stitcher of shoe–leather by trade. There were older Jews than he on the cemetery.

Alter Trus received these facts from personal conversations he had with the Bransk Christians who were forced to be present on the Bransk Jewish cemetery when all seventy Jews were shot there.

Avrume Verpikhovsky asks the Germans to be the last to be shot. He has a duty, a holy duty to fulfill. He is the Khevra Kadisha member and must do the right thing for the deceased Jews according to Jewish law. The Germans are big–hearted and agree to his request.

With courage, Avrum'ke stands at his post. He lays out the fallen bodies as if for burial, men separate, women separate, and recites verses. How the Christians tell of "his prayers."[2] He takes his time, arranges each person properly. His eyes fill but no tear appears. He says goodbye to each one, closes their eyes with his hand, says goodbye to his wife Sorah, and does not permit anyone to cry. He remains the last at the open pit. He summons a peasant over, an acquaintance, gives him the money he had with him: 'Take this money and with it you should not chase any Jews out who sometimes come to you asking for a piece of bread. Give it to him. I am paying you in advance', and with this he was shot, the last one.

[Page 299]

And so Bransk's greatest hero fell a victim.

The following are the fallen Bransk Jews at this horrific scene:

Shabbat Khomsky 55 years old,	Yekhiel Don 50
Sorah Khomsky 55 years old,	Feygl Don 50
Khaim–Yosl Shapiro 60,	his children 12, 14, 17
Avrum Verpikhovsky 50,	Shloyme Lazer from Bocki 75,
Sorah, his wife 50,	Rokhl Lazer from Bocki 70,
Shlomo Kukafke 50,	Khaim Klode from Bocki 55,
Sorah Kukafke 45,	Klode's three children 6, 11, 8,
Leybke Vainer 55,	Isser Bransky 55,
Mares Leybe Vainer 50,	Yankev Kashtan 25,
Sorah Rubinshteyn, Itskhak Rymer's girl 22,	
Rivka Bialystoksky 25,	Dovid Panitz 55,
Hershl Shroyt, Berl's son 18,	Tsirl his wife 50,
Alter Gadibrotsky's grandchild,	Panitz's girl 17,
Daniel Kagan, Alter Gadavratsky's son–in–law 45,	
Daniel's wife, Alter the Gelen's daughter 42,	
Feyge Kestin 70,	Daniel's child 8,
Shepsl Katlavitch, Khaim Beker's son 22,	

[Page 300]

Maishe Flaisher, the Red
Rooster's[3] son–in–law
25,

His wife 22, her daughter Their two children 2, 5,
Sorah 18,

Avruml Itche Gimpel's
wife 55,

Esther Bransky,   2 children, Braine 15, and
Shakhraike's 45,   Berl 19,

Her son Bertche 16,   Shloyme Smurzshik's
                         younger son 20,

Bayle Vaynshteyn,
Maishe Hersh the Deaf's
daughter about 55,

Shloyme Vaynshteyn, her Leybl Hurwitz and
son 18,   Fraidl's son 25,

The remaining names –
not known.

Shabbat Chomsky

Important activist in all town undertakings - the first to be shot

Footnotes (Rubin Roy Cobb)

1. See Maps Numbers 2 being pages 2/8 and 3/8 under the name of Khomsky; and Number 6 being page 1/2 under the name of Verpikhovsky. The well–kept tombstone that was erected over this mass grave (per Map Number 2 page 3/8) by the Poles of Bransk which last saw when he visited Bransk in 1998 with his son Gavin Aryeh Cobb, and presumably is still there, was erected as two of the captives were Polish [looters]. The only two Jewish names that appear on the tombstone are those of Khomsky and Verpikhovsky. When visited Bransk with Jack (Yankl) Rubin in 1991 we were shown this tombstone and were shocked to see a cross above it as well as flowers arranged in the shape of a cross on the ground above the mass grave. The Poles, Zbigniew Romaniuk and his friend, who showed us the tombstone could see our absolute outrage and removed the portable cross from the top of the tombstone and explained that it was placed there when the anniversary of the murders was commemorated. The flowers forming a cross was unexplained. 68 Jews are murdered but a memorial stone with a cross (albeit portable) is erected and a flowerbed in the shape of a cross above the mass grave is planted because 2 Catholic looters are also buried there!! Ironic isn't it?
2. The word molytve as it appears in the text, is Slavic, and means a Christian prayer.
3. Shimon Rubin was known by this name because he had a large swollen red nose, thus the nickname Red Rooster. He was related to Rubin Roy Cobb through 's paternal grand-mother Gelie (Genia) Rokhel Rubin–Kobylanski.

[Page 301]

The Fire in the Empty Ghetto

There remain only those Jews who are hiding in other cellars of the ghetto because Yeshaye Tsuker did not know of all the hiding places as they had been arranged in the greatest secrecy.

Those Jews who were still in the cellars already knew what had happened to the Jews who had been discovered through Tsuker. Their situation is now even worse, defenseless. They do not venture out of their cellars, they notice the reflections at night that throw fear into the cellars' residents. They understand the ghetto is still well–guarded. There is no talk of trying to get out.

Leybl Polyak's wife starts a fire beneath the houses and stables of Itche Gimpl and Khana Sokolavitch, figuring that in the tumult of the fire, they would succeed in fleeing the ghetto. Regretfully, the plan also didn't work. In the confusion of the fire the ghetto was guarded even more closely.

Those who make an attempt to escape the ghetto are shot by Polish policemen or turned over to the Germans.

During the terrible night of November 15th–16th, 23 victims fell. All paid with their lives for making an attempt to sneak out of the ghetto.

The following paid with their lives on that terrible night:

Leybl Polyak's wife and daughter 17 years old.

At the fence of the ghetto where they were shot:

[Page 302]

Kive Yamshin 24 years, Meir Khaim Kanafyate, 21 years old, Avrum Yentchman, Khaye Sorah Yentchman, Avrume's wife, a 5 year old child who was with Avrume in the hiding place. These three are caught by two Bransk Christians, Stashek Poplovski and Stazshek Kutlinski. They are robbed and turned over to the Germans. Avrume, his wife Khaye Sorah and the unknown child who was with them, are shot near Arke Katsev's house. On the night of the 15th–16th November 1942.

Avrum Burak, Khaim Burak's the butcher's son makes an attempt together with his wife, Yenkl Zavl's daughter and two children to escape, the policeman Zshevutski, notices them and a fight between Avrume and the policeman erupts. Avrum Burak grabs a gendarme by the neck. A shot rings out and Avrume Burak falls. His wife and the two beautiful children are shot near the pharmacy on the night of November 15th.

At Bobe Gershon Berl's in the basement a young woman was shot. No one knew her name. The Christians told this story. Many other names are also not known. The total of 23 victims is confirmed. All 23 were buried by Bransk Christians in the Jewish cemetery.

HershlShpak, the only survivor from the above–mentioned Jews in the ghetto relates the following:

"I hear a shout, it is burning! I notice, it is light. The fire is quite near. At that time I was at Skavronek the shoemaker's in the attic. I am restless. I grab a pail and go to put out the fire. How foolish I was. I am on the street and I encounter two Christian youths. They begin to shout: Oh Hershko! I retreat. I hear shooting, heart–rending screams, dying screams. I already know what this means. I calm down somewhat. I go over to the Christian neighbor Zshire on Shayer Street. They become afraid of me. I tell them that I will leave them. I have no difficulty getting across the fence.

[Page 303]

A little further on, I am noticed by Polish policemen. They are ready to shoot me. Suddenly Ramak, a Christian, Dzhezhinstchikhe's grandchild shouts: "Let Hershke go". They let me go, and several minutes later, I was in the Bransk forest. I lived through everything."

There still remained Jews in the ghetto. On the 20th of November Liebe Jaskolke, Reizl the blacksmith's step daughter with her three year old son Naute were caught by the Germans' agent Mikhal Panashuk, Liebe and her son were shot.

On the 21st November the same Panashuk discovered the hiding place of Jews in the ghetto, in Yenkl Voytek's basement. There was shot Alter Gotlieb, Yankev Yentchman's son–in–law and two children of 11 and 14 years, Yankev Tcheslyak, Yitskhak the baker of buckwheat's (?) son–in–law and his two sons Avreml 19 years and Khaim17 years. This is the record of the Historical Commission at the Bialystok Provincial Committee, according to list number 17/17.

On January 22nd 1947 I entered a complaint in Bialystok against the murderers Panashuk, Zhevutski, Kotlynski, Poplavske. There are no results at this time. Those murdered during the attack and those caught by Panashuk are buried in the Bransk cemetery.

The ruling of the Historical Commission about the Polish policeman Murkowski, a terrible beast, who was known as the murderer of little Jewish children, is noted according to 17/47.

The attack on Jews takes a horrible form. They search for Jews in order to take their money. The rumour is that Jews have a lot of money. To this end, they hated Jews that in previous years had money. (?)

The vulgar men of Shayer Street shot Yosef Kapelotsh, Fishel Spishinger's grandson, 22 years, Leybl Hurvitz, Hershl Hurvitz's son, 28, Leybl Shereshefsky, Alter Shereshefsky's son, Maishe Gusikhe's grandchild 26, and the five year old Shaike Broyde.

[Page 304]

Makofski would wait with his firearm, where little Jewish children would wander about looking for their fathers and mothers. Poor things, they did not know their young innocent lives were about to be ended. This is how Makofski near Shayer Street, caught Yoske Menukhe's grandson of 9 years, Khane Shvartz's grandson 12 years, this Khane Itsl Avrum Ber's.

Both children were neighbours on the street, and both murdered by one bandit.

He also murdered Leybl Burak's son of 16 years.

After the liberation, he was arrested. The result: he was freed. His crimes against Jewish children were not great enough to punish him.

I pressed charges against Markofski, but he is in hiding somewhere.

[Page 305]

The Fate of the Bransk Jews in Neighboring Villages

Alyekshon,[1] Patok, Khaieve,[1] Dolovove,[1] Khoyeve,[1] Glinik, Zanye[1]

Every Bransk resident is familiar with these neighboring villages. Tens of Jews would visit these villages almost daily, doing business with the Christian population there. They were connected through many generations. The older Christians respected the Bransk Jews, visiting their homes as friends, old acquaintances.

The Bransk Jews who fled the ghetto thought they would be safe from the Nazis in the homes of their Christian neighbours. Having nowhere to go, many of the Jews sought out their old village acquaintances.

Regretfully, a new generation grew up in the villages, a generation that absorbed well the former Polish anti–Semitic agitation. These elements now had an opportunity to implement their devilish plans. They were most especially talented in their rush to capture Jews and bring them to the Germans, and to murder them themselves to get rid of them.

The better Christians admonished the Jews: "Why are you running away? You know your generation must disappear." There is no help for this. This was so–called, giving them courage.

Those Jews who had fled the ghetto did not believe they were falling into a terrible fire that in a short two months would wipe out everyone and everything.

[Page 306]

From previous chapters we know what happened to the more than 100 Jews who remained in the ghetto.

Now we will see the fate of the Jews who had fled to the villages around Bransk.

The story of the death of 27 Bransk Jews in the Bransk forest in Kozhe (?) between the villages of Glinik and Zani

This was during the last days of November, 1942. There were about 80 Bransk Jews there in the forest. They lay in trenches, having run away from the Bransk ghetto, unarmed. Provoked by the Christians there suddenly appeared gendarmes accompanied by Polish policemen. People run. The following succeeded in running away: Velvl Halperin, Inditchke's grandchild, Niske Nidelman, Khaim Kevlyaker, Motl Kevlyaker's son, Yisroel Brener, Pesakh the miller's grandchild, Leybl Stelmakh's grandchild and Binyomin Vayinavitch from Benduge.

The gendarmes order everyone out of the trench. They assure them they will take everyone to Bransk. When all of them emerged from the trenches, the gendarmes opened fire with machine guns. Everyone perishes.

I was successful in obtaining a partial list of names. There were some
names I could no longer find.

Motl Vrubel, 65 years old
Hershl Vrubel, 24 years old
Sheyne Halpern, Hindetchke's daughter–in–law, 60 years old
Hershl Halpern, Hinditchke's grandchild, 30 years old
Yerakhmiel Brener, Pesakh Milner's grandchild, 18 years old
Itche Valkavitch, Pesakh Milner's grandchild, 22 years old
Avrum Voynovitch from Benduge, 23 years old
Reyzl, his sister, 28 years old
Feygele, Avrum Voyinovitche's sister–in–law, 30 years old
Khaviva, Feygl's child, 3 years old
Velvl Yerusalimsky, Pesakh the scribe's son, 19 years old
Yosl Broyde, Kesilke Shaike's son, a butcher, 35 years old

[Page 307]

Note Broyde, Yosel's child 8 years old,

Yakhe Susel, Maishe Susel's daughter 25 years old,

Menukhe Hurvitz, Hershl's daughter 27 years old,

A Jew from Sakole, name unknown 40 years old,

Kham Hersh Rotenshteyn, Mendl Toker's son 40 years old

Yankev Rotenshteyn, Enakh Leybl Stylemakh's 40 years old,

Pesakh Kaplan, Shloyme Volfke's son–in–law 47 years old,

Berl Yatz, Shloyme Volfke's son, 50 years old,

Malke Yatz, Berl's girl 18 years old,

Sholemayke the teacher's grandchild 24 years old,

Hershl Pulshanski, Tchebtche's son 18 years old,

Tsalye Broyde, Shayke's grandchild 28 years old,

Berl's daughter Malke Yatz   Berl Yatz
and Shimshon Bransky

I cannot locate the rest of the names. Those few who fled stopped on a small hill and watched and saw the execution. All were buried in the trench. After the liberation all 27 who had perished were brought to the Bransk cemetery for a proper Jewish burial, thanks to Khaim Vrubel's hard efforts.

From the Historical Commission records 17/47, accordingly.

Many Bransk Jews perished by the hand of Bransk commandant, police chief Monik Zavatske.

[Page 308]

Jews would come to Bransk during the night to reclaim from the Christians significant items they had hidden with them, but the Christians did not want to part with these treasures and return them willingly.

Zavatski's[2] victims numbered 12. Regretfully, I can only give the names of: Khaim Piekucki,[3] Babtche's son 16 years old and Yankl Piekucki,[3] Maishe Khanale's son, 23years old.

I filed a complaint against Zavatski with the prosecutor in Bialystok on the 21st of January 1947.

This is how the Polish bandits acted towards the defenseless and weakened Jewish people of Bransk. In addition, their being unorganized and unarmed resulted in a Polish victory over the Jews.

There were still Jews in other villages.

Alyekshon

The village of Alyekshon is located near Bransk in a swampy forest area. Jews who had fled from the ghetto were hiding in these swampy forest areas thinking no one would notice them there.

The Jews did not have any food with them so they were forced to creep out of the swamps to go to the villages to beg for a little bread or to buy some with money.

There were many who actually did give the Jews bread, but the fact remains that Jews were in the neighborhoods and therefore this was common knowledge in the village of Alyekshon.

The Alyekshon village–magistrate Jozef Adamtchik called a village gathering. There he demanded all Christians of the area to not help the 'zhides'[4] in any way. He demanded they capture the Jews, tie them up and bring them to the Germans.

That same evening, Adamtchik forced a number of Christians, and others took this on voluntarily, to participate in a wild chase to capture Jews. They capture, bind the Jews like sheep. They are held, bound in a barn for a couple of days and then the German arrive and shoot all the Jews.

[Page 309]

Eleven Jews were captured in this area. All were shot in Alyekshon on the way to the village of Klikhe.[5]

A second hunt was organized by the same hooligan Adamtchik during which five Jews were captured. These five were taken to Bransk where they were shot.

These are the victims of the bandit Adamtchik:

Esther Oskard, Mordekhay Oskard's daughter–in–law, Yisroel–Khaim's wife 55
   years old,

Mordekhay Oskard, Yisroel–Khaim's son, 5 years old,

Kozak, first name unknown, Maishe Pribut's son–in–law, 56 years old,

Ruben Kozak, grandchild of Maishe Pribut, 20

Leye Kozak, Maishe Pribut's grandchild, 18

Yosl Pribut, Tepltsime's son, 35

Pinye Tchigelsky the barber's son, 26

Yankev Rotnshteyn, Maishe Mendl Toker's son, about 21,

Leybl Rose, Alter Shloyme Hitzl's son who had fled from Bielsk from the train, 12 years old,

Peshe Rozen, Dovid Shmid's grandchild 20 years old

Naftali Awol, Rikl Beeber's[6] grandchild 16 years old,

Shimon Branski, Yoske Menukhe's grandchild, 16 years old

Avrum Davidovitch from Kolnye, Sane's grandchild 30 years old,

Sorah Tabak from Vishonk, her father was some big shot, about 25 years old,

One is unknown.

I submitted this fact to the Bialystok Historical Commission of the Jewish Committee under the number 3–1–47, accordingly. Through the efforts of the commission I submitted a complaint to the court officials. Jozef Adamtchik is arrested, the witnesses against him are those who escaped the grasp of the Alyekshon Christians. They are: Maishe Oskard's, Zakhrye Shnayder's son, whom a friendly Christian sheltered in his home in the town, Khaim Velvl and Yosef Pribut's two brothers, Shmulye Potlover's grandchildren. He resisted them with a pitchfork, sticking those who wanted to approach him. The Christians, young mischief–makers became frightened and scattered. His brother Yosef saved himself by escaping from the stable, hiding beneath a turned over barrel that was standing in the courtyard. Yosef did not survive [see further of later attacks]. The complaints against Jozef Adamtchik were signed by the Bialystok Jewish magistrate Mr Turek. On the basis of the two witnesses, Maishe Oskard and Khaim Velvl Pribut, and my [Alter Trus] signature were the main reasons for the prosecution of the murderers.

[Page 310]

Mr Burshteyn, the current president of the Provincial Committee in Bialystok, sent me a notice that Adamtchik had been arrested.

Remarks by Julius Cohen:

'The relief committee in New York has photocopies of all the reports and complaints against the Polish bandits who participated in helping to murder Jews.

The complaints were signed by all the witnesses who were present at these scenes. The most responsible for bringing these Jewish murderers to the court is Alter Trus, who did not allow anything to get in his way. Threats did not deter him from his purpose. The sworn witnesses also behaved like true heroes because their lives were also in danger and yet, the refugee remnant of Bransk Jews brought to the court numerous murderers of Jews among whom was Jozef Adamchik. We include herewith the sworn photocopies of the complaints. Now, March 9th, (1948). I received a notice from the Bialystok Historical Committee in which they inform me that Jozef Adamtchik was sentenced to death by hanging on February 27, 1948. The sworn testimonies of Bransk Jews played an important role at the trial which lasted three days. A heartfelt thanks to you, Bransk courageous heroes, for your brave stance.

We have more than 30 pages of photocopies documents. Due to the heavy costs of reproducing them in this book, we included only the letters that are in regard to the complaint against Adamtchik.

[Page 311]

On the 1st March, 1948 the trials of the murderous Ritch[7] brothers of Khayeve began as well as that of the bandit Kaminski, when the book was already at the printer. Therefore we do not know whether we will be able to bring the results of the trials in time.'

The slaughters near Patok, Khaieve, Dolokhove

There were Jews hiding in the village of Patok. They had fled from the Bransk ghetto.

Two Patok Christians, the brothers Toyur, captured the Jews. Half–dead, beaten and bound, they brought them to Bransk to the gendarmes where they were shot. Following are the victims: Leyzer Skavronek, Ahron Tcheslyer's son–in–law, 60 years old, Manes Skavronek Leyzer's son 23 years old, Nisl, another son, 21 years old, and a Jewish youth from Lapy, name unknown, 25.

In the summer of 1943 the partisan detachment was already organized to some degree. They came to Potok at night seeking food and the same two Toyur brothers captured Yankev Olyentsky (Maishe Alyentsky's son) 30 years old. Somehow, their pistol did not work properly, so they gave him a good beating and brought him to the gendarmes. The gendarmes gave him an additional beating, trying to force him into giving up the names of the other partisans. The partisans had already evacuated the area. Yankev Olyentsky is shot in the forest as they went to the hiding–place. The partisans buried him after the liberation, bringing him to a proper Jewish burial on the Bransk cemetery.

I registered a complaint against the two brothers Toyur to the prosecutor on the 7th January, 1947, with the stated reasons of the Jewish Historical Commission in Bialystok, No. 7/47, accordingly.

The brothers Toyur were arrested.

Khaieve

In the village of Khaieve at the end of November there were Bransker who had fled, the Krukofsky family, the family is attacked by a band of Christians, the brothers Dlugolenski and others. They are beaten, bound up and brought to the gendarmes at Rutke,[8] and there they were shot there. The following are the victims:

[Page 312]

Yosl Krukofsky, 53 years old,

Leybl, Yosl Krupskiy's son 21 years old,

Khana, Yosl's daughter 24years old,

A child of 9 years old,

And Krukofsky's brother with the nickname of Tegale 25 years old,

Right: Rubele, the rabbi's grandchild,
Centre: Avrum Grazhinsky's son,
Left: Maishe Taker's girl

Yankev Alyenktsy

I brought in a complaint against the Christians through the Jewish Historical Commission in Bialystok List Number 7/47 accordingly. Up to this day, there has been no word of any results. There is missing evidence.

Dolovove[9] – In this village during the month of December there were attacks by Christians whose names we were unable to determine. Upon the following Jews: Berl Pam, Kopke's grandchild 25 years old, Elye Rubinshteyn, Zavl–Hersh Khasid's grandchild 23 years old and Itche Rhymer's son 23 years old, they were all victims of this attack.

The following were murdered by Lyeshnik Koshak and his helper Yohanutch.

These were armed leshykes (forest guards) at Ploneve–Spishin. These are their victims:

Ayzik Vaynshteyn, the deaf Maishe Hersh's son–in–law 52 years, bound and brought to the Bransk gendarmes and shot.

Yosl Okronglye, Berl Klikher's son, 21 years old,

Yosl Pribut, Leyzer Schmidt's son, 55 years old,

Yosl's daughter, Toyve 20 years old,

and Khana Esther Pribut 18 years old.

[Page 313]

In the village of Klikhe[10] the Lyeshnikes murdered Yosl Pribut's two little children, In the village of Klikhe, the lyetchnikes murdered Yosl Pribut's two little children Yenkl 10 years old and Mordekhay eight years old. They robbed and murdered the Bransk Jewish attorney and his wife. They also captured and bound Maishe Lyev 24 years old, Puder's grandchild, brought him to the gendarmes who shot him.

Maishe the quilter, Volkovitch, Pesakh Milner's son 60 years old, Bashke, Maishe the quilter's wife, 52 years old were also murdered by them.

They stalked and attacked the 2 brothers Goldvaser, Mende Leyb 65 years old and Leyzer 54 years old, Meir Khilikhe's sons. The two brothers escaped. They were later captured by the Germans and shot.

Also in 1943 they caught Nokhum Kleinot, Elber the shoemaker's son 30 years old, wounded and brought to the gendarmes to be shot.

This Koshak[11] at the beginning of 1944 was handed a death sentence by the partisans, which was carried out.

I entered a complaint against Yohanushen through the Jewish Historical Commission to the prosecutor, Number 5/47 et seq, accordingly. To my regret, he is in hiding.

The Death of Yosl Shpitalne – Yosl Shpitalne 21 years old, was the only one of the family to survive when all the others were taken to Treblinka. His father–mother and another brother, a teacher. He was alone, remaining in the liquidated ghetto, he always took his better belongings to a Christian acquaintance, Trushkofske. This Trushkofske at that time lived in a colony near the forest near Bransk.

Young Yosl always came to Trushkofske for a little bit of money or clothes.

[Page 314]

Trukofske wants to get rid of Yosl so that he can keep everything. When Yosl once came to him he gave him a good meal and then asked him to go to the barn to thresh and clean the corn. Yosl did this. Trukofske went to Bransk, within a short while, Trukofske returns with the infamous murderer Markofski, the Polish–German policeman.

Yosl Shpitalne now sees his tragedy. Markofski orders Yosl to run, Yosl begins to run, and Markofski aims his revolver, and shoots Yosl in the back. Yosl Shpitalne falls dead with the first shot, after accomplishing this piece of work Trukofske feels assured of keeping the Jewish miller's belongings. There will no longer be anyone to claim or inherit anything. He prepares the table and he and Markofski enjoy a drink together while the gramophone plays, 100 feet from where lay Yosl Shpitalne's body in a pool of blood. No one is punished, Markofski cannot be found.

Khayeve – Three sturdily–built Bransk Jews were hiding in the village of Khayeve, big heroes. They were, Bertche Yentchman 35 years old, Yenkl's son, Shlome –Hersh the khasid's grandchild, and the Portseleynik's two grandchildren Pesakh Yosl Toptchevsky 40 years old and Nokhum Leizer Toptchevsky 24 years old.

The Soltis Kaminski and the Ritch[12] brothers organized an attack on them in which 20 Christians participated. They mounted a strong defense, but at the end they were overcome. They took their money, bound them and took them on wagons to the Bransk gendarmes. They are shot there near the river, not even being properly buried. The foxes tore the bodies apart.

Not far from the village of Khayeve, there were hidden in a trench in the field Khana Yentchman 22 years old, Khaytche Yentchman 32 years old, Bobtche's daughter and Riva Leye Tcheslyak 45 years old, Itskhak the baker of buckwheat cake/rice's daughter. The Khayeve Christians were very friendly with them. The Ritch[13] brothers, Poles from the village of Khayeve, attacked them, robbed them, undressed them naked and shot them. They fell into the same trench in which they had been hiding.

[Page 315]

Riva Leah Tcheslyak

Bertche Yentchman

Itskhak Kashnik's daughter and son–in–law ????

The Ritchs kept hidden the belongings of those who had been murdered, wanting to be certain of their inheritance. At this same time, they noticed in the Nuretz River the floating bodies of Yenkl Yentchman, Shloyme–Hersh the khasid's son, 70 (?) years old the top criminals charged. It was confirmed that the Ritch brothers also did this because Yenkl's belongings were hidden by them.

Sometime later the body of Maishe Smurzshik, Leyzer Katsev's grandchild 20 years old was found in the river. This too, was a murder committed by the Khayeve Christians, the Ritch brothers, because it was known that Maishe Smurzshik was hiding with them.

The drowned bodies were found tied up, hands and feet, first murdered and then tossed into the river.

While compiling the material against Kaminski and the Ritch brothers, the Historical Commission personally listened to Bransk survivors: Yankl Rubin,[19] Leybl Trus, Leybl Pribut, Maishe Oskard, Khana Okon and Maishe Yentchman. On January 22nd, 1947, the investigation was concluded and sent to the prosecutor of the Bialystok Regional Court as per record number 7/47. Regrettably, neither Kaminski nor the Ritch brothers could be found. They were in hiding.

On January 9th, the Bransk Jews Fishl Gruder and Avrume Pyetkover saw Kaminski in Bielsk. Kaminski was detained by Avrume Pyetkover. The Bielsk police did not have any information regarding Kaminski and wanted to release him, so they called me [Alter Trus] on the telephone in Bialystok and told me the story. I immediately contacted the President of the Bialystok Jewish Regional Committee, Magistrate Turek. This resulted in the prosecutor ordering the detention of Kaminski. This is how Kamkinski was arrested through the help of Fishl Gruder and Avrume Pyetkever.

The Ritch brothers were arrested in July, 1947. Their trial will take place in 1948.

Others of those who had fled, older people, could not accommodate to living in the cold and wet forests. Their old bones simply could not suffer through such a life. The frosty nights and wet mud during the day ravaged their bodies and they could not even stand on their feet any more. Christians did not want to take them into their homes. People such as these begged the Christians to take them to Bransk. They did not want to die somewhere in the protected forests. If they were to die, let it be by German bullets, at least let it be in Bransk in their home.

[Page 322]

Hershl Firshkhaler
This photo was sent by a Christian who knew him

Yosl Firshkhaler

Maishe Pribut, Maishe, Elye Dovid's the Damsker tailor in his 80s year, cannot remain in the forest, cannot tolerate the cold that is wreaking havoc with his 80 year old crooked bones. He dragged himself around to the village of Voytke with his daughter Rikl. He begs the Christians to take him to Bransk. He wants to die in Bransk. The Christians bring the 80–year old broken man to Bransk, turn him over to the gendarmes. Maishe Pribut is not frightened. He asks the Germans to shoot him on the cemetery. His request is fulfilled. Maishe dies by Nazi bullets, satisfied.

Mirke Noske Katsev's daughter and two children and Bere Leibishe's two daughters wander around. No one will take them in after they left the ghetto. They return and turn themselves over to the gendarmes. Their fate is unknown. They go together with the Bransk community to Bielsk on November 7th 1942 to the burning gas chambers and crematoria.

[Page 323]

Bransk After Removing the Jews to the Gas Chambers

The Christians of Bransk and neighboring areas grabbed Jewish belongings like hungry wolves. They dressed in Jewish costumes, overcoats, took to their homes Jewish furniture, linens and bedding. Even though the ghetto was still guarded, the Christians still entered, rummaging in the Jewish houses.

Moshe–Berl Penkherzh

Khaim Verpikhovski

The Germans claimed the best things for themselves, and divided the rest as a reward for helping to capture and murder Jews. They also sold all the items that had been brought in as collateral, and the Christians made haste to get bargains.

Many Jewish homes were sold. The Christians tore them down and built their own houses from the material of the old. They sold the houses for groshens. If someone had helped to capture Jews he earned the right to be the first to buy. In this way, the New House–Of–Prayer/Study was sold, Avrum Abe the turner's house, Hershl Burak's house, Leyzer Rubin's[20] house, Mordekhay Sherer's, Khaim Katlavitche's, Berl Baker's and Itche Gimpl's houses, Avrume Ripke's and Yankitchke's houses and many others, were sold.

[Page 324]

We must note here about the swindles the Christians pulled on the Jews. They took small Jewish children to hide in their homes. Demanded to be paid in dollars and good clothing. At the end when they had received everything, they took the children to the gendarmes.

This happened with Kive Yamshin's 2 ½ year old child. They took 200 dollars from them and afterwards took the child to the gendarmes. They, the gendarmes played with the nice little boy, gave him food and entertaining themselves with him, they shot the innocent child. Brakha Shpak,[21] who was married to Bevl Pam took their child to a Christian to be raised, paid good money for this. The child was brought to the gendarmes as a gift and was shot. Fishl Lyev Itche Orliarnik's son gave the child who had been left without a mother, a six–year old little girl, to Christians for a goodly amount of money. The child was turned over to the Germans and was shot. The mother of the child, Dyntshe Zeifman's had been killed on September 7th by German airplanes.

Khaim and Matl Finklshteyn, Rokhke's from Benduge gave their three–year old little girl to a Christian from the Taptchever area, paying good money. They took the money and the child was brought to the Germans to be shot.

The Jewish cemetery was vandalized. The fences were taken apart by Bransk and Brezhnitser Christians. The headstones were taken down to be used as sidewalks from the stable to the house. Others made them into grinding stones. Everything that had been Jewish was destroyed.[17] Even the Jewish dead were desecrated.

This is how in the year 1942, only in two months, so much was destroyed. This is the report about the eight weeks of November 2nd 1942 until the end of the year.

We will begin the year 1943 in the following chapters.

Footnotes (Rubin Roy Cobb)
1. See Maps Section 2 Page II.
2. When Rubin Roy Cobb travelled to Bransk with Jack (Yankel) Rubin [related to through his paternal grandmother Gelie (Geni) Rokhel Rubin–Kobylanski] to film the documentary "Shtetl" for PBS in October 1991, at the end of the visit as we were already sitting on the bus to depart, Jack Rubin got off the bus to greet an elderly Pole bent over with a walking stick. believes this might have been Zavatski or maybe some other Polish policeman that was active in Bransk during November 1942. After he shook his hand and then reprimanded or asked whether or not he had a conscience I don't know. He told us when he returned to the bus that this former Polish policeman said to him that if the Jews had left the ghetto earlier they would have survived!
3. Related to Rubin Roy Cobb through his maternal grandmother Henye Rivka (Anni) Piekucki–Skornik.
4. Derogatory word for 'Jew' in Polish.
5. See Maps Section 2 Page II.
6. See Maps Section 2 Page II.
7. Sister of Rubin Roy Cobb's paternal grandmother Gelie (Genia) Rokhel Rubin–Kobylanski whose family lives in Atlanta, GA today.
8. In the PBS documentary Shtetl shot in 1991 in Bransk, the producer interviews the surviving Ritch brother who shows no remorse whatsoever.
9. See Maps Section 2 Page II.
10. See Maps Section 2 Page II.
11. See Page 312.
12. The surviving Ritch brother was interviewed by Marian Marzynski during the shooting of the PBS documentary 'Shtetl' produced/directed by him on 10/11/1991. Ritch showed no remorse whatsoever.
13. Yankel Rubin (aka John Rubin) lived in Melbourne, Australia when he left Bialystok, Poland 'in a hurry' in 1967. His father was a brother of Rubin Roy Cobb's paternal grandmother.
14. A brother of Rubin Roy Cobb's paternal grandmother.
15. Related to Rubin Roy Cobb through his paternal grandmother Gelie (Gelia) Rokhel Rubin–Kobylanski
16. Related to Rubin Roy Cobb through his paternal grandmother Gelie (Gelia) Rokhel Rubin–Kobylanski
17. Related to Rubin Roy Cobb through his paternal grandmother Gelie (Gelia) Rokhel Rubin–Kobylanski met him in Melbourne, Vic., Australia in the 1990s. He was known as 'John' Rubin and was the first cousin of 'Jack' Rubin of Baltimore, MD.
18. When visited Bransk with Jack Rubin in 1991 he was shown the entry to the barn where they are buried.
19. Yankel Rubin (aka John Rubin) lived in Melbourne, Australia when he left Bialystok, Poland 'in a hurry' in 1967. His father was a brother of Rubin Roy Cobb's paternal grandmother.
20. Rubin Roy Cobb met Brakha Shpak at a celebration (wedding or bar mitzvah) given by Evelyn Silverboard (nee Iteld) in Atlanta in the 1990s. She and her husband found refuge in Cuba after the war and became very wealthy, but when Castro came to power they had to flee once again penniless, this time to Charlotte, NC where once more they were successful. She believed that a baby of hers whose body was never ever found was taken by Poles and raised as a Pole without knowing of its Jewish origin.
21. Evidence of this is seen in the PBS documentary 'Shtetl' produced/directed by Marian Marzynski on 10/11/1991.

The following pages (316 to 320) were inserted but are a separate section onto themselves and are placed here {note by Joel Alpert}.

Pages 316 to 320 inclusive were translated by Ania Zilberkant and edited by Rubin Roy Cobb

Pieces of a torn passport
All that remains of Dovid Yentchman's family

WOJEWODZKA
ŻYD.KOMISJA HISTORYCZNA
BIAŁYSTOK, dnia...........
L.p.....................

Zeznanie Prybuta Arie-Lejba

o mordach dokonywanych na brańskich Żydach przy pomocy miejscowej
ludności.

Prybut Arie-Lejb, urodzony w Brańsku w 1907 r., z zawodu rolnik,
przebywał w brańskim ghetcie, następnie w partyzantce. Obecnie zamieszkuje w Białystoku, Nowy Świat 23.

Świadek zeznaje, że sołtys wsi Oleksin, gmina Brańsk, powiat
Bielsk-Podlaski, Adamczuk Józef, oraz pomocnicy jego Byczkowski
Bolesław i Nieróda Edward w nocy 14 na 15 grudnia 1942 r. na
własną rękę (Niemcy nie brali udziału) urządzili łapankę na Żydów,
którzy zdołali uratować się z akcji urządzonej przez Niemców 2-go
listopada 1942 r.
Zebrali 16 Żydów, imiona ich są następujące:
1. Oskard Batera, lat 40
2. Oskard Mordchaj, lat 5
3. Oskard Sara, lat 16
4. Kozak Liba   lat 48
5. Kozak Rubin lat 19
6. Kozak Leja   lat 17
7. Prybut Moel (przezwisko Cynes), lat 52
8. Szczygielski Pinia, lat 23
9. Hotamsztajn Jankiel, lat 21
10. Chawal Naftoli, lat 17
11. Dawidowicz Abram z Kolna, lat 18
12. Tabak Sora, lat 23
13. Rozen Pesach, lat 20
14. Rozen Lejb, lat 15
15. Brajnski Szymszon, lat 14

Nazwiska jednego Żyda świadek nie pamięta.
Podczas likwidacji ghetta w Brańsku, wyżej wymienieni Żydzi
zdołali uciec, łamiąc płot ghettowy, przepłynęli rzekę Nurzec
i zdali się w stronę wsi Poświny i Oleksin.
Ciekawy jest fakt wiejski.Rosse Lejba z pociągu wiozącego
Żydów do Treblinki. Wyskoczył z pociągu, pieszo przyszedł do wsi
Oleksin. W ciągu dwóch tygodni był ukrywany przez gospodarzy Oleksina. Należy zaznaczyć, że gospodarze Oleksina wykopali jemu duże
serce, codzień karmił go inny gospodarz, a gdy Adamczuk Józef przyszedł chłopca zabrał, leżał w łóżku, gospodarz Jaworowski sprzeciwił
się, nie chciał go oddać.
Pomocnik Adamczuka, Byczkowski Bolesław, wyciągnął go siłą za
nogi z pościeli i nagiego poprowadził.
Skydor Ludwik, gospodarz wsi Oleksin znalazł w swojej stodole
Kozak Libe, Kozaka Rubena i Kozak Leje, własnoręcznie związał tych
ludzi i oddał w ręce Adamczukowi.
Ogorek, gospodarz wsi Oleksin, szwagier sołtysa popędził konno
galopem do Brańska po żandarmerię.Czy pojechał po swojej woli, czy
był zmuszony przez Adamczuka świadek nie może stwierdzić.
Wszystkich wyłapanych Żydów Adamczuk zamknął w Ogorka w spich-
rzu. Trzymali ich związanych w zamknięciu dopóki nie przyszli Niemcy.
Niemcy dali rozkaz, żeby nieszczęśni Żydzi wykopali dla siebie
mogiłę przy pierwszej znniej za gościńcu, który prowadzi z Oleksina do Klichów.
Z wyżej wymienionych Żydów Niemcy zastrzelili 11-tu.Pomoc-
nicy Adamczuka mogiłę zasypali.
Pięciu ludzi: Kozak Leje, Kozaka Rubena, Kozak Libe, Rozen
Pesto i Brańskiego Szymszona, związanych dostarczono do brańskiej
żandarmerii, gdzie zostali również w kilka dni później rozstrzelani.
Ci 5-ciu nie zostali odrazu zgładzeni, gdyż obiecali dać
złoto, które było aby schowane w Brańsku.
Jednocześnie świadek stwierdza, że Adamczuk i Byczkowski
Bolesław zamordowali 2 Sowietów. Jeden z Sowietów chował się
u gospodarza Szafrana w kolonii Oleksin, drugim gospodarza De-
mina w tejże kolonii. W nocy ci dwaj poszli do wioski, tam przy-
łapali ich Adamczuk z Byczkowskim, zastrzelili i własnoręcznie
pochowali na Konstupil (teren wsi Oleksin).
To wszystkie fakty może potwierdzić Symajło Jakob, który
przeżył razem z świadkiem w lasach, a obecnie znajduje się
w Białystoku, Nowy Świat 23.

Świadek   _p̲r̲y̲b̲u̲t̲_   Protokolant
                                                         Mgr.B.Faks
                                                         1947

Przewodniczący
Woj.Żyd.Komisji Historycznej
Mgr.M.Turek

Authority

Jewish Historical Commission

Bialystok, ? 1947

p. 3/47

<u>Aryeh–Lejb Prybut Complaint</u>

Testimony of Arie Lejb Prybut regarding the murder of the Jews of Bransk committed with the assistance of local residents.

Prybut Arie Lejb, born in 1907 in Bransk, farmer by trade; lived in the local ghetto before joining the underground army. He currently resides in Bialystok, on 23 Nowy Swiat Street.

According to the witness' accounts, on the night of December 14, 1942 Jozef Adamczuk, the village headman from Oleksin, located in Bielsk–Podlaski district, and his two henchmen, Boleslaw Byczkowski and Edward Nieroda, on their own initiative (without the Germans' participation) carried out a roundup of Jews who had managed to escape a massacre carried out by the Germans on November 2, 1942.

They captured the following 16 Jews:

> Ester Oskard, age 40
>
> Mordechaj Oskard, age 5
>
> Sara Oskard, age 16
>
> Liba Kozak, age 48
>
> Rubin Kozak, age 19
>
> Leja Kozak, age 17
>
> Joel Prybut, (nickname Tsynes), age 32
>
> Pinia Szczygielsky, age 23
>
> Jankiel Rotenshtejn, age 21
>
> Naftoli Chawal, age 17

Abram Dawidowicz from Kolno, age 18

Sora Tabak, age 23

Pesza Rozen, age 20

Lejb Rosse, age 15

Szymszon Brajnsky, age 14

The witness does not recall the name of one of the victims.

During the liquidation of the Bransk ghetto, the above mentioned Jews managed to escape by breaking through the Ghetto wall and swimming across the river Nurzec toward the villages of Poplawy and Oleksin.

Lejb Rosse managed to escape from the train carrying Jews to the concentration camp in Treblinka. He jumped from the train and walked to the village of Oleksin. Over the period of two weeks he was helped by the local farmers who took turns providing him with food and shelter. When Jozef Adamczuk came to take the boy away, the farmer who was hiding him that night refused to give him up.

Adamczuk and his henchman Boleslaw Byczkowski, forcefully removed the boy from the bed where he was sleeping not allowing him to even get dressed.

Ludwik Szydor, another farmer from Oleksin, after he discovered Liba Rubin,[14] and Leja Kozak hiding in his barn, he tied them up and turned them over to Adamczuk.

Another farmer from Oleksin by the name of Ogorek, (Jozef Adamczuk's brother–in–law) rushed on horseback to Bransk to call the gendarmes. The witness did not know if Ogorek did it on his own accord or if he was forced to do so by Adamczuk.

All the Jews who were captured were tied up and kept in Ogorek's barn until the arrival of the Germans.

The Germans made the captured males dig a grave by the road from Oleksin to Klichow and shot eleven of the Jews listed above. Following the killing, Adamczuk's henchmen buried the victims.

Five of the victims, Leja Rubin,[15] and Liba Kozak, Pesze Rozen, and Szymszon Bransky were taken to the gendarme headquarters in Bransk where they were also shot a few days later.

The reason why they were not killed right away was that they promised to turn over the gold that had allegedly hidden in Bransk.

The witness also testified that Adamczuk and Byczkowski were responsible for killing two Soviets who were hiding in nearby farms owned by a couple of local farmers by the name of Szafran and Demian. Adamczuka and Byczkowski shot them and buried them in Konotopja (part of Oleksin).

All these facts can be confirmed by Jakob Symojla, who survived the war hiding in the woods with the witness, Arie Lejb Prybut, Bialystok, on 23 Nowy Swiat Street.

Signatures *A.L.Prybut* Recorder

B.Fuke

Mgr. Fuke Court reporter

Head of the Jewish Historical Commission

Mgr. M. Turek

[Page 317]

Do

Wojew.Komitetu Żydowskiego

w Białymstoku

Od Altera Trusa zam.w
B-stoku przy ul.Pieknej 2
prezesa koła ziomków z m.
Branska w Białymstoku

P O D A N I E
- - - - - - -

Jestem w posiadaniu materiału opisującego likwidacja
Żydów m.Branska,miedzy innymi figuruje nazwisko Adamczuka Józefa
ktory był za czasów niemieckich sołtysem wsi Oleksin gm.Bransk
pow. Bielak-Podlaski,ktory współpracował z niemcami przy wyłapywaniu
ukrywajacych sie Żydów w lesie i w terenie,oraz zmuszał swoich ludzi
do pomagania mu.Wyłapywanych Żydów związywał i dostarczał do poblis-
kiej żandarmerii.gdzie zostawali rozstrzeliwani.

Podaje liste ofiar,które zginely z jego reki:

Oskard Estra 1.40
Oskard Mordko 1.5
Oskard Sora 1.16
Mozak Liba 1.46
Kozak Ruwin 1.19
Kozak Laja 1.17
Prybut Josel 1.32 (przezwisko "Cymes")
Szpzygielski Pinia 1.23
Rotensztejn Jankiel 1.21
Chawel Naftali 1. 17
Dawidowicz Abram 1.18 (z Kolna)
Tabak Sora 1. 23
Bozen Fesza 1. 20
Rozza Lajb 1. 15
Branski Szymszon 1.14

Co moge stwierdzić nastepujacy swiadkowie:
Moszka Jeszmien Wroclaw ul.Sępa-Szarzynskiego 6/4
Oskard Doszko B-stok " Piekna 2
Trus Lajo B-stok ul. Piekna 2
Oledzki Abe " " Rabinska 16
Alpern Wolf " " Rabinska 13
Okon Chana " " Mazowiecka 1
Prybut Arja Lajb " " N-Swiat 29
Dasiaziuk sołtys wsi Bruchaty gm.Bransk
Byczkowski Cieniek wies Oleksin gm.Bransk
Turaski wojt gm.Bransk

Prezes Koła ziomków Branskich
w B-stoku

Alter Trus /

Complaint Against Adamtchik Attested to By Witnesses

Bialystok, December 2, 1946

To: Jewish Committee

in Bialystok

From: Alter Trus

residing on Piekna Street 2

?????

Bransk in province of Bialystok

STATEMENT

I am in possession of documents describing the liquidation of Jews in Bransk. One of the names being mentioned is that of Jozef Adamczuk who was the village headman in Oleksin, in Bransk County, Bielsk–Podlaski Region. He cooperated with the German in rounding up the Jews who were hiding in the nearby forests and in the village. He forced other residents to help him. He tied up the captured Jews and delivered them to nearby gendarmes where they were shot.

The names of the victims are listed below:

Estera Oskars, age 40

Mordko Orkard, age 5

Sora Oskard, age 16

Liba Kozak, age 48

Ruwim Kozak, age 19

Leja Kozak, age 17

Josel Prybut (nicknamed Tsymes), age 32

Pinia Szczygielsky, age 23

Jankiel Rotensztejn, age 21

Naftoli Chawol, age 17

Abram Dawidowicz (from Kolno), age 18

Sora Tabak, age 23

Pesza Rozen, age 20

Jejb Rosse, age 15

Szymszon Bransky, age 14

This can be confirmed by the following witnesses:

Moszko Jeczmien, Bialystok, 56/4 Sepa– Starzynski Street

Moszko Oskard, Bialystok, 2 Piekna Street

Lejo Trus, Bialystok, 2 Piekna Street

Aba Oledzky, Bialystok, 16 Habinska Street

Wolf Alpern, Bialystok, 13 Habinska Street

Chawa Okon, Bialystok, 1 Mowiecka Street

Lejb Arje Prybut, Bialystok, 29 Nowy Swiat Street

Dawidzuik, village headman from Bruchaty, Bransk County

Cieniek Ryczkiwsky, from Oleksin, Bransk County

Wojt Hurasky, Bransk County

Head of the Jewish Community of Bransk

Bialystok

Alter Trus

[Page 318]

WOJEWODZKA
ŻYD.KOMISJA HISTORYCZNA
BIAŁYSTOK, dnia.7.X./47
L.p....714...

Do
Wojewodzkiej Żydowskiej Komisji Historycznej

w Białymstoku
————————————

Od Trusa Altera b.mieszkanca m.Bransk,
prezesa Koła Żydow branskich w B-stoku.
Obecnie zamieszkuje w B-stoku, Piekna 2.

P O D A N I E
————————————

W zebranych przezemnie materiałach o likwidacji branskich
Żydow figuruje nazwisko Pietraszko. Pietraszko za czasow niemieckiej
okupacji był sołtysem we wsi Pietraszko, gmina Bransk, powiat
Bielsk-Podlaski. Zajmował sie dobrowolnie wyłapywaniem [...].
Na wieś Pietraszko na poczatku 1943 r. przyszli dwaj Żydzi,
bracia Ptak (przezwisko Baltorze) Joel lat 27 szewc i Karol lat 24,
krawiec, zamienic ubranie na chleb. Schowali sie w lesie na terenie
wyżej wymienionej wsi. Sołtys Pietraszko sledził za nimi, zatrzymał
ich, zmusił swoich ludzi do zwiazania ich, przyprowadził żandarmerie,
poprowadził ofiary na pole ze strony Domachowa, razem z żandarmeria
rozebrał Żydow do naga, rozstrzelał i pochował tamze. Dostał ubranie
zamordowanych Żydow, jako wynagrodzenie za swoja "prace".
Pietraszko sledził za 2 dumi przechowujacymi sie na terenie
swojej wsi.
Wysledził w lesie schron, w ktorym ukrywali sie Sliwko Mendel
lat 30, kolesnik, Rybko Chaim-Rubin stolarz, oboje z Branska. Sprowa-
dził żandarmerie do schronu, tam rozebrano obu Żydow do naga i roz-
strzelano. Ubrania dostał Pietraszko.
Zajmował sie rowniez wyłapywaniem ukrywajacych sie Sowietow,
tych odprowadzał do żandarmerii. Bransk partyzancki oddział im.
Żukowa, ktoremu była wiadoma jego mordercza robota, poszukiwała go,
ale nie dał sie złapac, ukrywał sie.
Należy zaznaczyc, ze miejscowa ludnosc była przeciwna działal-
nosci oskarzonego.

Podaje swiadkow, ktorzy moga powyzsze fakty stwierdzic.

1. Oskard Moszko, mieszkaniec Białegostoku, Piekna 2
2. Segmien Moszko   "   Wrocławia, Hupa-Barzynskiego 56 m4
3. Tykocki Moszko   "   Szczecina

A.Trus
Prezes Koła Branskich Żydow w B-stoku.
Były prezes Zarzadu gminy wyznaniowo-
zydowskiej w Bransku.

Przewodniczacy   Protokolant
Woj.Żyd.Komisji Historycznej   Mgr.B.Fuks
Mgr.M.Turek

Complaint Against Pyetroske

Brought by Maishe Oskard, Maishe Yentchman and Maishe Tikotsky

PROVINCE

DISTRICT HISTORICAL COMMISSION FOR JEWISH AFFAIRS

BIALYSTOK date 7–1–1947

Page 6'42

Province Historical Commission For Jewish Affairs

Bialystok

From: Alter Trus, former resident of Bransk,

Head, Bransk Jewish Association in Bialystok

Now residing in Bialystok, 2 Piekna Street

TESTIMONY

The name of Pietraszko appears repeatedly among the documents I collected pertaining to the liquidation of the Bransk Jews. During the German occupation Piretraszko was the village headman in Pietraszko, county Bransk, Region Bielsk –Podlaski.

On his own accord he captured Jews. Early in 1943 two Jews, brothers by the name Ptak, came to the village. Joel was 27 and Zawel 24, tailor by trade. They came to exchange clothes for bread. They were hiding in the forest near the village. Pietraszko followed them, stopped them and forced some village men to tie them up. He called up some gendarmes and with their help he lead the victims to the fields outside the village, stripped them naked, shot them and buried them. As a reward he was allowed to keep the victims' clothing.

Pietruszko searched for Jews who might have been hiding in the area surrounding the village.

He found a shelter in the forest that was occupied by Mendel Sliwko, age 30, Kolensnik Rybka and Khaim Rubin,[16] carpenter, both from Bransk. Again he called the gendarmes to the shelter, stripped both victims naked and shot them. He kept their clothes

Pietraszko also captured some Soviets hiding in the village whom he turned over to the gendarmes. The unit of the underground army was searching for him to retaliate for his murders, Pietraszko, however, was able evade them. It is important to note that the local population was against Pietraszko's actions.

Listed below are the names of witnesses who can verify this testimony:

Moszko Oskard, residing at 2 Piekna St, Bialystok

Moszko Jeczmien, residing at 56/4 Sep–Starzynski Street, Wroclaw

Moszko Tykocky, residing in Szczecin

Alter Trus

Chairman of the Bransk Jews Association in Bialystok,

Former Head of the Jewish Community of Bransk

*A.Trus*c Court reporter Recorder

Head of Jewish Historical Commission Mgr. B.Fuks

Mgr. M. Turek

[Page 319]

WOJEWODZKA
ŻYD. KOMISJA HISTORYCZNA
BIAŁYSTOK, dnia. ....
L.p...........

Do
Wojewodzkiej Żydowskiej Komisji Historycznej

w Białymstoku

Od Trus. Altera b.mieszkańca m.Branska
prezesa Koła Żydów branskich w B-stoku.
Obecnie zamieszkuje w B-stoku, Piekna 2.

P O D A N I E

We wsi Patoki, gmina Brańsk, powiat Bielsk-Podlaski dwaj bracia Taur, jeden krawiec, drugi kowal pracowali ...., etc.
Zajmowali się wyłapywaniem Żydów wśród woli mieszkańców ... i sołtysa Sobolewskiego.
Na drugi dzień po likwidacji ghetta w Brańsku bracia Taur strzelili dwóch Żydów branskich Skavrenka Lajzera lat 55, właściciela .... elewatorowego i syna jego Skavrenka Lamesa lat 19. Zwięzali ich, zameldowali o nich sołtysowi, żeby dostarczył do Brańska. Sołtys odmówił. Sami sprowadzili Niemców, razem z Niemcami zabili dwóch wyżej wspomnianych Żydów.

W końcu 1943 r. Jankiel Olendski przyszedł na wieś Patoki po chleb, ukrywał się wtedy w lasach na terenie tej wsi. Bracia Taur jego złowili, związali i własną furą zawieźli do branskiej żandarmerii. Tam został rozstrzelany.
Oskarżeni zajmowali się także wyłapywaniem ukrywających się Sowietów.
Fakty te potwierdzą następujący świadkowie:
1. Olendski Dawid, Białystok, Rabinska 13
2. Olendski Aba "   "
3. Olendski Byna "   "
4. Sobolewski b.sołtys wsi Patoki.

A. Trus
Prezes Koła Branskich Żydów w B-stoku.
Były prezes Zarządu gminy wyznaniowo-żydowskiej w Brańsku.

Przewodniczący   Protokolant
Woj.Żyd.Komisji Historycznej   Mgr.B.Fuks
Mgr.M.Turek

Accusation against the Taur brothers for the murder of the Skavraneks

PROVINCE

DISTRICT HISTORICAL COMMISSION FOR JEWISH AFFAIRS

BIALYSTOK date 7–1–1947

Page 7'48 [?]

Province Historical Commission For Jewish Affairs Bialystok

From: Alter Trus, former resident of Bransk,

Head, Bransk Jewish Association in Bialystok

Now residing in Bialystok, 2 Piekna Street

TESTIMONY

There were two brothers, residents of the village Patoki, county Bransk, Region Bielsk– Podlaski; last name Tur, one a tailor by trade, the other a smith, who were working for the occupation government. Against the will of the local residents and the village head, Mr. Solbolowki, they were searching and rounding up Jews.

The day after the liquidation of the Bransk ghetto, the brothers Tur captured two Jews, Lejzer Skowronek, age 55, owner of a truck, and his son, Jego [?] Skowronek, age 19. They tied them up and delivered them to the village headman demanding that he delivers them to Bransk. The village headman refused so they summoned some Germans and with their help executed the above mentioned Jews.

Toward the end of 1943 Jankiel Glondzky, who at that time was hiding in forests nearby, came to the village Patoki searching for some bread. The brothers Tus captured him, tied him up and drove him to the gendarmes headquarters in Bransk where Jankiel Glondzky was shot to death.

The accused were also guilty of catching Soviets who might have been hiding in the vicinity of the village.

These facts are verified by the following witnesses:

Dawid Olandzky, residing at 13 Rabinska Street, Bialystok

Abe Glendzky

Dyna Glendzky

Sobolowski, village headman from Patok.

Alter Trus

Chairman of the Bransk Jews Association in Bialystok,

Former Head of the Jewish Community of Bransk

Court reporter Recorder

Head of Jewish Historical Commission Mgr. B.Fuks

Mgr. M. Turek

[Page 320]

WOJEWÓDZKA
ŻYD. KOMISJA HISTORYCZNA
BIAŁYSTOK, dnia.....
L.p.....

Zeznanie Rubina Jankiela

O mordach dokonanych na brańskich Żydach przy pomocy miejscowej
ludności.

Rubin Jankiel urodz. 1905 roku w Brańsku, cieśla, przeżył w lasach
okolicy Chojewa-Kieronowa, obecnie mieszka w Białymstoku, Rynek-
Kościuszki 40 mieszkanie 17.

Świadek zeznaje, że Kamiński lat 40 i bracia Bycz mieszkańcy wsi
Chojewa, gmina Brańsk zajmowali się wyłapywaniem i mordowaniem
ukrywających się Żydów i Moskwian.

Świadek zeznaje, że na początku 1943 r. obrał się w stodole
na wsi Chojewa, widział jak znani Kamiński i bracia Bycz wieź-
li na dwóch furach związanych trzech Żydów:
1. Jęczmienia Berkę, 2. Topczewskiego Pejsacha i 3. Topczewskiego
Lejbera.

Świadek słyszał jak Żydzi krzyczeli: "Kamiński ratuj".

Dnia przedtem wieczorem na wsi mówiono, że Kamiński i bracia
Bycz złapali Żydów, to za to dostaną od Niemców mąki czarnej.

Wyżej wspomnieni Żydzi przyszli do wioski Chojewa po chleb, a
tam zostali przytrzymani przez Kamińskiego i braci Bycz. Noc przele-
żeli związani, a znani Kamiński i bracia Bycz powieźli ich na furach do brańskiej żandarmerji, gdzie zostali rozstrzelani. Zwłoki
zostały pogrzebane w Brańsku koło stodoły gryzistej, gdzie ipo
dziś dzień leżą.

Świadek zeznaje, że Kamiński i bracia Bycz w końcu 44r. doko-
nali mordu na trzech żydowskich kobietach: 1. Jęczmień Chajcze
2. Jęczmień Rywa 3. Ciesluk Fryma-Leja.

Świadek w lesie spotkał się z Jęczmieniem Jankielem lat 65,
z którym poszedł do wioski Kieronowa, wracając mieli
się w kierunku schronu Jęczmienia, gdzie znajdowały się wyżej
wymienione kobiety. Nagle usłyszeli, że idzie fura. Świadek razem
z Jęczmieniem schował się w krzakach w jrłowca. Ochrzan poznali
Kamińskiego po głosie i po wyroście jest on wujrzątey we wsi,
poznali również braci Bycz. Świadek i Jęczmień przed wojną co-
dziennie bywali we wsi Chojewa i bardzo dobrze znali ludność tej
wsi. Świadek słyszał, że Kamiński i bracia Bycz rozmawiali między sobą
o ubraniu, komu się dostaną obrączki i.i.p. Ze swojej kryjówki
też widzieli, że na furze leży ubranie, suknie i koce.

Gdy fura odjechała świadek razem z Jęczmieniem, poszli do
schronu i tam zobaczyli zabite kobiety całkiem nagie. U Jęczmień
Chajcze była ścięta głowa, a z ust wyjęte złote zęby, u Ciesluk
była odrąbana ręka, a na niej odrąbane dwa palce, a trzeciej kobiety była przerżnięte szyja.

Ludność wsi i okolicy wie, że ten mord jest robotą Kamińskiego i
braci Bycz.

Za kilka miesięcy ci sami złapali Jęczmienia Jankiela i utopili
w rzece Narwec, trup wypłynął w Brańsku ze związanymi rękoma i łopami,
trup był w jednej koszuli.

W Brańsku często znajdywali zwłoki utopionych ludzi ze związanymi
rękoma i nogami. Powszechnie jest wiadome, że topieniem Żydów
zajmowali się Kamiński i bracia Bycz.

Kamiński i bracia Bycz związali Trusa Lejba lat 25 i wrzucili do
rzeki, ten cudem się uratował i żyje.

Ten fakt może potwierdzić Trus Lejb, mieszka w Białymstoku,
Piękna 2.

Świadek wyraża życzenie, aby powyższe zeznanie zostało skiero-
wane do prokuratury, oraz być świadkiem dla potwierdzenia tych zbrodni.
Te zbrodnie chcą potwierdzić pozostali przy życiu Żydzi brańscy:

1. Olendski Abe	mieszk. Białegostoku,	Łubiatka lo
2. Alpern Hellka	"	13
3. Cukt Chawa	"	Kupiecka 1
4. Prybut Arje-Lejb	"	Nowy-Świat 23
5. Trus Lejb	"	Piękna 2
6. Oszard Mojsze	"	
7. Jęczmień Mosze	Wrocław	Sępa-Szarzyńskiego 26 m.4

Świadek   Protokolant

                      Mgr. B. Fuks

Przewodniczący
Woj. Żyd. Komisji Historycznej
Mgr. T Turek

Complaint against Kaminski and the Ritch brothers (signed by Magistrate Fuks.)

PROVINCE

DISTRICT HISTORICAL COMMISSION FOR JEWISH AFFAIRS

BIALYSTOK date 4–1–1947

Page 9'17 [?]

Testimony of Jankiel Rubin[17]

Regarding the murder committed on the Jews from Bransk with the assistance of local population.

Jankiel Rubin born in 1909 in Bransk, a carpenter by trade, survived the war hiding in the forests in the vicinity of Chojewo Kiersneve, [?] he currently resides in Bialystok, 40 Rynek Kosciuszki Street, unit # 17.

The witness testifies that Kaminski, age 40, and brothers Rycz, residents of Chojewo, county Bransk, were engaged in the capture of Jews and Soviets who were hiding nearby.

The witness testified that in early 1943 while he was hiding in a barn in the village he saw one morning Kamiski and the brothers Ritch transporting three Jews on the hay wagons. The names of the captives were 1. Berko Jeczmien, 2. Pejsacha Topczynsky, 3. Lejzer Topczynsky.

The witness testifies that he heard the Jews crying "Kaminski, have mercy".

The day before there were rumours circulating in the village that Kaminski and the brothers Ritch had caught some Jews and were expecting to

receive a meter of sugar from the Germans as a reward.

The above mentioned Jews came to the village in search of some bread when they were caught by Kaminski and the Ritch brothers. They spent the night tied up and in the morning Kaminski and the Ritch brothers loaded them on a couple of hay wagons and took them to Bransk to turn them over to the gendarmes who then shot them to death. Their bodies we buried in

Bransk, near a barn belonging to a church organ player, and they are still buried there to this day.[18]

The witness testifies that Kaminski and the Ritch brothers were also responsible for a murder of three Jewish women committed toward the end of 1942. The victims' names were: 1. Chajcze Jeczmien, 2. Rywa Jeczmien, and 3. Leja–Rywa Ciesluk.

The witness testifies that on that day he met Jankiel Jeczmien, age 65 and together they went to the village to get some bread. On the way back they walked toward the shelter where the three women were living. Suddenly they heard a sound of a wagon so they hid in the bushes. They recognized Kaminski by his voice and size (he was the tallest man in the village) and the Ritch brothers. The witness and Jeczmien had visited the village daily before the war and thus knew its residents well. The witness heard Kaminski and the Ritch brothers talk about who is going to get the clothes, the wedding band, etc. From their hiding place the witness saw some clothes, dresses, and blankets piled on the wagon.

After the wagon passed, the witness and Jeczmien went to the shelter and found the naked bodies of murdered women. Chajcze Jeczmien's head was cut off and her golden teeth were removed. Leja Rywa Ciesluk had her hand and two fingers cut off. The third woman had her throat slit.

The villagers were aware that the murders were committed by Kaminski and the Ritch brothers.

A few months later the same men caught Jankiel Jeczmien and drowned him in the river Nurzec. The body washed ashore in Bransk. The victim's arms and legs were bound and he was only wearing a shirt.

There were a lot of incidents in Bransk of bodies with bound arms and legs washing up ashore. It was a common knowledge that Kaminski and the Rycz brothers were behind these drownings.

Kaminski and the Rycz brothers caught Lejb Trus, age 25, tied him up and threw him into the river. Miraculously he survived and is alive to this day.

Lejb Trus can confirm this account. He currently lives in Bialystok, 2 Piekna Street.

The murders can be confirmed by other surviving Bransk Jews:

Abe Olandzky, residing at 16 Rabinska Street, Bialystok

Wolfke Alpern, residing at 13 Rabinska Street, Bialystok

Chawa Okon, residing at 1 Mowiecka Street, Bialystok

Arje –Lejb Prybut, residing at 23 Nowy Swiat Street, Bialystok

Lejb Trus, residing at 2 Piekna Street, Bialystok

Mojsze Oskard, residing at 2 Piekna Street, Bialystok

Moszke Jeczmien, residing at 56 / 4 Sepa– Starzynskiego Street,

Wroclaw

Signed Court Reporter

Mgr. B Fuks

Court reporter

Head of Jewish Historical Commission

Mgr. M. Turek

[Page 325]

1943 Beginning of the Resistance

Russians Do Not Permit Any Bransk Jews in the Forest – Heroic–Deeds by Bransk Youths

It becomes quite evident after the events of the last few months of 1942 how and through whom all those who were hiding with Christian acquaintances, or who found themselves near the villages and in trenches, perished and about which the Christians knew. These were the Bransk Jews whose possessions, many of which were quite substantial, were given away to the Christians who had been their acquaintances for many years.

We must note that those who were hidden by the Christians, usually at a high financial cost, were separate from the rest of the Jews of the ghetto. There was no longer any communication between those who were in hiding and the others who had fled. Possibly they felt more fortunate because their Christian acquaintances had taken them under their wing.

Regretfully, those who had been hidden were the first victims. The Christians, with their thirst to inherit Jewish belongings, robbed and murdered their victims in the most brutal ways, showing no pity. They wanted to ensure that there would not be anyone who later could claim the stolen possessions they had acquired.

The category of people who were hidden in the trenches in the ghetto perished because they were betrayed by spies, by Polish policemen. All of them during these two months – November and December of 1942 were murdered.

[Page 326]

There were others who owned nothing, so they ran to the forest, not entrusting their lives to anyone and living from whatever they could find. Later on, there came to the forest those who had already been robbed of their possessions. A natural bond and warm friendship developed among them, like brothers of one family. However, this did not develop easily.

First–of–all, there were those who felt the forest was theirs and complained about why was everyone coming there? The first problem was that there were Soviets who had fled to hide in the forest to escape German capture, as well as a number of deserters who were also hiding in the forests. They did not permit Jews in general in the forest. At the first opportunity, the Soviets who had fled took clothing, shoes and everything the Jews had and left the Bransk Jews naked in the greatest frosts.

And this is how those who fled from the ghetto were faced with a third enemy: the Germans in the town, the Poles in the villages and the Soviets who stole from them and lived off these stolen items and who were always drunk. The end was that the Russians were little–by–little murdered by the Germans, because with their behavior they didn't possess the foresight to be watchful. They slowly fell into Nazi hands.

Eventually it became possible to form a tie with the remaining Soviets, forging a friendship thanks to little Hershele Rubin[1] and Maishe Rubinshteyn. However this did not come easily.

Hershele Rubin, a 17–year old youth, small and skinny, was Yankl Shimon's grandchild. He was very good–looking and intelligent, a well–read young man. He was friends with my younger son Ozer Trus. They were two friends who were well–informed sympathizers of the progressive workers' idealism.

[Page 327]

During the ghetto days Hershele collected weapons which he received from a German soldier friend, Heinz, a Communist. This Heinz advised the Jews to arm themselves with weapons and flee to the forest.

By the time the Bransk ghetto was liquidated, Hershele and his sister Dore, were already in the forest and well–armed. There in the forest he meets his school friend, Maishe Rubinshteyn. Hershele decides he will shoot all the Soviet deserters because they do not permit Jews to enter the forest. Maishe Rubinshteyn, Yozefinekh's (?) grandchild, does not agree with this plan. He says they have to make an attempt for a good outcome. Maishe Rubinshteyn warns the Russians to avoid little Hershele, that he is heavily armed and a good shooter. They were very afraid of Hershele. The result was that they became friendly and dubbed Hershele 'the brave Ershko.' This led to closeness between the Russians and the Jewish groups in the forest.

Hershele does not sit idle. He always keeps his revolver close by and uses it quite often. The whole area is now aware of the little Hershele. The Germans place a price on his head. Hershele receives support from the Polish intelligentsia, from the teachers, from the priest. They bring him food and weapons, ammunition. Following his example they all seek to find weapons. The gathering point is in the Polish *smentarzsh* (?) and is also where the Polish supporters meet.

He spreads fear across the entire area. He stands on the Bielsk–Bransk road and shoots at those riding past. He spreads propaganda among everyone, urging them to take a stance and confront the enemy. Branskers ridicule him.

Hershele goes to the village of Markeve, eight kilometres from Bransk. The Germans had set up a school in Markeve where they trained hunting dogs in helping to capture Jews in the forest.

Suddenly Hershele attacks the dog–training school. The guard flees.

[Page 328]

Hershele shoots all the dogs. Panic ensues among the Germans. Hershele becomes even more popular in the area.

Polish weddings would take place during carnival time. German gendarmes would be invited to these weddings as honored guests. Hershele says: "We suffer without food, wander around like dogs and they conduct celebrations and bring the Nazis in as guests. No, this will not happen." He organizes a group to do something about this. Such a wedding was going to take place in the village of Poplov at the home of the Pole Zarski. The group makes its preparations. They come out of the forest across the river to Poplov, not yet encountering any guests. The door is guarded and they make a toast with a good drink, enjoy a good meal and then they pour kerosene over the wedding finery and prepare the baked goods to take back with them. Hershele says to the parents that 'this is because you invite the German gendarmes to your celebrations. This is only a warning. It will be worse the next time.' You understand that the guests were closely guarded by the pointed revolvers. The door was locked from the outside. They leave this place and head back to the forest through different ways.

The gendarmes arrived at the wedding ten minutes later. The following day it is known throughout the area about Hershele's work. No more German gendarmes were ever again invited to Polish weddings. He had taught the Bransk Jews how to handle firearms, and to watch out for themselves. However, he himself was not careful and this brought him to anearly and untimely death.

During the summer cutting time he is betrayed. Poles discover that he is in the village of Polyetl. A large number of gendarmes arrive. They attack him. Hershlpistol jams, and as he stands face–to–face with the enemy he could not even take revenge for anyone. He falls dead along with his sister Dore.

The Polyeteler Christians bury them with great respect in the village of Polyetl near Bransk.   Honour their memories

[Page 329]

Hershele's death led to better ties with everyone in the forest. In addition, they now saw they must not be in a village but only in the forest.

Jews who had held themselves aloof now get together, and now make communal hiding–places (trenches). Arrangements are made for food to be supplied for everyone.

Murders in the Villages – The same hunt continued in the villages. If anyone was caught in the field, he would pay with his life.

In the spring of 1943 there were several Jews hiding in the village of Smurle. The Smurle Christians tied them all up and brought them to Bransk. The following were shot:

Hershele Rubin in the Forest

[Page 330]

Kive Sashin, 24 years old,

His wife, Blume

Alyh Sashin, Kive's brother, 19 years old,

Nokhum Shroyt's girl drags herself to the village of Olyentsk at the beginning of the winter of 1943, hands and feet frozen as well as her nose and entire face, begging to be taken to the Germans. The Christians do not want to do this. They see there is already nothing left to take there. They take her to Toptcheve to the gendarmes. The girl begs them to shoot her and they oblige.

MaisheVigder Katsev's grandchild, 6 years, is found in the village of Zalyeshe. A Christian captures the little boy, takes him to the gendarmes in Toptcheve. They take him with them to the forest, carrying a shovel with them with which to bury him. In the forest they shot into the air, told the little boy to flee, and told him not to return to this area. The boy disappeared. According to certain Polish rumors, he was murdered.

Berl Shroyt, Avrum–Meir the painter's, escaped the ghetto, hiding somewhere in fields and forests, when finally at the end of summer 1943, he is captured by Poplover Christians. He no longer had the possibility of escaping the troubles he has endured. He is brought to Bransk and the gendarmes shoot him near the river where he is buried.

Berl Okon, Khaim Burak's sister's son, a very fine young man, escaped from the ghetto along with two sisters, and Leah. They hid in the area near Klikhe, Ploneve, Alyekshin, endured much from the Germans and Poles. At the end of 1943, Berl set out to find some food. He wandered into an attack. He hides in a cellar, but suddenly gendarmes appear there, capturing him and taking him to Alyekshen [sic]. MCG Berl is shot at the wall of Pilinske's barn by the gendarme Shumanski. He was buried there.

Berl Tabak, Asher Damsken Shnaider's son–in–law, 30 years and seven Vishink Jews, names unknown, are murdered in the village of Myen near Bransk. The murderers are unknown to this very day.

[Page 331]

In the Rutker Forest – in the heavily wooded Rutker forest a group of Jews was in hiding in a deep trench. The Pole Skavronek from the village of Rutke noticed the trench and came with gendarmes, pointing it out. The gendarmes blew up the trench with hand–grenades. This same hiding–place became the grave for the following:

MaisheOrlyansky, Yenkl Zavl's son 45 years,

Frume Arlyansky, [sic] Maishe's wife, 42 years,

Zelde their daughter, 10 years,

Khaike their daughter, 7 years,

Hershl Orlyansky, Yenkl Zavl's son 47 years,

Itche Yenkl Pribut, Lazer the blacksmith's son 37,

Maishe's 5 year-old child, name unknown

A special investigation confirmed that the Pole Skavronek had discovered this hiding–place. A complaint to the prosecutor through the Bialystok Jewish Historical Commission, Number 4/47, accordingly, was filed.

[Page 332]

Pyetrask – Many Jews died near the village of Pyetrask by the murderous hand of the Pyetrask village magistrate by the name of Pyetrashke. There were two hiding–places there.

Yosl Ptak, a shoemaker, 27 years old,

Zavl Ptak, a tailor, 24 years old,

Mendel Shlifke, a wheelwright, 33 years old,

Lazer Rifke, Yankev Maishe Rifke's son, 21 years old,

The village magistrate Pyetrashke discovered both hiding–places and brought gendarmes. Pyetrashke orders the victims to come out. They are shot and are buried in their trenches. Their clothes are taken by Pyetrashke as a reward for his work.

The Ptak brothers were discovered at the beginning of winter, 1943. The other two were discovered in the spring of 1943. Pyetrashke was responsible for both of these in the same murderous manner.

A complaint to the prosecutor was entered on January 7th, 1947 to the Historical Commission, Number 6/47, accordingly.

Christians from the village of Lyendive did not give the Germans the pleasure of shooting Jews. They did this themselves by their own efforts. Why give the gendarmes the pleasure. The war is in full swing. The Nazi army must be supplied with meat, butter, tobacco, tea. Let the gendarmes concentrate their efforts on the transports. They will take care of murdering the Jews themselves. The Armia Krajowe[2] was supposed to fight against the Germans, but instead devoted their efforts to murdering Jews. The following were the victims of the Lyendiver beasts:

Khaim Raibak, Shaye Afrikaner's[3] son, 70 years old,

Shepsl Broyzman, Shepsl Treger's grandchild, 17 years,

Lerman dentist, 42 years,

Lerman's wife 40 years,

Stelye Lerman, their daughter, 18 years.

Ten Jews from the village of Sakole, names unknown.

A Warsaw girl, name unknown.

A Tchekhenovtser[4] boy, name unknown.

Shloyme Olyentsky, partisan and Berl Okon

[Page 333]

Zaluske – Leybl Itche Krinsky's son, the hat–maker, was hidden in the village of Zaluske. In the spring of 1943, a Pole by the name of Aldikhovski captured Leybl. Leybl defied him. The Pole hit him over the head with an axe and he falls into an unconscious condition. He is taken to Bransk to the gendarmes. He is shot at the mountain and is buried there. The Pole Aldikhovski, for his work, receives Krinsky's clothes and a half–kilo of sugar.

A complaint is filed in the Historical Commission 17/47 accordingly.

Rishke Tsuktlyer, Ben Tsiyon the lame teacher's daughter was noticed as she was walking from the village of Shvirikh to the village of Zaluske during the summer of 1943. The Christians set out to capture her. She had already spent nine months in the fields, was hungry and weak. Naturally she did not have any more strength to run, so she was quickly captured by the well–nourished drunk Christians. They bound her and she begged and cried, but regretfully, they brought her to the gendarmes. They took her shoes off and she was shot near Leyzer Katsev's cellar. The Christians also received the reward of a half– kilo of sugar. This was now the usual prize for capturing Jews. Up to this day, it cannot be confirmed who the Christians were who participated in this instance.

Sheyne Volkavitch, Pesakh the miller's grandchild, Maishe the quilter's daughter, 22 years, was hiding together with Maishe and Perl Penkherzh in a trench. Some kind of argument took place there and Sheyne leaves the trench. She goes to the village of Glinek to meet Jews in the forest near Bransk. She knew that her cousin Yisiroelkele is somewhere in the forest. This is summer 1943, She is captured by a Glinik Pole, is brought to Bransk to the gendarmes. They beat her mercilessly to force her to tell them where and with whom she had been the entire time. Sheyne did not reveal anything despite having been chased out of the hiding–place. She did not betray anyone. She was made to run a gauntlet as punishment, shot and was buried there. Honour her memory. This is true heroism.

[Page 334]

Itche'ele Burak, 13 years, Leybl Burak's youngest son, fled the ghetto, wandering about in fields, forests and villages. He was very capable of finding food for himself. He met his uncle, Velvl Burak, and they were together for a certain length of time, and Itchele was able to find food for Velvl and himself.

Something occurred that Velvl allows his nephew to leave. If Itchehad been able to reach the Bransker in the forest, he would possibly survived. However, he hid in the area between Kersnave–Kalnitse Summer time he lay hidden in the corn stalks. A gendarme standing high up in the Kersnover [sic] windmill noticed him with his binoculars, aimed his revolver and shot him. Itche'ele lies in a pool of blood, in the corn stalks.

His uncle Velvl later comes to the forest and survives.

Rumours abound that the Bialystok ghetto has not and will not be disturbed because of various reasons. They wanted to believe it was true, so secretly a group of Bransk Jews organized for the purpose of reaching Bialystok ghetto where the Jews live. This was at the beginning of 1943. The group consisted of:

Shimon Rubin[5], 35 years, Shtyopke's son,

Khaitshe Shimon's wife, 29 years,

Shimon's two year old son,

Mair Rubin[6], 40, Leyzer Rubin's son,

Menukhe Rubin, Mair's wife, Elke Rive's daughter,

Mair's two children

[Page 335]

Zelig Kestin[7] (Kuptchi Zhelozes), 23 years,

MaisheKhaim , Batker the teacher's grandchild, 22 years,

Niske Nudelman, Itchke (Zalisher's son), 26 years,

Blume Kasarsky, was married to a cousin, American,

A Pyekuter youth who had lived in Bransk for several years.

The group found a wagon and make an attempt to reach Bialystok.

In the area of the Pyetkever forest, they are betrayed by someone. They are met by Germans and everyone is shot.[8]

Khatskl the ritual slaughterer's son 16 years, is in hiding in the area of Klikhe–Voytke near Bransk. He is captured by Christians, taken to Bocki to the gendarmes. In Bocki he is shot.

The two sisters Finklshteyn, Avikhe's grandchildren and the wife of Pesakh–Yosl Taptchevsky with her three year old child are somewhere between Kersnove and Kalnitse. Because of a report by a Christian Bablyevitch from the village of Mervizne near Bransk, in the summer of 1943, the gendarmes attack the area and the above are shot there.

At the same time, a Kersnover Christian, Yanek Stepanoves brings the Germans to the trench hiding–place between the village of Kalnitse and Kersnove, where the following are hiding:

Bentsl Rubin, Yosl–Shimon Farber's son, 21 years,

Khone Piekucky[9], 16 years, Babtche's son,

Leybele Yentchman, Bertche Yentchman's son, 8 years,

Two Visaker Litovsker Jews, names unknown

All are chased from the trench and shot. Their rotted clothes are taken by Janek Stepanoves as a reward for his work. He throws all the bodies back into the trench and that is where their grave remains.

Excerpt from the Historical Commission 10/47 accordingly. Complaint against Janek. 9/1/47.

In the month of April 1943 there is an attack in the area of the swamps on the way to the Rutker forest. There were Germans and Polish police. This was possibly the result of a betrayal. They are following the scent of the hidden Jews. Shooting breaks out from both sides during which DovidPribut, 55 years, Shmulye Poplover's son falls dead from a bullet. Leybl Sashin, Yosl Pribut and Elye Yentchman succeed in fleeing during the shooting. This is now the second time Elye Yentchman has managed to run away.

[Page 336]

A couple of months later in 1943, a second attack takes place in the same area. The bandits come to a trench with Jews. As a result, LeyblSashin 22 years, Ruven Katsev's grandchild, falls dead and the well–known Poale Tsiyonist Elye Yentchman, 44 years old.

With the death of Elye Yentchman the entire account of the Bransk Jews on the way to Treblinka is lost. He was the only Bransk Jew who had fled from Treblinka. He had much to tell. He did not live to tell the world the facts of the Bielsk–Bialystok–Malkin–Treblinka trip that he knew. He took this story with him into his deep grave. Honour his memory. Elye Yentchman, courageous fighter, Bransk hero!

Elye Yentchman his wife Dvorke and son Dovidl

Yosl Pribut, 15 years, was only wounded in his hand. He fled to Bransk Bendige to the river. The Germans met him with bullets. Yosle hides in a cellar with potatoes. The Germans search for him and cannot find him. They demand of the Christians that within a half–hour they turn him over. However, thanks to the help of the Christians, they did not find him.

[Page 337]

At night, with the help of a Christian, Pilinske he made contact with the group of Bransk Jews in the forest. His brother KhaimVelvl Pribut, was there. They healed him of his wounds. He remained with the forest group. However, he perished later. About his death – in later chapters.

Exhausted and Weakend Bransker Die – By this time almost all were so starved and exhausted that there was no longer any strength left to survive the terrible suffering. Many died a natural death in the forest and in the field and not from direct gunshots by the Germans or Poles. They simply passed away.

I tried to gather the facts but not everyone is mentioned here.

Elye–Moshe Menashe's 19 years dies in the forest at the end of 1942. He was unable to endure the two months of living in the forest. He is buried by Maishe Oskard and the Ptak brothers. They were still alive at that time.

Gedalye Krinsky, hat–maker, approximately 43 years, dies alone in the swamps between Poplov, Alyekshin near Bransk, frozen. No one knows if or where he is buried.

Leybl Kamen 20 years, Yudl Galise's middle son dies from a wound he had sustained from a rusty nail that was used to make a new trench near the village of Patok. The trench they were in was noticed and so they had to make another. This was summer, 1943. His brother Maishe, with the help of Perl Penkherzh buries him in the field near Patok.

Avrumele Gradzhinsky, 55 years, Itche Gimpl's son dies in his trench, hidden near the village of Dominove. Avreml was there with his son 15 years old, nicknamed Gril. The Christian who had taken their money to bring them food once in five days, saw that the money was running out and stopped bringing the food. Avreml died of hunger. His son buries him near the village of Dominove. The 15–year old boy, after his father's death, lost his mind. The Christian, two months later, brought him to Bransk to the gendarmes. He is shot in the horse market.

[Page 338]

Zelig Rozen 46 years, a blacksmith, Dovid the blacksmith's son was somewhere in a trench with his son Pesakh near the village Luvishtch near Bransk. He was already swollen [from hunger] for the two months prior to his death. His son Pesakh, 20 years, buries him in the forest near the village.

And so ended the lives of the Bransker who had fled, been captured, shot, murdered or died swollen from hunger pangs.

Footnotes (Rubin Roy Cobb)

1. Related to Rubin Roy Cobb through his paternal grandmother Gelie Rokhel Rubin Kobylanski.

2. Wikipedia – abbreviated AK was the dominant Polish resistance movement in World War II German–occupied Poland. It was formed in February 1942 from the Zwiqzek Walki Zbrojnej (Armed Resistance). Over the next two years, it absorbed most other Polish underground forces. It's allegiance was to the Polish Government–in–Exile, and it constituted the armed wing of what became known as the "Polish Underground State." – – – While the Home Army largely untainted by collaboration with the Nazis during the Holocaust, some historians have asserted that, due to anti–Semitism, the Home Army was reluctant accept Jews into its ranks. – – – According to Antony Polonsky, General Stefan Grot–Rowecki, the Home Army's commander, made it clear in an order of 19 November 1942 that the Home Army did not regard the Jews as "part of our nation", and that action was not to be taken to defend them if it endangered other Home Army objectives. [Mayevski, Florian (2003). Fire Without Smoke: Memoirs of a Polish Partisan. Page 3: Mitchell Valentine & Company. p. 168. ISBN 978–0–85303–461–2].

3. South African (as Amerikaner refers to the USA).

4. See Maps Section 2 Page III.

5. Related to Rubin Roy Cobb through his paternal grandmother Gelie Rokhel Rubin Kobylanski. All the Rubins referred to here are of the same family descended from Shimon Rubin who owned the tavern in Bransk.

6. Introduced the parents of Rubin Roy Cobb as per Brakha Weiner–Harris in Johannesburg in the late 1980s.

7. Rubin Roy Cobb's father, Henry Cobb [Khlawna Kobylanski] of neighbouring Bielsk–Podlaski was apprenticed as a cabinet–maker to a Kestin in Bransk.

8. In 1991 Jack (Yankl) Rubin showed the place where the murders took place and told him how it happened. It was about midnight in the forest in the Pyetkever area on the way to Bialystok from Bransk when they came across a Pole walking on the path. They left him and later on as they came to a rise Jack saw some distance in front of them a wagon drawn by two horses which Jack immediately saw was a German wagon as the Polish wagons were led by only one horse. He immediately screamed for everyone to jump off the wagon. He jumped to the left and ran for his life and eventually arrived at a Polish peasants' house. He knocked on the window and asked for something to drink and eat. The man of the house was deaf but his wife gave something to Jack but was afraid to let him stay there as the Germans might come and if they found Jack they would also kill the Polish man and his wife. Jack eventually made his way to Bialystok, secretly entered the ghetto there. He was hoping to meet his fellow travelers in the Bialystok ghetto and after a few days realized that they would not come. He stayed on for a few months and just before the final liquidation in mid–1943 he managed to escape. The late Nathan Kaplan of Chicago, whom met in Chicago in 1990 and through him presented the videoed interview with Jack Rubin done by the Spielberg Foundation, to Marian Marzynski resulting in the making of the documentary "Shtetl" for PBS in 1991. In Nathan Kaplan's editing of PART III 'Bransk Destroyed' of the Bransk Yizkor Book loosely translated by Dr Gol of Chicago [originally from Bransk, of the Goldwasser family]. Dr Gol graduated from a Medical School in Switzerland and   ed to Bransk in 1938 after graduation. But because of anti–Semitism he could not become registered and so went to the United States. His family committed suicide rather than be transported to Treblinka. This is related in the documentary 'Shtetl' by a Pole who was very friendly with the Goldwassers who came to say goodbye to him just before they committed suicide in November, 1942. On pages 35 and 59 of Nathan Kaplan's edited book dated 12/22/1995 Jack Rubin confirms that the following were on the wagon: ShimonRubin (Jack's brother); Khaitshe his wife; their two year old son; Mair Rubin; Brindel Rubin; their daughter (?) Menukha and two other children; the brothers Zelig and Shlomo Kesten; MaisheKhaim Dobrowsky; an unidentified woman – not Niske Nudelman. After the Germans retreated the corpses were transferred to their final resting place at the Jewish cemetery in Bransk. But the body of Shimon and Kaitshe's two year old son was never ever found. Jack thought that maybe he is still alive today and obviously does not know of his origins.

Whenever spoke to Jack he always felt guilty as to why he could not do more to save the lives of his family and others that were on the wagon and murdered by the Germans.

9. RubinRoy Cobb's brother, Charlie Cobb, is named after Khone Piekucki (ca 1860) who was our maternal great grandfather.

[Page 339]

A Small Number of Jews Remain in the Forest

Heroic Battle of Rokhl Tcheslyak and Bobtche Rubinshteyn – Armed Partisan Detachment Formed, Death Sentence Carried Out on a Betrayer

At the beginning of 1944 the situation of the small number of remaining Bransk Jews in the forest greatly worsened. The Polish armed bandits of the Armaia Krayowa attack and create much trouble.

There is a spontaneous organization of a defense detachment. The time was ripe for the formation of this detachment. The Nazis are pushed back by Russia. There is already grass growing on the Nazi graves in Stalingrad.

The members of the Soviet underground still keep their distance.

Thanks to MaisheRubinshteyn a friendly atmosphere developed with the Soviet underground members, those who had previously not permitted any Jews in the forest. There are frequent encounters between the Soviets and the Jews. No longer are they taking away the Jews' weapons.

Possibly the news from the front which reports Soviet victories had something to do with this.

MaisheRubinshteyn later worked his way up to become the secretary of the forest detachment at the Komsomol.[1]

After the liquidation of the Bialystok ghetto on August 15, 1943 new people show up in the forest, among them Yankev Povritske, a Bialystok attorney, Alek Gzushevin, former head of the academic youth in Warsaw, Mates, a Bialystok poet. Several also came from Tchekhenovtser.[2] Abtche Lifshitz, Shloyme Oks grandchild, and his Polish friend Gravazh, who later becomes one of the murdered by the gendarmes.

[Page 340]

At the same time the Polish bands gain strength. We receive reports of mass murders of Jews.

A Bialystok girl Edye Katz, is found in the village of Hodishove badly wounded by the Polish band, with the name of "Hanul Shmirtch." Hershl Lype and Khaim Vrobel take her to them and devote themselves to her recovery. They got medicine for her, you understand of course that money made this possible. It took five months until she regained her health. She later married Hershl Lype. They now have a fine son.

Edye Katz and a group of others had run away when they were on the road, as they were being taken with everyone else from the Bialystok ghetto to Treblinka. They slowly made it to the Bransk area near the village of Hodishove where they settled into a forest trench. The Polish Armei Krajowa, bandits discovered the trench and threw hand grenades into it. Everyone died.

Khaim Vrobel the Kevlyaker went to bury them and found Edya Katz still alive. He took her with him. His efforts were not in vain.

The activities of Khaim Vrobel consisted of helping to supply the Jews in the forest with food and medicine as well as clothing and shoes. He also helped to find hiding–places.

The following fact is very characteristic. At the end of 1943, wintertime, Khaim Vrobel finds in the village of Hodishove a 9 year old Bialystok girl, Stella Tcheslyanske. She too, jumped from the train while it was on its way to Treblinka. The little girl crept about in the forest alone. Khaim took her with her feet frozen, with him to his hiding–place. Several Christians had pointed the little girl out to Khaim. He clothes her.

[Page 341]

She recovers and becomes accepted into the Bransk group under his guidance. They suffer great difficulties from this child during the time of attacks. Yet Stella lived through everything. She is now in Palestine. misses her as if she were his sister.

Khaim Vrobel, Kevlyaker earns the greatest respect for his heroic and devoted work under such difficult circumstances.

A little Jewish girl of about twelve years shows up in the village of Olyentsk near Bransk. Christians encountered my son Leybl and told him that somewhere a young girl is wandering about. Leybl arranges with the Christians to leave the girl on a certain day near the well. At the correct time my son Leybl Trus, Maishe –Ber Penkherzh and Shloyme Olentsky show up at the well. The little girl, sick, was standing at the well, feet frozen. They take her to the forest. Her name is Lube Frank. She was born in Kovne [Lithuania] and found herself in the Bialystok ghetto. She was being taken to Treblinka, and on the way she fled. She wandered about alone until she came to the Bransk area. They give her clothing, medicine and help. She becomes a member of the Bransk group, helped by my son Leybl Trus with food, clothing and medicine. She survives the war, and is now with her relatives in Australia.

[Page 342]

Left: Luba Frank, She wandered into the Bransk forest and was rescued.

Right: LeyblTrus, partisan

For the purpose of being more secure, they are divided into small groups and take off in different directions in the forest and field, carrying small firearms.

Yosef Katlovitch, now in Israel and Khaim Vrubel in Camp Farenvald

There is a betrayal at the end of 1943. A Shvirider Pole by the name of Dnyestor, the watch–commandant of the village of Shvirid brings Germans to a hiding–place which is between the villages of Shvirid and Olyentsk. The following Branskers were in the trench at that time: Maishe Kleinot, Elber the shoemaker's grandchild, Leybl Pav from Tchizhev, who had lately lived in Bransk, Binyomin Pribut, 18 years, Shmulye Paplaver's grandchild, Rokhl Tcheslyak, 18 years, , Itskhak the porridge –maker's grandchild and, Babtche Rubinshteyn, the Yozefiner's grandchild.

The Germans order them out of the trench. They respond from within the trench with a hail of bullets upon the Nazis and Dnyestor. After a couple of hours, they run out of bullets. There is nothing more with which to defend themselves. The men make an attempt to flee and fall dead. There remain in the trench only Bobtche Rubinshteyn and Rokhl Tcheslyak. The Germans approach the trench, throwing hand grenades in Rokhl Tcheslyak and Bobtche Rubinshteyn catch the hand grenades and throw them back to the Germans.

[Page 343]

Rokhl Tcheslyak Yitzkhak the porridge–maker's daughter

Bobtche had already lost one hand. They do not give up. The betrayer Frank approaches with bundles of straw, throws them into the trench. They are burning bundles of straw. The fire and choking smoke force Bobtche and Rokhl'n to come out of the trench and they are shot.

There are five heroic Branskers lying at the edge of the trench, young Bransk martyrs. They defended themselves bravely and fell as heroes.

This incident forces everyone to look for ways to respond to this mass murder. At a consultation, the Soviet underground workers recommend a death sentence to be carried out on Dnyestor'n, the betrayer. There is unanimous agreement in favor of the death sentence. The best workers volunteer. The commandant of the detachment Radzin, Pyetke, Nikolay Tsigan and two who are unknown. On a Shabbos evening, when it was still light, they enter the village Shvirid, find Dnyestor's house, and go in with a grand greeting. They take out a paper and ask who is Franek Dnyestor? There was a neighbour in the house. He becomes frightened as this means death, so he immediately points to him: "This is Franek Dnyestor."

[Page 344]

"Why did you throw burning bundles of straw into the trench? Why did you bring Germans to the hiding place?" "I will not do this anymore," Franek answered. "We will ensure that you do not do this anymore," – the detachment members say. "Franek, there is a death sentence handed down to you by the partisan detachment for you to be shot." They instruct Franek to sign the death sentence. The neighbour also signs.

Pyetke then rewards Franek'n with 5 bullets. Franek Dnyestor falls onto Pyetken who throws him off his body with his foot.

The commandant Radzin warns that no longer will betrayers be tolerated.

Radzin says to Franek's wife that she should bring her children up in a better way than the one their father led. He says goodbye and they leave. (*Excerpt from the Historical Commission in Bialystok.*)

The next day this information about the sentence has reached everyone in the area. The local press makes an uproar. The Soviets and the Jews are murdering innocent people of the Polish population. The residents of the villages are frightened. Some of them say it was a good thing, Franek should not have told on them.

After Franek Dnyestor's judgment and death, the Poles did not capture any more Jews. They did not try anymore.

In the village of Glinyek a group of Soviet organizers from the detachment asked a gentile for bread. The Pole raged, threatened he would bring Germans to them. You understand that he is immediately dead. This resulted in the beginning of respect for the partisans.

Two days after the death sentence is carried out on Franekn, the partisan detachment was once again organized. They formed new ranks with political commissars and an official recorded journal. They put in place an armed watch at specially designated areas that were always changed when necessary.

[Page 345]

They also put in place the planned methods on how to obtain food. The detachment had already been in existence, but it had not worked as anorganized entity. It was especially important to reform their methods of obtaining food. Up until that time they went out for food individually, each for himself, not in an organized fashion. Anyone who was capable found food.

According to the explanation in Velvl Golde's letter, he writes the following: "when winter fades and when it became somewhat warmer we, had to leave the peasant's house where we had been staying, my sister and I. We went to the forest. I was very frightened. I crept around the entire day thinking that I could possibly find some Jews. I found no one. Several weeks passed this way. Occasionally we got food from Lyenshnikes whom we knew. It was impossible to be with them. During calm periods they were very friendly. Now they were totally different people.

Eventually I did find Jews. They brought me to Leyb lTrus and I was there for a long time. I joined the partisans and I was given a rifle. The first day I went with Leybl to the village to get food. The Christians gave me whatever we asked for from them. They had respect for me and my rifle. The rifle was what counted.

Right after fleeing the ghetto we went to ask for food. There were those who did give something."

The Polyeteler lord would always bring food for the Jews. The Germans had murdered his eldest son and therefore, he was good to Jews. Adelye Shteiynmanave always brought food for Gitl Yozefyner and the children who were in the forest.

[Page 346]

In 1939 the Germans murdered many Christians in the village and therefore they were a bit friendlier.

Pharoah's Third Plague – Maishe Berl Penkherzh was from the village of Povikre, of late he had lived in Bransk and was always with my son Leybl. They came to a Christian by the name of Dankevitch, in the village of Polyetl to ask for food.

Dankevitch says to them: 'What, you are still alive? There are Germans in the village.' He tells his son to lock the door and he immediately runs to the German gendarmes. Maishe Berl and Leybl run away from there before the Christian boy even made a move. The boy lay sick for several days. He could not come to himself due to having been frightened.

Sometime later the Palyeteler lord told Maishe Berl' that Dankevitch was bragging to all the Christians how he had frightened the two "zhidkes."[3]

Maishe Berl Penkherzh and Mulye Rekhlzon, partisan

Maishe Berl decides to seek revenge on Dankevitch'en.

In the winter of 1943 Maishe Berl is living in the forest. There is nothing to do. There are plenty of insects, so he scoops them up and places them in a little container. Now he has to figure out where to put them.

At the beginning of the evening he goes to this same DankevitchHe greets him with extensive 'good evening'. Dankevitch is perplexed. 'You are still alive Moshke?' – Dankevitch asks.– 'Yes,' Maishe replies. 'and everything is alive with me.' "Get out of here, for if you don't I will bring the Germans," – says the gentile. "Mr Dankevitch, give me a little piece of bread," Maishe Berl begs. "Go, go, get out of here" – he yells with fury. "I only want to see the clock," Maishe Berl answers. The clock was hanging on the wall over the bed. Maishe Berl opens his little container, releases the living insects onto the bed. And this is how he got revenge with Pharoah's third plague on Dankevitch'en.

[Page 347]

Upon my return from Russia I met with the Polyeteler nobleman and he told me this story while laughing, how Dankevitch scratched himself and cursed Maishe Berl'.

There were now other methods used to find food. At first they went to steal food, and then lately, they obtained food using weapons.

Mulye Rekhelzon, Dvora Dine's grandchild, was the specialist. He kept a record of the fattened sheep and calves and pigs. Why take small skinny ones if they can get big fat ones so it would be enough for everyone. Yes, he was a specialist first class. But he depends only on stealing. He does not carry weapons because it is safer. He would do the slaughtering in the barn, make portions for each group separately, and for himself and his group, he would take the smallest portion. There are more sheep, so they will take more a second time. This is what he would say. However, he did not forget to leave the feet, the head and the innards for the Christians leaving a note: 'this is for your work in making the calves and sheep fat.'

Dovtche – Olyentsky Voitek's, was a real artist. He would go to get food for the detachment. He never broke a lock. He would crawl in through a window at the Christian's house, take the little key, open the barn, or the stable, take what he wanted, lock the stable and creep into the house, hang the key on the wall. This was safer because the Christian did not notice what was missing and they could come a second time.

[Page 348]

The best method was using weapons, demanding and receiving bread, meat and other food.

Then another method was to steal from other villages. Then do the same thing in other villages, never in the same village again. This was easier.

New Misfortune – Armaia Krayowa – this was supposed to be a Polish army, helping the war effort and partisans against the Germans. They returned from the Russian provinces. But they attacked and murdered Jews.

The Jews who were in the forest were safer because they were grouped and well–armed. However the ones who were still alive and hiding in or near villages were now becoming victims of the Armaia Krayowa bandits.

The news reaches the forest.

At the end of 1943 and the beginning of 1944, in the village of Soltsye, the following were murdered by the A.K.: Yoske Smurtchik 56 years, Leyzer Katsev's son, Keyle Smuztchik, Yoske's daughter 25 years, Yoske Smurtchik's son 30 years, whose name I do not know. He was Motl Rhymer's son–in–law, and Motl Rihmer's four sons in the same village.

> Meir Valtchinsky – 28 years,
>
> Yankev Voltchinsky, 23 years,
>
> Shimon Voltchinsky, 21 years,
>
> Yosl Voltchinsky 16 years,

These same bandits murdered in the village of Kersnove Khaim**Error! Bookmark not defined.** the baker's (Khaim Katlavitch's) youngest son, 16 years, name unknown , Yoske Katlavitch, Khaim Baker's eldest son 27 was only wounded.

In the village of Rutke, at the end of 1943, the Polish bandits with the help of gendarmes, murdered Maishe Shuster 23 years, Dovid**Error! Bookmark not defined.** the blacksmith's grandchild, Baylke Faynsod's 20 year old girl, Alter Katsev's grandchild.

In 1944, in the village of Prushanke, there were murdered the brothers Halpern, Inditchke Shloyme the peacemaker's two sons, Yankev Halpern 45 years, and Shaye Halpern 38 years, the group discovered them and both had been murdered by Christian acquaintances.

[Page 349]

In the summer of 1944, just a few days before the liberation, there were murdered in the village of Koshive by the same group Avrum Gadobrosky, 40 years, Alter the red head's son. The investigation revealed that the young Christian of the village of Koshyev, Krososki, was the murderer.

Also in the Bransk forest during the summer of 1944, the attorney Gzshebin from Lodz and Mates a well–known Bialystok poet were murdered, as well as an unknown Jew from Keltz. They had all been sick, unable to help themselves.

The only picture of the forest group, Dovid Olyentsky on the left, is alive

Yankev Olyentsky Dora Rubin[4] and Maishe Kleinat perished

All these stories of the new sort of murders of Jews near Bransk served to bring those who remained even closer together all the remaining Jews who were alive. They formed larger groups with everyone armed. They became closer to the Russians. Their number in the forest increased substantially.

Everyone learned the trick of obtaining food for all – one communal pot. Every night they go to obtain food, not to steal or beg, but to take it with weapons. They prepare stocks of potatoes so as not to have to go to the villages so often.

[Page 350]

There are rumours of an imminent attack. Everyone evacuates to another forest. They look around and discover that Dovid Vigotsky is missing. Naturally, they now understand that he has been captured. They decide not to leave until they will rescue Dovid. They formulate a plan. They spread out on the road from Glinik to Bransk to wait until they will lead Dovid out. It is already daylight, 8 in the morning, 10 in the morning, already midday. No one is being led out. Someone shows up with a report that Dovid is already here. Where was he? Dovid tells them that as they were evacuating from the forest, he cooked something to eat. He was tired, so he lay down to sleep and slept for sixteen hours. This shows how united they were. Everyone had agreed to risk their lives to rescue Dovid and not to run away from this place despite the great danger.

Footnotes (Rubin Roy Cobb)
1. The Communist Youth Organization.
2. See Maps Section 2 Page III.
3. Polish derogatory term for Jews.
4. Related to Rubin Roy Cobb through his paternal grandmother Gelie Rokhel Rubin Kobylanski.
5.

[Page 351]

"The Partizanke"

This was the official name of the Bransk Jews in the Soviet detachment.

They taught methods of resistance and showed the Bransk boys and girls how to use the weapons. They battled spies who were always to be found in the forest, searching. They found out about an episode where a large number of armed men questioned the shepherds about the "partizanke."

It later turned out that these had been Ukrainians vlasovtses, Hitler's collaborators.

They arrange a permanent watch. Pavel Radzin, an educated and much respected Russian was the commander. His work was of much use. However, there was no communication with other groups of partisans. Even though they knew there were other partisan detachments, but communication between them did not exist.

Resistance – On the 8th December 1943, a German group led by the infamous Shumanski attacked the Bransk forest. As the group approached the trench, they opened fire. Vanye Zhubater, the Russian takes aim and shoots Shumanski and the German flee.

A road is being built from Bransk to Drogetchin. The foreman, a German, was a bandit, Vanye Zhubater arrives in the middle of the day, at the end of 1943, shoots the foreman before everyone's eyes. He instructs all the workers to place their shovels on a hill and everything is burned.

[Page 352]

Lube Goldberg – a Tchekhenavtser young woman from Alt Shtot, is hiding in the Bransk forest with the Bransker partisans. At the attack on their trench on the 8th December 1943 she shows how brave she is. Lube Goldberg stands in the trench and is visible from the waist up and she is shooting. While Vanye Zhabate shoots, she prepares more weapons for him. She hands them to him and shouts bravely: "shoot, Vanye" while using the automatic pistol herself and directs Vanye. In March 1944 Lube Goldberg is transferred to another detachment near Bocki. Because she is a good typist, her name is well–known in the partisan headquarters as a brave young woman. She survived.

Maishe Oskart   Lube Goldberg

However, in a nearby trench there were the Jews: MaisheOskart, (sic) MGC Khaim Velvl Pribut and Yosef Pribut. They left their trench during the shooting. Maishe Oskard and Khaim Velvl Pribut fled successfully. Yosef falls with a wound to his leg. The Germans threw him into the trench, blowing it up with hand grenades. And so this is how the brave Yosef Pribut fell. Twice he had escaped death and now he has perished.

(Excerpt from the Historical Commission 17/46 accordingly)

[Page 353]

On 28th March 1944, the trench near the Bransk forest was attacked. There were seven Bransk Jews hiding there: Hershl Shpak, his daughter Brokha, Leybl Trus, Yisrael'ke Brenner, Dovtche Olyentsky, Maishe Berl Penkherzh and Yokheved Golde.

Brokha Shpak notices a dog from afar. She tells this to the others. They laugh at her. How does a dog come here? However, they are already shooting into the trench. They fire 70 rounds. Everyone is covered with the earth which falls into the trench. Their eyes are covered with sand. They hear footsteps overhead. Is this now the end? The little Yisrael'ke Brener grabs the revolver from Dovtche Vaytek's hand and shoots all seven rounds. The Germans flee. They must now run away from this trench in case larger groups of Germans appear. We ask: "Everyone alive?" 'Yes,' They stick a hat out of the trench. No one shoots at the hat. Leybl Trus is the first to leave the trench, followed by everyone else. It was terribly hot in the trench so everyone was in their underwear. It is cold in the field because of the snow and frost. There was no talk of taking any clothing with them. They ran naked to Christian acquaintances, and then Yisrael'ke Brener notices that he had been wounded. There is a trail of blood behind him.

They barely dragged themselves seven kilometres to a second forest, met with another group of Jews and Russians. Yisrael'ke's wound is bandaged. At night they return to the trench and take their clothes.

After such incidents a group of Jews and Russians decided to go through to the front. The offensive of the Russian army is underway. The front was near Orshe Vitebsk Kovel. On the road near the Bialovizher forest they encounter the spies from the Soviet partisan detachments and tell them to go back to the Bransk forest. They promise to communicate.

(Excerpt from Historical Commission 19/46 accordingly)

[Page 354]

Jew–Murderers Sentenced to Death

Lyeshnikes are forced to spy for the partisans, Bransk partisans join the Soviet partisan headquarters, given the name of Bransk Zhukov Partisan Detachment

At the beginning of 1944 the first group of partisans of the Major Kapuste brothers Martinov appear in the Bransk forest.

Four partisan groups in four areas are organized. The largest group is called Zhukov and is the Bransk group.

The first order of business of the Bransk group consists of destroying the telephone connections which were located on the Bransk Tchekhenoftse road. This was the direct line to the front at Warsaw. In one night the telephone wires on this road were cut in several places. The poles for a distance of 2 kilometres were torn down. The entire Bransk group of partisans participated in this.

At this same time a Boyevoyer detachment is set up as well as a family camp. Included in this camp were the families who were in the forest. There were a number of complete families in the forest – Khaim Finklshteyn, his wife and three children, Gitl Rubinshteyn 65 years old and her two daughters. And others. Khaim was the commander of the family detachment.

Death Sentences

The Bransk detachment decides to take revenge on the Pole Koshak, the betrayer and Jew murderer.

At a meeting of the detachment heads, it is decided to hand down the death sentence to Koshak.

[Page 355]

The armed men are given the job of carrying out this order. Among them are Mulye Kleinot and Yosl Broyde.[1]

The road to Koshak is a long one and they need to pass through the entire town. The snow makes their footprints easy to notice. This would total about forty kilometres. They cannot cover this distance in one day. The group decides to stop along the way and spend the night until the following evening.

Left: Sonya Rubinshteyn,[2] centre   Right: Shloyme Pat, partisan

They stop at a Polish colonist. He must give them food and remain with them the entire evening and day. He cannot leave the house. The door is guarded.

They set out once again when darkness falls and come into Koshak's house, who, upon seeing the 'guests' turns pale. They ask him for food and receive it, including alcohol. The men do not permit themselves to forget their purpose and keep clear heads.

After eating, Commander Radzin says to Koshak: "*khazaien,* (?) now we must make a reckoning."

Koshak, frightened, says: 'Go, you owe me nothing. I do not need to take any money from you poor people.'

[Page 356]

"No," says Radzin, "you stole, murdered and served the Germans well. Therefore we must make a reckoning."

They tell him to sit and not dare to move. 'First, return all you stole from your victims:' They then give him several blows. He returns the gold, dollars, clothing and a nice little knife. The knife was recognized immediately as having belonged to the Bransker 19–year old Itskhak Okronglies, one of Koshak's victims. He also turns over all his weapons. A special guard goes with his wife and takes all the weapons he had. They then read to him the death sentence: "In the name of the united councils, in the name of the field court of Bransk Zhukov partisan detachment, you, Koshak, are sentenced to death by shooting."

He is asked to sign the death sentence. An Alyekshener gentile girl is there, and she is also required to sign the decree as a witness. Frightened, she signs the paper with trembling hands.

Mulye Kleinot, the partisan, is honoured with carrying out the death sentence.

Mulye remembers well how Koshak had brought his uncle Nakhum, tied up, to the German gendarmes to be shot. Mulye shoots twice with his revolver. Koshak lies motionless. They check his pulse, dead. The time the decree was carried out is noted in the diary. They write a notice to the population that Koshak has been killed by the Zhukov partisan detachment of the Bransk forest for his murders and robberies. The gentile girl is given all the papers and strictly ordered that the papers be hung in a public place.

Radzin does not forget to mention to the mother that she should bring her children up in a better way.

The following day there were reports of this incident, and the partisan detachment was given even more recognition by the population.

[Page 357]

The detachment forced the Lyeshnikes to give them information about all suspicious happenings. Out of fear, they disclosed valuable information.

One of the Lyeshnikes reports to the detachment that a certain person always comes to him to inquire how many partisans there are? Do they have a lot of weapons? He asks the lyeshnik not to tell anyone about his visit.

The detachment now knows about this. They look for this person. Finally, the lyeshnik points him out. They meet with him. He is touched to have the opportunity to meet with the partisans.

After a brief examination, they note this man is wearing white underwear, fine boots and has enough money and good cigarettes. His explanation that he has been in the forest for six months is discounted and they now see he is a spy, and with no questions asked, the order is given to shoot him.

The detachment also forced many Christians to be spies. To tell them everything they had seen or carried as messengers which could only be done by the Christians. They were threatened with death, with burning their houses. They obeyed. Much necessary information came from the forced spies. They called themselves "ligalnikes."

For a certain length of time there came to the detachment a Russian partizanke. She was a young, pretty Russian woman who came to spend a little bit of relaxed time. She is suspected of spying. It is decided that a definite investigation must be carried out. When she comes again, she is followed by one of the ligalnikes. He follows her from afar and notices she is going to Bransk from the forest. The first place she goes is to the gendarmerie.

At that time there were high officials of the central Zhukov detachment, parachutists and other who had come from the central command. In a word, important officials. The danger was that if the gentile woman had told them everything, the Germans would attack.

[Page 358]

If she had not noticed too much she would certainly return again. The situation becomes serious.

They establish a front guard on the side of Bransk near the forest. One of the partisans is stationed on a tree with binoculars and they wait. He notices her approaching from afar and she is alone. They greet her in a friendly fashion. They spend some pleasant time with the Russian gentile girl. Then the political commander Danski, commander of the detachment and also the party representative in the forest interrogates her. After a severe questioning and a personal examination, they find a revolver and a German confirmation from the Gestapo. The partisan court decides to hang her immediately.

Young Itchele Broyde earns the honour, shoots her, but she is wounded. The commanders order her to be hanged. Everyone carries out the sentence. Now there is one spy less.

Very often parachutists, come to the Bransk forest. The brigadier commander Martinov also come often with ten aides. Also the major of the partisan detachment Vesolov. Martinov's wife, a parachutist.

They make known their very good opinion about the Bransk detachment. The population is the best organized.

They improved the discipline when summoned for diversified work for the battle against the Germans and Polish bandits.

A permanent group of parachutists remained in the Bransk forest. There was now constant communication with the headquarters and other detachments. Newspapers were brought every day from Moscow of the Partisan Post.

Reports from the front were sent from the Bransk forest every day.

The detachment issues an order that all Russians who are with Christians to report to the partisan detachment. The detachment is greatly increased.

[Page 359]

The civilian population is warned not to hinder the partisans in their activities. Those who do will be handled accordingly.

The Polish 70–year old lame Dr. Tsivinski is mobilized. He is forced to come every day to the forest, supply medicines, help the wounded partisans. They sent a wagon for him to bring him to perform various operations and to bring with him various medicines. We must note that Dr. Tzivinski's trip from Bransk to the forest had to be conducted in secrecy. However, he performed his work like a hero.

Bransk Jews and Russians were sent for work. They acknowledged and praised the heroic work of the partisans – Yosl Broyde, Mulye Kleinot, the brothers Olyentsky, Khaim–Velvl Pribut.

There were some partisans who wanted to get rich in the forest. Because of this they meddled in certain necessary work.

There was special mention of Khaim Vrobel (Motl**Error! Bookmark not defined.** Kevlyaker's son). His work resulted in good things for everyone. He personally did not seek to make use of the forest to become rich.

There was other work going on that would hinder the Nazi effort to wipe out the food contingent. There was a collection point in every village for food for the Germans. The partisans used to attack these collection points and take everything and destroy what was left. The central collection point for milk was also attacked. The milk was poured out.

Bridges were ordered to be burned. However, they were well–guarded. There was a large watch at each bridge. There were attempts made several times but they were unsuccessful. Then the bridge from the Bransk road to the Shepetove main road, central to the highway from Warsaw to Byalevyezh was burned by the partisans.

A second group at the Bialystok Warsaw railway track near Shepetove, twice dismantled the railway line. This led to a railway line catastrophe.

In honour of the 1st of May an attack is organized on the Vyelkove estate near Bransk. The estate is managed by a German administration. Four Russians and eight Jews take part in this attack. Shooting begins, but after a half–hour, the partisans retreat without losses.

[Page 360]

As they returned, the group is attacked by some Armaia Krayowa who had been hiding.

During this sudden attack, the Bransk Jew Yeshaye Tabak, 24 years old, a Vishinker, who had worked in Bransk for several years, by trade a master at repairing valuable tools falls dead. Wounded are Shloyme Olyentsky, Yankev Voyitek's son and Mulye Kleinot, Elber's grandchild.

The wounded Russians are taken through Bransk to Tchaie. Dr. Tsivinski goes to treat them until they recover. The 12 wounded Jews are quartered with Christians and the same Doctor Tsivinski comes to treat them.

On the 8th of May 1944 a large group of people are noticed nearing the forest. They quickly find out that 600 Germans and Ukrainians and their death battalions have blockaded the forest. The situation at that moment was serious. 28 experienced fighters take a stand against 600 armed Germans and Vlosavtses (Ukrainians) (?) There are at that time in the family camp 40 women and sick children. It becomes necessary to evacuate the family camp from the forest. There is no opportunity to do this because the large band of Germans in the forest. The partisans heroically defend the forest. There are victims on both sides. The fascists pull back.

The family camp is set up in another forest. Dead as a result of this attack were Meir Vishnevitch, 20 years, Kopke's grandchild and one Russian.

The following day there were write-ups in the press that the Germans had wiped out the Bransk partisan detachment of Russians and Jews.

The central organ of the partisans, "Partisan" wrote that 28 partisans were victorious over 600 Germans and Vlaslavtses (Ukrainians), (?) and thereby crediting the Bransk Zhukov partisan detachment.

Of course you understand, that after this attack the forest can no longer be used, so they decide to relocate to the Bielsk area to the Popokhovs detachment. However, attacks had also occurred on this detachment by Polish armed gangs. But an order arrives from headquarters to return to the Bransk forest. We settle in again into forest near Pyetkeve.

[Page 361]

They Take Prisoners – The front nears

The Neman near Grodno is now the battlefield. The partisans watch takes 19 Vlaslavtses prisoners, well–dressed in German uniforms. They always have with them leaflets that the Russian airplanes have distributed.

The partisans are not led astray. They take the German clothes from them. This now becomes very necessary. The roads are now filled with returning Nazis. They cannot go for food in their old clothes, so they make use of the new German uniforms. Twelve men don the uniforms and set out to the Christians. They bring back calves, sheep, bread, butter. Some Poles were unsure whether these were really Germans, so they cursed and nevertheless gave.

The question of water became very important. They can no longer go to the town for water. They decide to dig a well in the forest. The 19 prisoners think we are digging a grave for them, and felt that they had no other alternative than to make peace with their fate that this was their grave.

The front comes closer with quickening steps. An order arrives that anultimatum should be given to the Polish underground gang to cease their operations near the partisans.

At a meeting with certain Polish educated partisans in the house of a peasant, Commander Major Vesolof openly stated that 'any day we shall surround the forests.' 'The Red Army is coming. Prepare yourselves to turn over your weapons.'

The front is now very close. They can clearly see the shooting around Bransk, there is fire around the town. Soviet airplanes are flying, covering the town with leaflets. The night is lit by huge projectors and the fires all around. The partisan detachment finds itself in the middle of the front.

[Page 362]

Vesalov orders them to form into small groups. They divide into small groups of three in trenches or other holes. There is military everywhere. The forest is full of infantry and artillery.

On the 2nd of August 1944, at 4 a.m., the partisans receive an order to leave.

After a short pause, the first advance of the Russian army appears. They know where the Zhukovtses are, i.e. the Bransk Zhukov detachment. They clasp the hands of the commanders, Vesolov and Radzin, Danski and all Soviets and Jewish defenders.

The officers of the headquarters of the Red Army order the Bransk partisans to return to Bransk because here in the forests around Pyetkever Glinik there will be a large battle.

We set out in groups to return to Bransk in little groups of six or ten people. We are a total of 64 people.

We stand in the Bransk big market. We have a horrific picture before our eyes. The ghetto is still fenced–in. Jewish Bransk is empty. An echo is heard, an echo of Jewish voices, of Jewish life, the echo of the last screams of mother and father, of children that one imagines have remained in the air. We hear clearly the word: 'Why? Why, God?'

How hardened we have become in the 21 months of living in the forest, a life of animals, not of humans and our hearts melted away, our eyes that long ago had lost the ability to shed tears, were suddenly filled with bitter tears.

We look at ourselves, our 64 people, tattered, traumatized countenances. We look at the empty, frightening fenced–in ghetto that stands veiled in sorrow and yearns for her children who will never return to her.[3]

Footnotes (Rubin Roy Cobb)
1. Rubin Roy Cobb met him in the 1990s at a wedding or bar–mitzvah given by Evelyn Iteld in Atlanta. He was blind and lived in Venezuela. He related how well he remembered the Piekuckis (maternal family of) and how argumentative they were amongst themselves. He wrote a manuscript on his partisan activities in Yiddish that has been translated and has a copy thereof.
2. Married to Jack Rubin (paternal family of Rubin Roy Cobb) of Baltimore after her first husband died.
3. Jack Rubin of Baltimore told Rubin Roy Cobb when they were in Bransk in 1991 how he watched German soldiers retreating, followed by Russian infantry advancing after them and how he carefully, with hands raised to the advancing Russians speaking Russian that he

was Jewish and advised to   to Bransk. There he met the other 63 Jewish survivors referred to here.

[Page 363]

One of the 64

As told by Zavl Rubinshteyn to Julius Cohen[1]

In this article we will present the story of one of the surviving Branskers who was fortunate enough to come to New York.

It took much effort on my part to persuade Zavl to tell his story about what happened to him from the first day when the Nazis entered Bransk until the second of August 1944, when he returned to Bransk, one of the 64 survivors of the entire Bransk Jewish population of almost three thousand.

Zavl is a great–grandchild of Zavl–Hersh the Khasid. He is a harness–maker by trade, mostly working with his father. This is a trade practiced primarily by Christians for their own horses. Therefore, he had many Christian acquaintances where he could hide from time to time.

And yet, he was the only one of a family of eight to survive. His parents, sisters and brothers all perished.

This is his story as he told it to Julius Cohen.

The first order issued by the Germans was for mobilizing all the horses in Bransk. The mobilization point was Shayer Street. There were investigations conducted of the saddle–makers to confiscate all material from the businesses.

The Nazis took everything from our house. They piled all the merchandise on my shoulders and instructed us to take everything to Shayer Street.

[Page 364]

I was laden down by the thugs, with reins, bridles. I could not move. I go with all the merchandise to the gathering–point. The German gendarme walks before me. I hold on to the walls, the fences near the houses and look at the

German. At the first opportunity I throw a couple of bridles over a fence. My load got lighter, easier. Little–by–little, I freed myself from almost half of my weight. Finally, all sweaty, I arrive at the gathering–point. The Nazi studies me, curious. There is something that disturbs him. He demands I prepare all the harnesses for the horses. I explain to him in a pure Yiddish–German that I do not have any tools. I send my brother Alye 19 years, who had followed me, to bring my tools, asking and telling him with a wink to take his time. Finally, I get the tools. I work until night and then I take my tools, wanting to go home. I receive a merciless beating and am accused of wanting to steal German tools.

The Germans take me to the magistrate, the familiar bandit Doctor Dambrovski who is thrilled with his first chance to shoot a Jew. He orders his Polish police to do a new search in our house. Police who only a couple of days earlier had been policemen for the Soviets. They conducted a thorough search. The thugs look for leather goods and other valuable items and stuff them into their pockets. My mother calls them Bolshevikes. The policemen also bring my mother to the magistrate Dambrovski who is now even happier. He telephones the German official representative that they have to shoot the first Jews and then the others will have respect for the new power. He accuses us of having hidden more merchandise and that we wanted to steal German possessions.

The German commander orders us to be brought to him. He wants to see us. Everyone in town knows we will be the first victims. He asks my mother why she insulted the Polish police? She points to Borkofsken and says he was the policeman for the Bolshevikes and is now wearing the same rifle. The acting–commander frees my mother. Then he asks me, how many people work in your factory? I tell him my father is a sick man and I work together with him. I had worked the entire day for the Germans with my own tools. Now I take the tools to work at home. He let me go as well, and Dambrovski is left with nothing.

[Page 365]

I worked for several days and prepared the horses and then I was sent home. At night, I collected my merchandise that I had slung over the fences. I saved something.

Then there was a request for a harness–maker to work in Pyetkever. There in Pyetkever were already working about 50 young girls aged twelve who were digging potatoes. These workers had already been sent by the Judenrat knowing they would be forced to go to work. I voluntarily reported for work to the Polish harness–maker Shtzervinski for twelve weeks. During this time I did work for private peasants who were badly in need of harnesses. This was with the permission of Shtzervinski. They came to me in Pyetkever and brought the work. I placed my life in danger. However, knowing the peasants would give me food for my family and me, I took a chance. They paid me well. They sent enough potatoes to my house and other food. I was very friendly with the German overseers and they pretended not to notice. When the work ended, I returned to Bransk and asked the Judenrat to help the children who were working with the potatoes and in the fields.

The Judenrat receives a second request for workers also under the Polish harness–maker Shtzervinski. The Judenrat, seeing I had received food when working under Shtzervinski decides their own person should be sent there to work. They send Motl the harness–maker's son.

Shtzervinski is not pleased with this worker and the Germans beat him and tell him to go home. Alter Yamshin, the president of the Judenrat, comes to find out what has taken place there and he too, is badly beaten by the Nazis.

[Page 366]

Maishe Tikatsky and Itskhak Finklshteyn of the Judenrat come to me with a smile: 'You are already a candidate so go to work over there.' Eventually I did agree to be sent once again to work. I find out the work is in Valke. There is a palace there and a large holding that belonged to Mrs Pilsudski and is now under the German commander by the name of Gogo. The man in charge is once again the Christian Shtzervinski. We find there a large stash of leather that the Soviets had left behind. We begin to work, cutting up the best leather to make bridles. I see that a shoemaker can also make a living. I go to the Judenrat and ask them to send KhaimTsiplinsky the shoemaker. He makes good boots from this leather for the Germans. I make good business and we send it to Gogo to his courtyard. The rest we make for the German needs. For local peasants there is also work using the leather. Once again I receive potatoes, honey and spirits for my family. Many times we find a good piece of leather mixed in with the potatoes. In the house we know what to do with these items. We get little nails from Maishe Tikatsky and slowly create the merchandise.

The work and leather in Valke runs out within two months. I must sign to attest that I will return to work in the spring or when they will get more leather. It appears that they did not get any leather because they did not require me to work anymore and the Judenrat did not send me for any work. So for the summer months I worked with my father in the house and somehow earning enough for some bread and putting my life in danger because it was forbidden to own any leather whatsoever.

November, 1942

At the end of October there is a noticeably large change in the behavior of the Christian population. The Germans who had worked in the ghetto's Jewish–owned workshops suddenly appeared and demanded the work to cease immediately. Some take unfinished work. They know about something that is going to happen. Jews wonder why is there such haste? It becomes clear. The ghetto is going to be surrounded by wire so no one can climb over. The gates are heavily guarded. There is a feeling that danger is close at hand. The days are numbered.

[Page 367]

I decide to take my family out of the ghetto. I ask my father to leave the ghetto and go to Christian acquaintances until we see what will happen further. My father takes my mother and three children and leaves the ghetto. Along the road they become confused, and this frightened them and they return to the ghetto. I take them by the hand and lead them out of the ghetto through the fields and tell them to go to Zshilinski. Itskhak Finklshteyn, the Judenrat member, sends his two daughters out with Shimon Rubin's[2] wife and child on a wagon. My sister Peshe, my cousin Sorah Klode and a cousin from Sokolove remain in our house. My brother was not at home.

I told my sister Peshe we must be prepared because I feel something will happen this night. I ask them to sleep in their clothes and be prepared for anything that can occur. I gathered together valuable items and buried them near the door of our house.

We did not have to wait long. In the early morning we hear the noise of the approaching very end. (?) We soon hear heavy footsteps around the ghetto. The cordon has arrived. The ghetto is surrounded. We leave the house, lock the door and go to the gate of the ghetto that leads to the forest. They must have noticed us because we hear shooting in our direction. We run and luckily, due to the darkness, not one of us was wounded.

We were in the forest for several days. There were other Jews there as well. We hear rumours that many Jews were safe near Alekshon. My sister Peshe goes to Zshilinski where our parents were supposed to be. Zshilinski tells her our father and a daughter left Friday to return to the ghetto and were taken out with everyone else on Shabbos. My mother went to Dolovove where she was born. She thinks there in the town she will find a place to hide with a Christian acquaintance.

[Page 368]

A couple of days later we meet our brother Elye and our cousin BerlPat in the forest. We decide to go to Dolokhove to find out where out mother is. However, we are afraid to be seen by the Christians. I meet again with Zshilinski but he cannot hide us. He gives us a letter to one of his in–laws in the village of Sheshke. There will be room there for three to hide. I tell this to Bevel who most especially wants to find his wife Brokha and the child whom he had left with the Christian Romakh Yavorski. He, Yavorski, returns many items to Bevel that he had kept hidden for him. He could not have taken Brokha and the child because they would certainly not be successful. Yavorski assures Bevel he will bring Brokha and the child to a certain place on the road the following evening, but we have to be there and take them with us. He gives us a letter to a gentile acquaintance by the name of Trushkofske who takes us by wagon to the paved road where we find Brokha and the child. We are now all in the forest.

I go to the village of Sheshke to find place for them at the Christian who Zshilinski had recommended. He permits only three people to stay with him. I find place for Bevel with his wife and child and at a second Christian by the name of Guglyefski in a colony near the village of Malyesher. My sister Peshe and my brother Ely and I remain in Sheshke. It is understood we paid well. At night we all met in the forest. Now that we had taken care of everyone having a place, we decide to go to Dolobove to find out where our mother and the children are – but we do not have any clothes – especially warm ones.

[Page 369]

Trushkofski tells us Jews come into the ghetto at night to remove things from their houses. This gentile Trushkofski tells us he will take us to the ghetto and wait there for us. We were successful the first evening. Berl went into the ghetto. Oley Zshevoytske says he will stand watch. He pretended to not hear. He tells them to come only during the hours he is on watch. On the second evening, Berl once again went to the ghetto to look for things, especially warm items.

It is extremely dark in the house with only the wall–clock continuing to tick. He strikes a match. The flashing light of the match brought Germans to the ghetto. Berl Pat and my brother Alye flee, barely escaping with their lives.

Berl tells us we must find weapons to be able to defend ourselves. Without them we are lost. He becomes acquainted with a young gentile who wants to sell him weapons. He establishes the price but the gentile does not give him any weapons. He instructs him to return a week later with the money. This is suspicious so we do not return to the gentile.

Berland My Brother Alye Become Victims

We must now go to Dolobove to look for my mother. Berl and Alye set out. Peshe and I remain in Sheshke.

Lyeshnikes come to their hiding–place. They are captured, turned over to the Germans and are both shot.

Guglyefski already knows Berl is dead. He will no longer get any money from Berl so he does not want to hide Brokha and her child. He says he is afraid of the Germans.

I go alone to Dolobove to search for my mother. Along the way to Kolnitse, I am met by Tetlitski, the lord from Voylker. He was a former Polish judge. He warns me that if I wish to remain alive I should not be in the forest but rather somewhere hidden in a house or stable. He himself would hide me in his courtyard even though there are German top level leaders there, but he is afraid for his own farmhands.

He tells me several farmhands were hiding a little Jewish boy in a stable. They give him food. He pretends not to notice. This was Yankele Rothstein, Mendl Toker's grandchild. He assures me he will bring food for Brokha to a designated place. He points out along the way a little hill near a rock and that is where he will come to leave food at night and I will be responsible. I thank him for his goodness and set out again.

[Page 370]

I meet the peasant Yanek Katseski who tells me my mother had been in the colony yesterday. She said she was going with a daughter to the village of Zaluske. He also tells me Finklshteyn's two girls are hiding with his neighbour. They *naihen* (?) for the peasant and that is why he is feeding them.

In Zaluskel find out my mother is no longer there. She went to the village of Kozovske. I finally get to Kozovske and find my mother and sister Shayne.

I take my mother and Shayne to the peasant Gurski. He allows four of us to stay with him. I also bring my sister Peshe from the village of Sheshke to Gurski. My mother wants me to be with them. When I had come to the village of Sheshke to get my sister Peshe, I heard someone coughing on the opposite side of the wall. I ask: who this is? The Christian says the priest from Toptshever had asked him to hide a Jew by the name of Arona Lapser doctor, and therefore, he could not hide us because he would not have enough food for everyone. So I took Peshe and left to go to Gurski. The following day that place was attacked and Doctor Aron is shot. The entire neighborhood defends the priest and the Christian family, who had hidden the Jewish doctor and they released them. My mother, two sisters and I stayed in Gurski the entire winter.

Mother and Sisters Become Victims

Gurski tells me that in the spring the Germans go to the villages to inventory the cows, horses and chickens. This means to determine how much each peasant has to give to the Germans. It would be terribly dangerous for us to remain with him because the Germans will find us.

[Page 371]

He helped us to stay in the forest for several days until the investigations will be conducted. We leave the peasant Gurski and we all come to the forest where we meet six other Jews: Berl Rozinke, Berl Yakobtsiner, Leybl Grazshinsky's son, Yenkl Mulyer's son and a Bialystok Jew who had jumped from the train, and Bobble's grandchild, a 12–year old boy.

We meet each other several times in the forest. We try to plan what to do further. It was impossible to stay with Gurski. First–of–all, our money had already run out. We now did not have anything with which to pay. Secondly, according to Gurski's explanations, the stable was already empty and there is nowhere to hide in there.

Berl Rozinka says we should now live in the forest because it is now summer. We can live in the forest and be safe. We will have to find food somewhere without money. We remain together in the forest. For now we have only to find a pair of boots for one of the group who was barefoot.

This was the first of May 1943, 26th Nissan.

I leave behind in the forest my mother, the two sisters and Bobble's small grandchild, and we go into the village to get a pair of boots.

They are all attacked and shot. We hear the shooting from afar. I already understand the victims are mine, they are of my flesh and blood. We inquire of the peasants – What had happened? Why was there shooting there? Did they want to capture us? We managed to get away from the peasants but still not knowing what exactly had happened. We come to Gurski's stable. He tells us Levandovske from the village of Tchaye was horseback riding and noticed the group in the forest. He brought gendarmes from Toptsheve. All were shot. Gurski felt guilty that we had left his house. "You know that it was impossible for me to keep you," he said to us.

[Page 372]

We leave Gurski. I am now alone in the world, one left of a family. Rozinka, Yakobtsiner, I and the small Ishyele set out to another forest, not knowing where we could hide. I had even lost the desire to hide. Life has no worth for me now.

BerlRozinka, himself a Bialystoker, says, we need now to go to Bialystok. The ghetto still exists there. Jews live and work there. I declined to go with them, but eventually I agreed and we head to the road to Bialystok.

On the road to Bialystok we come to the village of Lutsaiev and go to a Christian by the name of Palkovski. He undertakes to hide us. He feeds us well. We remained with Palkovski for two weeks. But he could not take all six of us. He has room for three, and the other three do not have where to spend the night. We decide that all of us will continue on to Bialystok.

Between Stroblye and Suraz we cross the Narew River with a raft. At night we wake the raftsman to take us across the Narew. He indicates the road we should take to get to Bialystok.

We stay together. We get to a point near the city and we are attacked by gendarmes. Everyone scatters in different directions. I remain lying in a hole in the middle of the field. I no longer see anyone around me.

Suddenly, I notice a young gentile far from me in the field. I give him my jacket as a present. He is pleased. I ask him to bring me an old summer shirt and water to drink. The gentile youth examines the jacket. He liked it. He returns later with water and a torn jacket with holes. I put on the summer jacket. I ask the gentile youth if there are Jews in Bialystok. "Yes," he says. 'Stay here in the hole until the evening when the Jews return to town after work and you will be able to join in the group and that is how you will go into Bialystok.' I thank the gentile and remain lying in the hole. Sweat is pouring from me. I am alone. My friends are not here with me. What has happened to them I do not know.

[Page 373]

In the evening I notice a large group of Jews marching in rows coming from work. I edge closer to the road, stand up and join the marching Jews who are returning home from forced labor. They quietly make a spot for me in the row so they should be straight and not noticeable. 'A Jew?' – someone asks. 'Yes' I answer him. He gives me a piece of his yellow patch. "Put this on quickly," he says. We march together. How proud I felt at that moment with this piece of yellow patch is indescribable.

I hear one of the marchers behind me mumble: "Give him something to carry." That is when I notice all the marchers carrying packages of tools. Only I have nothing with me. My situation is not safe. I think to myself: "Take it." Someone in the line shoves a package into my hand. "Here, carry," he says. Now I am the same as everyone else. I am carrying a package and wear a yellow patch. I am going together with all the Jews from forced labour, returning to the ghetto in Bialystok which is strange to me because I have never been there. How lonely I was. In those minutes I was the most fortunate person in the world: A Jew among Jews. I was happy, proud and safe among my own.

We come to the gate where we are stopped and searched. I examine my package. I see that in the package there are eggs, certainly a terrible item because food is surely not permitted to be brought into the ghetto. My heart pounds again with fear. What will happen now? They come to my row. The German opens my sack. He finds eggs. He is happy with this. He takes them from me with joy. I see that the eggs will rescue me. Yes, the German allows me through the gate.

In Bialystok

This was in the middle of May, 1943. I enter the ghetto. Someone tells me where to go to find a place to spend the night. The people in the house give me food. The next day I am already a Bialystok ghetto Jew. They give me anaddress. I go there and they give me work in the ghetto which consists of assembling rifles from small parts that are smuggled into the ghetto through various secret means.

[Page 374]

This was a secret underground organization. They experienced much danger. In particular there were three brothers from Slonim with the name Yudkofsky who caused much trouble in the ghetto.

The organization wants me to show them I am devoted. I assure them I will do everything to seek revenge for my parents, sister and brother. They believe me on my word. They see that I am troubled.

I Receive Weapons

In the place where I sleep, I hear someone tell that he works in the house of a former officer as a painter. He noticed two revolvers there hidden in the wall. I ask him to take me with him to work tomorrow. He refuses. I threaten him and it works. In the morning he gives me a pot of whitewash and rags and we both go to work. We get to the house. I ask him where he had seen the revolvers. He does not want to say. My threats work. He shows me the wall. I remove a little box with two new revolvers. In the evening I wrap the revolvers in a rag, cover them with the whitewash and carry them into the ghetto.

I take the revolvers to the organization. A girl whom everyone called Yudite is the chief order giver. They are pleased with the weapons. They give me 20 rubles and say I can keep one revolver for myself and that I would need it during further work.

The underground organization had to carry out much work in the ghetto and outside of the ghetto. They sent me every day to work outside of the ghetto. They felt the ghetto would eventually be liquidated. There is a secret house in the ghetto at Leybl the baker on Nai Velt Street where the weapons are assembled. Many of those who work here are not suited to this work. The entire house is blown up and burns. Three people lost their lives. The gendarmes begin aninvestigation. They know these were explosions and the fire was not of the usual kind.

[Page 375]

Too my greatest astonishment, I meet in the ghetto Berl Rozinka and Berl Yakobtsiner. They arrived in the ghetto through other means a week after I arrived. We are happy with each other and stay together. We are in Bialystok until the middle of August. I become well–known in the underground organization. They have trust in me.

The work outside of the ghetto was fraught with danger vis–à–vis my leaving and returning. I ask them to give me work in the ghetto because I do not have any papers and with every failure I will pay with my life.

I am agonized with a longing to leave Bialystok. I still have the feeling my mother begs me, requests: "Zavl, leave the ghetto."

The day of the liquidation of the Bialystok ghetto draws near. We decide to divide our strengths with some being in the forests around the city, waiting for several days.

The Bialystok ghetto meanwhile is surrounded by three cordons. There are 45 of us in the forest. We hope we can find those who fled from the ghetto. I know that hundreds of Jews had fled from the Bransk ghetto. Regretfully, no one from the ghetto came to the forest. The Bialystok ghetto is now empty. No one survived. Our work has finished. There were a few Russians in the forest, but they advised the group to divide the weapons among the 45 people and hide in small groups of five. Rozinka, Yakobtsiner and I get our portion of weapons. We decide to return to Bransk.

[Page 376]

On the way to Bransk, behind the village of Malinove, we come to a peasant, Marzhvinski. We ask him to hide us for several days so we can rest. We hide our weapons in the forest. He tells us he himself does not have any food and therefore he cannot give us anything. We assure him we will not need his food. He permits us to sleep in the stable.

We retrieve our weapons at night and go to distant villages. There is respect for the rifles. We bring enough food. We give Marzhvinski some food as well. He is pleased to hide us. We went once a week to get food. We took everything we could get: sheep, pigs, potatoes, flour and brought these to Marzhvinski. We were so careful that he never saw us with the weapons. We meet Itche Grazhinsky, Shyele and a Bialystoker in the forest. We give them food as well. This is how we lived through the entire winter with the peasant. Spring approached. The nights are getting shorter. We cannot go too far to find food. We did not want to go in this neighborhood because Marzhvinski would also be blamed. We decide we must prepare food for the entire summer.

We set out with a wagon that the peasant gave us. We fill a wagon with food, meat and flour. We have to take it to the village to the peasant so he can salt [the meat] and put it away.

The night passed quickly. Day is beginning to dawn. We drive into the village. It is possible some peasants were already awake and had noticed the wagon of food and other merchandise arriving at Marzhvinski's and had become suspicious.

We are not aware of this. The entire load of food is prepared, well–packed with salt. We are certain we will now have food. We will not have to look for food the entire summer. We sleep in the stable.

[Page 377]

Marzhvinski had during the winter eaten quite well. The Christians wonder about this. His wife wears a new Jewish dress we had given her as a present. At the same time there were rumours circulating in Bielsk that Jewish bandits steal from good Polish citizens and Marzhvinski is spied upon.

We are all in the stable. We hear dogs barking at night. I peer through the cracks see flashlights lighting the road. Our weapons were in the stable at that time. I grab my weapon and crawl down from the stable. I am noticed. There is shooting and I am lightly wounded. I respond with fire. Berl Rozinka and Maishe the Bialystoker shoot from within the stable. The group pulls back. When we remain quiet they do not shoot back thinking we were no long alive. 15 minutes later, we come out into the courtyard. The Christian woman comes out of the house. We warn her not to divulge any names. She makes the sign of the cross and assures us she will not say a word.

Wounded I crawl away twelve miles to the village Kozuske to meet Gurski. I arrive at three o'clock at night and knock on the door and Gurski says to his wife: "Zavl is at the door."

She opens the door and I come inside. Gurski sees my weapon and says: 'Zavl, what is it with you?' I answer him that I have been wounded by the gendarmes. I tell him that Berl Rozinka finds himself somewhere in the forest, when he asks about ne, he must tell him that I am somewhere in the village.

I had arranged to meet Berl every three days near the forest at the two mills. If someone did not show up it would mean that he was dead.

Several days later, I began to notice something. The Christians were acting differently. They whisper to one another so I would not hear. They either suspect me or want to turn me over to the Germans. I go to the stable to check the weapons I had hidden. Gurski's son follows me from a distance. I see that the weapons have been touched but everything was there. This means that Gurski now knows my friends and I have weapons.

[Page 378]

I meet with Maishein the forest near the mill. Berl Rozinka is not there. Is he dead? It is impossible. We decide to wait another day. We must now leave Gurski. The following day, Gurski's little boy tells me someone with a green cloak had inquired about me. So Berl is here. We meet in the forest late at night and decide to go to Alekshon.

The Christian Stanislav Kroyze lives in a colony near the village of Alekshon. We come to her house. She is pleased to hide us: "With me you will survive the war," she says. The front is now near, at Brisk.[3] We were in the colony with Kroyze three months. We had to find food with our weapons. Stanislav knew we had weapons and how we got food.

In the middle of summer the Polish police who had been devoted Nazis up to this point realized the Russians were near and they now have to become, once again, Polish patriots. 25 Bransk Polish policemen together with a few young men organized in the Armia Krajowe in Polish partisan groups. They, with all their weapons, came to the forests. Jewish partisans suffered great trouble from these Poles. Their first work was to betray the Jews whom they found in the forests.

One night we left from Alekshon to get food. We get bread, eggs and butter. We are ready to take our packages and return to our hiding–place. Berl Rozinka says he had seen a pot of cream at the peasant's house. He does not want to leave it. It has been a long time since he ate cream. We wait for him and then return to the Christian woman.

Meanwhile the Krayovtses arrive. They notice us. They think we are Polish. They ask us for a password. They had expected to find some of them in the stable where they slept.

[Page 379]

In any event they left us, taking their pals and left together. As they left, I heard them say: 'Who were these people who did not know the password? They were not ours.' They shoot several rounds and leave.

We crawl into the stable and lie down to sleep. In the early morning we hear Kroyze milking the cows, speaking to them so we can hear: 'Two bands met here yesterday. Ten of them slept in the stable.'

At the end of the month of July, on a Sunday, the front was already near Alekshon. Germans retreat. The Russians arrive in the forest. We watch the battle from the stable. All the houses around the village are burning from the gunfire. We will have to leave the stable because it will probably at any minute begin to burn. We cannot get out of the stable. We will certainly be noticed by either the Russians or the Germans. We cannot cause any difficulties for Kroyze who had been good to us.

The Germans come looking for horses to retreat. They find a young gentile girl. They carry her away to the forest and forget about the horse.

We climb down from the stable, hide in the high oats. The Germans take up positions. They shoot all of Alekshon. The Russians are located on the other side of the village. Bullets fly over our heads. We lay in the oats and suddenly we hear a German panzer leaving the road and drive into the field. We now fully expect our death, to be squeezed by the terrible monster that is about 20 feet from the spot where we lay in hiding. Luckily, the Germans turned the tank around almost near our bodies and begin to shoot towards the forest. It is evening. The sounds of Russian artillery can be heard closer. The German artillery pulls back. We crawl in the stable once again which, through a miracle, remained standing, not burned and lie down. Have we truly survived? Or are we yet to become victims of the flying bullets.

[Page 380]

Kroyze comes in the early morning and tells us there are no Germans to be seen. They had been cleared out of the village.

An officer arrives. I recognize he is a Soviet officer. He asks us who we are and we tell him we are the remaining Jews. He tells us to go to Bransk.

We enter the village of Alekshon, now free people. We come to Adamtchik the saltim, the biggest bandit. His wife receives us like dear guests. She gives us our first breakfast. She is a totally different to Adamtchik. Her husband was not there.

We get to Bransk in the morning. It is a rainy, dreary and cold morning.

We find Maishe Yentchman and Dovtche Olyentsky in town.

This is the story of Zavl Rubinshteyn.

Zavl Rubinshteyn

Footnotes (Rubin Roy Cobb)
1. Married to Sonya after the War and when he died in the US she married Jack Rubin of Baltimore, a paternal cousin of Rubin Roy Cobb.
2. Related to Rubin Roy Cobb through his father's mother.
3. Brisk de'Lite (Brest Litovsk)

[Page 381]

Bransk After the Liberation

We slowly begin to recover. We begin to evaluate our situation, begin to comprehend the entire tragedy.

Later, a top Soviet official makes an appearance. I think he was a railway engineer. He questions everyone. He is most especially interested in finding information about the Tsukerman family, the family of the Bransk rabbi. Perhaps it is possible that someone is still alive. He launches a special investigation. It does not take too long. He discovers the terrible truth that not one member of the rabbi's family is among the living. He was Rabbi Tuckerman's grandchild, serving in the Soviet army. He had come to look for members of the family and found destruction.

People begin to do some kind of work. The Polish mobs do not allow us to settle in Bransk. Every morning there are placards warning Jews to leave Bransk.

The Jewish homes are occupied by Poles. The trade, work – is all Polish.

Heartbroken, we watch as the Christians went to church dressed in Jewish clothing. One recognizes one's father's suit.

There were still Soviet military in Bransk until Warsaw was liberated, and therefore the Poles could not exert much influence. Later, when the Soviets pulled back, Jewish life took a turn for the worse. After working during the day, at night we would all gather together at Itskhak Gotlieb's brick house on the second floor. Some of us, with our weapons, slept while others stood guard.

Page 382]

Murders After the Liberation

In March, 1945 Zisl Taptchefsky (Lipe Portselainik's) and Maishe Tikatsky's sister–in–law went to work at the Shtainmanove on Benduge. The Shtainmanove had a tailoring workshop. The Shtainmanove brought food to the Jews when they were in hiding in the forests. Suddenly a tumult breaks out, someone was shot. People come to the Shtainmanove and find both girls and the Pole Shtainmanove had been shot.

Sometime later Itchele Broyda and a youth from Drogetchin were traveling to the village, were both murdered along the road.

The Jew Poktcheve who had escaped the gas chambers of Treblinka had kept a girl near the village of Shemyon was on his way there when he was murdered.

Action to Bring Jews to a Proper Jewish Burial

Khaim Vrobel the Kevlyaker (?) organizes the work of bringing from the many scattered areas where Jews were known to have fallen to give them a proper Jewish burial. Groups are organized in Bransk. We make coffins. Each group sets out to different villages to gather together the fallen Branskers to bring them for burial. This was truly heroic work because their lives were placed in jeopardy as they traveled to the villages. And yet, they carried it all out in one day. Zavl Rubinshteyn even relates how dangerous this was. Almost everyone helped with only a few who declined to participate.

Since I was in Bialystok no one could give me precise information who had been buried, until I received it from Velvl Golde in the camp in Germany.

[Page 383]

This is the list of those who received a proper Jewish burial:

Meir Rubin, Leyzer Rubin's son,[1]

Menukhe, his wife and two children,[1]

Zelig Kestin,

Sorah Kusarsky, Perl Yankl Olshver's daughter,

Rokhl Tcheslyak, the Koshnik's grandchild,

Bobtche Rubinshteyn, Yazefinerkegrandchild,

Maishe Kleinot, Elber's grandchild,

Leybl Pav, from Tchizev,

Shimon Rubin, wife and children,[2]

Yankev Olyentsky, Maishe Alyentsky's son,

Binyomin Pribut, Lazer Schmidt's grandchild,

Khaim–Hersh Rotenshtein, Mendl Toker's son,

Yankev Rotenshtein, Leybl Stelmakh's grandchild,

Shayne Halperen, Inditshke's daughter–in–law,

HershlHalperen, Inditchke's grandchild,

Menukhe Horvitz, Hershl's daughter,

Yokhe Susel, Maishe Susel's,

Avrum Vainovitch from Benduge,

Reizl Voinovich,

Feygl Voinovich,

Khaviva Voinovich, 2 Years,

Rakhmiel Brenner, Pesakh Milner's,

Berl Yatz, Shloyme Valfke's son,

Malkhe Yatz, Shloyme Valfke's grandchild,

Yosl Broyde, Shayke's son,

Tsolke Broyde, Shayke's son,

Note Broyde, Shayke's grandchild,

Pesakh Kaplan, Shloyme Valfke's son–in–law,

VelvlYerusalimsky the scribe's, ,

Shalemaike the teacher's grandchild

Hershl Pulshansky, Tchotchke's son,

[Page 384]

Yitskhak Volkovitch, Pesakh Milner's grandchild,

Motl Vrobel, Kevlyaker,

Herzl Vrobel, Motl's son,

Niske Nudelman, Itche Zalitcher's son,

Maishe Khaim Dombrovsky, Botker Melamed's grandchild,

Khlavne Beeber, Rikls Beeber's son,[3]

A Pyekuter youth, name unknown

A strange Jew from Sokale, name unknown,

All these were identifiable.

There were many more who were buried whom we could no longer recognize and know who they were. Many were identified because of the papers they had carried with them. It was impossible to recognize those who had undertaken this noble work of gathering the dead and bringing them to a proper Jewish burial, so the only thanks we can offer is to Khaim Vrobel.[4] It would have yet been possible to bring more, but life was uncertain, most especially out–of–town.

It became known that in the nearby neighboring towns, within one day, there would be organized attacks upon Jews. Five fell in Simyatchitz five were killed, in Sokale, fifteen, in Tchekhenoftse four, in Tchizhev twelve, in Bocki one, and in Drogetchin four.

It now becomes impossible to remain in Bransk and therefore, we decide to leave.

Passover, 1945, all Bransk Jews must leave, barely escaping with their lives.

We will no longer derive anything good from Bransk. As we left Bransk, the Christians stood by, smiling, laughing at us and enjoying their new homes, beautiful clothing, new furniture and everything that had been Jewish. Now no one will come to claim their inheritance.

Many of the survivors set out not knowing where to go, once again wandering, dragging themselves across mountains and waters, across different borders.

[Page 385]

Some were successful in reaching the D.P. camps in the American zone of Germany and Austria.

Wherever there are remnants of survivors there can be found a few from Bransk.

There were those who no longer had the strength for new wandering and remained in the Polish towns of Lower Silesia.

A small number settle in Bialystok.[5]

Bransk remained free of Jews.

Khaim Finklshteyn, the former commandant of the family camp of the Bransk partisan detachment came to the Bransk market on February 24, 1947, and in the middle of the day, in the centre of the market, was shot.

Bransk had begun with Jews from the area settling hundreds of years ago and ended with the murder of Khaim Finklshteyn on February 24, 1947.

This is the story of our hometown, Bransk, of its 140 year–long life, striving, hopes, battles and eventual destruction. Bransk, only a small town, is anexample of all Jewish European influential existence that changed during the years from 1939 to 1944. Five years and so many victims. Will all these victims have died in vain?

We always complain the eternal complaint

That has never yet reached the heavens

And perhaps will never reach the heavens

Why? Why? And once again, Why?

(From Bialik's "In the City of Slaughter")

'zot kratnu v'saparnu b'shinun' (*Heb.*) – 'This happened to us and we have described it clearly.' With this we fulfill the will of Bransk's last rabbi of Bransk, Rabbi Yitskhak Ze'ev Tsukerman, of blessed memory, who perished at the head of the entire Jewish community of our hometown, Bransk.

[Page 386]

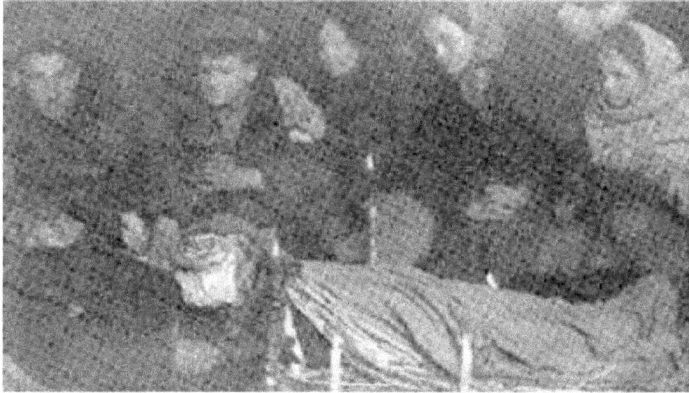

Yitskhak Finklshteyn of the Bransk detachment, the last

Jew in Bransk, murdered February, 1947 by Poles[a]

Footnotes (Rubin Roy Cobb)

1. Related to Rubin Roy Cobb through his paternal grandmother. Jack Rubin of Baltimore told him in 1991 during a visit to Bransk that they were together on the wagon going from Bransk to Bialystok in early 1943 when they were all shot by the Germans, Jack being the sole survivor. He was amongst those of the survivors who reburied the corpses in the Jewish cemetery in Bransk. Brakha Harris–Weiner, a Bransker living in Johannesburg told during a visit there in the 1990s that Meir Rubin introduced 's parents, Jospa Skornik and Khlawna Kobylanski (Cobb) to each other in the late 1920s.
2. Related to Rubin Roy Cobb through his paternal grandmother. He was a brother of Jack Rubin and was on the same wagon as that referred to in above.
3. Rubin Roy Cobb's father's first cousin, his mother Rikl Beeber being a sister of Gelie (Genia) Rokhel Rubin–Kobylanski. Khlavne is a very unusual first name and exists only in the Brest Litovsk – Bialystok area, the name originating in Bohemia in the eleventh century CE. does not know after whom Khlawna Cobb (Kobylanski) is named after, but as his first cousin was also named Khlawne it must be an ancestor of Shimon Rubin, a tavern keeper in Bransk, the father of Rikl and Gelie, either from Shimon Rubin's father's family or his mother's (name unknown) family. Three of the Beeber brothers and a sister move to Atlanta, GA before World War I. Descendants of two of the brothers still reside there. Jack Rubin of Baltimore told that when he escaped from the Bialystok Ghetto just before its liquidation in 1943, this Khlawne Beeber asked to join Jack, but as Jack felt that he (Khlawne Beeber) would not have the strength to keep up with him, he could not take him with.
4. Jack Rubin of Baltimore told that he was one of those who participated in the burial.
5. This included Yankl (John) Rubin {related to Rubin Roy Cobb through his paternal grandmother Gelie [Genia] Rokhel Rubin–Kobylanski) who only left Bialystok for Melbourne, Australia in 1967 as told to by him when visited Melbourne in the late 1990s

Footnote (Mindle Crystal Gross)

1. Please note he states Khaim Finklshteyn was the last Jew shot in February, 1947 (in the body of the writing) and yet he identifies the photo as Yitskhak Finklshteyn. Which is it?

[Page 387]

Bransk Jews in Various Armies

To give an account of all Branskers who participated as armed soldiers or in the role of higher-level officers, we must approach various armies because Branskers were represented everywhere.

At the beginning of the war in 1939, it is understandable that many Branskers were indicted into the Polish army. During the early days, they immediately fell:

Motke Olyentsky,

Meir Friedman, Khone Raizke's son,

In Maidanek near Lublin, there were in German prisoner–of–war camps ten Branskers from September 1939. Bransk received letters from them until the end of 1942. You understand they were taken to the gas chambers of Maidanek at the end of 1942. They were:

Mordekhai Turovitch, Yankev–Meir Kharlap's grandchild,

Mendl Lievartovske, Alter Radishaver Schmidt's son,

Maishe Mordekhai Perlman, Avrum Ber's,

Kaplan, Yenkl Vasser Treger's grandchild, Avrum's son,

Melekh Goldvaser, Mende Leyb's son,

Maishe Goldvaser,

Finklshteyn, baker from Benduge,

Mordekhai Khashe's, Alyentsker Shuster's son, two are unknown,

Yoske Weiner, Yankev Weiner's son (according to Christian friends' explanations and Yoske was missing in action on the battlefield.)

[Page 388]

On June 22, 1941, more than 100 were drawn into the mobilization. Many returned later but many fell.

Niske Golob, Avrum Abe the Toker's

Mordekhai Fraimener, Deborah Dyne's son–in–law,

Khatz, a quilter, originated from Orla,

Pyetrikovsky, bank bookkeeper,

Yosl Bransky, Aryeh Leyb's son, Beyle Feyge's great–grandchild,

Artchik Semyatitsky, Maishe Abe's son, Bashe Syme's grandchild,

Itche Fakhter, Yenkl Binyamin's son,

Yenkl Burak, Leybl Burak's son,

Kukafke, the watchmaker,

Hertzke Rypke, Mordekhai Hersh Melamed's son,

Yudl Kratz, Sholem Kratz's son,

Yisroel Grazhinsky, Avrum's son,

Leyzer–Lype Gutman Tchone's son–in–law,

Yankev Katlavitch, Kapuste's son,

Berl Deitch, Preiysl Schmidt's,

Itche Mann, Yenkl Marvinker's son,

Shloyme Grakhovsky, Shloyme Beker's,

Leyzer Susel, Shloyme Ephraim's son,

Maishe Yosl Truss, Motye Abe's son,

Maishe Khondovsky, Ayzik Zaifman's stepson,

Itche Levin, Shmuelke Beker's son,

Maishe Meckler, Kersnover Shnaider's son,

Patsovske, Dovid Liev's son–in–law,

Artchik Shpak, Hershl Gelen's son,

Sender Kontchik, Khatskl Shokhet's son,

Avruml Bransky, Yelke Benduger's son,

Podratchik, Alter Farber's grandchild,

Zabludofsky, Bertche, Naphtali Dominover's grandchild,

Artchik, Khaile Tikatsky's friend.

[Page 389]

There are certainly more, but I was not successful in finding any further information.

In the fall of 1944, when Bransk was already liberated and the battle was continuing near Pultusk. Three letters arrived from the front from Branskers in the Soviet military. They were: Benye Medvet, Faivl Shuster's son, Dovid Bombe, YenklVasser Treger's grandchild and Meir Rive, Yosl Voygeser's son. They inquired at that time about who of the Branskers were alive. Regretfully, no one answer them. They did not even have any addresses. In the summer of 1946, certain people inquired about them, but I regret I cannot respond because there is uncertainty. There were big battles in these areas, but it is possible they are living elsewhere.

Bransker in the Russian armies:

Hershl Bransky, Avrum Shkop's son, returned,

Shloym'ke Truss, Motye Abe's son, returned,

Avrum Yudl Vasser, Maishe Aron Klektor's son, fell in 1945,

Bai Piltusk was already 50 years old,

Asher Vyertchin, Berl Fidel's grandchild was in Anderse's army and near East and lately in England, Khaim Vaynshteyn, Maishe Hersh the deaf,

Khone Mann, Marvinke's,

Kalman Tskhtlyer, Ben–Tsiyon Melamed's grandchild,

Yeshaye Tchizetsky, Malke Zitserke's grandchild,

All of the above served in Kostchyaske's division. All returned, many with medals and awards.

Bransk Jews as Officers During the War:

Shloyme Truss, Shloym'ke Motye Abe's, participated in battles in Kursk, Stalingrad, Oryol, Kharkov, Kiev, Carpathians, Romania, Czechoslovakia, battalion commander. Last title captain. Several times wounded, received award from Red Cross and other medals. Was very loved by the officer's corps.

[Page 390]

Hershl Bransky' participated during the war in the Soviet Union as an officer with the rank of First Lieutenant, was Director of the music corps, performed outstandingly several times.

Khone Mann, was an officer of political education in and was only 22 years, but very talented.

KhaimVainshteyn, choirmaster advanced officer, with the Kastchyaske division at age 21 years.

Bransk Jews in Other Partisan Detachments

Dr. Datner from Bialystok, was one of the best partisans in the "Revenge" detachment. He describes in his writings and memoirs heroic battles by the "Revenge" detachment, about the heroic deeds of Bransker. He is speaking of Yekhiel Zaifman, the son of Yosl Zaifman, Artche's grandchild. Yekhiel is named after the famous Bransk community activist Yekhiel Leyb Zaifman.

Yosl was active in many branches of Bransk life as a teacher, leader of the folk–school, editor and publisher of the local Bransk newspaper "Bransker Life" and other timely activities. Yekhiel received a traditional–national education. He was a pioneer.[1] Doctor Datner has asked me personally to bring this out in the Bransk Yizkor Book. This is brought out.

Yekhiel Zaifman was very active around Bialystok in the "Revenge" detachment in which he worked as a former Polish soldier. He was a good marksman and machine–gunner and was a participant in all heavy work. His specialty was causing the trains to derail between Bialystok and Valkavisk.

He received a thank you note for his work. The daily record of the "Revenge" detachment also notes that Yekhiel is a brave hero.

He had to carry out a death sentence on a lyeshnik (forest watchman) who agreed to become a German spy with two of his friends. He comes to the lyeshnik on Sunday afternoon. He finds many guests at the lyeshnik. Yekhiel stands at the door with a broad 'good morning.' He holds a revolver in his hand, an automatic. They want to throw themselves on him, but Yekhiel in those seconds fired a series of bullets which resulted in the spy and his two German guests to fall dead immediately.

[Page 391]

On October 25, 1943, he fell in the battle with a band of Gestapos. He defended himself bravely and fell as a hero.

The partisans conducted a memorial for Yekhiel Zaifman with the greatest partisans' honour.

Hodes Susel, the dark young woman, Maishe – Susel's girl or Maishe Zalman Avrum's as her father was called, until the war was a member of the youth movement 'He'khalutz.'

After the Bransk ghetto was liquidated on November 7, 1942 she ran away to the forest where she encountered a group of Soviet deserters and is immediately enmeshed in their work. She did everything to help the enemies of the Nazis, even spying, and was successful in many cases.

In the summer of 1943, they are accosted by a large group of Germans. The battle lasts an entire day. German officers fall dead. Hodes stands in the middle of the fire, loads the weapons for the Russians to enable them to shoot more quickly. There is shooting from all sides. Hodes does not leave her position until she falls along with her compatriots. Honour her memory.

Footnote (Rubin Roy Cobb)
1. Hebrew is khalutz, being a pioneer in the Zionist socialist group who trained to immigrate to then called Palestine to establish Jewish settlements there. Rubin Roy Cobb's father's brother, Naftali Kobylanski, who after the establishment of the State of Israel in 1948 changed his family name to Yogev. He immigrated to Palestine in 1938 from Bielsk–Podlaski that was near Bransk.

[Page 392]

List of Bransk Jews Who Survived

Where They Were During the Period 1939–1944

Alpern, Velvl Hindetchke's grandchild, in the forest,

Alpern, Maishe Yosl, Hindetchke's son, in Russia,

Olyentsky, Dovid, Yenkl Vote's, in the forest,

Olyentsky, Abe, Yenkl Voyitek's, in the forest,

Olyentsky, Shloyme, Yenkl Voyitek's, in the forest,

Olyentsky, Dina, Maishe Alentsker's, in the forest,

Okon, Khava, in the forest,

Okon, Leah, in the forest,

Askard, Maishe, Zakhriya's son, in the forest,

Adelman, Shakhna, in Russia,

Bider, Maishe, Maishe Aharon Vaser's grandchild, in Russia,

Burak, Velvl, Hershl Burak's son, in a bunker,

Brenner, Yisroel Pesakh Milner's grandchild, in the forest,

Broyde, Yosl, Lazer Broyde's son, in the forest,

Bag, Shloyme Fishl Bag's in Russia,

Broyde Shayne, Shaye Tsalke's grandchild, in Russia,

Broyde, Avruml, Niske's grandchild, in Russia,

Broyde, Itche'ele, Lozier's son, murdered in 1945, in the forest,

Golde, Velvl, Slave's grandchild, in the forest,

Golde, Eva, Slave's grandchild, now in America, in the forest,

Goldberg, Yeshaye, Babele Beker's grandchild, in the forest,

Gradzhensky, Meir, in the forest,

[Page 393]

Gradzhensky, Itche, in the forest,

Dalinsky, Khaim Kartoflye, in a bunker,

Dalinsky, Dovid Kartoflye, in a bunker,

Virtchin, Asher Fidel's, in Russia,

Vaser, Sholem, Maishe Aron Vaser's grandchild, in the forest,

Vaser, Menukhe, Maishe Aron in a bunker,

Vrone, Leyzer, grandchild of Benduge, in the forest,

Vrone, Khanah, in the forest,

Vainshteyn, Shoshke, Maishe Hersh's now in America, in the forest,

Vrobel, Khaim Kevlyaker's, in the forest,

Vygotsky Dovid, Aydel's, in the forest,

Voinovich, Binyomin, Benduger's, in the forest,

Zilbershteyn, Avrum, Yenkl Vaser Treger's, in Russia,

Zalyefsky, Motl, Noske Katsev's, in Russia,

Khazn, Shayne, Mendl Gursker's, in Russia,

Toptchefsky, Zisl, Lype Partselainik's, murdered 1945. in the forest,

Tikatsky, Maishe, now in America, in the forest,

Tikatsky, Khanah, in the forest,

Tshizetsky, Yeshaye Malkhah'les, in Russia,

Trus, Alter, Motye Abes, in Russia, now in Sweden,

Trus, Leybl Alter's son in the forest, now in Sweden,

Tcheshainske, Stella, found in the forest,

Iteld, Shome, Alter Iteld's now in America,[1] in Russia,

Yentchman, Maishe, Avrum's son, in the forest, now in Poland,

Lievartofsky, Minke Schmidt's, in a bunker,

Lype, Hershl Tchone's, in the forest,

Lyev, Mulke, Dovid'ke's, Camp,[2]

Lyev, Fishl, Alyarnik's, in a bunker,

Lyev, Khaiah Sorah, Avrum Rifke's daughter, in Russia,

Lyev, Binyomke, Shaiye Tsalke's grandchild, in Russia,

Lyev, Treine Shaiye Tsalke's grandchild, in Russia,

Lyev, Peshe, Shaiye Tsalke's grandchild, in Russia,

[Page 394]

Lyev, Gitl, Shaiye Tsalke's grandchild in Russia,

Maggid, Yankev, the old ritual slaughterer's son, now in America, in Shanghai,

Melamed, Dovtche, Yentitshike's grandchild, in Russia,

Mann, Khanke Marvinker's, in Russia,

Shmurzhik, Dvorke, Leyzer Katsev's grandchild, in Camp,

Sukman, Zalman, Pyetkever, in the forest,

Sukman Freydl, Pyetkever, in the forest,

Sukman, Khaye, Pyetkever, in the forest,

Sakalovitch, Berele Khone's, in the forest,

Samoyle, Yankev, Yenkl–Hershl Schmidt's grandchild, in the forest,

Fraynd Nekhemye, the Khazan's son, in Russia,

Pas Simkhah, Borukh–Velvl's, in the forest,

Fenekherus Perl, Zalman Rutker's, in bunker, now in Israel,

Posesor, Syme, Tuckerman's, in Russia, now in Camp,

Pav, Maishe, Shmulye Paplaver's son–in–law, in Russia,

Pakhter, Shloyme Binyomke the shoemaker in Russia,

Finklshteyn, Khaim, Rakhke's from Benduge, murdered 1947, in the forest,

Finklshteyn, , in the forest,

Finklshteyn, Avreml, in the forest,

Finklshteyn, Shoshke, in the forest,

Finklshteyn, Khanah, in the forest,

Pribut, Aryeh Leyb, Hershl Schmidt's grandchild, in the forest,

Pribut, Zalman, in Russia,

Pribut, Khaim Velvl, in the forest,

Pribut, Esther, in the forest,

Frank, Lube, found in the forest, in the forest,

Tsukhtlyer, Kalman, Ben Tsiyon Melamed's grandchild, in Russia,

Kaminetsky, Dore, Daktershe, in a bunker,

Kamen Maishe, Galise's, in a bunker,

Kotlovitch, Yosef, Khaim Beker's, now in Eretz Yisroel, in the forest,

Kestin, Yankev, now in Italy, in the forest,

Kleinot, Mulye, Elber Shuster's, in the forest,

[Page 395]

Kestin, Yosef–Betsalel, now in Palestine, in Russia,

Kontchik, Khatskl, Shloyme's in Russia,

Kontchik, Shayne, in Russia,

Kontchik, Leybe, in Russia,

Rubinshteyn, Gitl, Yozefiner, died in 1945,

Rubinshteyn, Maishe, Gitl's son in the forest,

Rubinshteyn, Sonya, in the forest,[3]

Resnick, Tzvia, Yozefynerke's grandchild, in a bunker,

Rekhelzon, Mulye, Dvora Dyne's grandchild, in the forest,

Rubin, Yankev [John], Royten Ons[4] son, in the forest,

Rubinshteyn, Zavl[3], Zavl Hersh the Khasid's now in America, in the forest

Royzen, Pesakh, Dovid Schmidt's grandchild, in the forest,

Royzen, Khone Basl, Melikhe's grandchild, in the forest,

Rotslav, Berl, Shaye Tsalke's, in the forest,

Rotslav, Perl, Berl's wife, in the forest, Rotslav, Glike, Berl's daughter, in the forest,

Rotslav Maishe's son, in the forest,

Rotslav, Freyde, daughter, in the forest,

Rotslav, Feygl, daughter, in the forest,

Shapira, Faivl, Bashe Sime's grandchild, in a bunker,[5]

Shapira, Leybl, Bashe Sime's grandchild, in a bunker,[5]

Shpak, Hershl, Alter Orke's, in the forest, now in Cuba,[6]

Shpak, Brokha, in the forest,

Shteyn, Pesakh, Meir Khaim's grandchild, now in America, in Shanghai,

Letters arrived in Bransk from the following four right after the liberation
Regretfully, no one answered them, so we are unable to verify their current
status.

Benye Medved, Faivl Shuster's,

Dovid Bonke, YenklVaser Treger,

Mordekhai Sukhavitch, Yankev Meir Kharlap's,

Ryve Maior, Yosl Vaneser's.

Footnotes (Rubin Roy Cobb)

1. Lived in Atlanta, Rubin Roy Cobb met him, and he remembered hearing that 's mother (Jospa Skornik–Cobb) had been killed in a motor accident in South Africa. He lived across the street in Bransk from her family [see Maps Section 1 Page 1 for overall view, and Map 2, Page 7 of 8 and Map 6 Page 2of 2 for detailed information].
2. Refers to DP (Displaced Persons) Camps established in the Western Allies Zones of Germany after World War II awaiting visas to resettle elsewhere – USA, Israel, Australia etc.
3. After her husband Zavl died she married Jack Rubin of Baltimore [paternal cousin of Rubin Roy Cobb]. Her daughter is Cynthia Rubinstein who lives in Baltimore.
4. Means Red Rooster referring to his huge red nose. First cousin of Jack Rubin of Baltimore, lived in Bialystok, Poland until 1967, then moved to Melbourne, Australia where he was called John. Has a son named Henry who is an accountant in Melbourne. Related to Rubin Roy Cobb through his paternal grandmother. met them in Melbourne in late 1990s.
5. Two Shapiro brothers that lived in Baltimore. met their families in the 1990s. Their wives passed on a lot of information about the shtetl. One of the brothers was murdered it is believed because he refused to raise the prices of items sold in his store when requested to do so in Baltimore.
6. Met his wife at a celebration of a Bransker in Atlanta. She believed that her infant baby could still be alive as after the liberation the baby's body could not be found and was brought up by Poles (or Germans) without knowing of his/her origins. Her husband had a very successful manufacturing clothing plant in Cuba, but when Castro arose they had to leave Cuba in a hurry penniless. In Charlotte, North Carolina he reestablished another successful plant.

[Page 396]

Bransk Relief Organizations

In New York

Bransker Relief Committee

Under the name of the Bransker Relief Committee activities of the Bransk landslayt[1] are conducted on behalf of the old home.

The Bransker Relief Committee was founded in 1918 at the end of the First World War. All the Bransk Societies in New York were represented in the Relief Committee.

The initial activities consisted of raising funds for the fellow–countrymen who had suffered from the war. At that time there were no possibilities of sending help directly to Bransk because of the destroyed financial institutions.

The style at that time was to send delegates to the towns to bring the money directly to the people. The Bransker Relief Committee was not anexception. The Committee at that time attracted many fellow–countrymen who worked like busy bees, visiting all the fellow–countrymen, receiving donations for the town of Bransk. In addition, individuals were interested in seeing that their money should reach their relatives directly.

The Committee's main office was located at that time in Mr. Zilbershteyn's store on Stanton Street. Thousands were raised and given to the messenger – Avrum Zilbershteyn, who travelled to Bransk to fulfill the duty.

Mr Zilbershteyn carried out his mission. But the time of the terrible inflation in Poland were not favourable for any substantial aid. The money that the people received within a short time lost its value. Most monies were sent by relatives for their immigration purposes. Regretfully, many people exchanged

[Page 396]

their dollars for Polish marks and were left with nothing, stranded in Danzig and asking for new money.

Only a few landslayt, those who did not exchange their money for Polish money, were able to reach the shores of America.

We must admit that the messengers, not being financial experts, were many times fooled by swindlers who took their American dollars and gave them Polish marks according to the daily rate. The Bransk messenger was not an exception.

When the situation in Poland stabilized somewhat, aid was sent through the local bank institutions. The Bransker Relief Committee sent regular substantial amounts of money for all the poor in town, most especially for those who were the most destitute and who could not expect any help from the local and broken poor.

The personnel of the Bransker Relief Committee were represented by all Bransk in New York.

Abe Steinberg and Yosl Turtshin of the Bransker Rudolf Sholem. AvrumYankl Sankes and Shimon Wilf of the Bransker Brothers. Julius Cohen also represented the Bransker Brothers as well.

Representing the Bransker Young Men's were: Charles Kessler, Avrum Maishe Bertche's, Morris Rosen, Jacob Becker, Leyzer Fraynd and Zelig Saltzman.

They were also joined by those who were not members of the three Societies: Willy Cohen, Jacob Richman, Hershl Domenover and Jacob Sofer. When Sam Verp came from Chicago he immediately joined their ranks.

The group of young and older landslayt worked hard to collect the Relief funds which were sent home. The head of the entire effort was Mr Julius Cohen who devoted himself with his entire energy to help the Relief collections.

[Page 398]

Bransker Relief Committee in 1918

Bottom row from the right: Jack Becker, Avrum Silberstein, Julius Cohen, Lazer Fraynd, Abba Steinberg, Willy Cohen

Top row from the right: Willy Fiels, Jacob Richman, Harry Rosenthal, Morris Rosen, Yosl Turchin, Jack Sofer, Gedalye Hurwitz, Avrum Brian and Charles Kessler

Sam Verp and his family during a visit to Bransk

Louis Verp at the Bransk cemetery

[Page 399]

He [Julius Cohen] addressed all gatherings, wrote letters and encouraged the landslayt to do their duty. All the younger members also threw themselves into this activity. The older ones were the honorary members. Committees visited the homes of the landslayt and were given substantial donations.

Over the years, a large number of the older landslayt passed away. The work was carried on by the younger ones with the same energy. The younger element attracted many other landslayt and together, they worked to raise all financial aid that was sent home for the poor for holidays or for a little heating which was terribly expensive, for clothing for little children, for institutions in town such as loan banks and Talmud Torahs.[2]

By 1922, there were already Branskers who had emigrated from the war period. Having recently arrived from home, they helped in the relief activity of the earlier Branskers.

A couple of years later Branskers made various pleasure trips to Europe and traveled to see their parents and friends, to settle them in there, help them with whatever was possible, and also to bring whomever they could to America. Trips such as these were made by Julius Cohen, Sam and Louis Verp and Binyomin Zelvin, as well as others.

This gave them an opportunity to become familiar with the situation in Bransk. When they returned to New York, they made the local landslayt aware of the terrible poverty that existed in the old home and strengthened the relief activities. At the same time, they established communication with responsible individuals in the old home who would distribute the money in a just manner.

Messrs William Cohen and Sam Verp together with Julius Cohen, were this entire time the most active members in the New York Relief Committee. The Landsmanshaft,[3] at mass gatherings, would always express their full trust to them and to their work.

In the early 1930's the Polish boycott of the Jews begins, against Jewish businesses, against Jewish artisans. Hitler's poison has seeped into the new Polish land that was supposed to become a free republic. Branskers, along with all Jewish cities and towns, suffer a lot economically. The Relief does its duty to help in any way possible.

[Page 401]

The boycott movement increases in strength. Christians are chased with sticks from Jewish businesses. This results in pogroms. Bransk feels the brunt of a full–fledged pogrom during the summer of 1937. The activities of the Bransker Relief increase in strength, raising money to ease the situation of those who are suffering and institutions in the old home.

The last financial aid for Pesakh was sent to Bransk in March, 1939.

[Page 402]

The Second World War puts an end to all communication with Bransk. By the end of the war, there was finally revealed to the world the sad news of what had happened to the entire Polish Jewry, including Bransk. Millions were choked [to death] MCG in gas chambers. Those who had hidden were murdered by the Nazis for whom we are now searching to give ourselves strength once again, and from Polish bandits. Only a limited number of people miraculously remained alive.

At the beginning of summer, 1945, the Bransker Relief resumes its activities. The older Bransk societies are no longer interested in the landslayt relief because most of those who have the word are now not familiar with the Bransker needs and consider themselves second generation Americans.

The Bransker Young Men's benevolent Association chooses a committee from among its members, to begin a relief action. The very same who had always been active throw themselves once again into the work. The first mass gathering in the Forward Hall in May, 1945 selects Rabbi Avrum Yitskhak Edelman as Honorary Chairman, William Cohen, Chairman, Sam Verp Treasurer and Mr Julius Cohen as Executive Secretary. Money is raised regardless of not knowing whether there are any surviving Bransker landslayt.

The Troika, as the Messrs William Cohen, Sam Verp and Julius Cohen are called, are no longer the young men of long–ago, and yet they the most energetic. The most active in creating means of mitigating the situation of landslayt when and where they are to be found.

In September 1945 a list of 64 survivors in Bransk appeared in the Yiddish newspapers. No one at these newspapers had any idea of how to get in touch with these survivors. The correspondence had arrived to the Canadian newspaper and had been sent from there to the United States.

Cables were sent immediately to the names on the lists with prepaid responses. They disappeared like in water. no replies. Packages of clothing, cigarettes and food were sent right away to firms that advertised that they would distribute them. Everything was lost.

[Page 403]

We did not actually know that the several tens of Bransker Jews who survived were now in even greater danger and have to once again, flee Bransk. They were not safe at home and to travel or go on foot somewhere was again placing their lives in danger.

We did not know that many of the surviving Branskers had already gone over mountains and rivers past various borders far and near countries, investigating to run away entirely from what had been home.

Khaim Vainshteyn, left with a group of refugees in Stuttgart.

[Page 404]

In November 1945, Khaim–Hersh Bransky, may he rest in peace, the Bransker landsman who for 25 years had been a member of the American Jewish Joint Distribution Committee [Joint],[4] first in Paris and then in New York, came to a meeting of the Society. He brought a letter he had received from Bialystok with the address of a certain individual. The address was written in such a manner that it required a special talent to know the its meaning. The Joint could not decipher the address.

I was at this meeting as secretary of the Bransker Society. Khaim**Error! Bookmark not defined.** Hersh gave me the letter and the address. Looking at the words, I suspected that I could turn the letter over to someone else. I take the letter home with me.

Early the following day I met with Julius Cohen and he was immediately on a train with the letter on his way to the person in White Plains, New York.

I quickly responded to the writer of the letter in Bialystok who was Khava Okon. I gave her the correct address of her relatives. I inquired of her if perhaps she knows something about other landslayt.

This was the first communication I entered into with the remnants of the refugees of Bransk. In January 1946 I received the news of the surviving Branskers, and of those who had gone away and their whereabouts were unknown. In general, the entire tragedy of the Jewish people in Europe was revealed in its entire horror and sadness.

This was the beginning of the important work of finding and connecting them with their families in America. This was the first, the most important desire of the moment.

At that time, I did not have any far–reaching correspondence with other American cities. Being secretary of both existing Bransker Societies for tens of years, I was in a position of being able to be helpful in this work.

Regretfully, not all the Bransker landslayt belong to the Bransker Societies.

[Page 405]

The work turned out to be very difficult. I devoted all my time, my entire energy to fulfill this. Using various methods, I obtained everyone's information. I notified the people by cable of their families and their addresses.

At this same time, Branskers were already spread in DP Camps that were under the wing of the American army.

The connection with Jews in Linz, Austria is interesting. In May, 1946, a certain Mr Bernson received a cable from Linz, Austria. Someone is asking him to find Branskers. He wants to give this cable to the newspapers. His wife hears about this and she tells it to a neighbour. The neighbour tells it to an American–born woman. She hears the name of Bransk and says she needs to ask her father–in–law. He is a Bransker and is active in the Relief. The neighbour was my daughter–in–law Evelyn Cohen. My daughter–in–law tells me about this. I speak with Mr Bernson and he gives me the original cable which is dated 7th May, 1946. I have the difficult job of finding who those who are being sought could be. I ask them via cable for other signs. I pay for a reply. On May 16th, I receive a cable from them and I brought together Leyzer Vrone and his aunt in Brooklyn.

If this had been printed in the newspapers which were then bombarded with such notices, it would probably have been months until it would have been printed, and then it sometimes happens that it is not read by any Bransker because most of the names have been changed.

This happening quickly became known in that DP Camp. I receive tens of letters from other unfortunate wanderers. They ask me to do the same for them. I make it my responsibility to fulfill the requests of these people. I become even busier with the work. I look up the landslayt societies or their synagogues, ask for whom they are searching. When I find them, I give them the letter from their relatives in the DP Camps. At the same time, the relatives are told by me who and where their friends are to be found.

[Page 406]

I am inundated with such requests. My name becomes familiar in the DP Camps as one who helps to find relatives in America. I do not give up even though the work becomes more difficult for me, demanding almost my entire time. I give very little time to my own business. The correspondence from the DP Camps to me and my responses reach into the hundreds.

In the Joint I was called 'the personal location service.'

The hundreds of letters I received from those whom I brought together with their relatives give me good satisfaction for the difficult work. At the same time, I receive a letter from Alter Trus who came from the Soviet Russia to Bialystok. There becomes a connection between the landslayt who are in Bialystok. Alter does an investigation to find the landslayt who are already somewhere on the way to various DP Camps to inform them of the Bransker Relief.

On the ship 4 Freedoms turned back from the shores of Palestine to Cyprus.

[Page 407]

The name and address of the Bransker secretary is on the wall of the office of the Bialystok Committee for anyone who wants to contact him if they need his help.

The word there was that the "Bransker secretary" will locate your family quicker than anyone else.

(According to a letter from Alter Trus to me in January 1948.)

The Bransker Relief aided refugees in Shanghai, Italy, Sweden and sends CARE packages to all refugees in the DP Camps, helped the Irgun Yotzi Bransk in Palestine, for them to go there to fulfill their duty to the refuges who come to Eretz Yisroel, and also supports the United Jewish Appeal.

Refugees arrive in numbers who did not know of the Bransker Relief. Eventually, Brenner, who was in touch with the Bransker Relief through his trips to Poland, Austria, Italy and Palestine, arrives. From there he is caught by the British military and brought to Cyprus.

Yosef Kotlovitch

Yankev Kestin and wife

New Year Greeting Card to Bransker Relief

[Page 408]

The Bransker meet in Cyprus and find out about the Bransker Relief. They get in touch with their families who take over the work of helping them.

The Bransker Relief, in the new year, helps a number of refugees who do not have anyone who can take an interest in them, by clothing them as well as in other ways.

The Bransker Relief, through the help of individuals, worked out affidavits to bring certain people from German DP Camps. Regretfully, the State Department refused these people, did not permit them to enter because they were caught at a terrible crime. They sold a package of cigarettes in the DP Camp so they are not worthy of coming to America, regardless that the Relief had paid in advance for their transportation.

The Bransker Relief, at mass meetings, obligated itself to print the story of the destruction of Bransk, when the facts of the remnants of the refugees will be gathered and sent to New York. Alter Trus was informed of the decision, and he, with the help of all the survivors gathered the horrific facts of the Bransker Jews.

The work of writing this book in its final form once again fell on Julius Cohen, who for six months dedicated himself to it. The plan to raise the money for the publication of the book were formulated and carried out by him, and was later agreed to at Committee meetings.

This is a short description of the activities of the Bransker Relief Committee led by a few people and carried out by the secretary of the Committee, Mr. Julius Cohen.

In writing this article, I want to thank all Bransker landslayt and everyone else for their warm response to every call of the Bransker Relief Committee.

[Page 409]

Bransker Relief Committee in the year 1945

Bottom row from the right: **Binyomin Spector, William Cohen, Julius Cohen, Rabbi**

Avrum–Yitskhak Edelman, Sam Verp, Sam Becker

Middle row from the right: **Harry Levin, Charles Kessler, Hyman Novak, Abe**

Brayen, Charles Berman

Top row from the right: **Avrum Friedman, Zaydl Zalefsky, Yosef Rosenblum, Jake Stoller, Izzy Fitel, Louis Verp, Benny Moss**

Footnotes (Rubin Roy Cobb)
1. Fellow–countryman.
2. Religious schools
3. Fellow Countryman's Organization.
4. Founded in 1914, aids Jews throughout the world.

[Page 410]

Bransker Aid Society in Chicago

This is the name of the Bransker Landsmanshaft Society in Chicago, the second Jewish center in America.

The Society was founded in 1928, through the initiative of Rebitsn[1] Feyge Alshvang, sister–in–law of the famous Bransker rabbi, Rabbi Shimon Shkop.

The motto of the Society is "a very noble thing to aid the fallen brothers." The Society fulfills with all its heart the duties it sets for itself. The founding of the Society is all a result of the years following the war, when Bransk needed to be helped, when its institutions and individuals were in dire need after the First World War.

Chicago was especially fortunate in having their number an individual such as Sholem Dovid Wein, the famous philanthropist who was recognized for the beautiful institution, the Free Interest Loan Society he founded through his largest personal contribution.

The Bransker Relief Society in Chicago became an important Jewish charity institution. They raise funds for various local and national Jewish purposes.

They can reach their goal because they do not have any fraternal responsibilities to the members. Raising money for charity purposes is their main function and it is to this end they dedicate their activity.

It is worth stating the fact that Mr Cohen, the son of Meir–Sholem Cohen, whilst in the U.S. army, serving in the American zone in Munich and working to cleanse the area of Nazis, served this purpose with devotion. He sent thousands of them to DP Camps and helped the Jewish refugees there to settle and gave them permission to work. Many, through his personal efforts, received permission to enter America.

[Page 411]

The Jews of Munich viewed him as a true friend, turning to him through the central committee for various favours which were always granted.

The young, 22 year old American officer made a special effort to find out if there were any Bransker Jews in any of the DP Camps. He found five and immediately sent their names to his father in Chicago via air mail. At the same time, he received letters from them and sent them to Chicago to his father who immediately sent the information to Julius Cohen in New York.

When I received the information from Chicago through special delivery airmail, I took the letters that very day to Philadelphia to the closest relative of theses of those being sought.

A dramatic scene took place in the store of the landsman to whom I had brought the letters from his relatives. Harry S. Boyten, the prominent philanthropist and activist of the United Jewish Appeal was present at this. He had come for a contribution to the Appeal. Mr Boyten was certainly touched by this scene of personal interest exhibited by landslayt. Mr Boyten invited me to dinner. He even contributed 25 dollars to the Bransker Relief in recognition of my devoted work.

It is unnecessary to say that the relatives are now here in America and benefitting from the freedom of our country.

This is a result of the interest of Mr Cohen, the son of the secretary of the Chicago Bransker Aid Society together with the personal interest of Mr Julius Cohen, the secretary of the New York Bransker Relief Committee.

[Page 412]

Matesyohu Cohen
Meir Sholem's son, and grandson of Bransker
Rabbi Meir Sholem Ha'koheyn, obm

Meir Sholem Cohen
Secretary of the Bransker Society of Chicago

The address of the secretary of the Bransker Aid Society is:

S. Cohen, 1417 South Central Park Ave.

Chicago 23, Ill.

Bransker Club in Atlanta

Is the name of the Bransker Society in Atlanta. Regardless that there are only a few Bransker families, the Club, under the leadership of Sam Baker, Trayne's son, Avrum Ber the beadle's grandchild, together with the wonderful help of Pesakh Tenenbaum and his wife, have managed to raise large amounts of money for Bransker during all times. It is remarkable how quickly the Landsmanshaft can be called together in Atlanta and even how quickly the money can be raised for all purposes to help. They have especially excelled in constructive help for Bransk when it was necessary. We can say Atlanta is the spiritual center of the Bransker Landsmanshaft in America. This is because there is a large number of landslayt there who were the culture–carriers as early as 1905. Individuals such as Yosl Libofsky, Shimon Rimer's son, who together with Khaim Baker, may he rest in peace, founded the first library in town. Mr Lowenstein also does his part of the work to benefit his wife's hometown. His wife is Artsye, the Fellers' daughter. The Beeber brothers[2] are prominent with their significant financial aid.

[Page 413]

From afar, we shake the hands of the Bransker landslayt in Atlanta.

Atlanta does its duty now with its full hands, thanks to Sam Baker and his co–workers. Their aid, to a large extent, made it possible to publish this book.

Sam Baker
Secretary, Bransker Club in Atlanta

Paul Tenenbaum and wife
Important active members

The address of Secretary Sam Baker in Atlanta is:

Sam Baker, 801 Washington St., S.W.,

Atlanta Ga

[Page 414]

In Argentina

Society of Former Residents of Bransk

This is the name of the Bransker Society in Argentina. The number of Bransker landslayt in this South American republic is small in comparison with the huge Landsmanshaft in the large North American cities. Yet, wonderful work is carried out here for Bransk and all the institutions that help Branskers.

Khaim Kestin, Secretary

Avrum Leyzer Zagel, President

I was overwhelmed to find such a nice, hearty and intelligent Landsmanshaft in Buenos Aires, Argentina, like that which is headed by Mr Zagel as President and Mr Kh. Kestin as Secretary, together with the help of the officers, Binyomin Golding, Yisroel Messer, Shmuel Tsukhtlyer, Ayzik

Penkharsh, Khaim Fishelev and Ruven Rotsky. Argentina has earned its place among the true heartfelt and friendly Landsmanshaft organizations that are always ready to extend a helping hand to all Branskers wherever they find themselves.

Dear friends of the Society Of Former Residents Of Bransk, together with all your members in Buenos Aires, you are greeted from faraway Argentina.

[Page 415]

The address of the President of the Bransker Landslayt Society in Argentina is:

> H. Zagiel, Tres Arroyos 771,
>
> Buenos Aires, Argentina

In Johannesburg, South Africa

Bransker Society In Johannesburg, South Africa

This is the name of the Bransker Society in Africa. The existence of the Society was news to me. At the beginning of 1946, with the help of great material aid they sent to surviving Branskers who were in Bialystok. I found this out through the Joint.

I was even more surprised by their warm interest in the work of the book "Bransk." that they named They begged me not to stop the work of the book that I will either write or rewrite/edit.

Now, in the Societies associated with the Bransker Relief, there is often correspondence sent to me, most especially from the active members, especially from Khane Smurzjik and Hinde Lees.

The work of all Bransker landslayt and members of the organization consists of raising funds to substantially help all Bransker in DP Camps, Cyprus, Eretz Yisroel and other needs.

The first transport of clothing and food arrived in Bialystok for the Branskers there from the Johannesburg organization. The president is Mr M. Peck,[3] Khonele[4] the dyer's grandchild. The New York Landsmanshaft had the pleasure of becoming personally acquainted with the President of the Society when he was a guest in New York and visited our meeting. His fine speech, his warm interest in Bransk, entranced us, especially with his charming English with the Oxford accent[5] that pleased all American who attended this meeting. It is worthwhile mentioning that at this meeting to greet Mr Peck, there were 200 attendees.

[Page 416]

At this same gathering, there were also present Berl Sassen[6] and his wife. He is Mordekhay Furman's son. They are among the more important activists in the Bransker Society in Johannesburg. Hinde Lees, the secretary of the Society is a daughter of this Berl Sassen. In this way they connected the Bransker landslayt in Africa with the New York members and together decided to continue their connection which will surely bring good results.

The 21 Bransk families in Africa maintain their relationship, especially in the interest in all Bransker activities which is very important to them.

We greet you all, landslayt, from Johannesburg, South Africa, Branskers in the entire world reach out to you, dear friends, a long, hearty sholem aleykhemm.[7]

The address of the Secretary of the Bransker Society in Johannesburg is:

H. Lees, 561 Jules Street, Marvern, (*Malvern*)

Johannesburg, South Africa

[Page 417]

Bransker Society in Johannesburg, South Africa[8]

First row from the right: Motl Peck Chairman, Lyna Shames, Artchik Peck, Khaye Milner and Shirley Sassen

Second row from the right: Jospa Skornik, Mikhye Adesnik, Rivke Sassen, Bobke Peck, Sorah Weiner, Reizl Albiter and Khane Rypke

Third row from the right: Khlavne Cobb, Zaydl Adesnik, Berl Sassen, Shaulke

Pribut, Itche Meir Peck, Khaim Pribut, Velvel Albiter and Khaim Rypke

Top row from the right: Harry Harris, Vice Chairman, Malkhe Levin, Avrum–Itskhak

Sassen, Gitl Birger –Sassen, Brakha Harris–Weiner, Avrum Lees, and Hinde Sassen–Lees Secretary

Footnotes (Rubin Roy Cobb)
1. A rabbi's wife.
2. First cousins of Rubin Roy Cobb's father, Henry (Khlawne) Cobb (Kobylanski) through their mothers who were sisters and whose father was Shimeon Rubin the tavern keeper who owned one of the few brick structures in Bransk. See Map 3, Item #31 ('Moyer – hotel [brick]').
3. Motl (Morris) Peck (Piekucki in Bransk) was the first cousin of Rubin Roy Cobb's mother, Jospa Skornik–Cobb (Kobylanski) through their father, Itche–Meir Peck and Henye Rivka (Anni) Piekucki respectively.
4. Their grandfather was Khone Piekucki the dyer after whom the brother of is named
5. Knew him well and he certainly did not speak with an 'Oxford' accent
6. He lived to 104, and nearly up to the very end was given the honour of blowing the shofar during Rosh Hashanah and Yom Kippur at the Orthodox Pine Street Shul in Johannesburg where the families of 's wife, Renee Davidoff, and her brother Brian's wife Sharon, the daughter of Anne Barber and grandparents, Reizl and Velvl Alberts from Bransk, attended. The older brother of Berl Sassen (whom it is said outlived 6 wives) was the first Bransker to immigrate to Johannesburg, sometime in the early 1900s. As was required, he guaranteed the livelihood of immigrants coming to South Africa, as was then necessary by South African law, by loaning such immigrant breadwinner the sum of 75 pounds sterling (then equivalent to about US$375.00). This was paid back to him via a 'sweat shop' labour by the new immigrant. In 1929 when the United States, the British Mandate of Palestine and everywhere else was closed, because the Pecks, uncle and cousins of 's mother, were already settled in the Union of South Africa (as it was then known as), they were able to enter. Some few months after their entry, the South African gates were also shut tight to Eastern European (i.e. Jewish) immigrants – and in 1936 to Central European (i.e. Jewish) immigrants.
7. Yiddish (from Hebrew) for Welcome.
8. Rubin Roy Cobb clearly remembers when this photo was taken at his then home at 17 Orlando Road, Kensington, Johannesburg in 1947 when he was 11 years old.

[Page 418]

Bransk Relief Organizations (cont.)

In Eretz Yisroel

Association of former Branskers in Tel–Aviv

This is the name of the Bransker Society in Eretz Yisroel.

After all the horrific experiences of the remnants of refugees of European Jewry, they are interred in the DP camps of the various zones of the occupation forces in countries in which they hope to realize and begin a life as independent and useful people.

The refugees in the DP camps are up to now still recipients of charity from Jewish committees. No country has room for them. All doors are closed to them. They are extraneous creatures in the world.

Every country has millions to help itself during the period from war to freedom, but not for any Jews.

There are plans to help every country to become strong and back on its feet. Millions of American dollars are distributed to help the Germans who had shown themselves to be the worst criminals world history has ever produced.

Furthermore, American millions are sent to England to bring it out of bankruptcy, notwithstanding how the false English obtained military assistance to help the Arabs at the time of the war who directly helped the Nazis.

The world is deaf and dumb to the Jewish situation. The so–called civilized countries have remained deaf to the last dying screams of six million innocent souls who perished in the gas chambers and crematoria.

The civilized countries have become silent. No one wants to say or dares to say the word "enough." Let there be an end to the terrible behavior on the part of the world towards the remnants of refuges which resulted in the greatest number of victims.

[Page 419]

Unwillingly the thought tears through that Hitler had won the war to eradicate the Jews. The fact alone that now when Hitler has been dead for three years, his plans vis–Ã –vis Jews are being carried out with devilish precision, no longer by his Nazis but now by all national civilized countries. At the top now is the country that was Hitler's biggest victim, the country that had paid the greatest price for its political help to Hitler. The country that has now become a second, or perhaps a third–class power has begun a frightening campaign against Jews, accepting the friendly support of Hitler's surviving coworker, the Mufti, and together they stand in battle against Israel's last hope of building a home for itself in Palestine.

When the United Nations made the decision to grant the Jews a part of Eretz Yisroel which, with their blood and sweat they turned a barren desert into a blooming land, England unabashedly stated that it would be pleased to help in every area that would be agreed upon and accepted by the Jews and Arabs, knowing full well that it has had the power of the mandate for the past 25 years, certainly the last of the poison to the Jewish pioneers who built the land and the possibilities for a friendly understanding that is not possible any longer between them, shameless.

England had hoped Israel would receive the death blow from the Arab armies it had trained and armed with its cannons, fed with its food, anointed with its English recognition and supported with the American dollars it has and will never repay.

The incapable foolish English swindler however, is visible to everyone. The Jews in Palestine saw the great wisdom of the British Foreign Office and prepared for the day when Bevin would be convinced that the Jews are in Eretz Yisroel to stay, and not as English or Arab underlings, but citizens of their own land, – Israel.

[Page 420]

And yet England's representatives pretend ignorance and continue the same Jew–bashing politic in the United Nations.

The world however, sees the other side of the coin, that England's goal in the Middle East could have been reached with a Jew–friendly politic better than through the pro–Arab agitation.

England can afford to spend millions of American dollars to help itself in this despicable undertaking, but the day of reckoning will come. The Jewish blood spilled in Israel will fall upon the heads of the guilty.

In the United States, the land of freedom, equality and fair–play, a law was finally passed to ease the immigration of refugees, victims of Hitlerism. This is a very fine thing, however the law project was worked out in such a way by the lawmakers of both houses, that the greatest victim of Hitlerism, Israel, will die first in the D.P. camps before he will be able to enter the United States. A new generation of desert wanderers was created by the Congressmen and Senators for 40 years.

This same was done by all the other countries that have thousand millions of empty land waiting, begging to be worked. For Jews, the doors are locked.

Is it then a wonder that the remnants of refugees, with Jewish stubbornness set before them a single goal, to reach the shores of Israel, knowing full well they will again need to enlist in the ranks of fighters for their old and never forgotten home?

Among the hundred thousand refugees who set for themselves the goal, there were also our Bransker landslayt. Little by little, after the greatest difficulties, they attain their goal and arrive in Israel where they enlist in the ranks of the brave Israel army that gave notice to the entire world that Jewish blood will no longer be worthless. No longer will Jews be led to the gas chambers like innocent little sheep. That the Jewish people will not be sacrificed on the altar of Arab oil. That England will pay the price for its *zogenanter* (stupid British Union policy) led by the widely known enemy, Bevin who walks in the footsteps of Chamberlain.

[Page 421]

Y.Tz. Efraty
Secretary of Former Branskers

The Association of former Branskers in Tel Aviv works to give the Bransk Jewish refugees a friendly hand, helps them with everything possible to settle there.

At the head of The Association of former Branskers there are prominent Bransker landslayt who set forth for themselves the duty of helping these Branskers. Mr Yosef–Khaim Heftman (Emanuel), the well–known editor, is the President of the Society and Y.Tz. Efraty is the Secretary.

The duty of the Bransker landslayt in the entire world is now to strengthen the hands of The Association of former Branskers so they will have the full possibility of benefitting from true help to all Branskers who have arrived and will shortly arrive in Eretz Yisroel and to be able to assist them in beginning a new life in the Land of Israel that will certainly outlive all its enemies and will live and be a source of pride to the world long after the British Empire will only be a page of history, a forgotten story.

[Page 422]

Greetings friends of The Association of former Branskers in Tel–Aviv. Bransker landslayt throughout the world are one with you.

The address of The Association of former Branskers in Tel–Aviv is:

Y.Tz. Efraty, Rekhov Akhad Ha'am 98,

Tel Aviv, Israel

Bransker Fraternal Organizations

Bransker Young Men's Benevolent Association

This is the name of the most important Bransker Landsmanshaft society in New York. It was founded in 1904 in opposition to the older Bransker societies already then in existence over ten years. Two of its founders were Branskers and the rest were Vishankers.

The new Society endured some very difficult times in the first years of its existence. It was legally duty–bound to pay large benefits to sick and needy members. Yet, it carried out its obligations in an honorable manner. Thanks to the true dedication of some young landslayt who exhibited true devotion to the Society. With true loyalty the young men worked to create methods of raising funds to strengthen the Society and enhance its prestige.

Many of its members are no longer with us. Time has taken them from us, some of whom were young. It is worth mentioning these people. They were: Maishe Yantches, Fraynk Bass, Zelig Zaltzman, Aizik Chadwick from Sokole, Dzshaikov Magiz and Louis Fox. The Society will forever remember the dedicated work of these deceased members.

We must also mention those who are currently in the ranks of active members, and who occupy an honored place in the landslayt Charles Kessler, (Shaul'ke Kashtan from the old home), Henry Stein, this is Zushe Shnaider's son–in–law, Hayman Novak, Hitsl's son–in–law. Many of the members who were active until recently are now for various reasons, not in any position to give the same amount of work they did when they were younger. They too, must be mentioned. They are such landslayt as Morris Zilbershteyn, Hyman Faks and Harris Greenberg.

[Page 423]

All of them, during their time helped the Bransker Young Men's a great deal and now occupy a prominent place in the Landsmanshaft.

The Bransker Society was fortunate that in the 1920's new members joined who took over with truly heartfelt dedication to its activities that any other

Society ever experienced. You understand of course these are the members who are now known to everyone as Sam Verp and Julius Cohen.

These two members brought in with them a new stream of young landslayt, newly arrived from Bransk after the First World War. The membership greatly increases through their influence on all those who come from Bransk.

They have of late become very prominent in raising financial means to strengthen and ensure the future of the Bransker Young Men's. They work together with the aforementioned persons and have become the leaders, the – word givers' in the Society which is constantly becoming known in the Landsmanshaft.

During the past 30 years there has begun to be an influx of members who are, in the main the children of landslayt, American–born and English–speaking. A new and modern spirit has entered into the Society. The Yiddish language has now become a bit Anglicized.

The position of president in the Society is now filled by the new young member, Binyomin Spektor, the son–in–law of Zelig Zaltzman.

Yosef Yaverofsky, Yankev–Itskhak the Toker's grandchild, also served several terms as president.

Yosef Rozenblum the Portzelainik's grandchild has for several years served as vice president.

Mr Julius Cohen is the financial secretary of the Society since 1931 when he was drafted to serve the interests of the Bransker Young Men's. His impartial behavior and his intelligence help in uniting the young Americans and the older landslayt.

[Page 424]

Important Members of the Bransk Young Men's

Bottom row from the right: **Yosef Rosenbloom, Julius Cohen, Binyomin Spektor**

and Hayman Novak

Top row from the right: **Sam Verp, William Cohen, and Charles Kessler**

The membership now numbers 240, and with the families the total is approximately 1000, may it multiply.

The every five–year celebrations the Society held were big holidays for the Landsmanshaft. We always had to look for larger venues that would hold the hundreds who attended these celebrations

One of the historic gatherings of the Society took place May 9th, 1943 in the ballroom of the Pennsylvania Hotel, where an honour roll of the names of more than 60 Bransk youths who served in the United States army was unfurled.

The speeches of the rabbi, Rabbi Avrum–Itskhak Edelman, Binyomin Spektor and Julius Cohen will forever remain in the memories of all the landslayt.

Page 425]

Bramsker Young Men's Benevolent Association

Honor Roll

In the Service of Their Country

1941 —

Herbert Cohen	Sidney Kessler	B.H. Rosenberg
Seymour Pollack	David P. Greenberg	Isadore Burak
Leonard Heckelman	Robert A. Pollack	Bernard Piels
Sam Appelbaum	Henry Smith	Paul Smith
Wilfred Singer	Louis Novick	Emanuel Novick
Max Silverstein	A.B Silverstein	Leo Silverstein
Herman Rosenberg	Bernard Wynshaw	David Wynshaw
Saul H. Wynshaw	Bernard Fein	Norman Fein
Jacob Levine	Harry J. Rossenberg	Sidney Fox
Sol Pittel	I.G. Diskin	Philip H. Cole
Melvin Powell	Irving Ross	David Horowitz
Benjamin Horowitz	J.M. Lubar	Jack Silverstein
William Silverstein	Abie Kantrowitz	Harry Burack
Isadore Narimofsky	Sam Rockmaker	Herman Cohen
Harold Webman	Harold D Webman	Leon Myssiorek
Harry Gottlieb	Harry Pollack	Stanley M.Feinman
Bernard Berman	Herman M.Kefkowitz	Stanley Goldstein
Bernard Bryan	Seymour S Weinberg	Louis Shuman
Milton Handel	Harold Bryan	Harry Wilkins
Dr.Charles Saltzman	Morris Schechter	Jacob Brown

BRANSKER YOUNG MEN'S BENEVOLENT ASSOCIATION HONOR ROLL

In the Service of Their Country 1941

Herbert Cohen	Sidney Kessler	B.H.Rosenberg
Seymour Pollack	David P. Greenberg	Isadore Burak
Leonard Heckelman	Robert A. Pollack	Bernard Piels
Sam Appelbaum	Henry Smith	Paul Smith
Wilfred Singer	Louis Novick	Emanuel Novick
Max Silverstein	A.B. Silverstein	Leo Silverstein
Herman Rosenberg	Bernard Wynshaw	David Wynshaw
Saul H. Wynshaw	Bernard Fein	Norman Fein
Jacob Levine	Harry J. Rosenberg	Sidney Fox
Sol Pittel	L.G. Diskin	Philip H. Cole
Melvin Powell	Irving Ross	David Horowitz
Benjamin Horowitz	J.M. Lubar	Jack Silverstein
William Silverstein	Abie Kantowitz	Harry Burack
Isadore Narimofsky	Sam Rockmaker	Herman Cohen
Harold Webman	Harold D, Webman	Leon Myssiorek
Harry Gottlieb	Harry Pollack	Stanley M. Feinman
Bernard Berman	Herman M. Kefkowitz	Stanley Goldstein
Bernard Bryan	Seymour S. Weinberg	Louis Shuman
Milton Handel	Harold Bryan	Harry Wilkinds
Dr. Charles Saltzman	Morris Schechter	Jacob Brown

Honours list of the members that served in the American army

[Page 426]

Captain Philip H. Cole, son of Julius Cohen, together with Sergeant Horowitz, son of Louis Horowitz presented the honour roll to the President of the Society, Mr Binyomin Spektor. There was an outburst applause and good wishes.

Sergeant Horowitz   and   Captain Philip H. Cole

Everyone, thank God, returned from the war healthy and unscathed.

This celebration has remained in the annals of the Society to this day as one of the most important.

The address of the President is:

Benjamin Spector, 150 Nassau Street,

New York 7, N.Y.

Bransker Brothers Aid Association

This is the oldest Bransker Society, founded in 1894 by two well–known Bransker landslayt from two prominent Bransker families, Shimon Wilk, Yankev–Mordekhay the Khasid's brother and Avrum Brown, Yankl Sanke's.

The Society which then consisted of the oldest Bransker immigrants lived through a difficult existence because at that time a society had to fulfill many obligations.

[Page 427]

The newly–arrived immigrants felt strange in the large world city and needed someone to give them direction and to find work for them. The members of the Society fulfilled these obligations nicely. Other than the legal obligations that a society has, the functions of the Society were also carried out well.

In 1906 Mr Julius Cohen became the Recording Secretary of the Bransker Society and for about 35 years as Financial Secretary. At the beginning of 1948 Julius Cohen resigned his position. He wanted to free himself a bit from the heavy social obligations that lay upon him for more than 40 years. In addition, the Bransker Relief demands much of his time, and the membership freed him, but unanimously elected him as President.

During the 54 years of its existence, the Bransker Brothers experienced various crises and always remained a strong Society. Its leaders of various eras were familiar Bransker landslayt of the older generation who were now no longer with us. Its first founder, Shimon Wilk, died a relatively young man in 1916. The second founder, Avrume–Yenkl Sanke's died in 1941.

Several of the earlier members are still with us and regardless of their advanced age active in the Societies' activities. They are the two veterans, both not Branskers' Yisroel Sandler, Khaye-Esther's son-in-law, the second is Mr Hyman Greenspan from Orla. He worked in Bransk blouse garments in 1880.

One of the most important and recognized leaders of the Bransker Brothers is Louis Kosofsky, a Bialystoker, Maishe Khasid's son. Louis Kosofsky has been active in the Society for about 40 years and is one of the most important officials as Treasurer.

The number of members in the Bransker Brothers grows steadily smaller due to death. There are no younger members joining.

At this moment the children of the first founders, Shimon Wilk made the decision to take the place of their father in the society. In this way Jacob Wilk and Samuel Wilk, Shimon's two sons, continue the chain their father began in 1894. The Bransker Brothers Aid Association always responded warmly to all local and national Jewish needs. Even though it was a smaller organization its contributions to Jewish appeals were more meaningful than that of the larger Societies.

[Page 428]

Louis Kosofsky
current treasurer

Shimon Wilk
first founder

Only now, when the membership is much smaller, the Society has been forced to cut the general budget and perforce, also the budget for all other Jewish organizations and institutions. The support to the United Jewish Appeal however, has been doubled.

The Bransker Brother Aid Association is today considered in New York to be among the old Jewish Landsmanshaft societies of the first period of Jewish immigrant activity on behalf of independence through fraternal means.

The address of the President is:

Julius Cohen,

2060 Ocean Ave., Brooklyn 30, N.Y.

[Page 429]

Bransker Rodeph Shalom

This is the name of the first Bransker fraternal organization, founded as a lodge of the old Jewish order Brith Avrum in 1888, when the order was gradually diminishing because it did not recognize the importance to include the modern scientific systems of payments according to the age of the members.

Yoshe Hersh Bransky, the oldest Bransker landsman

The Rodeph Sholem Lodge tore itself away in 1917 and became independent, calling itself Congregation Rodeph Sholem.

The oldest Society that was founded by Avrum Zilbershteyn and Yoshe Hersh Bransky of the oldest Bransker immigrants but did not attract the large number of arriving landslayt, remaining a small unimportant Society. Its membership now is negligible, and yet it exists. With great difficulties it maintains a small synagogue for Shabbos and holidays on the East Side of New York thanks to the tireless work of the oldest Bransker landsman in America, Rabbi Yoshe Hersh Bransky.

The secretary of the Society is Joseph Watnick, Maishe Aron the hat maker's grandchild. His address is:

Joe Watnick,

1970 East 18th Street, Brooklyn, N.Y.

[Page 430]

Bransker Ladies' Auxiliary

This is the name of the Bransker Ladies' Organization in New York, which was founded in 1937 through the initiative of the Bransker Young Men's Benevolent Association.

During the 11 years of its existence, the Bransker Ladies' Auxiliary became animportant women's organization. It devotes itself most especially to raising money to support local charity organizations. The Auxiliary also supports the United Jewish Appeal, Histadruth, and all other important Jewish institutions.

The Ladies' Auxiliary contributed much to making the members of the Bransker Young Men's become more interested in their meetings.

Through the help of Sister Fanny Cohen the Auxiliary became interested in helping Bransker refugees in various D.P. Camps with food packages. Fanny Cohen, had experienced the First World–War in Bransk even though she was born in New York, became interested in the Bransker Relief work when she came to the first immigrants as an American citizen. She continues her interest until the present.

Through her help she has influenced Nathan Steinberg in sending the first transport of food to Bialystok to the Bransker who were there in 1946. For this we must thank Nathan Steinberg and Fanny Cohen.

The Auxiliary responded warmly in contributing to the fund to help realize the publication of this Bransk book.

The most important members in the Auxiliary are Sister Lena Stoller, the founder, now President, a very intelligent woman.

Laye Pollack, the wife of landsman Julius Pollack, together with her daughter, Ida Zelman and Sore–Leybe Kaplan, Bishke Shnaider's grandchild and her daughter–in–law Gertrude Orlinsky, who do their work with dedication.

[Page 431]

The Werp sisters–in–law, Khane and Bessie, and Bessie Cohen the wife of William Cohen, the Vice Presidents Khama Novak, Shloyme–Hitzl the Khasid's daughter, and the former President Mrs Goldsteyn, the wife of landsman Hyman Goldsteyn, the *Sjhpakyer* (?)MGC *binoculars* (?) are also important co-workers for the Ladies' Auxiliary.

The Officials Of The Bransker Ladies' Auxiliary

Sitting from the right: **Leye Pollack, Lena Stoller, Khama Novak**

Standing from the right: **Mrs Zaleski, Ida Zelman, Hanna Greenberg, Mrs Pitel**

The secretary, for all 11 years is the well–known Mrs Anna Greenberg, the daughter–in–law t of the founder of the Bransker Young Men's, Harris Greenberg who had large accomplishments in helping in the communication of all the members of the Auxiliary.

The Bransker Ladies' Auxiliary is one of the most important women's organizations in New York in the field of support for all city charity institutions.

The Bransker Ladies' Auxiliary, just like the Bransker Relief Committee, are under the aegis of the Bransker Young Men's Benevolent Association.

The address of the Secretary is:

Mrs. Hanna Greenberg

201 Linden Boulevard, Brooklyn, N. Y.

[Page 432]

Julius Cohen Short Biography

Written by him at the direct request of Alter Truss

Among the landslayt who through their own efforts earned a worldly education, I must also include Julius Cohen, born in Bransk in 1888.

In the [old] home he was called Yudl Yentchman, his parents' youngest, the 8th child of his parents. Up to the age of 12 years he studied in Bransk with the best teachers, such as Binyomke, Khaim Groshun's and Maishe Hertsken. He then travels to Bialystok, where he comes to the Jewish Religious School to prepare to study at Rabbi Pinkhas in the yeshiva. He suffered much there because the head of the yeshiva expected much more from him, explaining that he had good talents but does not want to make use of them.

From Bialystok he arrives in Sokolke at the famous yeshiva head Rabbi Shimon Katzenelenboygen. There, together with Yisroel Mikhlen, the son of the Bransker older Maishe Hitsls, who died as rabbi of a community in a town in Kovner Province.

He then decides to travel somewhere to the larger city of Tkhum where he intends to devote himself to a worldly education. He travels usually as a blind" investigator, i.e. under cover, he cannot buy a ticket.

It happened that he was caught by an official of the trains. They drag him out from under the bench and throw him out at a station, this was the city of Pinsk.

He is in the waiting–room in the Pinsk station, and his greatest fear is that someone might ask him for his passport, which he did not have. It was a cold morning, so he inquired how to get to the city. He arrives at a synagogue during the day on the *linishtzyes* (?) and sits down to read a gemora (Talmud).

[Page 433]

He was heartsick. He was yet still a child 15 years old and alone. He poured out his entire sorrow in the melody of the gemora.

Ezriel Vokhernik's son, a well–known learned young man, was at that time already in the synagogue/house of learning. He asks him from where he came. Instead of an answer he receives heart wrenching sobs. He becomes interested in him, finds places for him to eat, and Yekhiel the sexton permits him to sleep in the synagogue/house of learning for several days until they will find a place for him to sleep.

Yudl remains in Pinsk, studies in the synagogue, and becomes beloved by the congregants who consist mostly of poor working men of the area. He uses this opportunity to get four books from the young men and he studies Russian and other worldly subjects.

In 1905 he returned home from Pinsk, a learned young man. He finds children to teach writing in Yiddish, Hebrew, Russian and arithmetic.

At this same time, the air around him is filled with the revolutionary spirit that had reached Bransk.

Together with Yosl Libofsky and Khaim Baker, Maishe Hitzl Mendel's, they establish the first library in Bransk. He is interested in the workers' movement even though he is one of the intellectuals. He addresses many secret meetings in the forest and beneath the mills. He becomes well–known as a good orator, most especially as one who can popularize the difficult pretentious subject and helping everyone to understand.

In 1906, when the danger for all who were considered to be revolutionary activists was great, he decides to leave for America.

The time comes for him to part from his parents, he finds out that his mother, Khana, about whom everyone in Bransk will agree, that there was no end to her goodness, a quiet, hard–working woman who helps supply a bit of food for children, lies with her head buried in the pillows, sobbing, unable to say goodbye to her youngest son.

[Page 434]

His father ShloymeHersh, a khasidic Jew, a Gerer khasid, took courage and said to his youngest son:

__ Yudl, you are going to America and I want to tell you in one word, that God, is also in America. He could not utter any more words. The proud Jew burst into tears.

In America

On the 7th of May 1906 he arrives in New York. He begins to work into the trade of tailor, learning for four weeks how to sew pants. He then had to receive three dollars a week. The owner, a well–known Mr Mager, of the worst type of sweat shop owners on Cherry Street, has his shop above a horse stable. The air in the shop is unbearable. The smell of the horses downstairs poisons one's breath.

When at the fifth week he expected to receive the three dollars, he is terribly shocked when Mr Mager handed him a half dollar.

With a bitter spirit, he leaves the smelly palace and went to work on Elizabeth Street for Miller and Kaplan, a firm that had existed in New York for almost 50 years. He worked there for 18 years, until gladly gave this trade up. According to Mister Max Perlman, the only one of the firm of Miller and Kaplan who still with us, who now tells us he felt sorry for the quiet, genteel young man and permitted him to work regardless of his work not being good at the beginning.

He joins the union as a talented speaker at gatherings during a time of strikes, that occurred every season. Because at the end of the season, everything they had gained from the previous strikes, was lost. The Union delegates, Nekhemyes, Weiss, and a little later, Goldberg, pin big hopes on him as the leader of the workers. But Julius Cohen, as he now called himself, is more interested in furthering his self–education. The rest of his time, after the long work–hours, was spent in studying English and in general, to become better acquainted with the American system of government.

[Page 435]

He becomes interested in helping the workers of his shop to become citizens, to make it possible for them to be able to vote at the elections, and to not remain silent followers. During the first campaigns of the Socialist Party, almost all his co–workers, through his help, became citizens. He taught them to understand how the city, state and federal governments were organized so they would not fail the examinations.

The first to make use of this was Joe Sillen, father of the well–known radical editor of the New Masses, Sam Sillen. Julius Cohen was then an insignificant naturalized citizen.

He also joined the Landsmanshaft Society and was elected as secretary. In this society he has been anofficial until today, for the past 42 years.

This brought him close to the landslayt, and during the First World War he becomes active in the Bransker Relief. He is involved in this work to this very day, devotes much of his best time to such activities, paying no attention to his own economic interests and suffering the results of this.

In 1924, he gladly gave up his trade and became an insurance broker, a business in which he is employed until now.

Being more or less self–employed, he has more time to help his landslayt in various ways.

In 1931 he is drafted by the Bransker Young Men's Benevolent Association to be its secretary. To this very day, even though he is 60 years old, he is not free of his heavy duties in the Society. He is forced from year–to–year to continue in his position.

At this same time, something happened that hurt him deeply. He saw in this the beginning of the Jewish tragedy. Believing in democratic America, he is disappointed when he noticed how his son, Philip, a graduate engineer from Cooper Union and New York University could not find any employment for two years. Many advertisements and newspapers called for people like he. He wrote letters to the firms but received no responses. His friends who did not have any particularly Jewish names did find employment.

[Page 436]

As a bitter joke he wrote a letter to a firm which he signed Philip H. Cole. He received the position. This forces him to change his name. And yet this was not an impediment when he enlisted in the United States army which for five years, he served with his unique talents and worked his way up to the rank of captain.

Julius Cohen foresaw in this the beginning of the hatred that was developing in America. Is this the beginning? Or only a passing occurrence?

Who knows?

In 1937 the Bransker Young Men's held a testimonial banquet for him as appreciation for his good and devoted work for the Society during the six years he served as secretary.

Julius Cohen was also the secretary of the Bocker Young Men's Club for quarter of a century. He conducted a well–known relief that grows larger every time, but he resigned as secretary of the Bocker to be able to devote himself to his primary work for the Branskers.

The Bocker landslayt recognized his work of 25 years and arranged a lovely banquet for him on November 15th 1947. There were 300 attendees and all wished him good luck and thanked him heartily for his active service.

[Page 437]

With his speech to those gathered there, he elicited great interest when he accused the world of being more interested in strengthening the hands of the

Nazis rather than helping the remnants of refugees, the victims of the Nazi murderous hands. He did not foresee the last situation that developed in a rush to help rebuild the world's greatest murderous country with an open hatred towards all Jewish hopes.

Officials of the Bocker Young Men's at a banquet in honour of Julius Cohen's 25 years of service

At the Golden Jubilee of the Bransker Brothers Aid Association in March, 1946, he published a journal in which he pointed out the continuous behavior of England against the Jews. He accused England of wanting to destroy the Jewish community in Eretz Yisroel because of its desire to provide itself with a half–civilized Arab country that would replace the Jews who are sliding out of their grip.

[Page 438]

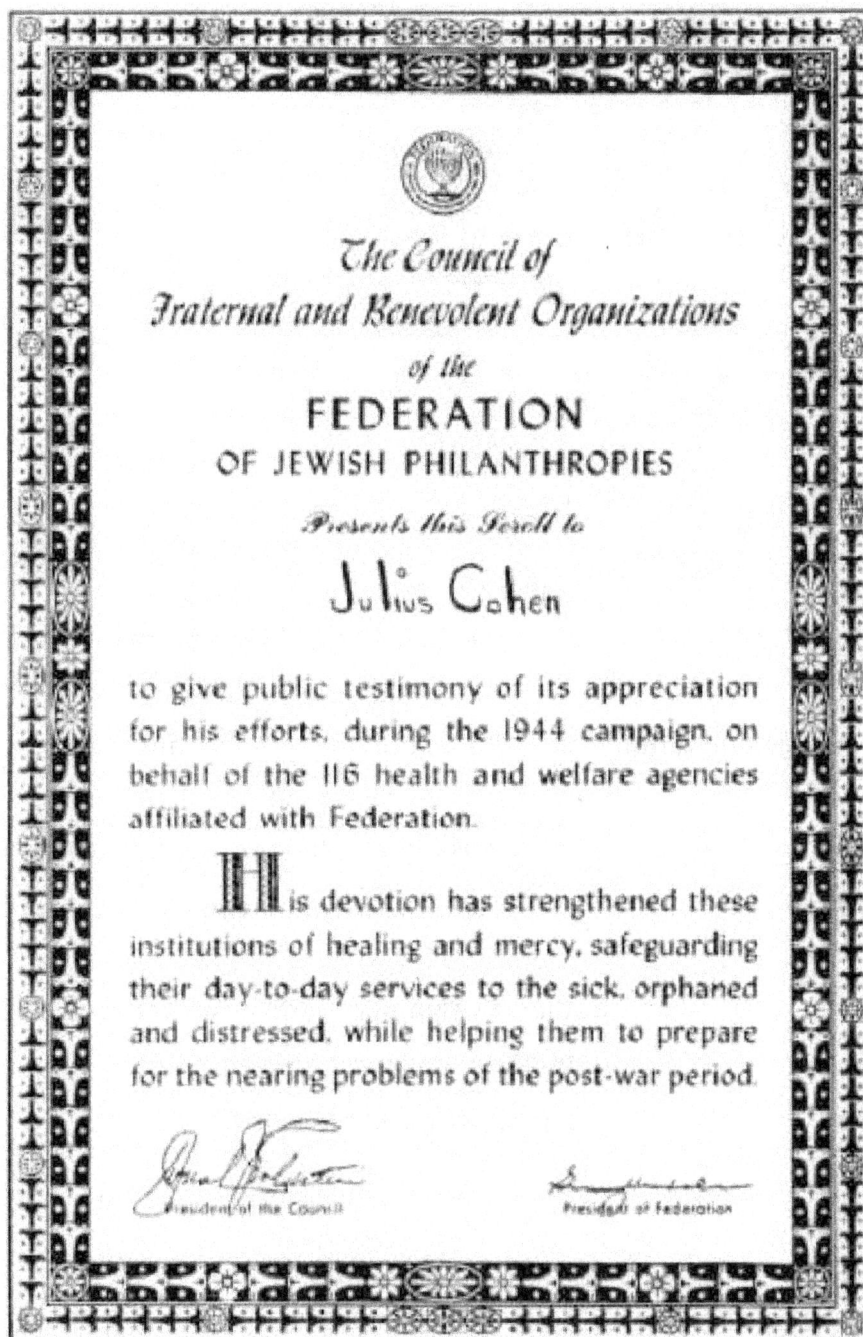

The Council of
Fraternal and Benevolent Organizations
of the

FEDERATION
OF JEWISH PHILANTHROPIES

Presents this Scroll to

Julius Cohen

to give public testimony of its appreciation
for his efforts, during the 1944 campaign, on
behalf of the 116 health and welfare agencies
affiliated with Federation.

His devotion has strengthened these
institutions of healing and mercy, safeguarding
their day-to-day services to the sick, orphaned
and distressed, while helping them to prepare
for the nearing problems of the post-war period.

President of the Council   President of Federation

The certificate to Julius Cohen for his help to the Federation of Jewish Philanthropies

[Page 439]

Julius Cohen and his family and closest relatives at the banquet of the Bodker Young Men's

From the right in bottom row: **Philip and Ida, his son and daughter–in–law, Avrum**

and Enye Richman, his brother and sister–in–law

Second row: **Philip Lutsky and wife Ida, his nephew, Sam and wife**

Esther, Evelyn and Benny, his son and daughters–in–law

Standing: **Julius Cohen and his wife Sarah**

[Page 440]

How true it has turned out today in light of current events.

Julius Cohen also dedicated a lot of his time to raising funds for the Federation of Jewish Philanthropies in New York, for which he was honored with a certificate from Judge Jonah Goldstein, the Chairman of the Organizational Council of the Federation.

During the war years he devoted much time in helping to sell government bonds. For this work he was also honored several times with special certificates.

Regarding his special efforts for the Bransker Relief, please refer to earlier chapters.

Special recognition to Julius Cohen for his help in selling war bonds

This is how Julius Cohen, from his very youth in New York, became part of the community social work. His work to publish the Bransk book for all to read is his primary goal at the present.

[Page 441]

In Memory

The Names of the

Bransker

Innocent Victims

Who Perished

Through Murderous

Hands During

The Time of the Second

World War

1939 – 1945

"May [Their] Soul[s] Be Bound in the Bundle Of Life"

[Page 442]

Blank Page

[Page 443

AS AN ETERNAL REMEMBRANCE

of my beloved parents

YITSKHAK ISSER LISS and wife **SORAH LEAH**

and of all the martyrs of our home Bransk –

those whom I remember and those whom I don't, and those whom I never

knew – may these words be as a dead anniversary light

for the snuffed–out lives, murdered

by the vicious hands in a world without emotion watched

and remained silent to their screams of pain.

We will never forget you, forever

will we sorrow for your

martyrs' death

From

REYZL WALETSKI

Bronx, New York

[Page 444]

AS AN ETERNAL REMEMBRANCE

Of our beloved parents, sisters and brothers, brothers–in–law and

their dear little children, victims of Nazi murderers. The innocent

spilled blood of your young lives will never be

forgotten by us.

'The lovers and believers in their lifetimes and in their deaths will never fall'[1]

HERSHL and **HENYE RUTZKY**

SORAH and **KHAIM LEYB LYEV**

their daughters

HAYTCHE and **RIVKA**

their son

MOYSH'L

DVORKE and **ELYE YENTCHMAN**

their son

DOVIDL

and daughter

KHANELE

our beloved brother

KHONE RUTZKY

three generations who went together to the slaughter not wanting to separate.

From

RUVEN RUTZKY and family Buenos Aires, Argentina

SHUAL RUTZKY and family Buenos Aires, Argentina

MOYSH'L RUTZKY and familyBuenos Aires, Argentina

FISHL LUTZKY and familyBrooklyn, New York

MALKHE FERBER and familyBrooklyn, New York

[Page 445]

AS AN ETERNAL REMEMBRANCE

of our not–forgotten

father **YANKEV PRIBUT**

mother **ETL PRIBUT**

brother **MAISHE PRIBUT**

from
HENYE WEISMAN
and husband
SAM WEISMAN
Plainfield

SHMUELKE PRIBUT
New York

KHAIM PRIBUT
Johannesburg, South Africa

SHAULKE PRIBUT
Johannesburg, South Africa

[Page 446]

FOR ETERNAL REMEMBERANCE

Our beloved father

ITSKHAK ROKHAMKIN

Our beloved mother

Feytche

Our sister and her husband

RIVKA–LEYE and **YANKEV TCHESLYAK**

Their heroic daughter

ROKHL TCHESLYAK

Their sons

AVRUM and **KHAIM TCHESLYAK**

Innocent victims of the wild Nazis

We will always remember you

YANKEV RICHMAN and family

Brooklyn

AVRUM RICHMAN and family

Brooklyn

[Page 447]

AS A REMEMBRANCE
of
My parents
SHLOYME HERSH and **KHANE YENTCHMAN**

My brothers
SHAUL and wife **YENTCHMAN**

HENAKH and wife **YENTCHMAN**

YANKEV and **HENYE YENTCHMAN**

DOVID and wife **MIRKE YENTCHMAN**

AVRUM and wife **YENTCHMAN**
My only sister

HENYE and family

All the children and grandchildren of my brothers and sister
Your memory will always be etched in our
hearts as heroic martyrs for the Jewish people
from
JULIUS COHEN and wife **SOREH**
My children
KHONE FISHL and wife **IDA**
BERTCHE and wife **EVELYN**
SHMUEL and wife **ESTHER**

[Page 448]

IN REMEMBRANCE

YANKEV–LEYB PENKHERZHSHIFRA PENKHERZHSIMKHA

PENKHERZH
and wife
ROKHL PENKHERZH

and son
YOSL PENKHERZH

From

KHANE VERP and family
Patterson

MEIR POLACK and family
New York

IZZY POLACK and family
Chicago

HERSHL POLACK and family
Chicago

SHMUEL'KE POLACK and family
Chicago

[Page 449]

FOR ETERNAL REMEMBERANCE

SHABTAY VERPIKHOVSKI

HINDE VERPIKHOVSKI

KHAIM VERPIKHOVSKI

ALTE VERPIKHOVSKI

SAM VERP and family

Patterson, New Jersey

LOUIS VERP and family

Patterson, New Jersey

[Page 450]

AS AN ETERNAL REMEMBRANCE

MOSHE PENKHERZH

GOLDE PENKHERZH

ETKE PITLAK

DOVID PITLAK

KHAYE KRESSIN

MOSHE KRESSIN

YENTE BYEDKA

ALTER BYEDKA

LEY'KE and **HUSBAND** from Simyatitch

KHAVE PENKHERZH and family

SHIMON PENKHERZH and family

AVRUM'KE PENKHERZH and family

From

MEIR GOTTLIEB and wife

LOUIS POLACK and family

HELEN and her family

[Page 451]

AS AN ETERNAL REMEMBRANCE

NOSKE ZALEFSKI

LIBE ZALEFSKI

HENAKH ZALEFSKI

MIRKE RIPKE

MENAKHEM RIPKE

SORE RIPKE

BERL PUKHALSKI

From

ZAYDL ZALEFSKI and wife

Brooklyn, New York

LILY SPERLING and family

Brooklyn, New York

[Page 454]

FOR ETERNAL REMEMBERANCE

ZAKHARYE OSKART and wife

YISROEL–KHAIM OSKART, wife and childen

FEYGL and her daughter **SORE** and son **SHMUEL'KE**

GEDALYE AYNEMER and family

DOVID VERPIKHOVSKI and family

FROYTCHE SHKOP and family

ZALMAN SHKOP and family

KHAIM–LEYB GOLDING and family

AVRUM YENTCHMAN and family

ITSKHAK RUBINSHTEYN and family

AYZIK VAYNSHTEYN and family

VELVL RUBINSHTEYN and family

KHAIM KLADE and family

SHLOYME TZIKHTLER and family

LEYZER PAT and wife

VEVKE SHIMANSKI and family

YANKL SPECTORSKI and family

From

WILLY and BESSIE COHEN – SORE–LIBE and the **BRANSKER** brothers

ESTHER–ROKHL SHKOP – LOUIS SHKOP and family

JACOB DISKIN – ZAVL RUBINSHTEYN and family

[Page 455]

IN MEMORY OF OUR BELOVED FATHER AND HUSBAND

DAVID GLASSER – DOVID–YOSL GLEZER – June 21, 1941

From

MRS. JENNIE GLAZER

JACK GLASSER and family

IRVING GLASSER and family

BENNIE GLASSER

MORRIS GLASSER and family

SAM GLASSER and family

ALEX GLASSER

ROSE LIPSON and family

ABIE GLASSER

MAX GLASSER

[Page 456]

AS AN ETERNAL REMEMBRANCE

YOSEF VINANKER and wife **BEYLE–MIRIAM**

HERSHL VINANKER, wife and family

YANKEV BAROVITCH, wife **FEYGL** and family

ZALMAN BRENNER, wife and children

FRADL BRENNER, husband and children

From
JACOB VYENER and family
Clifton, New Jersey

[Page 457]

LET US REMEMBER

Our parents

ITSKHAK–GEDALYE SAMOLSKI

KHAYTCHE SAMOLSKI

(Hershl Burak's daughter)

Our sisters

RINA SAMOLSKI

RISHE SAMOLSKI

From

AVRUM–NOAKH BURAK

MOLLY BURAK

Bronx, New York

[Page 458]

FOR ETERNAL REMEMBERANCE

Our parents

BERKE and ROKH'ELE FINKLSHTEYN

Our brother

KHAIM FINKLSHTEYN

Who was murdered by Polish bandits in February, 1947

He took care of the family in the forest detachment – for the weak women and children

MURDERED IN COLD BLOOD

We will always remember you.

DAVID FINKLSHTEYN and family

Bronx, New York

CHARLES FINKLSHTEYN and family

Brooklyn, New York

ESTHER COHEN and family

New York

[Page 459]

FOR ETERNAL REMEMBERANCE

My parents

SHLOYME VOLFKES YATZ

And wife

KHAYE

My brother

BERL YATZ, wife and children

My sister

SHEYNE–MISHE and husband **PINKHAS KAPLAN**

My brother

HARRY GOODMAN

(Died in New York, 1938)

From

DAVID GOODMAN and family

Brooklyn, New York

[Page 460]

We join the ranks of the mourners for the innocent victims of Hitlerism who perished as martyrs in the gas chambers and crematoria of Treblinka and those who perished through Polish bandits in Bransk and villages around Bransk.

May your innocent spilled blood not be silent.

THE BRANSKER YOUNG MEN'S BENEVOLENT ASSOCIATION

THE BRANSKER BROTHERS AID ASSOCIATION

THE BRANSKER RELIEF SHOLEM SOCIETY

THE BRANSKER LADIES' AUXILIARY, NEW YORK

THE BRANSKER AID SOCIETY IN CHICAGO

THE BRANSKER CLUB IN ATLANTA

THE BRANSKER UNION IN JOHANNESBURG AFRICA

THE SOCIETY OF FORMER BRANSKER IN TEL–AVIV

THE BRANSKER L.L. UNION, ARGENTINA

[Page 461]

FOR ETERNAL REMEMBERANCE

To our parents

GEDALYE VILK

ESTHER VILK

Our brother

MOSHE–LEYZER VILK

From

BERL VILK and family

Brooklyn, New York

NEKHOME GOLDBERG and family

New York

[Page 462]

AS AN ETERNAL REMEMBRANCE

Our beloved parents
YANKEV and **YEHUDIT PITLAK**

Our brother

DOVID and his wife **ETKE PITLAK**

Their children

KHAYTCHE and **RIVKA PITILAK**

Our sister
SORE and husband **VISHNEVITZ** and son **MEIR**

Our brother

YOSL PITLAK and family

MOLYE PAT and family

From
ESTHER VEBMAN and family
Bronx, New York

ROKHL LINKE and family
Asbury Park, New Jersey

[Page 463]

Special recognition to Julius Cohen for his help in selling war bonds

SOCIETY OF FORMER RESIDENTS OF BRANSK IN ARGENTINA
BRANSKER LADIES' UNION
BRANSKER LANDSLAYT UNION
REMEMBER!

To the holy memory of those who perished in martyrdom.

May your spilled blood not be silenced and may your torture not be in vain (?)

HONOUR THEIR MEMORY

Avrum Zagel; President, BinyominGolding, Vice–President, Khaim Kestin, Secretary, Yisroel Mesel, Treasurer, Shmuel Tsakhtler, Ayzik Penkhazh, Khaim Rishelov, Ruven Rudski,

MEMBERS:

Itskhak Pribut, Kh. Sh. (?) Pakhter, Leyb Khasan, Hersh Kasovitski, Shmon Krotz, Leyb Goldman, Zalman Golding, Sheyne–Rokhl Golding de Galant, Khane–Batya Golding de (?), Zaydl Shkop, Moshe Tapitser, Shmuel Penkharzh, Rokhl Fishelyev de Likhtenshtayn, Itskhak Levick, Khaim Sokolovitch, Pesakh Sokolovitch, Avrum Shurek, Lois Pakhter de Zhikovski, Rokhl Vrane de Zimmerman, Sheyne Mesel de Sivovitch, Leyb Golde, Reyzl Golde de Rose, Rokhl Kestin de Rosenblatt, Khaytche Golde de (?), Menukhe Golde de Leyzerov, Rivka Golde de Melnik, Mordekhay Klinkovitch, Eshaye Klinkovitch, Hersh Klinkovitch, Shaul Rudski, Moshe Rudski, Mordekhay Grinsheyn, Shloyme Blayman, Rokhl Tapitser de Kalmanovitch

next name has seal stamped over it,

Raykhe Tapitser.

Argentina memorial page of the Bransker Landslayt Union in Buenos Aires, Argentina

[Page 464]

THE FOLLOWING INDIVIDUALS AND SOCIETIES MADE POSSIBLE THE
PUBLICATION OF THIS BOOK WITH THEIR CONTRIBUTIONS:

BRANSK YIZKOR BOOK

Iteld family	Rubin, Keyle
Baker, Sam	Richman, Yankev
Bikher Brothers	Alter Richman
Burak, Yisroel	Ross, Moshe–Hitsl
Burak, Elye	Spak, Sam
Burak, Avrum	Salefski, Zeyde
Cohen, William	Sashin, Berl Africa
Cohen, Meir–Sholem	Smerling Brothers
Aylin, Mr. and Mrs.	Shayevitz, Sol
Federal East Corp.	Shuster, Columbia, South America
Friedman, Avrum	Tennenbaum Brothers
Goodman, David	Werp, Sam
Glasser Family	Werp, Louis
Gottlib, Meir	Vaysman, Enye and Sam
Goldshteyn, Hyman	Wilk, Berl
Golden, Mrs.	Wein, David
Hurant, Binyomin	Valetski, Rose
Huervitz, Louis	Zeytin, Mrs. (?)
Kelner Family	Bransker Young Men's
Lutski, Fishl	Bransker Club, Atlanta
Levsky Brothers	Bransker Landslayt Association
Libofski, Yosl	Argentina Bransker Ladies' Auxiliary
Yentchman Family	Moss, Benny
Bransker Aid Society	Chicago Bransker Brothers Aid Association
Madoff, William	Bransker Vereyn Johannesburg
Novak, Hyman	Pitlak, Yisroel
Rutski, Shaul'ke, Argentina	Rutski, Ruven Argentina
Rutski, Moshe Argentina	Bransker Society Johannesburg

In the name of the Bransker Relief Committee in New York

Julius Cohen

Footnote:

Translated by Micah Akiva Frankel, grandson son of Rubin Roy Cobb, named after his
great–great grandfather Akiva HaCohen Skornik

Maps of Bransk, not in the original Yizkor Book

Details given by Jack [Yankel] Rubin z"l (passed away 2/13/2011) on flight from New York to Warsaw to film documentary for PBS titled "Shtetl" on 10/11/1991 to Rubin Roy Cobb. An Excel file containing more information about the maps can be found at

http://www.jewishgen.org/Yizkor/Bransk/bra900.html

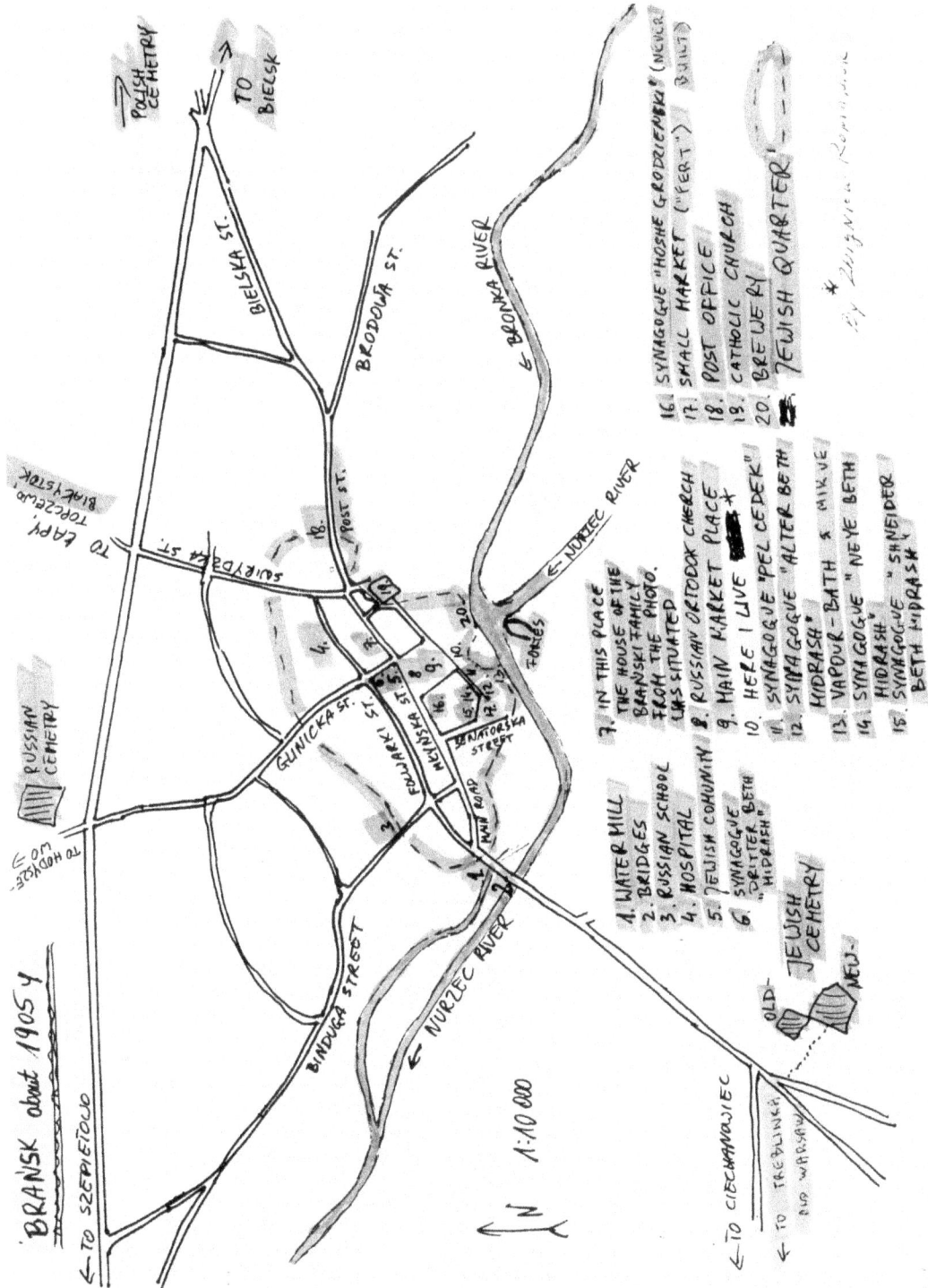

Map Dated 1905

Map labels and legend:

- TO BIELSK
- POLISH CEMETERY
- BIELSKA ST.
- BRODOWA ST.
- BRONKA RIVER
- TO ŁAPY, TOPCZEWO, BIAŁYSTOK
- SWIRYDOWA ST.
- POST ST.
- NURZEC RIVER
- RUSSIAN CEMETERY
- TO HODYSZE
- GUNICKA ST.
- FOLWARKI ST.
- MLYNSKA ST.
- SENATORSKA STREET
- MAIN ROAD
- BINDUGA STREET
- NURZEC RIVER
- BRANSK about 1905
- TO SZEPIETOWO
- 1:10 000
- N
- TO CIECHANOWIEC
- TO TREBLINKA and WARSAW
- JEWISH CEMETERY (OLD / NEW)
- By Zbigniew Romaniuk

Legend:

1. WATER MILL
2. BRIDGES
3. RUSSIAN SCHOOL
4. HOSPITAL
5. JEWISH COMUNIN
6. SYNAGOGUE "DRITTER BETH MIDRASH"
7. IN THIS PLACE THE HOUSE OF THE BRANSKI FAMILY FROM THE PHOTO. WAS SITUATED
8. RUSSIAN ORTODOX CHURCH
9. MAIN MARKET PLACE
10. HERE I LIVE
11. SYNAGOGUE "PEL CEDEK"
12. SYNAGOGUE "ALTER BETH MIDRASH"
13. VAPOUR-BATH & MIKVE
14. SYNAGOGUE "NEYE BETH MIDRASH"
15. SYNAGOGUE "SHNEIDER BETH MIDRASH"
16. SYNAGOGUE "HOSHE G-RODZIENSKA" (NEVER BUILT)
17. SMALL MARKET ("FERT")
18. POST OFFICE
19. CATHOLIC CHURCH
20. BREWERY
★ JEWISH QUARTER

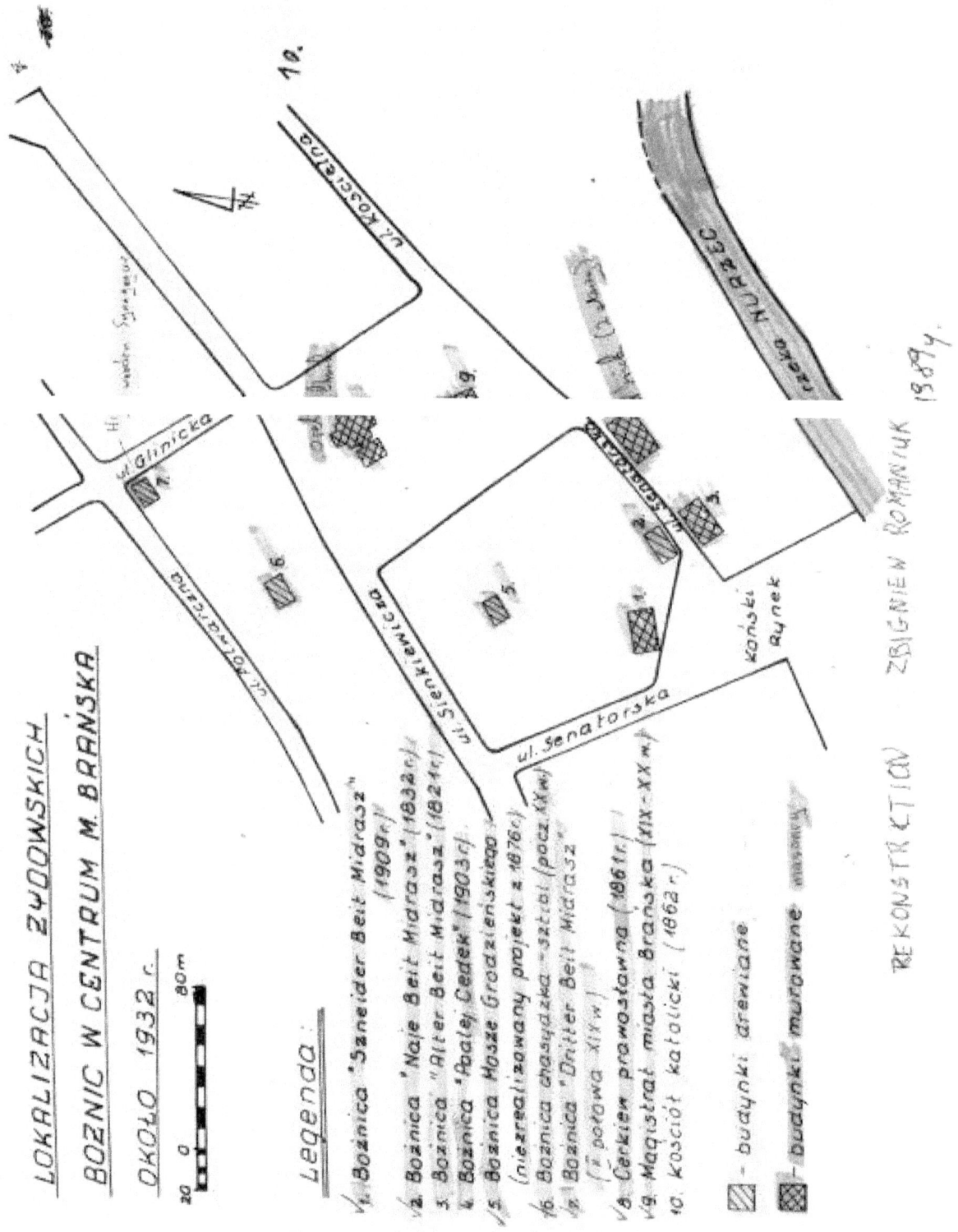

Map dated 1932

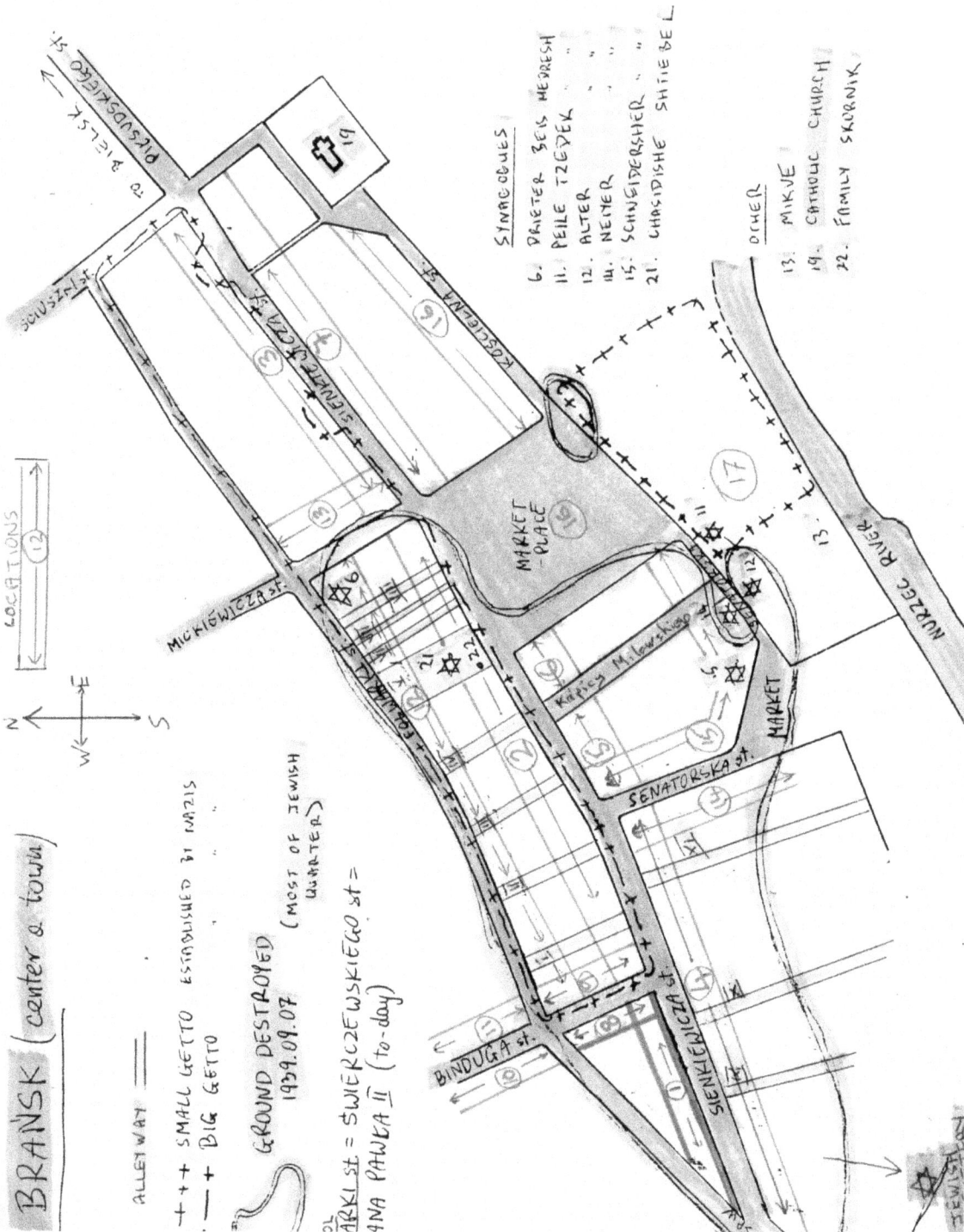

Map Dated 1942

SPIS CZĘŚCI RODZIN ŻYDOWSKICH ID W BRAŃSKU (opis do planu)

I.	Pinkielsztein (rolnik)	52.	Konopiate (melamed)
2.	Wojnowicz	53.	Burak (przewóz)
3.	Mendel (stelmach)	54.	Burak
4.	Kopka		Sekerowicz (fotograf)
5.	Pytlak (olejarnia)	55.	Rubin (hotel)
6.	Weinstein	56.	Wyrobnik (fryzjer)
7.	Rubinstein (melamed)		Chaim Klode (melamed)
8.	Doliński		Brański
9.	Paw (kierowca)		Pachter (kamasznik)
IO.	Rozen (kowal)	57.	Baker (piekarnia)
II.	Pulszański	58.	Piekucki (piekarnia)
	Izaakowicz (fryzjer)	59.	Gold ("Pod Bocianami")
I2.	Rubin (gęsiarz)	60.	Cepeliński (szewc)
I3.	Alpern (Halperin)	6I.	Goldberg (piekarnia)
I4.	Pentman	62.	Rochelson (właściciel młyna
I5.	Man (stolarz)	63.	Klejnot (szewc)
I6.	Okoń (fryzjer)	64.	Edelman
I7.	Kaufman (dentystka)		Goldwasser (zboże) grain
I8.	Gold (olejarnia)		Jęczmień
I9.	Ginsburg (melamed)	65.	Oskard (krawiec)
20.	Szczupak	66.	Klode
	Prybut	67.	Susel (woda mineralna)
2I.	Chomski (skład apteczny)	68.	Wilkański (stolarz)
22.	Suseł	69.	Kamień (samochody ciężarowe
23.	Orlański	70.	Zeifman
24.	Kruk	7I.	Rubinstein (rymarz)
25.	Wasser (rowery)	72.	Golde (drewno)
26.	Ajnemer (krawiec)	73.	Wasser (melamed)
27.	Kamień (transport)	74.	Szpitalny (młynarz)
28.	Iteld (sklep z materiałami)	75.	Bider
29.	Trus (czapnik)	76.	Szapiro
	Tykocki (kamasznik)	77.	Man (stolarz)
30.	Krac (krawiec)	78.	Cymbał (kowal)
3I.	Szrojt (farbiarnia)	79.	Wróbel
	. Alpern		Rubin
32.	Mejsie Juda (szames)	80.	Brener
33.	Kasztan (krawiec)		Wołkowicz (wiartak)
34.	Mordche Ersz (melemed)	8I.	Rubin (gęsiarnia)
35.	Kukawka (zegarmistrz)	82.	Rochelson (młyn)
36.	Tykocki		
	Sekerowicz		
37.	Makowski (restauracja)		
38.	Baker		
39.	Szeroszewski (drejasz)		
40.	Szpak		
	Arke (rzeźnik)		
	Pam		
4I.	Werpachowski		
42.	Grodzieński		
43.	Rotenstein (kołowrotki)		
44.	Ajneker (krawiec)		
	Wasser (handel płótnem)		
45.	Olendzki (handel końmi)		
46.	Glazer		
47.	Okrongły (kamieniarz)		
48.	Jęczmień (rzeźnik)		
49.	Lew		
	Cołka (stolarz)		

INDEX

Kasovitski, 450

Kass, 241

Katavitski, 75

Katchmarsky, 161

Katlavitch, 235, 271, 335, 373

Katlovitch, 329

Katseski, 355

Katsev, 12, 29, 41, 55, 61, 62, 93, 107, 116,
117, 120, 121, 128, 156, 186, 215, 226, 244,
246, 255, 257, 258, 264, 274, 288, 290, 316,
320, 322, 335, 378, 379

Katz, 96, 327

Katzenelenboygen., 421

Kazak, 192, 193

Keller, 117

Kerensky, 147

Kessler, 383, 384, 395, 410, 412

Kestale, 128

Kestin, 41, 42, 43, 54, 69, 108, 160, 163, 185,
201, 214, 225, 271, 321, 325, 367, 380, 393,
401, 450

Kevlyaker, 277, 327, 345

Khafetz, 185, 189, 190

Khaike, 101

Khaikin, 114

Khaim, 10, 31, 40, 43, 49, 53, 54, 55, 60, 63, 76,
86, 107, 138, 141, 160, 169, 172, 185, 188,
189, 193, 229, 260, 264, 281, 327, 335, 338,
340, 399, 404, 450

Khanah, 167

Khanale, 279

Kharif, 12, 109

Kharlap, 90, 190, 372, 381

Kharlop, 41, 43, 73, 74

Khasid, 63, 64, 73, 86, 120, 285, 349, 416

Khatskel, 250

Khatskl, 62

Khatz, 373

Khazn, 54, 63, 144, 169, 378

Khilikhe, 125, 285

Khilye, 59

Khofetz, 241

Khomsky, 131, 271, 273

Khone, 137

Khukar, 36, 37, 80, 210, 257

Klade, 55, 264, 266, 440

Kleinat, 336

Kleinot, 285, 329, 341, 342, 345, 367, 380

Klektor, 374

Klikher, 285

Klinkovitch, 450

Klode, 42, 263, 271, 353

Kloden, 266

Klodke, 72

Kobriner, 63

Kobylanski, 42, 62, 109, 158, 173, 176, 202,
216, 225, 232, 237, 242, 249, 253, 262, 273,
293, 325, 337, 371, 376, 405

Kodlubofsky, 55

Kofke, 185

Kokhlyarnik, 122

Kokitze, 87

Konopyate, 174

Konopyates, 66

Kontchik, 34, 53, 69, 373, 380

Kopelikhe, 96, 183

Kopiliekhe, 89

Kopke, 128, 185, 244, 285, 346

Kopkes, 55

Koshak, 285, 340, 341, 342

Koshnik, 367

Kosofsky, 416, 417

Kosovitski, 73, 75

Kotch, 193

Kotlovitch, 380, 392

Kotlovitsh, 12

T

Z

www.ingramcontent.com/pod-product-compliance
Lightning Source LLC
Chambersburg PA
CBHW062018090426
42811CB00005B/893